THE TURKS OF BULGARIA

Published by
The Isis Press,
Şemsibey Sokak 10, Beylerbeyi
81210 Istanbul. Tel. 321 38 51

First Printing 1990

ISBN 975-428-017-7.

THE TURKS OF BULGARIA:
THE HISTORY, CULTURE
AND POLITICAL FATE OF A MINORITY

EDITED BY K. H. KARPAT

THE ISIS PRESS
ISTANBUL

Kemal. H. Karpat

INTRODUCTION: BULGARIAN WAY OF NATION BUILDING AND THE TURKISH MINORITY

The publication of this book of research articles by leading authorities on Bulgaria was prompted by the Bulgarian governement's campaign starting in late 1984 when the Bulgarian government opened a well-planned campaign to force the Turkish population of the country to abandon their Islamic names and adopt Christian Slavic names. The Bulgarian government has claimed that the Muslim population changed names voluntarily, but there is not a single report in any western newspaper, journal, or book to support this claim. Even the Soviet press has kept silent on this issue, while the Russian statesmen, when questioned, have evaded, saying that this is a "matter between Turkey and Bulgaria." The forced changes of names—a type of forced "baptism" in the eyes of Islam—is fully attested by the reports of Amnesty International, the bulletins of the Helsinky Watch Committee, and the records of the United States Congress.[1] The changes of names has been accompanied by the closure and destruction of mosques and the prohibition of Islamic rites, such as fasting, circumcision, and even burial of the dead in Muslim cemeteries.

According to western estimates, over 1,000 persons who resisted changing names have been killed, several thousand have been arrested, and many interned on the Belene island. Resistance was actually far more widespread than officially reported. Many villages dug trenches and for days held off the attacks of government troops riding in tanks armed with the latest Soviet weapons. Today, visiting those villages is prohibited even for Bulgarian citizens. In some areas the resistance is continuing. There have been sporadic reports about the bombing of buildings, acts of sabotage, and hostage-taking on the part of the Muslim resistance fighters within Bulgaria. Visitors who have spoken with these oppressed Muslims believe that they will rise *en másse* at the first opportune moment. Other reports state that the Muslims are now making a special efforts to speak only Turkish among themselves, leaving out all Bulgarian words or expressions that had infiltrated the vocabulary in the past. The Pomaks also are now trying to learn Turkish

---

[1]See *Hearing Before the Commission on Security and Cooperation in Europe,* 99th Congress, Washington, D.C., June 25, 1985, pp. 182-83; Amnesty International, *Bulgaria: Imprisonment of Ethnic Turks,* (London, 1986; larger updated version, 1987); Radio Free Europe, *Radio Liberty Bulletin,* 2 no. 1, (January 1986). Reports appearing in the West European press have been gathered in several volumes by the Turkish General Directorate of Information ; see Basın Yayın v Enformasyon Genel Müdürlüğü, *Turkish Minority in Bulgaria,* 6 vols. /Ankara 1985-87/.

and thus avoid speaking in Bulgarian—their native tongue. In fact, a number of western observers who have spent time in Bulgaria claim that national sentiment among the Turks has risen to an exceptionally high level.

Meanwhile, in Turkey the immigrants from Bulgaria or their descendents—amounting to some ten million people—and the rest of the country's population as well have been emotionally mobilized against Bulgaria. A side effect of the Bulgarian government's action has been to deflate the claim of the Turkish communists that a communist regime is the only one capable of achieving brotherhood and equality among different national and ethnic groups, regardless of which group holds power. The results of the elections of 1987 showed that leftists in Turkey have been weakened greatly. The reports summarized only briefly above prove beyond any doubt that the Muslims' name change in Bulgaria was a forced act, and one of which the consequences for Bulgaria may be more damaging than imagined.

This volume, then, is dedicated to the Muslims—particularly the Turks—living in Bulgaria today. The articles herein explore the history, culture, and condition of this population. Written by European and Turkish scholars and based on information gleaned from objective factual research, these articles show that, contrary to assertions by the Bulgarian government, the modern Turks of Bulgaria are the descendents of people of genuine Turkish stock. Some of their ancestors had settled in the area before the Bulgars arrived, while the majority were immigrants from the Anatolian peninsula during the Ottoman era. Under the Ottomans the Turkish communities developed their own Muslim culture that was different from that of the Bulgars. Eventually the Bulgar communities came together as a sort of nationalist political group that succeeded in gaining autonomy (1878) and then independence (1912).[2]

Bulgaria's Methods of Nation Formation

Bulgaria was not a nation in the modern cultural, ethnic, or political sense of the word at the time the Russian army made the newly created Principality autonomous in 1878. The fledgling state felt the urgent need to develop immediately a national-historical *raison d'être* and thus adopted the idea of an absolute ethnic-national homogeneity as its principle for nation formation. Thereafter, the government worked to either assimilate or liquidate all of its national minorities. The device employed to give credence to its actions was that of declaring a particular area and the people inhabiting it

---

[2]There are a number of good scholarly works on the history of Bulgaria. The best, despite pro-Bulgarian bias, are by Konstantin Jirecek, *Geschichte der Bulgaren* (Prague, 1876) and *Das Fürstenthum Bulgarien* (Vienna, 1891); see also Nikolai Botev Staneff, *Geschichte der Bulgaren* (Leipzig, 1918). For a recent work, see Richard J. Crampton, *Bulgaria, 1878-1918: A History* (New York, 1983); one may form an opinion about the quality and spirit of the contemporary Bulgarian writers merely by reading Bistra Cvetkova, *The Heroical Resistance of the Bulgarians against the Turkish Invasion* (Sofia, 1960); D. Kossev, H. Hristov, *Bulgaria, 1300 Years* (Sofia, 1980). The Turks who emigrated from Bulgaria have established several associations and published periodicals and books containing excellent firsthand information on the situation of their kin left in Bulgaria; see the views of one of the leaders, himself a recent refugee from Bulgaria, Mehmet Çavuş, *Bulgaristanda Soykırımı* [Genocide in Bulgaria] (Istanbul, 1984).

as having been "Bulgarian" at some point in history, however spurious the supporting evidence might be. Among the territories alleged to have been "originally Bulgarian" are lands today held by Bulgaria's neighbors: Thrace (Greece), Macedonia (Yugoslavia), Eastern Thrace (Turkey), and Dobruca (Romania). In 1885, in open defiance of the Berlin Treaty of 1878, and despite the fact that the area was culturally, economically, demographically, strategically, and historically an organic part of Turkey, she successfully annexed Eastern Rumelia (the area south of the Balkan mountains). However, being unable unilaterally to fulfill her territorial ambitions, Bulgaria allied herself with larger powers : Germany in World Wars I and II and the USSR after 1944. During WW II Bulgaria, as an ally of Hitler, occupied the long-coveted territories of Macedonia in Yugoslavia and northern Greece and promptly sought to bulgarize them. However, when Hitler eventually lost his war, Bulgaria had to give up these spoils. Macedonia is now one of Yugoslavia's six republics and enjoys recognition as a distinct ethnic-national entity despite the mixed religious composition of its inhabitants. Other areas were not so fortunate.

The large and flourishing Greek community centered in the Philippolis area (the Bulgarians changed the name to Plovdiv) and the ancient Greek towns on the Black Sea disappeared, through either emigration or assimilation. The Gagauzes, Turkish Muslims who settled on the shores of the Black Sea around Varna and became Christians at the end of the thirteenth century but retained their languages and traditions, were long ago declared "Bulgarian."[3] The same happened to the Romanians who lived along the southern shores of the Danube and to the Latin Vlahs (descendents of the Romans) living in the Pirin and Rhodope mountains. The small but influential group of Bulgarian Catholics—some 50,000 of them—who strove to abide, partially at least, by the political standards of the West were subjected to extraordinary pressure and persecution (except sporadically when the government of Bulgaria needed western sympathy and finance).

As the above brief summary of the Bulgarian government's policy towards its nationalities makes clear, the current treatment of the Turks and other Muslims falls into a well-defined historical pattern, although the Muslims in general (the Pomaks were less fortunate), and the Turks in particular, were spared the traditional assimilation pressures until well into the second half of the twentieth century, presumably due to the sheer size of this population—a good 20 percent of the total—as well as to the wide gulf of difference of religion, language, and culture separating the Turkish Muslim population from Christian-Orthodox Bulgarians. The existence of Turkey as a near neighbor also was a deterrent until Bulgaria agreed, under Breznev's urging, to assume her traditional role as proxy for Soviet policy in the Balkans.

---

[3] This group, consisting of some 20,000 people, still speaks its own Turkish language, even though its intellectuals have been among the vanguard in the Bulgarization campaign. (Dr. Emil Boyeff, a teacher of Turkish at Sofia University, is one of the most outstanding examples of the Bulgarized Gagauz.). The contemporary existence of the Gagauzes has been fully ascertained by some Bulgarian authors. One of the best known is A. I. Manov, an army officer who collected his material while serving in the Gagauz districts; see *Potekloto na Gagauzitei tehnite obicai i nravi v dve casti* (Varna, 1938). (A Turkish translation, *Gagauzlar,* was published by Varlık Publishing House [Istanbul, 1940].)

Scholars well acquainted with the demographic history of the Balkans know that the large Turkish population has always posed a thorny problem for the nationalist-minded rulers of Bulgaria. Historically, Bulgaria was part of the heartland of the Ottoman state and still preserves its Turkish character—as does the population, despite the many changes brought about by the assimilation policies of the government. Ottoman mosques, *vakıfs* (pious foundations), *hans* (inns), and *imarets* (business and social establishments) still dot the entire country.[4] The Bulgarian government tried to eliminate these Ottoman monuments as soon as it took power.[5] Meanwhile it pressured the Turkish population to emigrate. From 1878 to the present time a stream of "surplus" Bulgarian Turks has flowed steadily into Turkey (but the community in Bulgaria has still maintained its fair size, as shall be discussed later). In 1951/52 Bulgaria expeled 152,000-156,000 Turks under Stalin's order, in the hope of undermining the Turkish economy as punishment for that country's participation in the Korean War and its joining of NATO.[6] However, the intractability of what it saw as the problem of the large Muslim population seems finally to have moved the Bulgarian rulers to resort to drastic means. In 1956—and subsequently in 1964, 1969, 1970, and 1984—the Communist Party's Central Committee adopted measures designed to achieve *priobshtavane* (homogeneity, or becoming a whole) so as to establish *edinna bulgarska natsiya* (one compact Bulgarian nation). Initially the "unification", that is, assimilation, measures were directed against smaller groups, such as the Macedonians, the Vlahs, and the Gypsies. Eventually, in the 1960s, the Pomaks (Bulgarian-speaking Muslims) became the target. The government launched against them a campaign, supported by a fictitious "history" of the group, to convince them that their religion—that is, Islam—had been imposed on them by force, after which some of them somehow had become Turkish speakers.

The traditional Bulgarian historiography accepted the view that some Christians converted to Islam during two short periods in the sixteenth and seventeenth centuries and that these conversions were voluntary. By the late 1960s, as the Pomaks became the target for assimilation, Bulgarian historiography had adopted the extremist view that all conversions to Islam had been forceful. The "nationalist" wing of the historians. represented by a young, extremist generation that sought the patronage of Liudmila Zhivkova, the late daughter of Chairman Todor Zhivkov, launched an attack on the older generation of historians, especially against those who had somehow begun to accept the positive aspects of Ottoman rule. Veselin Traykov, Petur Popov, Bistra Svetkova, Hristo Hristov, Straşimir Dimitrov, etc. headed the anti-Ottoman attack aimed at, among others, Nicolai Todorov, a highly intelligent historian of Greek and Gagauz ancestry, educated in Moscow and befriended in the West, who had offered a more

---

[4]One of the best-documented works on the Turkish monuments is Machiel Kiel, *Art and Society of Bulgaria in the Turkish Period,* (Asen/Maastricht, 1985). For a more extensive bibliography, see *The Turkish Presence in Bulgaria,* published by the Turkish Historical Society (Ankara, 1986).

[5]On the destruction of the Turkish monuments, see Bernard Lory, *Le Sort de L'Héritage Ottoman en Bulgarie. L'Exemple des Villes Bulgares, 1878-1900* (Istanbul, 1985). There are also Bulgarian works —which justify this destruction as the liquidation of feudalism and capitalism; see Georgi Georgiev, *The Liberation and the Ethnocultural Development of the Bulgarian People, 1878-1900* (Sofia, 1979), in Bulgarian.

[6]See II.L. Kostanick, *Turkish Resettlement of Bulgarian Turks, 1950-1953* (Berkeley, 1957).

moderate and accurate interpretation of Turkish rule in Bulgaria. Todorov survived the attacks.[7] (He was a recent candidate for the top position at UNESCO. For a few years he was out of circulation as Bulgaria's ambassador to Greece, while the nationalists had the field to themselves.)

The new breed of nationalist historians produced "documentary studies" designed to prove the government's point.[8] A quick glance at these documents show that the authors relied on false evidence, that they did not use the basic Turkish documents, and that where they did use Turkish source, they were so unaware of the ethnic, confessional, and social organization of the Ottoman state as to be unable to understand the meaning of what they read.[9] The chief source used by all Bulgarian studies to document the "forced conversion" to Islam is a note of several pages supposedly written by Methodii Draginov, a Bulgarian priest, on the final page of a liturgical manuscript dated ca 1666.[10] This note, in its published version, states that Pehlivan Mehmed Pasha, on his march towards Morea in 1666, went through the Rhodope mountains. Gavril, the Greek bishop, informed Mehmed Pasha that the peasants had failed to pay their taxes to the (Greek-Christian) Plovdiv metropolitanate and were, therefore, rebels. Mehmed Pasha would have executed the Christian notables and the local priest for this offense, except for the interventian of a Muslim *imam*—Hasan Hoca—who suggested that the tax delinquents be spared their lives if they converted to Islam. Altogether it seems that the inhabitants of seven Chapni villages were converted. Those who did not convert fled into mountains and their houses in the villages were destroyed. Dennis P. Hupchic, who has studied this "conversion" in Bulgarian sources, claims that its roots were both social and legal. According to him, Chapni villages in the Rhodopes were given autonomy from the Greek patriarchate in Istanbul at the time of conquest in the fourteenth century in exchange for some military service. Then Suleyman the Lawgiver (1520-66) declared the area a *vakıf*, and this freed the villagers from other taxes and services. The Chapni Bulgarians "whether due to an outside threat to that religious autonomy—e.g. the Plovdiv Greek Orthodox Metropolitanate—or the existence of Ottoman laws applying to wakif lands which permitted wakif inhabitants to convert *en masse*... may quite possibly have decided that conversion to Islam was the only alternative open to them in order to maintain their priviledged status under an increasingly fanatical Muslim regime."[11] No reliable scholar has ever studied the

---

[7] See nn. 2 and 4 for bibliography.

[8] See P. Petrov, ed., *The Assimilatory Policy of the Turkish Conquerors. Collection of Documents with Regard to Islam and Conversion to Islam. 15th-19th Centuries* (in Bulgarian) (Sofia, 1962). Petrov has several other works of the same genre, none supported by any basic source, including K. Jirecek's classical works.

[9] In the "Documents" section of this volume we have reproduced a sample of the documents, selected by the Bulgarian government especially for the western public.

[10] The original, in Bulgarian, was published in the *Geographical-Historical Statistical Description of the Tatar Bazarcik* (Vienna, 1870). The original document disappeared immediately after publication and has never been seen by any other person. In fact, the language employed in the note attributed to Draginov is that spoken in the nineteenth century, not the seventeenth, showing that the note must have been added much later.

[11] Dennis R. Hupchic "Seventeenth Century Bulgarian Pomaks: Forced or Voluntary Converts to Islam," in *Society in Change: Studies in Honor of Bela K. Kiroly,* ed. Steven Bela Vardy (Boulder, Co., 1983), p. 311.

original document, and, in fact, scholars well acquainted with Ottoman history and Bulgarian affairs are in agreement that it must have been a forgery. Dr. Machiel Kiel, a Dutch scholar who has spent considerable time working in Bulgaria, states that some leading Bulgarian historians informed him in private that the document was not authentic.[12] There is a great deal of evidence—both internal and external—pointing to its spuriousness.

It is well known that there were in the Balkans voluntary conversions to Islam of large groups of Bogomils. The Bogomils were Slavic Christians, adherents of the Manichaean doctrine; thus, according to the tenets of the Catholic and Orthodox churches, they were heretics. So they were vigorously persecuted by their Christian brethren. When the Ottomans conquered the territory they put a stop to the persecution of the Bogomils, giving them reason to welcome the new administration. Furthermore, as their reasons for clinging to Bogomilism had almost as much to do with protecting their ethnic identity in the face of a monolithic Byzantine orthodoxy as it did with firm religious conviction, they were quick to see the advantage of becoming, by the simple expedient of accepting Islam, members of a ruling religious group that recognized and tolerated ethnic differences and was not organized to persecute "heresy."

Thus, the conversion of several villages need not necessarily have been forceful. The fact that the document holds both the Greek church and the Turkish administration responsible for the conversion is internal evidence that it was forged: one of the contentions of the Bulgarian nationalists is that the Turks and the Greeks were accomplices in the stifling of the Bulgarian national spirit. The fact that the area allegedly involved was Chapni also gives lie to the story: the name derives from the Chapni, a branch of Kızılbaş (Alevis) who reside in the Sivas area in Eastern Anatolia. Obviously some of these Turkish peoples were settled in that area of Bulgaria, so the villagers would already have been Muslim.

The Bulgarian government went so far as to ask an upcoming party member with literary ambitions, Anton Donchev, to write a novel to back the historians' contention that the Pomaks were forcibly Islamized. Donchev wrote the novel, *Vreme Razdelno* (Time of parting), in just 144 days after he had supposedly spent two years living among the Pomaks. He was awarded the Dimitrov Prize in literature, given only to "remarkable creative work," and his novel was translated into western European languages.[13] The story revolves around a Turkish military unit commanded by Kara Ibrahim (Abraham the Black), a Janissary chief, who was sent by the Porte in around 1668 to convert the Bulgarians of the Elindenya valley in the Rhodope mountains. The other characters in the novel include Muslim religious men, Sheik Shaban and Molla Zulfikar Softa (the author's unfamiliarity with Muslim names and ranks is immediately apparent), and Hassan Hoca (a Pomak). Kara İbrahim's military force is confronted by Manol, the fearless Bulgarian shepherd leader, with his sons and various other types of

[12] *Art and Society,* p. 5.

[13] The Bulgarian edition appeared in 1964; the English version, translated by Marguerite Alexieva, was published in Great Britain in 1967; in the USA it was published by William Morrow and Company, New York, 1968. Recently a movie dealing with the subject of "forced conversion" to Islam, prepared under the supervision of the Bulgarian government and financed by it, has been released in Western Europe.

persons chosen to represent the Bulgarians. The story, which is based on the spurious Methodii Draginov document discussed above, ends, as one might expect, with the Janissaries engaging in rape and massacres and the execution of those who say, "My head I'll give—my faith I will never give." Thus historians and novelists at the beck and call of the Bulgarian government sought to provide "moral-historical" justification for the policy of "Bulgarization" of the Pomaks. This policy in the 1960s was brutally enforced without causing any unfavorable world comment, although the "justification" advanced was totally baseless. The Pomaks—inhabiting the southwest part of Bulgaria—are probably the descendents of the Cumans, the Turkic-speaking group that settled in the area in the eleventh and twelfth centuries and later adopted the Slavic language. Some embraced Christianity in its Bulgarian form and then accepted Islam. Apart from those Cumans who migrated and settled in eastern Hungary and eventually adopted Calvinism (probably to distinguish themselves from other Hungarians, who were Catholics), the Pomaks are staunch Muslims and consider themselves Turks (as shown by their mass migration and settlement in Turkey), despite the fact that they speak a Bulgarian dialect.

The party cadres engaged in the 1960s campaign sought not only to persuade the Pomaks that they had been forcibly Islamized but also to prepare themselves for bigger tasks in the future. Several groups in Turkey criticized the forced change of names among the Pomaks but without any visible success.[14] The Turkish government saw it as an isolated incident that did not impinge upon the religious and cultural freedom of the rest of the Muslims and, as usual, adopted an extremely conciliatory attitude towards Bulgaria. At that time it was preoccupied with internal terrorism (the arms for which were supplied by Bulgaria); additionally, it did not want to damage relations with the eastern neighbor whose higways were used by millions of Turkish workers traveling to and from Western Europe. Contrary to foreign press reports, the Turkish governments in general have refrained, under the prodding by the Foreign Ministry, from defending the cause of Turks living outside Turkey until forced by public opinion to do so, as happened in the case of Cyprus in 1963-67 and Bulgaria in 1985.

The Turks of Bulgaria and Their Treatment

The Turks of Bulgaria have been under continuous pressure and suffered the denial of political rights almost ever since the country gained its autonomy in 1878, despite the provisions of the treaty of Berlin, which accorded them national and religious rights, and of several other treaties negotiated between Ottoman and (later) Republican governments and Bulgaria. (See section on international agreements.) However, immediately after 1944, when the Soviet troops occupied Bulgaria and installed a socialist regime, the Turks' position improved considerably. The number of Turkish schools increased dramatically, while periodicals and newspapers were published in all

---

[14]See, for instance, *Rodop-Bulgaristan Türkleri Tarihten Siliniyor mu?* [Are the Rodop Turks of Bulgaria eliminated from history?], published by the Association for Culture and Solidarity of the Rhodope-Danube Turks (Istanbul, 1976).

the main cities inhabited by Turks. Local Turkish literature began to emerge, along with a variety of studies dealing with the language and culture of the Turks in Bulgaria.[15] As late as 1975, several Bulgarian leaders praised development of the Turkish language and literature and promised help to aid its future expansion. However, by 1975 the Turkish schools, newspapers, periodicals, etc.—except for a few left to be shown to the visiting foreigners—were suddenly closed. By 1984 the entire panoply of historical works was revised, and all mention of the Turks was taken out of books and articles. In fact, many distinguished Bulgarian scholars were forced to rewrite their books and articles to eliminate any reference to Turks, except as Ottomans.[16] It seemed that the Bulgarian government had decided to eliminate absolutely everything in the country that could remind the Turks of their ethnic identity, as though they could by decree wipe out the entire past.

The reasons for the Bulgarian government's abrupt change of policy towards the Turks stemmed, first, from the Bulgarians' deep historical inferiority complex that has infected every ideological, tactical, or even occasionally *bona fide* effort by the Bulgarian regimes to adopt the standards of the civilized world. Bulgaria has always remained outside the moral confines of Europe. Many visitors entering Bulgaria from easy going Romania, sentimental Serbia, *laisser-faire* Turkey, or jovial Greece are struck by the urban Bulgarians' grim faces and unfriendly attitudes. The Bulgarian peasant is a hardworking, honest, reliable, individual, but the intellectual appears to be in the grip of a continuous crisis of identity, of feelings of insecurity and inferiority that he tries to overcome by engaging in endless—and for the most part false—diatribes about the glorious past of Bulgaria and the unjust treatment it has received from its neighbors, from Western Europe, etc.

The Bulgarian intellectuals are always trying to justify their regime's futile efforts to stand against the tide of history and civilization. Thus they have been accomplices when Bulgarian governments, driven by ambition, have sacrificed their dignity and moral integrity for petty territorial gain and have oppressed the country's minority citizens. The intellectuals helped the government undermine the Bulgarian church, which was older and stronger than any other institution in the country and was the real source of the Bulgarian identity and culture. The facist nationalist regime that

---

[15]İsmail Ağlagül, a director of the Ankara State Theatre and himself an immigrant from Bulgaria, is presently preparing a work on the Turkish writers of Bulgaria. According to preliminary information, the Turkish authors published in 1960-1968 a total of 34 novels, 36 collections of short studies, and 17 volumes of poems; see Bilal N. Şimşir, *Bulgaristan Türkleri* (Istanbul, 1986), pp. 303-306. A comprehensive bibliography on the study of Turkish spoken in Bulgaria was compiled by a member of the Turkish Institute of Bibliography; see Türker Acaroğlu, "Rumeli Türk Ağızları Üzerine Türkçe ve Yabancı Dillerdeki Başlıca Araştırmaların Açıklamalı Kaynakçası 1904-1981" [The annotated sources of the main researches in Turkish and foreign languages on the Turkish dialects of Rumelia 1904-1981 (Balkans)], *Halk Kültürü* 4 (1984): 13-40. One should mention also the linguistic studies undertaken by two well-trained linguists, Riza and Mefküre Molla (Mollov); see, e.g., "Traits de fusion dans le dialecte turc du Rhodope de l'Est," *Balkansko Ezikoznanie* 14, no. 2 (1970):57-81. (In 1985 Riza Molla was brutally murdered by the Bulgarian police after he refused to abandon his Turkish name.) Scholars of Bulgarian origin, such as Peter Miyatev and Stefan Mladenov have also produced works on the Turkish language of Bulgaria.

[16]For example, one writer of Muslim origin, Mustafa Müslimoğlu, in 1967 described the Turks as the largest minority in Bulgaria; in a recent rewriting of the same work he declared that there are no Turks in Bulgaria (meanwhile his name became Petar Letrov).

ruled Bulgaria from 1933 to 1944 used the church for its own political purposes and, in the process, substituted a materialist-nationalist ideal for the spiritual vision of the church. The materialism subsequently preached by the communist regime further undermined the church.[17] Even worse, after 1944 the Bulgarian people were almost forced by their leaders to adore and imitate the Soviet Union and thus deny their own culture and identity. It is well known that Zhivkov actually asked the Soviet Union to accept the country as another Soviet Republic and thus put an end to its independent national existence. In a relatively recent article, David Binder, who was a *New York Times* correspondent in Eastern Europe in the 1960s, told how Zhivkov paid his public dues to the USSR with remarks such as "The Soviet Union and Bulgaria breathe with the same lungs and the same blood flows in our veins," and actions such as participation in the invasion of Czechoslovakia in 1968.[18] The reaction of the average Bulgarians against the servility of their leaders towards the Soviets since 1944 (and towards Germany in World War I and II) has been the ultra-nationalistic outbursts in which the Turks are the scapegoats. In the 1970s the nationalist banner was unfurled by Todor Zhivkov's own daughter, Liudmila Zhivkova.[19] Zhivkova appealed to Bulgarian national pride with words such as, "It is to our generation ... that the historical responsibility and honour has fallen of standing at this vantage point [the 1300th anniversary of the First Bulgarian State] from which past and future are to be considered."[20] Another example of the Bulgarian leaders' low prestige in the eyes of their own people is provided by Georgi Markov, the Bulgarian writer who was confidant of Zhivkov until he fled to the West and broadcast bitter criticism of Bulgaria. (As one might expect, he paid with his life for daring to criticize the rulers of Bulgaria. While in London he was stabbed with an umbrella tip containing poison, and he died four days later.) In his memoirs Markov describes an interesting scene that took place in Arkutino, the resort town of the Bulgarian technocratic elite. Vulko Chervenkov (d. 1980), Bulgaria's "Little Stalin," came to spend New Year's night at Arkutino and entered the bar, which was full of young Bulgarian intellectuals. Upon seeing Chervenkov, the intellectuals began to sing "Shumi Maritza" (Maritza flows), the old national anthem of pre-Communist Bulgaria. The forbidden anthem was sung in order to remind Chervenkov and, later, the

---

[17]Yet the atheist government of Bulgaria does not hesitate to exploit for propaganda purposes that church the values of which it has undermined; see the brochure, *Religious Denominations in Bulgaria,* issued by the Press Agency (Sofia, 1987).

[18]*The New York Times Magazine,* 8 December 1985, p. 156.

[19]Zhivkova died of a mysterious illness in 1981. The former top ranking Soviet aide at the United Nations, Shevchenko, claimed in his memoirs that a KGB general expressed utter dissatisfaction with Liudmila's Bulgarian nationalism and vowed to liquidate her.

[20]"Unity Between Past, Present, and Future," *Palaeo Bulgarica,* III, 1979, 1, p. 3. The extensive festivals in 1981 celebrating the establishment of the "first Bulgarian state" were actually the expression of frustration and insecurity. There is little organic connection between the first, second, and, finally, the third (est. 1878) Bulgarian states except the name. It is interesting to note that the so called "1300 years of existence" of Bulgaria consisted merely of four centuries of independence—an independence that amounted to a continuous struggle for survival due to Bulgaria's inability to get along with its neighbors.

police who came to investigate the incident that they were not true Bulgarians.[21] (In the 1970s, during my visits to Bulgaria, several intellectuals expressed to me their admiration for the Turks, who, despite mistreatment at the hands of the Bulgarians and Russians, had maintained their ethnic identity, while the Bulgarians vied with one another to emulate everything Russian. By eradicating the Turkish community in the name of a nationalist policy, Zhivkov may hope to eliminate such exemplars of ethnic pride.)

The source of Bulgaria's historical animosity towards Turks and Turkey are well known. The early Bulgars, who came into the Balkans in the seventh century, abandoned their Turkish mother tongue and adopted the language of the Slavs, whom they ruled. Such events have occured many times in history, as rulers have become assimilated by the people ruled, but the Bulgarian case was different because the rulers of Bulgaria always remained aloof from the masses and stayed in power themselves, more often than not, by serving some bigger power. The Ottoman rule in the Balkans was challenged repeatedly by Greeks, Serbians, Albanians, Montenegrins, and Romanians—but not by Bulgarians. History does not record a single instance of Bulgarian uprising until the nineteenth century, a fact that the adversaries of Bulgaria are prone to cite very often. Bulgaria emerged overnight as an autonomous national state in 1878 as a direct consequence of the Russian victory over the Ottoman army. Russia desired to create a large, strong, but also loyal, proxy state that would promote her own interests in Southeast Europe. Today, as it was during the tsarist times, Bulgaria dutifully carries out in the Balkans all the roles assigned to her by her patron and, in exchange, receives economic, military, and diplomatic support and, occasionally, territory. Some writers go as far as to say that the USSR uses Bulgaria to test a new policy before applying it to her own people. According to the late A. Bennigsen, the forced change of names imposed on the Turks of Bulgaria may be the experimental prelude to a similar policy contemplated by the USSR for the Muslims living there.[22]

Nearly all the Bulgarian historians blame the Ottoman Empire (that is, the Turks) for having prevented Bulgaria for five hundred years from achieving national fulfillment and cultural and economic development. They also blame, even more strongly, the Greek patriarchate in Istanbul, which supposedly used religion and the universality of the Orthodox church to wipe out the national culture of the Bulgarians and hellenize them. As mentioned, some support a theory of a Turco-Greek conspiracy : "The Turks oppressed and exploited us physically while the Greeks robbed us of our national identity and alienated our leaders." (Bulgarian notables often became hellenized, as they sent their children to the Greek schools, the only ones available).

Behind the senseless persecution of the Turks lies the perennial Bulgarian fear that Turkey may be tempted one day to use the Turks of Bulgaria for her own purposes.

---

[21] Georgi Markov, *The Truth That Killed* (London, 1983); see the section entitled "Nationalist Serenade for Vulko Chervenkov," pp. 99, 107. Vulko Chervenkov was educated in the USSR. He took the place of Dimitrov, the veteran Bulgarian communist leader, after the latter died in 1949. Chervenkov was replaced by Zhivkov (b. 1911) who was Prime Minister in 1962-71, then chairman of the State Council and *de facto* dictator of Bulgaria till November 1989.

[22] Bennigsen expressed this view several times to this writer in many personal talks in France and the USA in the period 1985-88.

Bulgarians are aware that Turkey's western border is difficult to defend because of its lack of territorial depth. They also know that they illegally occupied East Rumelia. Thus, Turkey may wish someday to revise the *status quo*. Some Bulgarians even fear that Turkey may one day try to revive the Ottoman Empire (a thought that anyone with the slightest knowledge of Turkey would find laughable). The Bulgarians cite the landing of troops in Cyprus in 1974 as proof of Turkey's neo-Ottomanist designs (although this action was carried out according to treaties signed in 1959 and 1960, and Turkey has made no attempt to annex the Turkish part of Cyprus). In fretting about Turkish territorial ambitions they conveniently ignore the fact that during the 1939-44 period, when Turkey was allied with England and France, she could with impunity have attacked Bulgaria, which was allied with Hitler. Indeed, Turkey refused to engage in war against the Axis powers despite the possibility that she might thus get back a large portion of the territory given to or seized by Bulgaria in previous years. Bulgaria worries particularly about the fact that the Muslims living there show a natural affinity towards Turkey and fears that they would not feel inhibited from throwing in their lot with her if the opportunity arose, if only to escape Bulgaria's oppression and inhumanity.

Meanwhile the population of Turkey is constantly growing (it stands at approximately fifty four million versus nine million in Bulgaria) and economic development there is relatively steady, while Bulgaria is teetering on the verge of bankruptcy. It is these fears that have moved the leaders of Bulgaria, with the encouragement of the USSR, to use every means to prevent economic development of Turkey and to destabilize her regime by methods such as supplying weapons to the anarchists and terrorists (1975-78) and to the Kurdish bands operating currently in southeastern Anatolia. (The Bulgarian involvement in widespread efforts to destabilize Turkey are multi-sided and well documented but cannot be dealt with here in detail.)

In sum, Bulgaria's five hundred year submission to Ottoman power, coupled with the denationalization pressure of the Greek patriarchate in the eighteenth century seems to have permeated and distorted the political thinking of the Bulgarian leaders to such an extent that they see themselves as justified in taking the most drastic action against the Turks living in Bulgaria. Obviously, leaders who do not have self-respect and a national identity of their own can hardly be expected to respect other people's national identity. In effect the Bulgarian regimes have baptised as Christians Turks living in Bulgaria (as explained, Muslims consider the adoption of Christian names a form of baptism) allegedly in order to create a cohesive nation that could withstand pressure from outside, including potential attacks from Turkey. That this reason is mere pretext is demonstrated by the fact that Bulgaria refused adamantly the proposal of Turkey that the Turks living in Bulgaria be permitted to emigrate and to settle in Turkey, as did millions of their kin in the past. Obviously, the emigration of the Turks living in Bulgaria would eliminate the danger of a Turkish "fifth column" in case of conflict. However, the policy towards the Turks of Bulgaria and the refusal to permit their emigration is, in fact, a reaction to a series of basic demographic and economic events, to be discussed in the next section.

Demographic and Economic Factors behind Bulgaria's Policy toward its Turkish Population

The rapid growth of the Turkish population in Bulgaria and the near cessation of demographic growth among ethnic Bulgarians since the mid 1950s are the key factors that have moved the government to adopt the Bulgarization policy towards the Turkish community. The size of the Muslim population of Bulgaria (including Dobruca and Eastern Rumelia) on the eve of Bulgaria's autonomy—calculated by taking into account the pervasive undercount, omissions, etc.—stood at roughly one and one-half millions as against about one and one-quarter million non-Muslims, most of whom were Bulgarian speaking.[23] During the war of 1877-78 approximately half of the Muslim population was forced to emigrate, and some 300,000 were killed by Bulgarian bands and Russian troops. A number of Bulgarians also moved from the periphery to settle in the Bulgarian principality. A. Ubicini, a well-informed aide to the French Embassy in Istanbul who had access to official Ottoman statistics, estimated the population of the sancaks of Ruschuk, Varna, Vidin, and Tirnova and of Sofia at 1,914,638 in 1878-79. In Ruschuk and Varna Bulgarians constituted slightly over one-third of the population, the rest being mostly Muslims. Only in Vidin, Sofia, and Tirnova were Bulgarians in the majority.[24]

The government of the autonomous principality of Bulgaria conducted its first census in 1881 and a second census in 1888. The results of these censuses were published and are available. The British government, apparently dissatisfied with the available information asked for and obtained from the Bulgarian government a copy of these census results.[25] The population figures for Bulgaria (excluding Eastern Rumelia) as supplied to the British were the following:

	1881	1888
Bulgarians	1,345,507	1,570,599
Muslims	527,284	480,593
Greeks	11,444	10,975
Various	123,684	131,267
Total	2,007,919	2,193,434

[23]The figures used as the basis of this calculation are in Kemal H. Karpat, *Ottoman Population 1830-1914: Demographic and Social Characteristics* (Madison, Wisconsin, 1985). The Salname of 1874, which was based on the census of 1866 conducted by Mithat Pasha (and was used extensively by Nicolai Todorov in his book on the Balkan town) gives the male population of the Tuna province (including Dobruca but omitting the area south of the Balkans) as 504,297 Muslims and 491,742 non-Muslims. The Muslims were concentrated in the east, around Ruschuk, Varna, Pazarcik, Shumlu, Razgrad, Silistre, and Hezergrad, and in the southwest in Kustendil, Orhaniye, etc. The census of 1877, which does not classify the population into religious groups, gave the male population of Bulgaria north of the Balkan range (including the districts of Niş) as 1,247,000; calculated proportionately, the Muslims *numbered about* 680,000.

[24]"La Principauté de Bulgarie," *Revue de Géographie* (July-December 1879): 81-100.

[25]See Public Record Office, Foreign Office 78, vol. 4032, O'Connor to Salisbury, 13 September 1887; also ibid., vol. 4230 "Memorandum on the Population of Bulgaria," pp. 120 ff.

To these figures one must add the Muslim population of Eastern Rumelia, annexed by Bulgaria in 1885. Figures appearing in the journal *Maritza* give the number of Muslims in 1880 as only 174,000, as against 573,231 Bulgarians.[26] This number is obviously low, as the official Ottoman statistics numbered the Muslims, if calculated on the basis of Bulgarian sources, amounted to 654,593 in both the principality and Eastern Rumelia, while the Bulgarians totaled about 2,740,830. Actually, we know, from Ottoman official statistics and from a variety of other sources as well, that the number of Muslims, despite deportations, killings, and migrations amounted to over a million, or roughly 35 percent of the population in 1888. Even if one were to rely solely on Bulgarian figures, still the Muslim population of Bulgaria in 1880 constituted about 23 percent of the total.[27] In 1913 Bulgaria took over the nine districts in the eastern part of Macedonia, with its population of roughly 160,000, of whom 92-95 percent were Muslim. In that same year Bulgaria lost southern Dobruca to Romania (she regained it in 1940). The Bulgarian statistics of 1910 listed the Muslim population of south Dobruca at 117,622. After annexing the area, the Romanian government conducted a census, according to which the Muslims numbered 165,788.

The Bulgarian population growth, according to official Bulgarian statistics collected since 1900, has been as follows:[28]

Patterns of Population Growth, 1900-83

Year	Birth Rate (per thous.)	Death Rate (per thous.)	Natural Increase (per thous.)	Total Population (thousands)	Urban Share (%)	Density (per km)
1900	42.2	22.5	19.7	3,716	19.8	38.9
1920	39.9	21.4	18.5	4.825	19.9	47.0
1940	22.2	13.4	8.8	6,368	23.0	61.7
1950	25.2	10.2	15.0	7,273	27.5	65.7
1960	17.8	8.1	9.7	7,906	38.0	71.4
1970	16.3	9.1	7.2	8,515	53.0	76.8
1980	14.5	11.1	3.4	8.877	62.5	80.0
1983	13.6	11.4	2.2	8,939	65.0	80.7

These figures are exceptionally revealing if properly interpreted. They show, first, that Bulgaria's population grew steadily in the period 1900-40, with the main growth occuring between 1900 and 1924, (due in part to population exchanges). The increase in the birth rate from 22.2 to 25.2 over the 1940-50 period was due to the re-acquisition of southern Dobruca in 1940 and the immigration of the large Bulgarian population from

---

[26]Copy of *Maritza* of 27 July 1880, reproduced in Great Britain, House of Commons, *Accounts and Papers*, vol. 82, 1880, p. 109-10.

[27]A variety of sources placed the number of Muslims in Bulgaria at 652,000, indicating also that this population had 1,293 schools with 64,422 students; see Alexandre Popovic, *L'Islam Balkanique* (Berlin, 1986), p. 74.

[28]See *Statisticheski godishnik na NR Bulgariia, 1982* (Sofia, 1983), pp. 29.

the north (exchanged for the Romanian colonists of Qadrilater). The Muslim population of the two districts known as Qadrilater in southern Dobruca—that is, the districts of Silistre and Pazarcik—totaled approximatedly 120,000. The Bulgarian statistics show that the national birth rate dropped steadily after 1950, reaching a mere 13.6 per thousand in 1983, when the total population of Bulgaria had reached 8,939 million. Meanwhile, the death rate of an aging population increased from 8.1 per thousand in 1960 to 11.4 in 1983. The rate of urbanization, rose drastically from 19.8 percent in 1900 to 23 percent in 1940 and then nearly doubled to 65 percent in 1983. Heavy capital investment, financed in part by the USSR, which wanted to have a strong ally to face the two NATO powers (Turkey and Greece), turned Bulgaria into an industrialized-urbanized nation almost overnight, however shaky the bases of that industrialization. According to Bulgarian sources, the national income, which rose steadily at a rate of 8.3 percent until 1975, had slipped to a 4.1 percent rate of increase by 1980; since then the income has become much lower. It is interesting to note that the investment in agriculture, which was 22.9 percent of the fixed capital investment in the late 1960s fell steadily to 12.4 percent in 1980, although the export of food and consumer manufactures based mostly on agricultural production remained at a steady 26.6 percent of the total Bulgarian exports.[29]

The true political significance of the figures provided above can be understood properly only if the shifts in population growth and the urbanization of Bulgaria are interpreted in the context of the ethnic and religious composition of the population. The Bulgarian statistics give Turkish population in 1956 as 656,025.[30] This figure excludes the Pomaks, who number about 160,000 and consider themselves Turkish, the government having abandoned the old religious classification and adopted instead an ethnic linguistic classification that allows the Bulgarian-speaking Muslim Pomaks to be classified as "Bulgarians". The last forced exodus of Turks from Bulgaria, involving some 152,000 people (some put the figure at 156,000) occurred in 1951/52. From that date onwards Turkish emigration dwindled to insignificance because industrialization increased Bulgaria's need for manpower. Thus, one can say that the growth of the Turkish population in Bulgaria after 1960 was not reduced by emigrations, as was the case from 1878 to 1944 and in 1951/52. Thus, according to Bulgarian offcial statistics the total of Muslims (Turks, with Pomaks added in) in Bulgaria amounted roughly to 860,000, or 12 percent of the population, in 1956. This total of 860,000 Muslims does not include the 197,000 gypsies listed in the statistics of 1956, although most of them were Muslims. If the gypsies are added to the total, then the Muslims in 1956 amounted to at least 14 to 15 percent of the population according to rounded Bulgarian official statistics. We know from a variety of sources that the Bulgarian government has manipulated the census figures so as to show the number of Turks as lower that the true figure. The reclassification of the Pomaks is one such manipulation. Taking into account the various omissions from the official statistics, one may reasonably place the

[29]Background information on Bulgaria's economy is found in John R. Lampe, *The Bulgarian Economy in the Twentieth Century* (London, 1986) and John R. Lampe and Marvin R. Jackson, *Balkan Economic History, 1550-1950* (Bloomington, Indiana, 1982).
[30]See B. Kayser, *La population et L'économie de la république populaire bulgare* (Paris, 1961).

total of the Muslim population of Bulgaria in 1960 at some 20 percent of the entire population, or, roughly, 1,600,00. (I believe that even this figure is too low).

The industrial development and urbanization after 1960 affected mainly the ethnic Bulgarian population. The occupation change from agriculture to industry and services resulted in the movement of a large number of ethnic Bulgarians from villages and towns to cities. Meanwhile, the Turkish population in particular, and the Muslims in general, with the exception of those from a few areas around Plovdiv, Burgas, etc., stayed in their villages and remained involved in agriculture. (Presently about 80 percent of the Muslims live in rural areas.) The Bulgarian government welcomed this development in the 1960s and 1970s because the industrialization and urbanization resulted in the upgrading of the quality of life for the ethnic Bulgarians. The government exploited the agricultural sector, in which the Muslim-Turkish population was concentrated, to finance its industrialization. It payed very low agricultural wages and, in the process, downgraded the living standards of the Turks. The agricultural labor force, which stood at 82.1 percent of the total labor force in 1948, dropped to 23.8 percent in 1980. One may assume that about half of the agricultural force consisted of Muslims, since their rate of movement into industry (except for mining and similar hazardous occupations) was very low. The ethnic Bulgarian peasantry became a blue collar working class overnight, while the Muslims stayed in agriculture.

The same condition prevails in the army, which, like its counterpart in the USSR, used the Muslims as work units. We do not have exact figures for the percentage of the Muslims in the Bulgarian military forces; yet, it is safe to assume that, in view of their high birth rate as contrasted with the low rate for the Bulgarians, the percentage of Turks and Muslims in general in the army amounted to some 30 percent in 1980. The Muslim units are not trained for battle; therefore, the fighting capability of the Bulgarian army, if measured in terms of the number of fighting men, has undergone a steady deterioration since the mid-1970s. The Bulgarian government, having oppressed its Turkish citizens since 1970, is fully aware that it cannot now count on their loyalty in case of war with Turkey.

The service and construction sectors, which together accounted for 32.8 percent of the labor force, were equally affected. The Muslims who lived in small towns or on the periphery of cities were used in mass to build roads, port installations, and a variety of other projects involving heavy labor.[31] Since agriculture relied on low-paid manual labor supplied by Muslims, the government invested relatively little in heavy agricultural machinery. Thus, the fact that the drop in agricultural investment from 29.7 percent of the total in 1960 to 12.4 percent in 1980 did not greatly affect the gross agricultural production can be explained by the fact that the government could exploit at will the working Muslim population.

The results of this economic policy based on the exploitation of the Turkish Muslim element were just the opposite from that expected. In the 1940s and 1950s, in order to win the support of the population, the government introduced sanitary services and opened schools, including professional schools, in the Turkish areas: the number of

---

[31]I have collected this information during my frequent trips through Bulgaria in the 1960s and 1970s; I have also interviewed hundreds of Turks from Bulgaria who emigrated to Turkey.

schools went up from 424 in 1943 to 1,199 in 1949/50, and the number of teachers rose from 871 to 3,037 in the same period. Consequently, the literacy rate among Turks, which was around 10 percent in 1940, went up to 50 or 60 percent in 1970, while the health services helped increase the survival rate of the newborns. (Even before the new regime took power in 1944 the sanitary services, as well as the general standard of life, were of a relatively higher quality in Bulgaria, than in all the other Balkan countries, including Turkey). Moreover, the relatively low consumption of alcohol and the dietary habits of the Muslims permitted them to maintain a healthy life: their cuisine uses practically any ingredient grown in the backyard or on small pieces of land around the house. Thus, while the ethnic Bulgarian population in cities had to wait for hours in line to receive second class foodstuffs, the Turks living in rural areas had plenty of homegrown food, however simple. Meanwhile the Bulgarian ruling party opened branches in the villages and created a local bureaucratic structure manned by the new, politically-minded Muslim intellectual elite. This elite was under the direct supervision of the ethnic Bulgarian chiefs, but it could occasionally articulate the demands and defend the interests of its own people. A few of the Muslim intellectuals made it to the top: that is, they were given seats in the legislature.[32] Finally, one must mention the fact that in the late 1940s and 1950s Bulgaria was used by the Soviet Union as a show case to illustrate the superiority of the socialist regime in achieving rapid economic development, especially in comparison with Turkey, whose economy was underdeveloped. (A substantial amount of literature depicting the happy life of the Turks in socialist Bulgaria was smuggled into Turkey in the 1950s and 1960s.)

The result of this policy was that by the mid-1950s the growth rate of the Muslim, and notably of the Turkish, population began to increase dramatically, while that of the ethnic Bulgarians dropped steadily. The death rate among the aged Bulgarians also increased, due to shortages of food in cities, the excessive work, and a variety of other ills associated with rapid industrial development. One may safely assume that by 1960 the annual growth rate among the Muslims of Bulgaria had increased by at least 3 percent, although there are no accurate statistics available. The Bulgarian government provided census figures which showed that the size of the Muslim population remained the same during a thirty-year period, although there was practically no emigration between 1952 and 1987, and we know for certain, from field observations and sporadic talks with local people in Bulgarian villages and towns, that the rate of growth of the Muslim population accelerated steadily after 1956. The number of children in an average rural Muslim family in Bulgaria increased in the period 1950-1985 from 2 to 3 (1940-1960) to 5 or 6 in 1980; the marriage age decreased from 22 to 20 to 18 in the 1960s, contributing greatly to the explosion of population among the Turks.[33] Meanwhile the

---

[32] Halil İbis, a former Turkish member of the Bulgarian legislature could not endure the pressure imposed on him and the servility requested in exchange for this position and finally sought asylum in the West and eventually came to Turkey. He appeared later before the United State Congress where he related openly the pressure exerted on him.

[33] I was told in 1978/79, by several people intimately familiar with the life of the Turkish villages in the Deliorman (Silistre-Tutrakan) area, that young Muslim activists formed teams among themselves and went from one village to the next urging Turkish families to marry off their sons and daughters early and to have as many children as possible. This occurred after the Bulgarian government

ethnic Bulgarian population was aging and by 1980 could not even replace itself—a phenomenon common in all of Eastern Europe. On the basis of the various available figures, one may assume that the Muslim population of Bulgaria (excluding the gypsies, whose number is now placed at 500,000) has been increasing at a rate of 3 percent yearly, at the least. If one takes as basis of calculation the entire Muslim population as of 1960 as we have it from unofficial but reliable sources, then the size of the Muslim (mostly Turkish) component of the Bulgarian population may be given as follows:

1960	1,600,000
1970	2,080,000
1980	2,624,000
1985	3,017,000

A student of Bulgarian affairs, who was born and raised there and had access to unpublished data, gives the following figures for the Muslim population:[34]

1892	1,212,986	
1900	1,182,956	
1910	1,107,644	
1926	1,430,329	(including western Macedonia, acquired in 1913)
1934	1,439,566	
1941	1,471,000	(including Dobruca)
1956	1,075,000	(Pomaks not included)
1971	1,450,000	(Pomaks not included)

Muslim emigration from Bulgaria for periods from 1935 to 1951 was as follows :

1935-1940	95,494
1941-1949	14,390
1950-1951	156,000

According to our calculations which we believe to be approximately correct, the current proportion of the Muslim population of Bulgaria is as high as 28 percent, which is normal, given Bulgaria's special ethnic and economic situation as described above. One may go as far as to say that the drop in growth of the Bulgarian population (from 9.7 per thousand in 1960 to 2.2 per thousand in 1983) occurred mainly among the ethnic Bulgarians. In fact, the national growth probably can be attributed entirely to the sharp rise of the birth rate among Muslims. (A similar demographic phenomenon

---

intensified its pressure and attempted to prevent the Turks from having many children by cutting down the child allowances, etc.

[34]See Halit Molla Hüseyin, "Muslims in Bulgaria: A Status Report," *Journal of the Institute of Muslim Minority Affairs* 5, no. 1 (January 1984):136-44. For a comprehensive study of immigration from Bulgaria, see Cevat Geray, *Türkiyeden ve Türkiye'ye Göçler ve Göçmenlerin İskâni* [Turkish emigration and immigration and settlement] (Ankara, 1962).

occurred among the Muslims of Central Asia, as indicated by various Soviet censuses. The parallel growth of the Muslim population in the USSR and Bulgaria are not coincidental, since in the history of the Muslims and their treatment in both countries has been similar).[35]

The growth in size of the Muslim population, accompanied by the emergence of native elites, produced alarmed reactions from the Bulgarian government, beginning in the mid-1970s, when it began to close the Turkish schools, newspapers, etc. The Turks reacted to these measures by demanding explanations and by voicing criticism. Long dormant nationalist feelings were awakened; it was rumored, for example, that some Turkish leaders had asked for autonomy in the districts where they formed a majority as a means of defending their ethnic identity. The Bulgarian government responded by increasing the pressure, only to cause further resistance and open defiance, as shown by acts of sabotage, bombings, and the like. Yet the government would not expel the troublesome Turks or even allow them to emigrate because it had become vitally dependent on their cheap, slavelike labor. Without Turks, the Bulgarian agricultural and services sectors would collapse. The Turks had become indispensable to the Bulgarian economy, even though they were detested and feared. The Bulgarian government, out of sheer greed and nationalist passion, had pushed itself into an economic and political corner: It did not want the Turks in the country, yet, it could not do without them. This situation explains the Bulgarian government's conflicting policies towards the emigration of their ethnic minorities. For instance, in 1920 the Greek population of Messembria and Sozopolis, two Black Sea ports which had been Greek since the sixth century B.C., were expelled without remorse. In 1913 the Bulgarians applied every possible pressure on the Turks of Qadrilater to get them to leave their lands, and in 1951/52 it expelled some 152,000 Turks.[36] Yet, since 1960 Bulgaria has refused adamantly to permit any Turk to emigrate, despite the oft-repeated offer of the Turkish government to accept all the Muslims of Bulgaria who want to settle in Turkey.

The Bulgarian government considered that it had no choice: If it let its Muslim citizens emigrate, its shaky economy would collapse overnight; if it kept the Muslims and they continued to multiply their numbers, then in a matter of twenty years the ethnic Bulgarians would have become a minority. It came inexorably to the conclusion, after trying unsuccessfully to stem the growth of Turkish population, that it would have to Bulgarize them. Hence the policy of baptizing the Turks as Christians, under the guise of merely changing their names.[37] Thus an atheistic communist government was

---

[35]There is an abundant literature on the birth rates among the Soviet Muslims; see, in particular, the work of Murray Feshbach, "The Soviet Union: Population Trends and Dilemmas," *Population Bulletin* **37**, no. 3 (1982):1-45.

[36]The best book source on the history of the Turks in Bulgaria is by a member of the Turkish Historical Society, the author of several important studies; see Bilal Şimşir, *Bulgaristan Türkleri* [The Turks of Bulgaria] (Istanbul, 1986). Şimşir attended elementary and high school in Bulgaria before emigrating to Turkey. He has an intimate knowledge of the Bulgarian government's policies as well as of the language and customs of the country.

[37]The actions of the Bulgarian government has caused consternation among some, but not all, Bulgarians abroad. Some scholars of Bulgarian affairs in the USA have, in the presence of this writer, expressed their satisfaction with the policy, stating that "if the Bulgarian government can get away with the baptism of the Turks, then it will be thanked by the next generations." For a bold Bulgarian

forced, in the end, to employ religion to advance its nationalist aims and by grim economic, demographic, and political reality to declare that "there are no Turks in Bulgaria."

Once more the Bulgarian leaders have misused the power in their hands and exposed their country and its people to endless peril. It may be appropriate, therefore, to end this sad story by citing David Binder's insightful conclusion to his article on Bulgaria:

> "The Bulgarians never liberated themselves" remarked a Macedonian from Yugoslavia, who is a keen observer of this country [Bulgaria], "and after the Russians liberated them [in 1878], they only won one war, a short one in 1885 [against Serbia]. Bulgarian history is discontinuity" he said, adding that "they chose the wrong side in three wars," suffering defeat in the second Balkan War, and again in World War I and II, when Bulgaria sided with Germany. Having made wrong choices at three critical junctures in the space of less than three decades "there is no fixed reference point" observed the Macedonian. "For Bulgarians, who is to say the choices they make now are not wrong?"[38]

University of Wisconsin, Madison

Postscript

After the above was written, the government of Bulgaria entered suddenly upon a new act of aggression against its citizens of Turkish origin. It abruptly forced hundred of thousands of Turks to leave the country and take refuge in Turkey. By 20 August, 1989, some 310,000 had already crossed the Turkish border. Finally the Turkish government decided to close the border in an effort to force the Bulgarian government to negotiate an agreement to permit the orderly emigration of the Turks and save some of their assets.

The emigrating Turks had left behind homes, land, moveable property, bank accounts, and even family members. According to the accounts given by thousands of these refugees, Bulgarian police and military units summoned them to various government stations, handed them passports prepared in advance, and told them to leave the country immediately. The Bulgarian government claimed that this exodus was "voluntary," that the Turks had taken advantage of "freedom of travel" and could return to their homes in Bulgaria if they wished. The so called "freedom to travel abroad," however, applies only to Turks—not to ethnic Bulgarians or to other minorities. Furthermore, the right to return home is hedged about with financial penalties. Turks who do not return within three months have to pay heavy fines, while a six-months stay abroad (that is, in Turkey) leads to an automatic loss of pension and other rights.

The Bulgarian government calculated that the ousting of the Turks would benefit it either way. If those exiled stay in Turkey, it means that their number in Bulgaria

---

criticism on the treatment of the Turks, see S.T. Raikin, "Problems of Communism in Bulgaria. Liquidation of the Turkish Minority in Bulgaria," *Free Agrarian Banner,* no. 45/46 (1985): 1-13.

[38]*New York Times Magazine,* 8 December 1985, p. 162.

would diminish, their assets etc., would become the property of the government, and accumulated pension benefits would not have to be paid; if some return to Bulgaria, they could be used as propaganda vehicles to expedite the bulgarization of the remaining Turks with descriptions of bad living conditions in Turkey and discrimination by native Turks against the immigrants. So far about 8,000 exiles have returned to Bulgaria and have been promptly brought before TV cameras and radios and asked to defame Turkey; some of these are considered to have been agents of the Bulgarian government.

The exile of these Turks is an admission of the Bulgarian government that ethnic Turks do exist in Bulgaria and gives the lie to its four-year-old contention that "there are no Turks in Bulgaria."

Bulgaria's decision to expel its citizens of Turkish origin amounts also to a confession that its brutal policy of bulgarizing the Muslim minority has met with dismal failure. Despite the killing and jailing of thousands of Turks, resistance increased steadily and eventually culminated in open defiance of the military and police units charged with carrying out the bulgarization policy. In fact, the mammoth demonstration by some 50,000 Turks in Shumnu in the spring of 1989 was started by the desperate stand of Turks in a village in eastern Bulgaria, where they bare-handedly disarmed several dozen soldiers sent to arrest them. The news of the villagers' action spread rapidly and soon thousands of Turks converged on Shumnu to protest the government's action.

The demonstrators were objecting to the forced change of their Turkish-Muslim names to Slavic-Christian ones and the prohibitions imposed on the practice of their faith and customs. They did not ask for an autonomous Turkish region or for territorial separation from Bulgaria but only for respect for their rights. The protest of these Turks was an entirely legitimate and natural reaction to the oppressive policy of the Bulgarian government, which at Helsinki, among other places, had solemnly agreed to protect the precise freedom and rights it was wantonly violating. Many Bulgarians, as usual, supported uncritically the actions of their government. They stoned cars, buses, and trains carrying the refugees, robbed thousands of them, and committed rape against women and even young girls of eight or ten.

This inhuman behavior on the part of the Bulgarians paid indirect compliment to the tenacity and temerity of the Turks, who preferred death or exile rather than the abandonment of their Turkish names and Islamic faith (whereas the Bulgarian leaders had voluntarily offered to give up their country's independence just to become another republic of the USSR). The warm reception accorded to the refugees by even the most extreme leftist elements in Turkey contributed further to the undermining of the myth of "socialist brotherhood" and "humanism" expounded for decades by East European governments. Belatedly, a group of Bulgarian intellectuals in the West have criticized the action of their government.

The reasons for the latest actions of the Bulgarian government are numerous. The villages of the Turks who were forced to emigrate to Turkey are strategically located in eastern Bulgaria and the Kirjali mountains close to Turkey. After forcing out the native Turks, the government hopes to settle there some Bulgarians brought from other regions and to install military units also, as the number of ethnic Bulgarians is too small to allow replacement of all the departing Turks by civilians. Thus, by expelling the Turks the government aims to establish firmer control of the areas around the Kustendil,

Razgrad, Shumnu, Silistre and Varna districts, where the Turkish villages are contiguous and where the government's policy of forced bulgarization appears to have no impact.

In the late fall of 1989 the Bulgarian government plans to expel other Turks from villages and towns located elsewhere in Bulgaria, but only after the harvest is complete, since it has no other field workers but the Turks. The reports indicate that Bulgaria has started importing workers from Soviet Moldavia, which is inhabited among other nationalities by some 260,000 Bulgarians. These were settled in Moldavia (the former Romanian province of Bessarabia) in the nineteenth century, and their current return to Bulgaria is a form of repatriation. Obviously, Bulgaria enjoys the tacit support of the Soviet government in this population transfer, indicating Moscow's support of and involvement in Bulgaria's government campaign against its Turkish subjects. The Russian ambassador in Ankara offered to mediate the conflict between Turkey and Bulgaria, but his offer appears designated to derail the Turkish government's efforts to bring the matter before international forums. There has even been talk of bringing Vietnamese to work the Bulgarian fields, but this news is regarded as a smoke screen to mask the settlement of the Soviet Bulgarians in the villages of the expelled Turks.

The closing of the border may have thwarted the Bulgarian government's plans. It is estimated that Bulgaria is trying to rid itself of a total of 500,000 to 600,000 Turks. Then, citing its own false statistics, it can declare once more that "all Turks have left Bulgaria," and proceed with even more stringent measures to bulgarize its remaining Muslim citizens (whose number is still close to two million). Bulgarians believe that the Turks are the most politically conscious group and enjoy the sympathy of Turkey. Their removal, therefore, will eliminate the most resistant and vociferous Muslim voice opposed to the policy of bulgarization.

It is not clear at the present time how the Bulgarian government will respond to the closure of the border by Turkey, since this measure seems to have undermined the immediate efforts to clear the Turks from the designated areas. However, with this blind fascist-nationalist policy, Bulgaria has quite likely gone past the point of no return and has triggered a series of events with catastrophic consequences. It has raised an international outcry and, particularly, attracted unfavorable attention from the U. S. Congress. On June 15 concurrent resolutions condemning Bulgaria's treatment of its Turkish citizens were introduced in the Senate, by Dennis de Concini, chairman of the Commission on Security and Cooperation in Europe, and in the House, by Steny H. Hoyer, co-chairman of the committee, and Steven Solarz. These resolutions detail the history of the campaign to bulgarize the Turks, from the various discriminatory acts of the 1950s to the expulsions of 1989, and cite the various international agreements being violated by Bulgaria in this policy. They call upon the U. S. administration to raise the issue "in all appropriate international fora." (*Congressional Record,* 101st Cong., 1st Sess., 1989, vol. 135, no 80). In August the US. ambassador to Bulgaria was recalled. The displeasure of the U. S. may be felt in other ways also. In an article in *The Christian Science Monitor* of 2 March 1988 (p. 19), Congressman Hoyer suggested that

the more recent "openness" on the part of high-level Bulgarian officials, spurred in part by the desire to gain full membership in the General

Agreement on Tariffs and Trade and to enhance Bulgaria's access to Western markets and technology can be met with a challenge [to the assimilation campaign].

Thus, if the USSR embarks on a full fledged retrenchment on her commitment to her East European satellites—as many feel she must and is even now beginning to do— Bulgaria's government may find that in ridding itself of the "Turkish problem" it has also destroyed any credibility with the rest of the international community, toward which it will need to turn for trade and aid in lieu of the Soviets. Thus, it will have created for Bulgaria a larger problem: one of survival on its own in a world that for the most past, finds its treatment of its Turkish minority abhorrent.

K. H. K.

İlhan Şahin, Feridun M. Emecen, Yusuf Halaçoğlu

TURKISH SETTLEMENTS IN RUMELIA (BULGARIA) IN THE 15TH AND 16TH CENTURIES: TOWN AND VILLAGE POPULATION*

Introduction

The migration into and settlement of the Turkish peoples in the Balkan peninsula, notably in Bulgaria, occurred during at least four major periods. The first period can be placed somewhere in the first millenium B.C., The second period began roughly in the middle of the seventh century A.D., when one branch of the Onogur people, who had been part of the Turkic-speaking kingdom of "Old Great Bulgaria" on the Volga until the death of their ruler Kovrat in 642, moved into the Balkan domains of the Byzantine Empire. These were the Proto-Bulgarians, that is, the ancestors of the Slavicized-Christianized Bulgarians, of today. The third Turkic wave began to cross the Danube at the end of the eighth century, and this southward movement lasted at least until the twelfth century. The Pechenges, Cumans, and Uzes crossing the Danube were eventually either assimilated or simply liquidated by the established population.

The fourth period, by far the most important one, began in the thirteenth century with the settlement of the followers of Izzeddin Kaykaus, the Seljuki ruler of Konya, along the western shore of the Black Sea. Kaykaus had been defeated by the Mongol, armies and, together with his followers, sought refuge in the Balkan territories of Byzantium. Many of Kaykaus' followers—known as Gagauzes, or the people of Kaykaus—converted to Orthodox Christianity, but they preserved their Turkish names and language until today.

The last and most significant immigration and settlement of Turkic peoples (which concluded the fourth period of migration) occurred beginning towards the end of the fourteenth century, that is, well after the founding of the Ottoman state in 1288. By this time the ethno-historical and cultural synthesis of the various Turkic peoples in Anatolia and the Balkans had resulted in the creation of a new ethno-religious entity with a distinctive linguistic, cultural, and political identity and personality of its own. These were the Turks of the Ottoman Empire, the immediate precursors of today's Turks and Turkey; therefore, their language, culture, and identity should be properly referred to as Turkish.

---

* This article was translated from Turkish by Nurhan İsvan and edited and completed by Kemal H. Karpat.

The massive immigration of the Ottoman Turks into the territory of present-day Bulgaria occurred under the combined effect of two rather different factors. The first was the Mongol invasion and occupation of eastern and central Anatolia, which forced millions of Turkish tribesmen and town dwellers to flee westward and thus created a huge pool of people seeking places to settle. After the Mongol retreat, during the last decades of the thirteenth century, many of these Turkish tribesmen became the backbone of the population of the thirty-odd Turkish *beyliks*—that is, small princedoms established in most of west and central Anatolia in the period 1200-1470. The second factor was partly a consequence of the first: these Anatolian Turkish *beyliks* were suppressed and annexed by the expanding *beylik* of Gazi Osman (1288-1326), initially one of the least important, except for its location in the immediate vicinity of the Byzantine Empire. The tribesmen who were affiliated in one way or another with the ruling families of the defeated *beyliks* proved to be a source of continuous trouble for the Ottoman rulers. This was particularly true for the followers of the ruling families that, in addition to their political power, commanded some religious charisma, such as the descendants of the Turkoman states of Karakoyunlu or Akkoyunlu (including Uzun Hasan, whose territories became eventually fertile ground for the spread of the Kızılbaş or Alevi, heresy). Thus the settlement policy undertaken by the Ottoman government in the fifteenth and sixteenth centuries in the area south of the Danube and Dobruca had at least three purposes: first, to provide sanctuary and the economic means to ensure the survival of large numbers of people in western and central Anatolia (the expansion of the population in these centuries is well known); second, to disperse the unruly and the unorthodox Kızılbaş and settle them in areas away from their own religious centers in east Anatolia and Iran; and, third, to guarantee the security of the Ottoman state by giving to the new settlers a role as the defenders of, and even as spokesmen for, the new Muslim-Turkish order being established in the Balkans under the Osmanli dynasty.

The immigration and settlement of the Turks was further spurred by the economic and demographic conditions in the Balkans. The population there, especially in Bulgaria, had been reduced substantially by foreign and civil wars, which had ravaged the country for at least a century prior to the arrival of the Turks. Probably the total Bulgarian-speaking population in the early fifteenth century consisted of barely 200,000 to 300,000 souls. Thus, the territory of present-day Bulgaria was largely empty. The lack of population had led to the abandonment of agriculture and, ultimately, to the unimpeded growth of dense forests over large sections of the area. Thus, the north-eastern section of the country was an ocean of trees, which provided refuge for many Kızılbaş tribes seeking to escape persecution by the orthodox Sunni. (Hence its name, which has been preserved until today as Deliorman, or Telcorman in Romanian— "Wild", or "Crazy Forest".) Many Turkish settlements were established after forests were cut down and agricultural land was made available; but many other villages—many of them inhabited by the Kızılbaş—were established in the woods, and the inhabitants made a living by producing charcoal, which found a market in cities and in the capital itself.

The record of the Turkish settlements is preserved in minute detail in various Ottoman registers, some going back to the fourteenth century. The Ottoman government had to maintain accurate records concerning the size of the Muslim and non-

Muslim population in order to levy taxes and control the cultivation of the land. It is interesting to note that the tribes played a major role in the early Turkish settlement of Bulgaria. Indeed, according to the Ottoman records the settlement of Rumelia was achieved mainly by making sedentary villagers out of semi-nomadic Turkish tribes, mainly from Anatolia. Several reasons account for the state's choice of the semi-nomads for its settlement activity. These included the fact that the tribes-people were more inclined than sedentary people to migrate—a result of their way of life—and that they needed vast pastures and productive lands. In addition, the Turkish tribes possessed an organizational structure and discipline that were conducive to performing military functions on the borderlands and in their settlement places.

Islam played a major role in the success of this settlement policy, since it provided the most important cultural and linguistic link between the various groups of new settlers, eventually superseding the ethnic and tribal identities and loyalties. Thus, by the middle of the seventeenth century, tribal identities appeared to have been forgotten as the new Muslim-Turkish identity superseded local and tribal allegiances. A new cultural-ethnic community had thus emerged.

The Ottoman rulers, true to the well-established Muslim tradition, classified their subjects according to religion only. Consequently, the classical Ottoman population records listed chiefly three categories: Muslims, Christians, and Jews. While the Ottoman records used in this study employ only the term "Muslim", we have used the terms "Turks", "Muslims", and "Muslim Turks" interchangeably, for until the seventeenth century, despite some conversion to Islam of non-Turks, the ethnic Turks constituted the bulk of the Muslim population of Rumelia.

The Turkish settlers in Rumelia brought with them the Turkish language and customs prevailing in Anatolia. They often gave their new settlements in the Balkans the names of their original villages. Moreover, they tended to settle as a group and seldom mixed with the local Bulgarians. (These had, in most areas, become, in fact, a small minority. They were left to reside in their original homes and became part of the Christian Orthodox *millet,* which was under the authority of the Greek patriarchate. Thus they had religious and cultural autonomy.) Most Turkish villages adopted Turkish names, although in a number of cases the old Byzantine or Bulgarian names of major cities were preserved by adapting them to the Turkish phonetics. By the seventeenth century one begins to see a revival of the Bulgarian population, which, thanks to the relative economic prosperity and political-military security brought by the Ottoman power, began to gain vitality and economic health.

As a consequence of the Ottoman government's settlement policy, in a relatively short time Rumelia became even more densely populated by Turks than many parts of Anatolia. The settlement methods varied during the early Ottoman period. The government settled the tribes by using harsh methods such as the deportation, especially with regard to the rebellious tribes. At the same time it sought to induce voluntary migration by establishing *imarets* (charitable institutions) and *vakifs* (pious endowments), and by building *tekkes* and *zâviyes* (sites for religious men), which often became the nucleus of the settlement. One must also mention the efforts of the colonizing Turkish dervishes, who played a very important role indeed in bringing about voluntary immigration. Thus Thrace, eastern Bulgaria, the Meriç (Maritza) valley, and the vicinity of Dobruca became intensively turkified in a short time, particularly during the late fourteenth and early fifteenth centuries.

The purpose of this collective work, based on *tahrir* registers (cadastral surveys) covering a large portion of present-day Bulgaria, is to study the settlement of the Turks there. We shall analyze, under separate headings, first, the settlement of Sofia, Filibe, Eski Zağra, and Tatar Pazari; second, the regions of Şumnu, Hezargrad, Silistre, and Varna in northeastern Bulgaria; and finally, the population and settlement of the *sancak* of Çirmen.

The Population and Settlement of Sofia, Filibe (Phillippopolis-Plovdiv), Eski Zağra (Stara Zagora), and Tatar Pazari

Documents that form the basis of our information indicate that the earliest immigration of Turkish tribes into and their first settlement in Rumelia occurred in 1357. In that year, a group of tribes living in the Karesi (Balikesir) region were colonized, first around Gelibolu (Gallipoli) and subsequently in Hayrabolu.[1] The migration of a larger number of tribes to Rumelia took place in 1400-01, when Yörüks wintering in the Menemen Valley in western Anatolia were deported to the Filibe region, having been found guilty of violating the customs regulations concerning the sale and import of salt in the *vilayet* of Saruhan (Manisa).[2] Similarly, Mehmed the Conqueror settled İsfendiyaroğlu İsmail Bey and his community around Filibe. İsfendiyaroğlu was the ruler of the *beylik* of İsfendiyaroğulları, which comprised Kastamonu and Sinop when these were incorporated into the Ottoman Empire.[3]

Tatar tribes also were colonized in Rumelia during the formative period of the Ottoman state. Some of these tribes were followers of Aktav, a chieftain who sought refuge with Bayezid I (1389-1402) after losing a bid for power in the Crimea; he and his people were subsequently settled in Filibe.[4] The Tatars of İskilip, who, in 1418, under Mehmet I (1413-1421), were settled in Konuşhisar in the vicinity of Filibe, constituted another such Tatar group.[5]

Records in Ottoman chronicles refer to periodic massive migrations from Anatolia to Rumelia; however, it is difficult to ascertain what numbers were involved or from which regions of Anatolia they came. Nevertheless, it is possible to learn the actual administrative, economic, and social structure, as well as the overall population numbers, for each city, town, and village in Rumelia from information provided in

---

[1] Aşık Pasa-zâde, *Tevârih-i âl-i Osman*, Âlî Bey edition (Istanbul, 1332), pp. 49-50; Mehmed Neşrî, *Kitâb-i Cihan-nüma*, vol. 1, ed. Faik Reşit Unat and Mehmed A. Köymen (Ankara, 1945), pp. 181 ff.; Oruç b. Âdil, *Tevârih-i âl-i Osman*, F. Babinger edition (Hannover, 1925), p. 18.

[2] Aşık paşa-zâde, *Tevârih-i*, p. 74; Mehmed Neşrî, *Kitâb-i*, p. 339. For the ban on salt trade, see *Kanunnâme-i Sultanî Ber Mûceb-i Örf-i Osmânî*, ed. Robert Anhegger and Halil İnalcık (Ankara, 1956), pp. 29,30.

[3] Oruç b. Âdil, *Tevârih-i*, p. 73; I. Hakkı Uzunçarşılı, *Anadolu Beylikleri ve Akkoyunlu Karakoyunlu Devletleri* (Ankara, 1969), pp. 137-38.

[4] Ömer Lütfi Barkan, "Osmanlı İmparatorluğunda bir iskân ve kolonizasyon metodu olarak sürgünler,"*İktisat Fakültesi Mecmuasi* (1955): 211-13.

[5] Âşık paşa-zâde, *Tevârih-i*, pp. 90-91.

tahrir defterleri (cadastral survey records), which were designed for taxation purposes and are currently kept in Ottoman archives in Turkey.

For this section we use seven registers. Three registers are for Sofia, the first being dated 1530 (the accurate date is 1516).[6] The second dates from 951/1544 and the third from 987/1570.[7] Thus, the information on Sofia is limited to the period from 1530 to 1570. Similarly, the surveys for Filibe are dated 890/1485, 922//1516, 1530, and 978/1570;[8] thus the information on Filibe covers the period from 1485 to 1570. The latter three Filibe registers contain data also on Eski Zağra and Tatar Pazari; hence the information on these two settlements covers the period from 1516 to 1570.

The city of Sofia was among the *sancaks* (counties) of the *eyalet* of Rumelia during the period under discussion, while Filibe, Eski Zağra, and Tatar Pazari were the administrative centers of *nahiyes* (neighborhoods) or *kazas* (districts) known by their own names, except that the district that had Tatar Pazari as its capital was called Saruhan-Beyli in the survey of 1516;[9] In subsequent surveys the district came to be called Tatar Pazari.[10] The fact that the *kaza* was called Saruhan-Beyli in 1516 is not likely to be a mere coincidence. It is plausible that the settlement of a substantial number of Turks from the Saruhan region in this area during earlier periods was the reason why the area initially had this particular name.

Before providing the population figures for Sofia, Filibe, Eski Zağra, and Tatar Pazari, it is necessary to explain briefly how town residents were recorded in the *tahrir* registers and how our figures were arrived at. Since these records were prepared as a basis for tax assessment, only married men who were heads of households and single males above the age of puberty were recorded. Therefore, it is necessary to employ some special methods of calculation to arrive at approximate total population figures. It is true that even the number of households (*hâne*) alone can give an idea of the population of a town. However, in order to form a more solid basis for the analysis of population in the modern sense, it is necessary to use a household multiplier. We can calculate the total population by multiplying the number of households by 5, the usual multiplier employed in these cases, and adding the number of single males to this figure, and this method was used to reach the population figures given in the following analysis.

In 1530 there were in the city of Sofia 1,023 households and 182 single taxable males, that is, a total population of approximately 5,000 to 5,200.[11] Almost 4,000 of these—some 80 percent—were Muslims, or Turks, while the remaining 1,200, or 20 percent, were non-Muslims, that is, Christians. By 1544 there were approximately 7,000 to 7,300 people in Sofia, of whom the Muslims still constituted 80 percent, non-

---

[6]Başbakanlık Osmanlı Arşivi, Tapu-Tahrîr Defteri (hereafter BA, TD), no. 370. The date of this register, which summarizes the results of the cadastral survey of a number of *sancaks* in Rumelia, is usually given as 1530. Actually the survey was conducted in 1516 during the reign of Selim I. It represents therefore an earlier period, but for the sake of consistency we shall refer to it as the *defter* of 1530.

[7]BA, TD nos. 236, 492.

[8]BA, TD nos. 26, 77, 370, 494.

[9]BA, TD no. 77, p. 632.

[10]BA, TD no. 370, p. 109 and no. 494, p. 716.

[11]BA, TD no. 370, pp. 191-92. We have reached these total urban population figures by adding up the numbers provided separately in the register book.

Muslims 12 percent, and Jews 8 percent.[12] Thus, from the first survey to the next, the city's population had increased by 40 percent, which is much higher than what may be considered a natural rate of growth in 14 years. The number of town quarters (*mahalles*) also increased by 10, which suggests that the population grew mainly as the result of immigration into the city rather than births. On the other hand, the total population of Sofia in 1570 was still only around 7,000, of which 70 percent were Turks, 23 percent non-Muslims, and 7 percent Jews.[13] It is not possible to assess definitively the reasons for the lack of population growth in the 26 years that elapsed between the second and third surveys; however, the fact that this last survey does not mention the names of some *mahalles* suggests that external factors such as natural disasters, epidemics, or war might have caused the dissolution of some sections of the city. (One may also postulate mergers of quarters as a cause of the disappearance of some old quarters.)

The 1485 survey for Filibe indicated that there were 918 households and 105 single taxable males in that year;[14] that is an estimated total population of 4,500 to 4,700. Out of this total, 4,000 (86 percent) were listed as Muslims, almost 450 (10 percent) as non-Muslims, and the rest as gypsies. In 1516, an estimated total of 5,000 to 5,500 people lived in Filibe, of whom 4,500 were Muslims, 500 were non-Muslims, 160 were Jews, and 175 were gypsies.[15] In other words, Muslims, who were practically all ethnic Turks, constituted about 85 percent of the population over the 30 years covered by these two surveys, and other elements were only 15 percent. The second *tahrir* indicates an approximate 10 percent population growth, which is normal for the 30 years that elapsed between the two surveys. However, the survey of 1530 gives the total population of Filibe as only approximately 4,500, showing a decline of 20 percent over the few years of intervening since the 1516 survey; of this population, 3,500 were Muslims and the rest non-Muslims, Jews, and gypsies.[16] Again, it is not possible to make a definitive statement about the causes of such a decline over a relatively short period of time, but we can speculate that natural disasters or an epidemic might have struck the city. The *tahrir* of 1570 indicates that the population of Filibe numbered 4,000 to 4,500 of whom approximately 3,500 were Muslims, with about 500 non-Muslims, and the rest gypsies and Jews.[17]

Another important settlement center after Filibe was Eski Zağra. According to the *tahrir* of 1516, there were a total of 521 *hânes* and 245 taxable single males in Eski Zağra at that time, which means an estimated total population of 2,700 to 2,900; this population was entirely Muslim Turkish.[18] The survey of 1530 similarly indicates an estimated population of roughly 2,700 to 2,800, again entirely Muslim.[19] In 1570, on the other hand, the population of Eski Zağra had risen to 3,100 to 3,300, of whom

[12]BA, TD no. 236, pp. 5-26.
[13]BA, TD no. 492, pp. 10-26.
[14]BA, TD no. 26, pp. 64-82.
[15]BA, TD no. 77, pp. 86, 107.
[16]BA, TD no. 370, p. 86.
[17]BA, TD no. 494, pp. 529, 531.
[18]BA, TD no. 77, p. 670.
[19]BA, TD no. 370, p. 67.

almost 3,200 were Muslims, the rest non-Muslims.[20] Thus, while the surveys of 1516 and 1530 record no non-Muslims living in Eski Zağra, the next survey shows that approximately 100 non-Muslims had settled there at some time after 1530.

Tatar Pazari was apparently a smaller town with a lower population capacity. It is recorded in the 1516 survey as having 168 households and 27 taxable single males, for a total population of approximately 800 to 900, all Muslims.[21] In 1530, Tatar Pazari still had an all Muslim population of 800 to 900.[22] By 1570, however, the population had increased to 1,100 or 1,200, of which approximately 1,100 were Muslim; a small community of about 100 non-Muslims had settled there at some time in the 40 years after the 1530 register was complied and were listed in the 1570 register.[23]

By comparing the sixteenth-century population figures for Sofia, Filibe, Eski Zağra, and Tatar Pazari with those of other cities for the same period we can get a better sense of how they stood as urban centers. Serez had a population of 5,000 in the period 1521-30 and 6,000 in 1571-80; Manastir (Bitolia) had 4,000 in 1521-30 and 5,000 in 1571-80; the population of Trabzon (Trebizond), an old imperial capital, numbered 5,000 in the 1521-30 period and approximately 9,000 in 1571-81.[24] The city of Adana, the capital of an old *beylik*, which later became the center of a *beylerbeylik*, had in the second half of the sixteenth century a population of 3,000 to 4,000.[25] Considering these other figures, it becomes clear that Sofia, Filibe, Eski Zağra, and Tatar Pazari were comparable to many other Ottoman urban centers in terms of population size and that they may be considered to have been fairly large for the sixteenth century.

The *tahrir* registers for Sofia, Filibe, Eski Zağra, and Tatar Pazari show also the division into the quarters that were indispensable features of the physical and social structure of Turkish-Islamic cities of the period. In 1530 Sofia had 32 quarters, of which 18 were Turkish Muslim; in 1544, the number of Muslim quarters in Sofia was 28 and of non-Muslim quarters, 11, making a total of 39; in 1570 there were 37 quarters, 23 of them Muslim and 14 non-Muslim.[26] In Filibe in 1485 there were 30 quarters, of which 26 were Muslim and 4 non-Muslim; in 1516 Filibe had a total of 33 quarters, 29 Muslim and 4 non-Muslim; in 1530, it had 28 Muslim and 4 non-Muslim quarters, or a total of 32; and in 1570, it had 30 Muslim and 4 non-Muslim quarters, or a total of 34 quarters.[27] As for Eski Zağra, the city had 18 quarters inhabited entirely by Turks in 1516 and in 1530 as well; by 1570, with the addition of one non-Muslim quarter, the total had increased to 19.[28] Tatar Pazari had also acquired one non-Muslim quarter by

---

[20]BA, TD no. 494, pp. 430-31.

[21]BA, TD no. 77, p. 635.

[22]BA, TD no. 370, p. 109.

[23]BA, TD no. 494, pp. 716-19.

[24]Ömer Lütfi Barkan, "Tarihî Demografi Araştırmaları ve Osmanlı Tarihi," *Türkiyat Mecmuasi* **10** (1953): 22.

[25]Suraiya Faroqhi, *Towns and Townsmen of Ottoman Anatolia: Trade, Crafts and Food Production in an Urban Setting, 1520-1650* (Cambridge, 1984), p. 303.

[26]BA, TD no. 370, pp. 191-92; no. 236, pp. 5-26; no. 492, pp. 10-26.

[27]BA, TD no. 26, pp. 64-81; no. 77, pp. 543-650; no. 370, pp. 85-86; no. 494, pp. 518-31.

[28]BA, TD no. 77, pp. 459-69; no. 370, p. 67; no. 494, pp. 422-31.

1570, and it had grown significantly also; it had 6 and 7 quarters, respectively, in 1516 and 1530, all settled by Turks; but by 1570 there were 14 quarters, of which 13 were inhabited by Muslims and one by non-Muslims.[29]

It is noteworthy that in the four cities studied above, the Muslim and non-Muslim quarters were fully segregated. It appeared that not only did non-Muslims avoid settling in Muslim quarters but also no Turks settled in the Christian quarters. This state of affairs provides clear evidence that the Christian element was not subjected to a policy of islamization.

It is well-known that the residential quarters in these early Turkish-Islamic towns in Rumelia consisted of settlements gathered around a *mescid* (a place of worship), a mosque, a *zâviye* (dervish lodge), or a *medrese* (religious school). The inhabitants formed a community of people who knew each other and/or had close or distant kinship ties and were united by social bonds. Upon closer examination, it appeared that the names of some quarters in Sofia, Filibe, Eski Zağra, and Tatar Pazarı derived from the names of the mosques or *mecids* around which they were formed. For example, in Sofia the quarters of Saruhan, Hacı Hamza Emine Hâtun, Karahisârî, Hacı Yahşi, Kara Danişmend, Karagöz Bey, Alaca and Hacı Mehmed were established around the *mescids* having the same names. In Filibe we see a similar pattern. The quarters of Yâkub Fakih, Aslıhan, Hacı Ahmed, and Köprübaşı were built around the *mescids* of those names, while the quarter called Câmi (Câmiᶜ-i Kebîr) had this name because it was located near a central mosque. Similarly, the quarters of Hacı Hasan (Terzi Yusuf), Hacı Malkoç, Hacı Mahmud, and Debbağan in Eski Zağra were established around *mescids* of these names, while Câmi (Câmiᶜ-i Atîk) was situated near a mosque. In Tatar Pazarı, the quarters of İshak Çelebi Câmii and Câmi (Camiᶜ-i Kebîr) were established around mosques; Kara Terzi Mescidi, Musalla Mescidi, Hacı Mahmud Mescidi, and Divâne Sefer Mescidi obviously had each a *mescid* as a nucleus.

The records in the *tahrir* registers also indicated that a part of the population of Sofia, Filibe, Eski Zağra, and Tatar Pazarı consisted of Turkish migrants. We can distinguish the places of origin of such people from their names. Among those who can be identified in this manner were three households from Anatolia and one household each from Persia and Karaman, immigrants who came to Sofia in 1570. Similarly, the immigrants to Filibe in 1485 included two households from Anatolia and one household each from Persia, Avratalan, Semendre, and Bergama; in 1516, three households from Anatolia and one household each from Vardar and Bosnia came to Filibe; and in 1570 the city gained 10 households from Anatolia and one from Gümülcüne. Immigrants to Eski Zağra in 1516 included 10 households from Anatolia and one each from Persia, Geyve, and Karaman; and in 1570 there were 2 households of immigrants from Anatolia. As for Tatar Pazarı, the immigrants of 1516 included 4 households from Anatolia, 2 households from Persia, and one from Karaman; in 1570, one household from Anatolia. Thus the records provide evidence of a population flow from Anatolia on a continuous basis during the rise of the Ottoman state.

It is also noteworthy that the foundations, such as mosques, *mescids*, zaviyes, *imarets* (soup kitchens), *khans* (inns), and *hamams*, (bathhouses), which were

---

[29]BA, TD no. 77, pp. 632-35; no. 370, p. 109; no. 494, pp. 716-19.

indispensable elements of Turkish social life, were established in all four cities. For example, we have found evidence for the existence of more than 30 *mescids* in Sofia in 1544. In 1570, in addition to these *mescids*, there were also approximately 10 mosques and 2 *zâviyes*, the latter carrying the names of Habîb Halîfe and Bâlî Bey. In Filibe there were 3 mosques, one *imaret*, one *medrese*, 10 *mescids*, 4 *hamams*, and 4 *khans* in 1530, while the number of *mescids* alone in the city had reached around 20 by 1570. The survey of 1530 for Eski Zağra lists 2 mosques, 2 *mescids*, and 5 bathhouses as well as the soup kitchen of Gümlü-oğlu and the *zâviye* of Karaca Ahmed; by 1570, the number of mosques had increased to 5 and of *mescids* to around 12. In 1530 Tartar Pazari had the soup kitchen of Evrenos Bey-oğlu Ahmed Bey and the *zâviye* of Pîr-zâde and also 2 mosques, 3 *mescids*, and two bathhouses; by 1570 the number of *mescids* in the city was around 6. In all four cities the number of such establishments kept pace with the population growth.

From the data we can draw the following conclusion: in the sixteenth century the Muslims—that is, the Turks—constituted the overwhelming majority of the population of Sofia, Filibe, Eski Zağra, and Tatar Pazari. These Muslims had emigrated from Anatolia and settled in Rumelia during the emergence and rise of the Ottoman state. Once more, as noticed by other scholars such as Ö. L. Barkan, the Turks played a very significant role in establishing (or reviving) the urban centers, swelling greatly the populations of Sofia and Filibe and constituting the entire populations of Eski Zagra and Tatar Pazari until sometime after 1530. It is safe to state, therefore, that the population of the Balkans was very low at the time the Ottoman Turks came into the territory. The existence of a small non-Muslim minority in Eski Zağra and Tatar Pazari in later years suggests that these settlements established and developed by Turks attracted the non-Muslim population as well, enabling the latter to partake of some of what we can all the blessings of civilization for that period. The fact that the survey registers list groups that can be identified as having moved to these cities from Anatolia show that the Turkish population in Anatolia provided a continuing source of population for this region. Large numbers of religious and social establishments served the Turkish population of these prosperous urban centers making them in many ways like other Turkish-Islamic cities in Anatolia.

The non-Muslim population of Rumelia began to increase in the seventeenth and eighteenth centuries and reached the zenith of its growth in the nineteenth century, for a variety of economic, social, and political reasons that worked to the detriment of the Muslim population.

Urbanization, Population, and Countryside Settlement Centers in the Silistre-Şumnu-Hezargrad (Razgrad)-Varna Region

It is well-known that during the early expansion into the Balkans the Ottomans established a frontier zone (*uç bölgesi*) in every newly-conquered region. They colonized immigrants from Anatolia as well as warriors belonging to Yörük tribes in these zones so as to lay the groundwork for new conquests. As the frontier zones moved westward with such new conquests in the Balkans, former frontier zones such as Edirne, Filibe, Serez, Sofia, and Silistre became inland towns, densely populated by Muslim-Turks.[30]

The city of Silistre was one of the frontier towns that developed in this manner; it was divided into 4 Turkish and 13 non-Muslim quarters, according to the *icmal defteri* of Rumelia compiled in 1530 to summarize the results of the cadastral surveys conducted at the beginning of the reign of Süleyman the Magnificent.[31] The estimated population of the city at that date was 3,900; there were at that time 1,000 Turks in Silistre, constituting approximately 25 percent of the total, and the 4 Turkish-Muslim quarters had 2 *mescids* and one mosque.[32] A subsequent *defter*, compiled in February 1570, indicates that Silistre's demographic and physical structure had developed considerably in 40 years:[33] the number of quarters inhabited by Turks had increased to 21, while the number of non-Muslim quarters rose from 13 to 15. The total population of the city had doubled, reaching 8,000, and the Turks had come to constitute the majority, being 52 percent of the new total; the Christian population accounted for 41 percent, while Jews and gypsies constituted the remaining 7 percent of the total.[34] According to the records of the intervening cadastral survey (1550-60), the total population of Silistre was approximately 6,500, with 4,000 of this total being Muslim (61 percent), 2,250 non-Muslim (34 percent), and the remainder Jews and gypsies (3 percent). The residential quarters numbered 20, with 8 of those being Christian quarters.[35] Obviously the Christian population failed to increase much after 1830.

The 300 percent increase in the Turkish-Muslim population by 1570 was due to immigration rather than to natural growth. The strategic importance of the fortress of Silistre must have been a significant factor in this expansion. In fact, a note in the register indicates that there were Turks serving in the fortress.[36] Other records refer to the construction activity undertaken by the Turks and to the fact that they cleared the forests around the city in order to open land for pastures, orchards, and vineyards.[37] The new quarters were often established on such cleared lands.[38] By 1570, 4 mosques, 14 *mescids*, each carrying the name of a city-quarter, and 2 *zâviyes* had been constructed and several *vakifs* established in Silistre.[39] This all indicates that the outlook of the town

---

[30]H. İnalcık, "Rumeli," in *İslam Ansiklopedisi*, vol. 9, pp. 768-70.

[31]BA, TD no. 370.

[32]BA, TD no. 370, p. 383. See the previous section for the method used in estimating the total population for towns discussed in this section.

[33]This *defter* is included in BA, TD no. 483. In addition, there are two more identical detailed (*mufassal*) registers on the *sancak* of Silistre that probably cover the cadastral surveys of 1550-60; see BA, TD nos. 701 and 688.

[34]BA, TD no. 483, pp. 241-56.

[35]BA, TD no. 688, pp. 176-92; no. 701, pp. 230-45.

[36]BA, TD no. 483, p. 239.

[37]BA, TD no. 688, pp. 192, 194-95; no. 483, pp. 257-60; no. 701, pp. 246-49.

[38]Twelve of the Turkish quarters were established in areas newly opened up for settlement; see BA, TD no. 688, pp. 194-95 and no. 483, p. 257.

[39]BA, TD no. 483, pp. 249-51. The *câmis* and *mescids* around which quarters were established were the following: Câmi-i Atîk, Hasan Bey Câmii, İsâ Bey Câmii, Seydi Efendi Câmii, Mirahur Mescidi, Harmancı Ahmed Mescidi, Seydi Ali Fakih Mescidi, Pazarbaşı Mescidi, Topçu Asım Mescidi, Rüstem Çelebi Mescidi, Kadı Ahmed Mescidi, Şeyh Mescidi, Hayreddin Mescidi, Karayazıcı Mescidi, Hacı

changed dramatically around the middle of the sixteenth century as it acquired the main characteristics of a typical Turkish-Islamic city.

It is noteworthy that the countryside falling within the district (*kaza*) of Silistre, which as the capital of the *sancak* of Tuna located along the shore of the Danube River, was densely populated by Turks. Although some of the villages in the district fell to the north of the Tuna River, in present-day Romania, most were located south of the Danube within the boundaries of present-day Bulgaria. Maps drawn at the turn of the sixteenth century indicate the names of a number of such villages.[40] The cadastral survey records supply interesting clues about the formation and settlement of these villages, of which Silistre district had 244 in the 1530s. The names of the villages demonstrate beyond the shadow of a doubt how much this region was like a region in Anatolia. As many as 200 villages have purely Turkic names, the majority taken from their founder. Examples include the villages of Saru Mahmud, Umur Fakih, Terzi Hamza, Yunus Pınarı, Receb Kuyusu, Adil Kuyusu, etc. In addition, many villages carried the names of the nomadic tribes that settled them (as confirmed by explanatory notes in the registers). Included among these were, e.g., Saruhanlu, Nasireddünlü, Yörük Sinan Cemaati, and so on. According to the records of 1530, there were 12,000 Turks in the countryside, whereas the non-Muslim population consisted of 3,500 to 4,000 people. The Yörük tribes accounted for almost half of the Turkish population (1,050 households, or 5,000 people), while the origins of the rest varied.[41] The subsequent cadastral survey (1570) provides further information about the population structure of Silistre *kaza*. At that date, the total population of the district, excluding the city itself, was 41,000 to 42,000 with the Turkish Muslims numbering 34,000 - i.e., 82 percent of the total. In the countryside there were at this time a total of 366 settlements. Most of the non-Muslims, who made up 18 percent of the population, lived in villages near towns, but some had settled along mountain passes.[42] The number of Turkish villages in 1570 was considerably higher than that of 1530, for new settlements were established during the period in between. Some of the people who gave their names to villages were still living there with their families, an indication that these rural settlements were quite newly established. The survey of 1570 provides numerous examples to illustrate how villages and quarters got their names. For example, the İskender-oğulları settled on the outskirts of the village of Kızıl Muradlu, and thereafter this settlement area was called the quarter of the İskender-oğulları. Similarly, a person by the name of Ömerce was living together with his two sons in the village called Ömerce.[43] It seems that the

---

Şirmerd Mescidi (Ilisarönü), Âşiyân-şah Hatun Mescidi, Hacı Bektaş Mescidi, and Sinan Paşa Mescidi; the two *zâviyes* were called Mahmud Baba and Baba Mahmud Şah.

[40]See, for example, F. Handtke, *Bulgarien und Ost-Rumelien* (Berlin: Carl Flemming Generalkarten, n.d.).

[41]BA, TD no. 370, p. 397. Among these Yörük groups, listed as *canbaz*, *yamak*, *küreci*, and *yağci* (all denoting military duties of some sort), some are recorded as *"sürgün"* (deported).

[42]In some villages around the city of Silistre, which were the sultan's *has*, large Christian groups were exempt from the *avâriz* tax and charged with the security of roads and passes, and some Christians were registered as *köprücü* (bridge keepers) in return for their tax-exempt status; see BA, TD no. 483, pp. 218, 338, 417.

[43]Ibid., pp. 224, 445.

turkification of the strategic region around Silistre through migration continued incessantly throughout the sixteenth century.

In the *sancak* of Silistre, the city of Varna, located on the coast of the Black Sea, lay within the lands serving the pious endowments (*vakıfs*) established by Selim I in Istanbul.[44] The estimated population of the Varna district in the 1530s was 13,300 including 232 villages. The overwhelming majority of this population—73 percent—consisted of Muslim Turks. Yörük tribes who migrated from Anatolia and colonized the Varna region were charged with specific economic obligations towards the state; they made up most of the Turkish population. Thus, a note in the *defter* indicates that 1,784 Yörük households were deported from Anatolia and colonized in this region at the turn of the sixteenth century.[45]

The town of Hezargrad (known originally as Yenice and then as Hezer-Grad, as Cedit, and as Razgrad) in the *sancak* of Niğbolu, which had a large Turkish population, does not appear in the record of the survey conducted at the turn of the sixteenth century. It is mentioned in 1543 as having a Muslim population of 104 households and no Christians, and it is mentioned again in the Niğbolu *defter* of 1565. The town lay within the scope of the pious endowments established by Makbul İbrahim Paşa, who built a mosque, a *medrese*, and a *zâviye* there and allotted the tax income of the town to the upkeep of these charitable institutions.[46] The Hezargrad area appears to have been depopulated in the fifteenth century, probably due in part to the destruction caused by the Hungarian armies of Janos Hunyadi (who in 1443 and 1444 forced the Orthodox Christians of the area to convert to Catholicism, executing thousands who refused to do so). Hunyadi was defeated at Varna in 1444, but the population did not recover until the Turkish settlement of the area began in earnest in the late fifteenth century. The Ottoman surveys show that no town of Hezargrad existed in the fifteenth century and that the Christian presence was confined to 16 villages in the area; the inhabitants of these villages, known as Torlaks Citah spoke an ancient Turkish language and apparently were the descendants of Pechenek and Cuman Turks.[47] Probably the growth of Hezargrad to become an urban center was due largely to the establishment of charitable foundations, for, as we know, many cities, small towns, and villages in the Balkans were formed around *vakıfs* and later flowered as large settlement centers, thanks

---

[44]BA, TD no. 370, p. 418.

[45]In the Varna region, where there were 864 *hânes* of Yörük groups exempted from the *avâriz* tax, some were specified as being deported from Anatolia to Dobruca: "Zikr olan taife bundan evvel Anadoludan Dobrucaya sürgün olan" (the aforementioned group was deported earlier from Anatolia to Dobruca); see BA, TD no. 370, p. 436. (In Ottoman times the boundaries of Dobruca were larger than the present ones; see "Dobruca," E.I. III, pp. 628-43).

[46]BA, TD no. 382, pp. 847-49.

[47]An article on Razgrad-Hezargrad by B. Cvetkova is fatally flawed because of a misreading of an inscription on the front of a building. She read the date as 1388, which would mean that the town existed at the time of the conquest of the region by Candarlı Âli paşa. Actually the correct date is 1488. That is within the period in which the Turkish settlement of the area was well underway and buildings were being erected. There is an overabundance of errors in works on the Ottoman period by Bulgarian historians due to their ignorance of Turkish. Of several dozen Bulgarian scholars dealing with Ottoman history, probably only two or three are capable of handling the Turkish sources properly (ed.).

to the trade and religious-cultural activities generated by these charitable foundations.[48] At this point in history some 10 to 12 percent of the non-Muslim population in the *kaza* of Varna consisted of Gagauzes, ethnic Turks speaking a pure Turkish dialect who were orthodox Christians and were classified as non-Muslims.

The entire population of the town of Hezargrad in 1565—about 1,000 souls—was Muslim Turkish.[49] The Christians lived in the nearby villages. There were 213 countryside settlement centers in the district of Hezargrad, but only 38 of these were non-Muslim; all the rest were Turkish villages, some of which were recorded in the *defter* as being located in the Deliorman region between the Danube and Black Sea.[50] The *defters* provide indications about the time and manner of the formation of these villages. Thus, there were villages that were recorded as "*hâric ez-defter*"—that is, those not appearing in the earlier cadastral survey but registered in the present one as new entries. Obviously, these were newly-established. For example, the village of Durakça in the Deliorman region, did not appear in the survey of 1530, but in 1570 Durakça himself was still living, together with his five sons, in the village he established.[51] Similarly, Sultan-oğlu Musa lived with his two brothers, six sons, and five nephews in the village of Sultan, which he apparently established.[52] The same pattern can be observed in the villages of Kütükçü Sinan, Terzi (tailor) Hasan, Selman Dede and Sâil Baba (these two were apparently established by religious men), Mustafa Halife, Koçak, and Derviş.[53] In addition, it is noteworthy that the village of Kalova (Kolowa, which still exists) to the north of Hezargrad was at the time a large Turkish settlement divided into eight quarters, and that each quarter was recorded by the name of a member of the family who came first to settle there. Moveover, some members who gave their names to the *mahalles* were still living in the village at the time the survey was conducted.[54] Eight of the villages in the region were established by the colonizing Turkish dervishes. The records show that Hasan Dede, Burhan Baba, Sâil Dede, Derviş Kuzguncuk, Burhan Dede, Selman Dede, Ali Dede, and Doğan Dede were still active in the *tekkes* in the villages that carried their names. They also appear to have been engaged as farmers in

---

[48]For the manner in which towns and cities in Bosnia developed stimulated by the *vakifs*, see Adem Handzic, "On formiranju nekih Gradskih Naselja i Bosni o XVI Stoljecu Uloga drzave i vakifa," *Prilozi*, XXXV (Sarajevo, 1979), pp. 133-69.

[49]The quarters of Hezargrad were called Câmi-i Şerîf (İbrahim Paşa câmii), Ahmed Bey, Behram Bey Mescidi, and İskender Bey. There were 4 *imâms*, 1 *hatib*, and 3 *müezzins* employed in the mosque and *mescid*, as well as one instructor (*muallim*); see BA, TD no. 382, pp. 847-49.

[50]See, for example, "*Karye-i Hüseyin Terzi, der-Divâne-orman*", listed ibid., p. 298. The fact that there are numerous records about such villages in Şumnu and Hezargrad suggests that the Deliorman region was opened up to settlement because of the settlement of the Turks.

[51]BA, TD no. 382, p. 275.

[52]Ibid., p. 297.

[53]Ibid., pp. 332, 334, 345.

[54]Ibid., pp. 307-309. The village had 87 households, 23 single taxable males, 11 *ellici yörük* (one family in 50 provides one soldier supported by the rest), 3 descendants of Timur Han (probably Tatars left from Tamerlane's army), and 3 *müflis*. The residential quarters were called Habil, Eynehan, Muslihiddin, Musa, Veli, Sinan, İzzeddin, and Mümin.

land cultivation. The total village population of Hezargrad consisted approximately of 38,000 souls, of whom 22,000, or 60 percent, were Turks.[55]

The population of Şumnu (Shumen), a large settlement to the southeast of Hezargrad, was numbered at 1,100 people at the beginning of the reign of Süleyman the Magnificent; 500 people living in the town at the time were Muslims, constituting, thus 45 percent of the total.[56] In a survey conducted probably shortly before 1550, the Muslim Turkish quarters in Şumnu had increased to 4 in number while the percentage of the Muslim population had increased to 55 percent, or 630 out of a total population of 1,130.[57] Records of the survey of 1565 indicate the existence of 5 Turkish quarters and 1,400 Muslims, making up 65 percent of a total population of 2,200.[58] These numbers demonstrate that the percentage of Turks in Şumnu increased throughout the sixteenth century and that, whereas they constituted a minority in the first survey, they came to constitute the majority by the second half of the century.

This trend is more pronounced in the countryside. A total of 183 villages belonged to the district of Şumnu in the 1530s. The Muslim population was fairly well dispersed, resulting in a large number of very small villages bearing Turkish names and inhabited by Turks. The number of non-Muslim villages, on the other hand, was small; but these appear to have been densely populated, since half of a total population of 20,000 living in the Şumnu district were non-Muslims. The records of the cadastral survey of 1565 show that in 30 years this situation had changed dramatically. The borders of the district had expanded through the establishment of new settlements and its population had increased rapidly, the number of villages in the district rising to 250. Only 36 of these were non-Muslim villages; the rest, including all of the newly-established ones, were Turkish. The *defter* of 1565 indicates that 24 villages in Şumnu had been founded shortly before that date and that their founders were residing in the villages at the time the survey was conducted. For example, Aydın Fakih was a resident and the *imam* of the village he had established.[59]

In the period between 1530 and 1565 the total population of the district of Şumnu increased from 20,000 to 45,000. Whereas in the 1530s this population was divided equally between Muslims and non-Muslims, during the following 30 to 40 years the Turkish population increased more than threefold, from 9,000 to 28,000. The rapid expansion of the Turkish population was no doubt due to immigration, as a result of which the new villages were established. The non-Muslims, on the other hand, continued to live in their old villages, and their growth rate followed a natural pattern, their total rising from 11,000 to 17,000. It is clear that the non-Muslims were not subject to a policy of islamization and that the size of the non-Muslim population

[55]Ibid., pp. 296, 350, 368-69. The area around Hezargrad and, especially, Deliorman, was populated by large groups of Kızılbaş from Anatolia; hence the abundance of names with "baba" and "dede," which were given to Kızılbaş leaders.

[56]BA, TD no. 370, p. 549.

[57]BA, TD no. 439, pp. 157-61.

[58]BA, TD no. 382, pp. 380-86. The Turkish quarters of Şumnu at that date were Söğüd-pınarı, Veli Kadı, Câmi-i şerîf, Yolcu, and Eski-pazar.

[59]Ibid., p. 472.

continued to increase, due to the relative security and the agricultural development brought by the Ottoman administration.

Indeed, economic factors seem to have contributed substantially to the population growth of the area. Eski Cuma was one of the villages of Şumnu which in the sixteenth century rapidly developed into a large settlement center due largely to its local market. The record shows that there was a market every Friday (*her cuma pazar olur*) and that market dues (*pazar bâci*) of 500 *akçe* collected in the period before 1550 had been increased to 1,500 *akçe* by 1565 a clear indication of economic development resulting in greater revenues.[60] Several other market towns were established throughout the region for the trading of agricultural commodities, being produced now in large quantity. In Cumalu, which was established as a Turkish village, there were 13 households and 5 single males in 1530; by 1550 the number of Muslim households had gone up to 31 and the single males to 13 and the village had also 5 non-Muslim households (a departure from the segregated quarters prevailing elsewhere). The 1565 survey recorded 78 Turkish households and 16 single taxable males, while the number of non-Muslim households had reached 10, with 7 single males also.[61] Thus, it is clear that the economic activity in Cumalu attracted not only a substantial number of Turks but also non-Muslims. One would think that there might be other examples of villages with a similar pattern of development.

The Şumnu district's villages, unlike villages elsewhere, which were unitary in structure, had distinct quarters attached to a center. This characteristic must be viewed as the consequence of continuous immigration. We can identify some 30 villages that fit this pattern; a number of them, including Topuzlu, Kovancılar, Kocacıklar, Ereğli, Tekeler, Türkeşler, Mezidce, Hacı Salih, and Akdere-yakası, had two to four quarters.

In sum, one can state that the total population of the districts of Silistre, Varna, Şumnu, and Hezargrad amounted to 133,000 in the second half of the sixteenth century (1550-1574). The Muslims-Turks numbered 90,000, or 70 percent of the total. Research has demonstrated that there was a large potential for the settlement of Turks in northeastern Bulgaria, which was quite deserted in this period; that the rapid growth of the Turkish population was not a result of forced islamization or of natural factors but was due to immigration; and that the process of migration continued throughout the sixteenth century. Archival documents clearly indicate that the Turks living in this region at present are the descendants of those Turkish farmers and semi-nomadic Türkmen and Yörük tribes who periodically migrated from Anatolia to establish new settlements in the region; they developed the towns and villages there through the establishment of charitable endowments, opened up and cultivated the land to raise a number of crops, including cotton and, in particular, rice, and were the pioneers in the development of the local economy.

---

[60]See BA, TD no. 439, pp. 220-21 and no. 382, pp. 527-29.

[61]BA, TD no. 370, pp. 550-55; no. 439, pp. 220-21; no. 382, pp. 527-29.

Population and Settlements in the Sancak of Çirmen

In the sixteenth century the districts of Çirmen, Hasköy, Akça Kızanlık, Yeni Zağra, and Çirpan formed the *sancak* of Çirmen in Rumelia province. In addition, the province of Tekirdağ (Tekfurdağı-Rodosto) in present-day Turkey was then within the boundaries of the Çirmen *sancak*. Except for Çirmen itself, which is a small village in Greece at present, most of the villages of the district of Çirmen are within the boundaries of modern Bulgaria, as is the rest of the territory (except for Tekirdağ) that made up Çirmen Sancak.

Çirmen was among the first Ottoman *sancaks* to be incorporated into the Empire during the conquest of Rumelia. It became subject to a systematic policy of settlement and thus acquired the characteristics of a Turkish region in terms of its institutions, populace, and physical features. The area was sparsely populated at the time of the conquest, which must have been the reason why settled peoples as well as semi-nomadic Türkmen groups were brought from Anatolia to give the *sancak* its new identity.[62] New cities, towns, and villages exhibiting Turkish-Islamic works of art were established by these immigrants, as shown by the cadastral survey record dated 921 (1515), which lists only 40 non-Muslim households in the town of Çirmen and none in the other towns in the *sancak*.[63] According to this *tahrir*, 92.86 percent of the population of Çirmen and its villages, 90.14 percent of the population of Hasköy, 100 percent of Çirpan, 65.86 percent of Akça Kızanlik, and 91.05 percent of Yeni Zağra were Muslim. In the *sancak* as a whole, there were 26,746 Muslims and 4,111 non-Muslims.[64] (See the table following this article for data from this and the two later surveys discussed below).

According to another survey, conducted during the reign of Süleyman the Magnificent (1520-1566) there were no Christians in the towns of the *sancak*.[65] The Christians inhabited the countryside and, consequently, they are recorded only in village surveys. For example, the Muslim population in Çirmen was then 78.43 percent of the total; in Hasköy, 97.64 percent; in Çirpan, 100 percent; in Akça Kızanlik, 73.19 percent; and in Yeni Zağra, 87.40 percent. Thus the total population of the *sancak* in 1530 was 85.63 percent Muslim and 14.36 percent Christian. It should be noted that these figures do not include the segment of the population known as *musellem* and *yamak*, although their number amounted to more than 10,000 throughout the *sancak*.[66] At that date there were 20 *imams*, 1 mosque, 2 *mescids*, 2 *zâviyes*, 1 bathhouse, 13 shops, and 20 mills in the district of Çirmen; Yeni Zağra had 3 *imams*, 1 *hatib*, 1 mosque, 2 *mescids*, 2 *zâviyes*, 1 bathhouse, 25 shops, and 4 mills; Akça Kızanlik boasted 15 *imams*, 1 mosque, 2 *mescids*, 1 bathhouse, 12 shops, and 1 *bozahane;* and

---

[62]For more information, see Tayyib Gökbilgin, *Rumeli'de Yürükler, Tatarlar ve Evlâd-i Fatihân* (Istanbul 1957), pp. 9 ff.

[63]BA, TD no. 50. There are 16 *defters* on Çirmen in the Başbakanlık Arşivi, but only three of those have been used in this study.

[64]Each *hâne* (household) is estimated to be equivalent to 5 people. The number of single taxable males (*mücerred*) has been added. Gypsies are not included in these figurs.

[65]BA, TD no. 370, dated 936 (1529/30).

[66]Ibid., p. 357.

Çirpan had 7 *imams*, 1 *hatib*, 1 mosque, 1 *mescid*, 1 bathhouse, and 1 *dink*. The total number of Muslims in the *sancak* at that date was about 26,852; of Christians, 4,505.

The cadastral survey conducted during the reign of Murad III (1574-1595) shows that the *sancak* had developed considerably since the previous survey was done.[67] The town of Çirmen, however, had lost its significance, while the nearby settlement of Cisr-i Mustafa Paşa, where a *menzil* (caravan station) and a *derbend* (mountain pass guardpost) were located, had become a large settlement. Thus, whereas the population of Çirmen dropped to 137 households, Cisr-i Mustafa Paşa, which is not even mentioned in previous survey records, emerged as a settlement center with 189 households. This survey records approximately 10,000 Turks living in the district of Çirmen, while the number of Christians is placed at 2,177 (82.13 percent and 17.87 percent, respectively). The survey gives the population of other localities as follows: Hasköy, 22,447 Muslims and 3,048 Christians (88.05 and 11.95 percent); Çirpan, 1,971 Muslims and 65 Christians (96.80 and 3.19 percent) ; Cisr-i Mustafa Paşa, 821 Muslims and 143 Christians (84.03 and 15.96 percent); and Akça Kizanlik, 13,868 Muslims and 2,216 Christians (86.22 and 13.77 percent). Yeni Zağra had a population of 10,030 Turks and no non-Muslims. Thus, in these districts belonging to the *sancak* of Çirmen, the total number of Muslim Turks reached 59,138, while the Christians numbered 7,701 (88.48 and 11.52 percent, respectively).

By taking into consideration tax revenue figures, collected from Muslims as *resm-i çift* and *resmi-bennâk* and from non-Muslims as *ispence*, we can also estimate the amount of land held by each community. In Çirmen, of the total revenues of 29,465 *akçe*, 20,990 came from *çift* and *bennâk* taxes and 8,475 from *ispence*, indicating that approximately 77.23 percent of the arable land was held by Turks, 28.76 percent by non-Muslims. For other districts the figures were as follows: Akça Kizanlik, with total revenues of 39,685 *akçe*, realized 21,640 (54.53 percent) from *çift* and *bennâk*, 18,045 from *ispence* (45.47 percent); Çirpan—4,111 *akçe* total, 3,786 from *çift* and *bennâk* (92.09 percent), 325 from *ispence* (7.90 percent); Hasköy—38,786 total, 33,718 from *çift* and *bennâk* (86.97 percent), 5,050 from *ispence* (13.02 percent); and Yeni Zağra— 13,708 total, almost all from *çift* and *bennâk* (only 25 *akçe* came from *ispence*), indicating that nearly 100 percent of the arable land in that district was owned by Turks. In the *sancak* as a whole, 93,817 *akçe* out of a total of 125,737 was collected as *çift* and *bennâk*, 31,920 as *ispence;* so approximately 74.59 percent of all the arable land was in Muslim hands, 25.40 percent in Christian ownership.

These figures provide some insight into the occupational structure of the population. The Christians, who were 11.52 percent of the population, held 25.40 percent of the arable land, indicating that they were mostly farmers; the Muslims were involved in both trade and agriculture. The most extensively cultivated products in the region were wheat, barley, rye, oats, and millet, while sesame, walnuts, flax, hemp, lentils, tobacco, and a small amount of cotton were also grown. Apiculture and stockbreeding also played a significant role in the local economy. The records of the cadastral survey conducted during the reign of Süleyman the Magnificent includes the *kannunnâmes* of Çirmen, Hasköy, Akça Kızanlık, and Yeni Zağra, which were issued as

---

[67]BA, TD no. 651.

special legislation intended to regulate the advanced commercial activity of these localities.[68] As in the other areas of Rumelia discussed here, the pattern of separate Muslim and non-Muslim residential quarters in towns and villages prevailed in Çirmen. It is noteworthy that during the reign of Murad III one could find Christians in 50 villages (out of the total of 282 rural settlements) but that in only 16 of these was the population mixed Muslim and Christian; and in all of the 16 mixed population villages the two groups lived in different quarters.

The names given to residential areas indicate that the overwhelming majority of the Muslims inhabiting the area were Turks of Anatolian origin. For example, there are the names of localities and town quarters such as Câmi, İmâret, Dabbağan, Tekye, Aydoslu, Akhanlı, Kara Dânişmend, Karaman, and Türkmen. Similarly, names of villages show the Anatolian connection; for example, Balıkesirli, Manyaslı, Saruhanlı, Bitlisli, Germiyanlı, Karesili, Karahisarlı, Aladağlı, Karamanlı, Kangal Ayvacık, Aydınlı, Ahlatlı, Gönenli, Ulubatlı, Karlı, Fındıklı, Kovancılı, Gödelü, Pusadlı, Kurtbasan, Keçi-deresi, Aytemürlü and Boğacık carry names that are the same as those of settlements in Anatolia. In fact, some of the names given to the villages in Çirmen are very common in Anatolia; for example, there are 48 Örenciks, 18 İgdirs, 25 Eymürs, 23 Danişmends, 24 Sorguns or Sorgunlus, 15 Karlıs, and 22 Kovanlıs or Kovancılıs in Anatolia.[69] A large number of the villages in Çirmen bear the names of Oğuz tribes from Central Asia who had settled initially in Anatolia—for instance, Dânişmendlü, Eymürlü, Salürlü, Kırmanlı, Avşar, Oğuzhan, Kadı Yörükleri, Alalar Yörükleri, and İğdirli, among others. Many of the above named villages arose between the time of earlier surveys and that conducted during the reign of Murad III. In fact, whereas the last *tahrir* registered 282 villages, the previous one had listed only 161.[70]

In conclusion, the information in the documents studied here clearly demonstrates that the Bulgarian Turks, contrary to some current arguments, have ties with Anatolia. Their ancestors migrated from Anatolia to Rumelia in a steady stream during the sixteenth century, established villages and towns there with the typical Turkish-Muslim support institutions, and continued to live in accordance with the Turkish-Anatolian customs and culture. As for the Christians, they too continued to follow their traditions, living in their separate villages, or in separate quarters within larger settlements, and prospering as the entire area prospered under the relative peace and security the Ottomans were able to provide.

Marmara University, and Istanbul University Istanbul, Turkey

---

[68]BA, TD no. 370, p. 319.
[69]See, *Köylerimiz*, İçişleri Bakanlığı İller İdaresi Genel Müdürlüğü Yayınları (Ankara 1968).
[70]BA, TD no. 370, pp. 321-42.

TABLE. THE POPULATION OF ÇIRMEN SANCAK IN THE 16TH CENTURY

Periods Recorded	Selim I (1512-20)				Suleyman the Mag. (1520-66)				Murat III (1574-95)			
	Muslims (Turks)		Christians		Muslims (Turks)		Christians		Muslims (Turks)		Christians	
	Hshld.	Single	Hshld.	Single	Hshld.	Single	Hshld.	Single	Hshld.	Single	Hshld.	Single
Çirmen Kaza												
Çirmen (town)	184	--	40	--	118	41	--	--	79	30	58	--
Villages	1414	316	87	--	1191	374	380	14	1801	571	355	112
Total	1598	316	127	--	1309	415	380	14	1880	601	413	112
Cisr-i Mustafa Paşa	--	--	--	--	--	--	--	--	150	71	26	13
Hasköy Kaza												
Hasköy (town)	271	--	--	--	192	108	--	--	392	35	--	--
Villages	1297	199	175	4	1648	328	44	12	3820	1352	586	118
Total	1568	199	175	4	1840	436	44	12	4212	1387	586	118
Çirpan Kazâ												
Çirpan (town)	150	94	--	--	172	80	--	--	226	169	13	--
Villages	118	44	--	--	104	23	--	--	128	32	--	--
Total	268	138	--	--	276	103	--	--	1971	201	13	--

Periods Recorded	Selim I (1512-20)				Süleyman the Mag. (1520-1566)				Murat III (1574-1595)			
	Muslims (Turks)		Christians		Muslims (Turks)		Christians		Muslims (Turks)		Christians	
	Hshld.	Single	Hshld.	Single	Hshld.	Single	Hshld.	Single	Hshld.	single	Hshld.	Single
Yeni Zağra kaza												
Zağra (town)	385	--	--	--	231	101	--	--	326	2	--	--
Villages	566	72	91	19	501	82	107	19	1611	343	--	--
Total	951	72	91	19	732	183	107	19	1937	345	--	--
Ança Kızanlık												
Kızanlık (town)	143	15	--	--	151	41	--	--	338	108	--	--
Villages	657	81	418	33	785	209	360	5	2307	535	403	201
Total	800	96	418	33	936	250	360	5	2645	643	403	201
Total Towns	1133	109	40	--	864	371	--	--	1511	415	110	--
Total Villages	4052	712	771	56	4229	1016	891	50	9667	2833	1344	431
Grand Total	5185	821	811	56	5093	1387	891	50	11178	3248	1454	431
Approx. Total Population	26.746		4,111		26,852		4,505		59,138		7,701	

SOURCE: BA, TD nos. 50, 370, and 651.
NOTE: The terms *"hane"*, *"mücerred"*, "Muslim", and "Gayri Muslim" have been translated, respectively, as "Households", "Singles" (males only), "Muslims (Turks)", and "Christians".

R. J. Crampton

THE TURKS IN BULGARIA, 1878-1944

     Although reliable statistics are difficult to find, it would seem to be safe to assert that in the middle of the nineteenth century approximately one-third of the population of what is now the People's Republic of Bulgaria was Muslim.[1] The vast majority of them, like most Muslims in the Balkans, were Sunnites of the Hanafite rite, although there were some Shiites near Razgrad and Rusé, and a small number of *bektashi* dervishes could also be found, as could tiny groups of *Kazilbashi*, or *alevi*.[2] These were located in the northeast of present-day Bulgaria, both in the fertile lowlands and in the eastern section of the Stara Planina mountains, where the largest concentrations of Muslims lived; even after 1878 it was the general rule that east of the river Yantra the Christians spoke Turkish whilst to the west of it the Turks spoke Bulgarian.[3] Other areas of compact Muslim settlement were along the edge of the fertile sub-Balkan plain around centers such as Zlatitsa, Karlovo, Kazanlŭk, Sliven, and Karnobat, while further south towards and on the floor of the Maritsa valley there were large Muslim settlements in and around Tatar Pazardjik, Haskovo, and Harmanli. In the northwest few Muslims were to be found, but there were communities in the south-west, especially around Kiustendil; there were also large Muslim populations in the Rhodope mountains.[4]

     The Muslims of Bulgaria were divided into four distinct ethnic or, at least, linguistic groups. The largest group by far was the Turks, who had settled in Bulgarian lands after the conquest of the fourteenth century and who retained their Turkish language and customs. Some nineteenth-century commentators who supported the Slavic cause pre-dated the present regime in Sofia in maintaining that a proportion of Turkish-speaking Muslims were, in fact, Bulgarians who had been Turkified; the noted Czech savant Konstantin Jiricěk, for example, asserted that a number of Muslims in the Eski Djumaya (Blagoevgrad) area had been islamicized in the early eighteenth century and that the older ones among them still, in the 1880s, spoke Bulgarian when they did

---

[1] Alexandre Popović, *L'Islam balkanique*, Balkanologische Veröffentlichungen, no. 11, Osteuropa Institut der Freien Universität Berlin (Berlin 1986), p. 71.

[2] Wayne S. Vucinich, "Islam in the Balkans," in A. J. Arberry, ed., *Religion in the Middle East*, vol. 2 (Cambridge, 1969), p. 237; S. M. Zwemer, "Islam in Southeastern Europe," *The Moslem World* 17 (1927) : 338 ; Alexandre Popović, "Les Turcs de Bulgarie, 1875-1985. Une expérience des nationalités dans le monde communiste," *Cahiers du monde russe et soviétique* 37. nos. 3-4 (July-December 1986): 395.

[3] Konstantin Jiricěk, *Pŭtuvane po Bŭlgariya* (Sofia, 1974), p. 86.

[4] Bernard Lory, *Le Sort de l'Héritage Ottoman en Bulgarie: L'Exemple des Villes Bulgares, 1878-1900* (Istanbul, 1985), p. 36.

not want their young folk to understand what was being said.[5] The Pomaks, on the other hand, were converts to Islam who had retained their native customs and language, the latter being sometimes preserved in remarkably pure form. The Pomaks lived predominantly in the Rhodope mountains but were also to be found near Chirpan, Xanthi, and Kavalla.[6] The third Muslim group, the Tatars, had arrived in the mid-nineteenth century, mainly as refugees from tsarist expansionism in the Caucasus and along the Black Sea littoral; they were settled primarily to the north of the Balkan mountains where they would, it had been hoped, strengthen Islam's northern frontier.[7] The fourth Muslim group, the gypsies, were dispersed throughout most of the Bulgarian lands.

In the areas of compact Muslim settlement in the northeast, the countryside as well as the towns were predominantly Muslim; but where Muslims were in a minority they tended to concentrate in the towns, a fact which was to have important social and political consequences. This was not true of the Bulgarians, who are overwhelmingly rural, the only purely-Bulgarian towns being found in the mountains, particularly the cloth-producing centers of the Stara Planina range such as Gabrovo, Teteven, Elena, Kotel, Kalofer, Panagiurishte, and Koprivshtitsa.[8]

In general relations between the various communities in the Bulgarian lands had been peaceful. In the towns different ethnic and religious groups lived in separate *mahala*, meeting seldom except in the *charshiya*, or commercial area. The political tensions, which caused and were in turn intensified by the stirrings of the Bulgarian national movement, were as often between Greek and Bulgarian as between Muslim and Bulgarian. This peace was shattered by the April Uprising of 1876, the massacres which followed it, and by the Russo-Turkish war of 1877-78. That conflict not only brought about the political liberation of Bulgaria but it also ushered in a decade of instability which was to do much to shape the face of the new Bulgarian political organism and to determine the climate of relations between the new *Staatsvolk* and their Muslim subjects.

Muslim Emigration from Bulgaria

The social development of Bulgaria after 1876 may be divided approximately into three distinct phases: the period of the war of 1877-78 and its immediate aftermath, a time of confusion and fluctuation; the period *circa* 1880 to the mid-1880s when Muslim and Turkish illusions were gradually dispelled; and the period after the mid-1880s, an era of steady if undramatic Turkish emigration.

---

[5]*Pŭtuvane*, pp. 945-47.

[6]André Girard, *Les minorités ethniques et religieuses en Bulgarie* (Paris, 1932), pp. 34-35.

[7]Mark Pinson, "Ottoman Colonisation of the Crimean Tatars in Bulgaria, 1854-1862," *VII. Türk tarihi kongresi, Kongreye sunulan bildiriler*, vol. 2 (Ankara, 1973), pp. 1040-58; also Herbert Wilhelmy, *Hochbulgarien: die ländliche Siedlungen und die bauerliche Wirtschaft*, no. 4 of the *Schriften des Geographischen Instituts der Universität Kiel*, ed. O. Schneider and H. Wenzel (Kiel, 1935), pp. 289-97.

[8]Lory, *Le Sort de l'Héritage*, p. 36.

The war itself caused a wave of Muslim emigration. Some Muslims had reason to fear retribution at the hands of the Russian army or, more probably, the Bulgarian *opŭlchenie*, or militia, and they took themselves off "bag and baggage." Others, innocent of any involvement in the killings of 1876, nevertheless fled in fear of war and its attendant, indiscriminate terrors. Of these there were enough. In some larger settlements the Russians had to restrain Bulgarian passions, which prompted acts of vandalism such as the attempted destruction of a library and the local archives in Chirpan.[9] In other villages vacant Muslim homes were burned because, in the mixed areas through which the Russian army advanced, the local Bulgarians sought both vengeance and a guarantee that the owners would not return. House-burning was also caused by the lack of an alternative supply of fuel for heating.[10] For many a Bulgarian Christian peasant an even more urgent need than to destroy the homes was the desire to seize the land that the departing Muslims had vacated; this was a desire so intense that one scholar has likened it to "les allures d'une reconquista à l'espagnole."[11]

The departure of Muslim landowners posed acute problems for those who administered the Bulgarian lands.[12] Some of the emigrants had rented their land to local Christians. A few had even sold it. In the vast majority of cases, however, the land had been abandoned without its ownership being transferred. This created a danger for the Bulgarians and their Russian sponsors. The Ottoman government and its protagonists, primarily Great Britain, would wish to protect Muslim property rights, hoping to retain in Bulgaria a Muslim presence and, with it, the excuse to involve themselves in Bulgarian affairs; nor would the Imperial Russian government be happy to see property rights entirely discounted. Both treaties of peace, San Stefano and Berlin, therefore guaranteed the property rights of Muslims who were not resident in the territories placed under Bulgarian control. (See Article XI of the San Stefano treaty, Article XIII of the Berlin treaty.)

The Russian Provisional Administration, which governed the Bulgarian lands in the period up to the withdrawal of the Tsar's armies in February 1879, handled this thorny question with dexterity and sensitivity. The land could not be left untended. Not only would this have mystified the local Bulgarians, naturally elated by the defeat of the

---

[9]Ibid, pp. 54-58.

[10]Ibid, pp. 36-37, 101.

[11]Alexandre Popović, "Problèmes d'Approche de l'Islam bulgare," in Rudolph Peters, ed., *Proceedings of the Ninth Congress of the Union européenne des arabisants et islamisants* (Leiden, 1981), p. 245. For an expanded English version of this article, see idem, "The Turks of Bulgaria (1878-1985)," *Central Asian Survey* 5, no. 2 (1986): 1-32, esp. p. 3.

[12]The following passages are based on Richard J. Crampton, *Bulgaria, 1878-1918: A History*, East European Monographs, no. 138 (Boulder, Colorado, and New York, 1983), pp. 177-85. The major sources used for that work were N. G. Levintov, "Agrarnye otnosheniia v Bolgarii nakanune osvobozhdeniia i agrarny perevorot 1877-1879," in L. B. Valev, S. A. Nikitin, and P. N. Tret'yakov, eds., *Osvobozhdenie Bolgarii ot turyetskogo iga. Sbornik Statei* (Moscow, 1953), pp. 138-221; Zhak Natan, V. Hadjinikolov, and L. Berov, eds., *Ikonomikata na Bŭlgariya* vol. 1, *Ikonomikata na Bulgariya do sotsialisticheskata Revoliutsiya* (Sofia, 1969), pp. 307-20; Gordon T. Todorov, "Deinostta na vremennoto rusko upravlenie po urezhdane na agrarnya vŭpros prez 1877-1879g.," *Istoricheski Pregled* 11, no. 6 (1955): 27-59; Hristo Hristov, "Nyakoi problemi na prehoda ot feudlizŭm na kapitalizŭm v istoriyata na Bŭlgariya," *Istoricheski Pregled* 17, no. 3 (1961): 83-107; and K. Irichek and M. Sarafov, *Raport na Komisyata izpratena v Kiustendilskiya okrug za izuchi polozhenieto na bezzemnite selyani* (Sofia, 1880).

Ottoman armies, but there was also a need to feed the thousands of Bulgarian refugees who were streaming in from Macedonia and Thrace. Bulgarians were therefore allowed to till and plant the vacant lands but, in conformity with Russian practice, these lands were placed in the temporary charge not of individuals but of village communes, and it was insisted that this temporary use of the vacant land in no way implied a transfer of ownership. The rent was set at half the value of the harvest and was to be paid to the departed owner, should he return, or to the Russian Provisional Administration if he did not. Frequently the local representatives of the Provisional Administration were not over-zealous in the collection of rents, but at least the legal niceties had been preserved, and the diplomatic opponents of Bulgaria deprived of a cause for complaint or intervention.

This solution worked well in the early summer of 1878, but after the signing of the treaty of Berlin on 13 July complications set in. The new settlement returned Thrace and Macedonia to Ottoman rule and made southern Bulgaria, or Eastern Rumelia, into an autonomous province in which the Muslim element might enjoy much of its former supremacy. Even the Principality of Bulgaria was required to give guarantees on personal and property rights for Muslims; there however, despite the availability of some land, there was little that could be done to restore Muslim domination: the compact Muslim communities of northeastern Bulgaria had survived more or less intact, and in those areas, west of the Yantra Islam had never encompassed a large element of the population. To the south of the Balkan range, on the other hand, there was not only a great deal of vacant land, abandoned by the Muslim refugees of the previous year, but also a realistic hope, raised by the Berlin treaty, of the restoration of Muslim domination. And this hope was bolstered by rebellions among the Pomaks of the Rhodopes and by the Muslims of the Aitos district. The Ottoman government was determined that as much as possible should be retrieved from the débacle in the Balkans, and, concentrating its attention upon Eastern Rumelia, it encouraged the return of as many as possible of the 150,000 Muslims who had fled in 1877-78, providing many of them with documentary evidence of their property rights.[13] This was a wise precaution because the 70,000 who did return to Eastern Rumelia faced considerable competition for vacant land and for political influence. After the end of the war 50,000 Bulgarian refugees from Thrace and Macedonia had also moved into Eastern Rumelia, where they expected to be given land; and a further 20,000 arrived after the suppression of the rising in the Kresna-Razlog area in 1878-79, while 20,000 to 30,000 others moved into the principality north of the Balkans to take advantage of its vacant plots.

The ultimate objective of the Ottoman government had been to redeem its political position and influence in southern Bulgaria, but by the middle of 1880 hope for the restoration of Muslim power was fading. The Muslims, and now more specifically the Turks, began to sell their land and leave. The second wave of emigration had begun. It was again massive, but this time it was permanent. From the time of the signing of the treaty of Berlin to the summer of 1880 only six Turkish *chifliks*, or large estates, had been sold voluntarily in Bulgaria and Rumelia; between the latter date and

[13] Georgi Georgiev, *Osvobozhdenieto i etnokul turnoto Razvitie na bŭlgarskiya Narod, 1877-1900* (Sofia, 1979), pp. 11-16.

September 1885 about 100 changed hands.[14] Smaller properties were also sold in large numbers, with total transactions from the spring of 1878 to 1 November 1883 involving 102,145,237 piastres, 72,229,516 piastres, or 70.70 percent of which came from sales by Muslims to Christians; 24.26 percent came from sales by Christian to Christian; 4.63 percent from those by Muslim to Muslim; and only 0.41 percent from sales of land by Christian to Muslim.[15] By 1900 six million dekars of Muslim land had been bought by Christians, and 175 villages had been deserted, 118 of them between 1878 and 1885.[16] The wave of selling and emigration weakened after the mid-1880s, but it then assumed a new characteristic in that Turks from the compact Muslim areas of the northeast now joined the exodus. So too did the Pomaks from areas such as Lovech, Pleven, and Vratsa; they lived far from the Pomak strongholds in the Rhodopes and fell easy prey to the proseletyzing *softas* sent from Constantinople to woo them with offers of land in Thrace and Asia Minor.[17] The Turks, who had formed 26 percent of the population in 1878 were 24 percent of the total, in 1880; 19 percent in 1887; 17 percent in 1892; and 14 percent in 1900.[18] (See Table 1 for precise figures) So serious a problem had depopulation become in some areas that in the early 1890s the prime minister, Stefan Stambolov, was reported as saying that if the Muslim exodus continued his government would be forced to import foreign laborers and settle them on vacant land.[19]

The Muslim political and social losses after 1878 were every bit as painful and penetrating as the military defeat sustained during the war; and they were inflicted despite the guarantees contained in the treaty of Berlin. The Bulgarian victories were achieved with considerable subtlety and within the confines of the law; they came about because the governments of Sofia and, even more so, of Plovdiv indulged, consciously and unconsciously, in the politics of disincentive. There was to be no outright discrimination against or restriction of Turk or Muslim, but the latter's established cultural and social attitudes and behavior were to be frustrated and sometimes affronted. Gradually many came to the conclusion that the new Bulgaria and Eastern Rumelia were not places in which Muslims could live in quiet and contentment. This policy evolved over a number of years and was pursued and applied with varying degrees of intensity at different times.

The process of finding ways to put pressure on Muslims within the confines of the law began with the mass return of Muslim refugees in the summer of 1878. As early as July 1878 the Russian Provisional Administration had come to an agreement with the Porte that returning refugees could be provided with armed escorts only on condition that the returnees surrendered all their weapons. For Muslims to go unarmed

---

[14]Natan et al, eds., *Ikonomikata na Bŭlgariya*, p. 324.

[15]Iwan Ekimov, *Das landwirtschaftliche Kreditwesen in Bulgarien* (Tübingen, 1904), p. 21; and Constantin Jiriček, *Das Fürstentum Bulgarien* (Vienna, 1891), pp. 190-191.

[16]Lory, *Le Sort de l'Héritage*, p. 79; P. Koledarov and N. Michev, *Promenite v imenata i statuta na selishtata v Bŭlgariya, 1878-1972* (Sofia, 1973), p. 6.

[17]Jirichek, *Pŭtuvane*, p. 965.

[18]Irwin T. Sanders, "The Moslem Minority of Bulgaria," *The Moslem World* 24 (1934): 357; Georgiev, *Osvobozhdenieto*, p. 13, n. 3, quoting from the various censuses.

[19]Edward Dicey, *The Peasant State. An Account of Bulgaria in 1894* (London, 1984), p. 156.

under the protection of armed Christians was in itself a sharp break with pre-war practices and socio-political values. In the following month a decree ruled that the returning refugees would not be immune from prosecution for excesses committed during the 1876-78 period and that those convicted would be deprived of their land. This decree acted as a sharp disincentive to a number of Muslims, and from the date of its promulgation, 21 July/ 2 August 1878, the flow of returning refugees began to decrease in volume.

The Russian Provisional Administration came to an end in February 1879. After that the new government in Plovdiv had to tread warily. The Porte and the British were as vigilant as before for the protection of Muslim rights, and the rulers of Eastern Rumelia obviously had nowhere near the strenghth of the Imperial Russian government. Rumelian courts were therefore ordered to enforce all legal decisions returning land to Muslims and were to report every fifteen days on the action they had taken in this regard; peasants were warned that if they obstructed a court decision of this type they would be deprived of the right to bear arms or to join gymnastic societies—a powerful threat when the bearing of arms was a symbol of liberation from Ottoman rule (under which Christians had been forbidden this privilege) and when the gymnastic society was often little more than a covert Christian militia. There were instances of coercion being used to remove Christians from land which returning refugees were claiming; even the villagers of Shipka, near the site of the famous battle of 1877, were forcibly ejected from properties they had taken over in the Turkish village of Sheinovo. Yet, legislation can only be effective if the local representatives of the state choose to enforce it, and frequently, in Eastern Rumelia, this was not the case. Most local councils and law courts were dominated by Bulgarians, who were far more favorable to the claims of their fellow-nationals than had been the mixed Turkish-Bulgarian commissions which had decided property claims under the Russian Provisional Administration. The Plovdiv government had preserved the appearance, and sometimes the reality, of protecting minority property rights, but its local arm had also shown enough flexibility to reassure the Bulgarians that there would not be an entire restoration of the *status quo ante* as far as land ownership was concerned.

In 1882 an even greater impulse to Muslim emigration from Eastern Rumelia came with the replacement of the tithe with a land tax. The tithe had conformed to the Muslim notion that temporary ownership was conferred by working the land (full ownership was the privilege of God), for the tithe was a levy upon the fruits of work rather than upon ownership. The land tax was a direct levy on ownership; and what was worse was that many Muslim landowners who did not rent out their property kept much of it fallow. Under the tithe this had incurred no financial burden, but now fallow land was to be taxed, although it was producing no wealth. The tax reform had been drafted in 1880 but was not applied until 1882; and it was that year which saw the highest incidence of sales of Muslim land to Christians.[20]

In the Principality of Bulgaria, as in Eastern Rumelia, the power to decide property disputes was transferred from mixed commissions to the local courts, which in many cases showed what in the circumstances was an inevitable bias towards the

[20]Todor Vlaikov, *Zemedelskiyat Vŭpros* (Sofia, 1897), p. 97.

Bulgarians. Because the settlement of 1878 had allowed the new authorities in Sofia much more freedom of action than those in Plovdiv, the Bulgarian government could be more adventurous in its domestic policies. Having little need to fear the intervention of the Porte or the latter's supporters in London or Vienna, it declared without compunction that, in accordance with a previous Ottoman law, all land that had been left untilled for three years would revert to state ownership. Initially the Bulgarian liberals attempted to differentiate between the wealthy Turkish landowner and the poor Turkish peasant; but this proved impossible, and in October 1880 it was decided that all vacant land should be subject to the three-year rule. Under pressure from the western powers the deadline for repossession was moved a number of times, and the law did not finally become effective until January 1885; but by then the prospective law had already sapped the confidence of many Bulgarian Muslims, who decided to remain in or emigrate to the Ottoman Empire; this was easier than fighting, and probably losing, a legal battle against the Christians over whom they had previously enjoyed an unquestionable superiority in the face of the law.

In general, returning refugees were a problem in only two areas of the Bulgarian principality, those to the south- and north west of Sofia. There, in the so-called *gospodar* and *chiflik* lands, the tenancies imposed upon Bulgarian peasants at the end of the eighteenth and in the early nineteenth century were harsher than elsewhere in the Bulgarian lands.[21] Significantly, Muslims coming back to this area did not bring with them original documents, either because such documentation did not exist or because it would reveal purchase prices so low as to be ridiculous; nor did the Ottoman authorities in Constantinople provide these Muslims with tax records in support of their claims because, once again, the information on purchase prices and rents could have proved embarrassing. In 1880, after a crop failure had magnified the problems of these areas, the Sofia government made its decision that vacant land should pass into state ownership, which made virtually impossible the return of more former landowners. The government was to compensate former owners from an especially-created fund of over a million *leva,* while the peasants were to buy the land from the central government in instalments paid over fifteen years. This was a powerful inducement to former owners to abandon all claim to their property in the principality and to settle on the estates the Porte was willing to provide in Thrace or Asia Minor.

The Ottoman government, in the meantime, was not prepared to let such legislation pass without retaliation. After the passage of the Law on Gospodar and Chiflik Lands, the Porte announced that it would no longer deal with Bulgaria as if were a sovereign state; rather, the Bulgarians, in view of the vassal status conferred upon them at Berlin, must approach the Porte through the Bureau for Privileged and Autonomous Provinces of the Empire. This the Bulgarians refused to do, and in March 1881 diplomatic relations were virtually severed. Between 1881 and 1883 more conservative administrations held sway in Sofia.[22] These made a number of minor

---

[21]For the origin of the *gospodar* and *chiflik* tenancies, see R. J. Crampton, "Bulgarian Society in the Early Nineteenth Century," in Richard Clogg, ed., *Balkan Society in the Age of Greek Independence* (London, 1981), pp. 265-68.

[22] Crampton, *Bulgaria, 1878-1918*, pp. 59-72.

concessions, but they were not prepared to repeal the Law on Gospodar and Chiflik Lands, the revenue from the sale of these lands providing a useful and welcome supplement to the national budget. In October 1882 the Porte capitulated and agreed to the restoration of diplomatic relations on the earlier basis, while the Bulgarians for their part relaxed the regulations enabling the state to take over ownership of vacant land.[23]

Legislation on the land issue, both in Bulgaria and Eastern Rumelia, clearly encouraged the Muslim drift towards emigration after 1880. That drift was intensified by the political settlement of 1878. There was little hope for Muslims and Turks in the principality, but the treaty of Berlin and the Organic Statute drawn up to define the political system south of the Balkans gave some hope that the Bulgarians would not enjoy undiluted political power in that region. Eastern Rumelia was to have a Regional Assembly with thirty-six elected deputies, ten of them *ex-officio* members, who were to include leaders of the non-Bulgarian religious communities, and ten of them nominated by the governor-general. The French delegate to the commission to draw up the Organic Statute had argued in favor of appointed members on the grounds that this would bring into the assembly Greeks and Turks who would, he said, compensate for the lack of an aristocracy or a bourgeoisie in Bulgarian society in Eastern Rumelia. The Russians had initially been dubious about the nomination of deputies but accepted it in return for a Franco-British agreement to the election of the Assembly's main executive organ, the ten-man Permanent Council. The western powers then diluted their concession by successfully pressing for a system of proportional representation, which they believed would ensure a Greek and/or Turkish presence on the council. The Organic Statute also gave assurances that the three major languages of the province, Bulgarian, Greek, and Turkish, would all be used in the Assembly and in regional political affairs. The governor-general, Aleko Bogoridi Pasha, a Greek-educated Bulgarian who had served in the Ottoman administration, also toured the province, assuring all its communities that there would be no discrimination against non-Bulgarians and, at the same time, stressing that the administration had taken and would continue to take measures to help Muslim refugees.

Hope in the political sector did not live long. No sooner had Aleko Bogoridi returned from his tour than he was signing all documents in Bulgarian only; and in the elections to the Regional Assembly on 7 October 1879 a well-organized Bulgarian electorate, supported by the Jews and the Armenians, secured thirty-two out of the thirty-six seats, notwithstanding efforts by the British consul to persuade all non-Bulgarians of the virtues of a Greek-Turkish coalition against the Bulgarians.[24] There was worse to come for the non-Bulgarian activists. On the day before the Regional Assembly began its first session the Bulgarian deputies, together with leaders of the gymnastic societies and other *prominenti* from the Bulgarian communities, met to decide upon common tactics in the forthcoming debates. It was a valuable exercise,

[23]Dimitur Kosev, ed., *Vŭnshnata Politika na Bŭlgariya: Dokumeti i Materiali*, vol. 1, *1879-1886*, no. 206, p. 430, n1. For more detailed documentation on the earlier history of the land and the refugee question see B. N. Şimşir, *Contribution à l'histoire des populations turques en Bulgarie (1876-1880)* (Ankara, 1966), and idem, *Rumeliden Türk göçleri*, 2 vols. (Ankara 1968, 1970).
[24]El. Statelova, "Izbirane, sŭstav i deinost na Pŭrvoto oblastno sŭbranie na Iztochna Rumeliya," *Istoricheski Pregled* 38, no. 2 (1983): 74-76.

which was frequently repeated, at least until Bulgarian political domination within Eastern Rumelia was unchallenged and unchallengeable. In December 1879 the Bulgarian Rumelians achieved their most notable victory: The Permanent Council was elected on 10 December and, despite a form of PR carefully contrived to ensure minority representation, all the elected deputies were Bulgarian. For this the Bulgarian camp could thank Ivan Salabashev, a deputy in the Assembly who had a higher degree in mathematics from Prague. By careful exposition and planning, and by putting his doubting fellow deputies through a rigorous dress rehearsal, Salabashev had ensured an exclusively Bulgarian Permanent Council.[25] In April 1880, in its first extraordinary session, the Regional Assembly successfully insisted upon the resignation of the province's director of finances, Adolf Schmidt. The significance of this incident was that Schmidt, with the backing of the Austrian and British consuls, had at first refused to resign; that he was forced to go showed that, even with the support of powerful foreign elements, a member of the Rumelian executive could not survive without the confidence of the legislature's Bulgarian majority.[26]

Bulgarian control of Rumelian politics was underscored by the prevalence of the Bulgarian language. Article 97 of the Organic Statute had stated that any of the three major languages of the province could be used to make proposals in the Regional Assembly, but even the commission on procedure in that body had published its guidelines only in Bulgarian. When a Greek motion that all documents for debate should be presented in the three languages was defeated, this was a *de facto* acknowledgement that Bulgarian would be the language of the Rumelian parliament. The handful of Greek and Turkish appointed or *ex-officio* deputies occasionally used their native tongue, but if they wished to be heard and understood they used Bulgarian, not least because the stenographers were competent only in that language.[27]

By the summer of 1880 the general political scene and the measures on the land question had combined to depress Muslim and Turkish morale; by 1882, with the Laws on Gospodar and Chiflik Lands in Bulgaria and the introduction of the tithe in Eastern Rumelia, depression had deepened. Those landowners with political awareness had for the most part already decided that there was no future for them inside Bulgaria or Eastern Rumelia. After 1880 this disillusionment spread further down the social and intellectual scale.

The transfer of power in both Bulgaria and Rumelia was accompanied by a series of symbolic changes that contributed to further depress Muslim morale in all social groups. The *Konak*, the symbol of local Ottoman power, was frequently destroyed or taken over by the new regime.[28] There was also a plethora of place name changes. In 1891 the Bulgarian scholar Mihail Sarafov detected no fewer than 150 changes of place names. Sixty-four of these were adaptations or modernizations of existing names, but

---

[25]For a lively description of this incident, see Ivan Salabashev, *Spomeni* (Sofia, 1943), pp. 8-17; as in the rest of the volume, the author does not minimize his own role in deciding events.
[26]Statelova, "Izbirane," p. 79; Alois Hajek, *Bulgariens Befreiung und seiner staatlichen Entwicklung unter seinem ersten Fürsten* (Munich and Berlin, 1939), pp. 140ff; Mih. Iv. Madjarov, *Iztochna Rumeliya: (Istoricheski Pregled)* (Sofia, 1929), pp. 191-200, 208-14.
[27]Statelova, "Izbirane," pp. 77-78.
[28]Lory, *Le Sort de l'Héritage*, p. 11.

the remaining eighty-six involved the imposition of entirely new names, most of them with Bulgarian patriotic associations and a number of them inspired by incidents or participants in the recent Russo-Turkish war.[29] A more recent study records for the years 1878-1912 a total of 114 changes, sixty-five being cases where Turkish names were replaced by the previously-existing Bulgarian ones, the remainder being villages where the inhabitants spontaneously changed the name.[30] Meanwhile, outside the villages, the depredation of the forests also offended the Muslims; and if the Koran had said that he who is against the forest is against God, then the Bulgarian poet Ivan Vazov judged the Bulgarian to be as beneficial to the tree as phylloxera was to the vine.[31]

Changing social attitudes and patterns of behavior also tended to emphasize the passing of the *ancien régime* and the shift of power away from its former dominant elements. The *charshiya*, the center of trading and the focus of much social life in the Ottoman town, fell victim to modernization and the desire to "Europeanize" Bulgaria. By 1888 the *charshiya* in Sofia had been demolished; and by the turn of the century few of these typically Ottoman institutions remained in any sizeable Bulgarian town.[32] The pattern of urban settlement also changed in many of the larger towns. The *mahala*, or self-contained ethnic quarters, had lost their legal status in Bulgaria by 1882, and the new arrangement for local government "ne laissent aucune autonomie aux minorités nationales des villes."[33] This did not destroy all ethnic settlements. Jewish, Greek, Turkish, and Armenian quarters were identifiable in Varna for many years after 1878, and even in Sofia there were separate Jewish and gypsy communities; but the surviving ethnic districts tended to be inhabited only by the poor and the uninfluential: the rich, successful, emerging bourgeoisie of all types usually built their homes in new suburbs or in redeveloped areas of the inner cities. The character of the quarter was determined more by economic and social status than by religious or ethnic identity. In Sofia, however, tradition did survive in the public baths, where there were separate days for Christians, Muslims, Jews, soldiers, prisoners, and other groups.[34]

The liberation also inflicted economic change and damage on the resident Turks. Some changes were psychologically painful: for example, the admission of Bulgarians into the ranks of the tanning guilds, which by tradition had been virtually confined to Muslims because Mahomet was said to have been a tanner.[35] Other changes were less psychologically disorienting but equally debilitating from the economic standpoint. The new Bulgaria opened its markets more readily than the Ottoman Empire to the factory-produced goods of Central and Western Europe, not least because the now dominant Christians saw in the adoption of "European" styles and tastes an outward manifestation of their separation from Constantinople. With German, Austrian, and British textiles,

---

[29]*Naselenieto v knyazhestvo Bŭgariya* (Sredets, 1893), p. 43.

[30]Koledarov and Michev, *Promenite*, p. 6.

[31]Lory, *Le Sort de l'Héritage*, p. 79.

[32]Ibid., p. 116. See also Georgi Georgiev, "Preustroistvoto na traditsionnata selishtna sistema v rezultat ot osvobozhdenieto," *Istoricheski Pregled*, 33, nos. 5-6 (1977): 111-126. The classic treatment of the Balkan town is Nikolai Todorov, *Balkanskiyat Grad* (Sofia, 1972).

[33]Lory, *Le Sort de L'Héritage*, p. 117.

[34]Ibid., pp. 69-79, 112-13.

[35]Ibid., pp. 88-89.

clothing, shoes, porcelain, glassware, furniture, etc., being *à la mode* amongst the urban Bulgarians, the traditional crafts declined, in many cases causing economic dislocation among Bulgarian as well as Turkish producers.[36]

At times the changing habits and customs of the new state came near to offending Muslim religious susceptibilites. Much of the Turkish emigration, particularly in its earlier stages, had been from the towns, and, as a consequence, the Bulgarian element in these towns increased substantially as a proportion of the total. (See Tables 2 and 3.) For many Turks and Muslims, more especially those beyond their youth, this made social and public life uncomfortable. In the words of Bernard Lory, the most intelligent and original commentator on the immediate post-Ottoman period in Bulgaria," Le voisinage direct avec des *giaour* était particulièrement pénible aux femmes musulmanes qui n'en avaient pas l'habitude et n'osaient plus sortir dans la rue."[37] The old system which required women to remain unseen was even more rudely challenged by the would-be sophisticates of new urban élite, with their mixed dinner parties, theatrical excursions, balls, picnics, and so forth.[38] Even in diet the end of the Ottoman Empire brought changes which the Turks often found humiliating or perhaps even offensive to their religious practices. After 1878 in northern Bulgaria there was a very rapid increase in the growing of the potato, which had no part in traditional cuisine.[39] If the Turks of Bulgaria found this objectionable, their co-nationals south of the Balkans faced even greater difficulties. In February 1879 the Russian Provisional Administration banned the planting of rice in the Plovdiv, Tatar Pazardjik, and other regions. The public reason for this prohibition on the cultivation of the Turks' staple food was that the paddy-fields in the Maritsa valley were a health hazard, providing a breeding ground for malaria-carrying mosquitoes.[40] No doubt they did, but there was more to the prohibition than the health issue. It was, in the first place, an affront to established Turkish habits; but it was also an overt assertion of Bulgarian domination, in that rice had earned especial unpopularity because the former Muslim landowners had levied a corvée to grow it. Not until 1884 was the ban on the planting of rice lifted, and by then most Turkish landowners, and nearly all the owners of the large estates on which rice had been cultivated, had left.[41]

The new social attitudes and the restrictions on rice-growing were irksome and humiliating, but they did not openly and directly offend Muslim religious feelings. Other actions by the new régime did. With the departure of the Turks many nationalist Bulgarians had come to resent the number of mosques remaining in the towns of Bulgaria, many of these mosques being former Christian churches converted after the Ottoman conquest. Sofia in 1878 had a population of no more than 20,856;[42] but it had forty-five mosques. In December, during a storm, Russian military engineers dynamited

---

[36]For a summary of this development, see Crampton, *Bulgaria, 1878-1918*, pp. 215-18; for a more detailed treatment, see Atanas D. Spassow, *Der Verfall des alten Handwerk und die Entstehung des modernes Gewerbes in Bulgarian während des 19 Jahrhunderts* (Greifswald, 1900).

[37]*Le Sort de l'Héritage*, p. 41.

[38]Georgiev, *Osvobozhdenieto*, pp. 179-80.

[39]Ibid., pp. 28, 170.

[40]Natan et al, eds., *Ikonomikata na Bŭlgariya*, p. 324.

[41]Lory, *Le Sort de l'Héritage*, pp. 82-83.

[42]Léon Lamouche, *La Bulgarie* (Paris, 1923), p. 37; the population figure given for 1880 is 20,501.

seven of them, using the crash of the thunder to disguise the explosions. Some of the more famous former churches, for example the Church of the Forty Martyrs in Tŭrnovo and St. Sophia in Sofia, were reconsecrated, but other mosques were put to uses which can only have dismayed and angered those who once worshipped in them; some were turned into storehouses, while other uses included a printing-house, a museum, barracks, a prison, and, later, during the Balkan wars, a center for housing Turkish prisoners-of-war.[43] In a number of towns, including Plovdiv, Lovech, Svishtov, Burgas, and Rusé, Muslim cemeteries were turned into public gardens where, no doubt, men and women mingled with un-Muslim public familiarity, while the headstones from the graves were unscrupulously used for building.[44] Regulations concerning marriage age were also an interference with religious autonomy. The Ottoman system had not distinguished between "church" and state, and the various religious authorities had been left to regulate matters such as marriage among their adherents. In 1884 the Bulgarian government enacted minimum ages of seventeen for girls and nineteen for boys; and in 1897 these minimums were raised to eighteen and twenty respectively.[45] Whether such laws could be enforced, especially in the rural areas, is open to doubt; but for the relatively few Muslims who remained in the towns it was yet another reminder that the new system was dismissive of Muslim tradition. Another such reminder was the defeat in 1884 of a proposal put to Plovdiv city council by Turks, with the support of the Armenians, that Ottoman hours should be restored in public during Ramadan.[46]

North of the Balkan range, the Muslims of eastern Bulgaria feared that they were being discriminated against in the immediate post-liberation period by the fierce suppression of brigandage in their region; this law enforcement action became particularly intense in the spring and summer of 1880, after a pitched battle near the village of Belibe (Bulair) and the murder of Madame Skoboleva, the wife of a Russian hero of the 1877-78 war. Units of the new Bulgarian army were concentrated in the area, and a vigorous campaign of disarmament was instituted; but this deprived the local Turks of any defense against the remaining brigands, not all of whom were Muslim and few of whom had any compunction in taking advantage of the Turks' defenseless condition.[47]

Some of the brigands against whom the new Bulgarian army took action were Muslim deserters from that very army.[48] Conscription was for the Bulgarian Muslim perhaps the most intrusive act of the new state. On 6 May 1878 the Russian Provisional Administration had decreed that all males between the ages of twenty and thirty were to enrol in the militia, but Turks could, if they wished, pay a tax in lieu of military service. This right was soon rescinded. On 14 June 1880 the Bulgarian parliament, the Sŭbranie, enacted the law that all Bulgarian adult male citizens under

[43]James Samuelson, *Bulgaria Past and Present. Historical, Political and Descriptive* (London, 1888), p. 55; Lory, *Le Sort de l'Héritage*, p. 107; Johannes Awetaranian, "Results of the War in Bulgaria," *The Muslim World* 4, (1914): 407-412.

[44]Lory, *Le Sort de l'Héritage*, p. 117.

[45]Georgiev, *Osvobozhdenieto*, pp. 28, 170.

[46]Lory, *Le Sort de l'Héritage*, p. 149.

[47]Crampton, *Bulgaria, 1878-1918*, p. 45; Lory, *Le Sort de l'Héritage*, pp.1 58-59.

[48]Jirichek, *Pŭtuvane*, p. 317 n8.

fifty-five who did not belong to a military organization must enlist in the militia; and in the following year an article in *Voenni Sbornik* (Military Miscellany) confirmed that, with the sole exception of ministers of religion, military service was obligatory for all men, including Turks. The period of service with the colors was to be two years in the infantry and three in the cavalry and specialist regiments;[49] a further eight years with the reserve was also required, although those with middle and higher education need serve only one year or six months, respectively.[50] Conscription, therefore, was in force at the time of maximum Muslim and Turkish disorientation and demoralization. Concessions were made to Muslims, who did not, for example, have to wear the cross on their uniforms, but they were nevertheless required to obey Christian officers and to eat non-Muslim food; life in the army was, therefore, another, and a very powerful, reminder of their reduced status in the brave new Bulgarian world. In the Bulgarian census of 1880 those questioned were allowed to register their nationality; that many Muslims elected to register themselves as Ottoman subjects had not a little to do with their desire to avoid conscription into the Bulgarian army. Eventually the Bulgarian government decided to release Muslims from the draft on payment of a hefty tax of 500 *leva*, but this was not so much an act of generosity as of circumspection: the Bulgarians could not imagine that they would cross swords with any state but the Ottoman Empire, and in such an eventuality they did not know whether their Muslim conscripts would remain loyal.[51] Nevertheless, the exemption tax was one relatively few could afford. In 1892 only 1,700 to 1,900 Bulgarian Muslims applied for exemption, while about 30,000 chose to, or had no alterative but to, enlist. In 1910 the tax burden was eased in that the payment period was extended to twenty years—the time an enlisted man would have to spend in the reserve. Muslims were not called to arms in the Balkan wars; but in 1915, when Bulgaria fought alongside Turkey, the previously unconscripted Muslims provided a very welcome reserve of manpower for an army already depleted by the exertions of the 1912 and 1913 campaigns.[52]

By the time of the Balkan wars the proportion of Turks in the total population of Bulgaria was less than half that of the time of the liberation; the census of 1910 recorded them as 11.63 percent of the total, whereas figures taken from the Bulgarian census of 1880 and that in Eastern Rumelia in 1884 showed Turks as 24.81 percent of the total (see Table 1).

The decline in the urban Turkish population was even more rapid than the overall rate. The true extent of this decline may be gauged from a study of the figures given in Tables 2 and 3. These give statistics from the twenty largest towns, Sistova excepted, in Bulgaria in 1880 or 1884;[53] these were the years in which the first censuses were taken respectively, in Bulgaria and Eastern Rumelia. Data from Burgas and Kavlaklii, two

---

[49]Lamouche, *La Bulgarie*, pp. 61-56.

[50]Spiridion Gopčević, *Bulgarien und Ostrumelien, mit besonderer Berücksichtigung des Zeitraumes 1878-1886* (Leipzing, 1886), pp. 417-25.

[51]Lory, *Le Sort de l'Héritage*, pp. 29, 59.

[52]Girard, *Les minorités*, pp. 155-58.

[53]The only copy of the *Liste des Localités* which I have been able to find in Britain, that being in the Library of the London School of Economics and Political Science, has a few blank pages, including that on which the data for Sistova was printed.

towns not in the "top twenty" but with large Greek populations, have been included for comparative purposes. The tables all refer to ethnicity as determined by mother tongue. This will, of course, include Pomaks with Bulgarians and the Gagauzes with Turks; in neither case, however, will this greatly distort the general pattern, because neither group had a large urban presence. The data for the Greek and Jewish populations have been included only when those groups constituted at least 5 percent of a town's population at the time of the first census. Figures for the smaller ethnic groups—Tatars, etc.—were not always included in the pre-1900 censuses, but once again their total numbers are usually so small that their initial exclusion does not invalidate the general picture given by the changes in other groups.

The figures illustrate clearly the decline of the Greek population after the turn of the century, with a halving of absolute numbers in Plovdiv and in Stanimaka; but the more revealing trend was for the Greek population to fall much more rapidly in the years 1900-1910. In Varna the Greek population of 1900 was 4.64 percent more numerous than in 1880, but the 1910 figure was 36.59 percent less than that of 1900; and while in percentile terms, the proportion of Greeks in the total population in 1900 was 26.44 lower than in 1880, the 1910 reading was 46.52 under that for 1900. In Plovdiv absolute numbers fell by 28.91 percent between 1884 and 1900 and by 59.80 percent from 1900 to 1910, with percentile declines of 44.77 and 56.28. Even in the Greek strongholds of Burgas and Kavlaklii the same pattern is discernible: in Burgas, between 1884 and 1900 the Greek population grew in absolute numbers by 84.35 percent, but from 1900 to 1910 it fell by 32.69 percent while in both periods the percentile changes were negative,—7.89 from 1884 to 1900 and—46.96 from 1900 to 1910; in Kavlaklii, where the Greeks formed 96.6 percent of the total population in 1884, they increased in numbers between that date and 1900 by 15.08 percent but declined by 25.56 percent in the following ten years; and here too, throughout the post-Ottoman period, the proportion of Greeks in the total population fell, with percentile declines of 0.41 and 4.00 in the two periods being measured. The rapid post-1900 decline in the Greek population owed much to an increase in tension between the Greek and Bulgarian communities, a tension which led to ugly pogroms against the Greeks in 1906.

The figures also illustrate clearly the growth of the Jewish population in many Bulgarian towns. Between 1880-1884 and 1910 the Jewish population, both in absolute number and as a percentage of the total, increased in Plovdiv, Vidin, Sofia, Stanimaka, Yambol, Tatar Pazardjik, Stara Zagora, and Kiustendil; only in Samokov did the total numbers fall, while the Jewish share of the total fell only in that town and in Tatar Pazardjik, Kiustendil, and Sofia.

With regard to the Turkish urban population the statistics make quite obvious its concentration in the northeast, with the five largest Turkish settlements, measured by the proportion of Turks to the total population, being Razgrad, Silistra, Shumen, Rusé, and Varna. Of the top five, measured by absolute numbers, Rusé, Shumen, Varna, and Razgrad, were in the northeast and only one, in the south. Of the 76,147 urban Turks listed in Table 2 for the years 1880-1884, 43,625 or 57.29 percent were to be found in the north-eastern towns of Pleven, Razgrad, Rusé, Shumen, Silistra, Tŭrnovo, and Varna. By 1910 the position was even more consolidated, with 27,230, or 68.06 percent, of the 40,006 urban Turks domiciled in the same northeastern towns.

All indicators for changes in the Turkish population, both in absolute numbers and in percentages, are negative except in three cases: Stanimaka, where the Turkish element increased in the second period, both in absolute numbers and as a percentage of the total; Pleven, where an increase in absolute numbers of almost one-fifth was accompanied by a fall of two-fifths as a proportion of the total; and Burgas, where a minimal increase in absolute numbers was offset by a fall of sixty percentile points in the other measurement. The Turkish population fell by half in thirteen towns—Varna, Plovdiv, Haskovo, Vratsa, Samokov, Sofia, Stara Zagora, Kavlaklii, Sliven, Tatar Pazardjik, Chirpan, and Kiustendil—although it is to be noted that this list of towns does not include those five with the highest Turkish share of the population. It seems, then, that the decline was most rapid in towns where the Turkish element was less well entrenched. But even in the five towns with the largest Turkish populations the Turks declined as a proportion of the total, with percentile falls of 35.05 in Razgrad, 34.18 in Silistra, 42.15 in Shumen, 59.25 in Rusé, and 70.49 in Varna. In fact, the percentile decline was less than one-third only in Stanimaka, where there was an increase of 9.62 percent, although the actual numbers involved were very small and the departure of the sizeable Greek population magnified the Turkish element of the population—a point underlined by the fact that between 1884 and 1900 the percentile change for the Turks was—25.48. The total percentile decline from 1880-1884 to 1910 was between a third and a half in five towns, all of them in the northeast: Shumen (42.15), Razgrad (35.05), Silistra (34.18), Pleven (40.43), and Tŭrnovo (45.50)—although in the latter the absolute numbers were again very small. In ten settlements the Turkish percentile decline was between half and three-quarters: Yambol (57.33), Rusé (59.25), Burgas (60.04), Sliven (61.71), Vratsa (64.64), Haskovo (70.01), Varna (70.49), Plovdiv (71.25), Vidin (71.70), and Stara Zagora (72.28). The percentile fall was over three quarters in Tatar Pazardjik (76.81), Samokov (88.52), Chirpan (90.56), Sofia (92.72), Kiustendil (95.36), and Kavlaklii, where the tiny Turkish population disappeared completely. Of the ten towns with the largest Turkish percentage of the population in 1880-1884—Razgrad (54.80), Silistra (49.83), Shumen (42.63), Rusé (39.19), Varna (36.26), Vidin (32.68), Haskovo (28.64), Burgas (21.62), Plovdiv (21.36), and Stara Zagora (17.03)—only in Rusé, Razgrad, Shumen, and Silistra was the absolute decline by 1910 as low as 50 percent; and only Razgrad, Silistra, and Shumen had experienced a percentile fall less than that figure. The same exceptions to the rule apply in the cases of ten towns with the largest Turkish population measured in absolute numbers in 1880-1884—Rusé, Shumen, Varna, Plovdiv, Razgrad, Silistra, Vidin, Haskovo, Sliven, and Tatar Pazardjik.

The decline of the Turkish element in those Bulgarian towns that grew most rapidly in the years from 1884 to 1910 is set out in Table 4, which shows that the Turkish component in absolute numbers fell by at least 50 percent in six of them and, in percentile points, by the same figure in nine of them. The Bulgarians, on the other hand, increased by at least 50 percent in all except Vratsa, although their increase as a proportion of the total population was not as dramatic as was the decline in the Turkish population.

Most of the departing urban Turks had taken part in the Ottoman administrative service, had been established traders, or had been part of the small Turkish professional or intelligentsia group, and their departure deprived the Turkish community of its natural leadership, just as the emigration of the large landowners broke the social power of the Turks in the countryside. At the same time, many of the incoming Bulgarian refugees, particularly those who came to the new state from Bulgarian communities in Romania and Russia, were the adventurous and the able. In effect, the intelligentsia and the commercial leadership cadres of the towns rapidly changed from Turkish to Bulgarian— which could only intensify Turkish dissatisfaction and harden the determination to leave. The quality of the new Bulgarian-dominated administration was sometimes lower than that of its predecessor; in his memoirs, the Bulgarian public servant Danail Yurukov admits that rapid promotion in Tatar Pazardjik placed him in a position where his reponsibilities far outstripped his qualifications and his knowledge, as a result of which he ruled according to the dictates of his conscience in the hope that these were not too divergent from the provisions of the statute law.[54]

In the countryside the fact that the majority of wealthy Turkish landowners had departed did in some cases lessen the gap between Bulgarian and Turk. Initially many of the less wealthy Turks benefited equally with the Bulgarians from the availability of land. The acquisition of new property in all probability created some loose ties of interest between them and the poor Bulgarian peasants who had seized or bought vacant land, and these ties were strengthened by a common antipathy toward the wealthier Greeks, who formed the mercantile élite in eastern Bulgaria and parts of Eastern Rumelia. Writing in 1898, the noted *Times* correspondent, James Bourchier, recorded that "In eastern Bulgaria the upper class are mainly Greeks, who have enriched themselves by mercantile pursuits ... between the Greek merchant who buys corn at fifty percent below its value, and the Greek tavern-keeper who charges him fifty percent too much for the *mastika* he drinks, the Bulgarian peasant does not run a particularly good chance of dying a rich man."[55] And if the Turkish peasant did not drink *mastika,* he did sell grain and therefore had an object of resentment in common with his Bulgarian peasant neighbour. It is instructive that when the first attempt was made to enforce teaching in Bulgarian in non-Bulgarian schools, the legislation was aimed primarily at the Greeks and did not effect either Turks or Jews.[56]

The most notable diplay of Turkish-Bulgarian solidarity came with the surprising contribution of Bulgaria's Turks to the victory over Serbia in the war of 1885. Turkish volunteers were reported marching from Varna in their national dress.[57] In addition, the regular army, including the cavalry regiment raised in Shumen, contained large numbers of Turkish conscripts as well as professional soldiers and NCOs. A number of decorations were awarded to Turks in that war.[58] Maj. A. Huhn, a German observer of the fighting, is worth quoting at some length on this and other effects of the war:

---

[54]*Spomeni: iz politicheski zhivot na Bŭlgariya* (Sofia, 1932), p. 51.

[55]"Social Life in Bulgaria," *English Illustrated Magazine* 7 (1889): 526-27.

[56]Crampton, *Bulgaria, 1878-1918,* pp. 149-50.

[57]Yoto Mitev, *Istoriya na Srbska-Bŭlgarskata Voina, 1885* (Sofia, 1971), p. 121.

[58]Jirichek, *Pŭtuvane,* p. 317, n8.

Together with the pride in their victories, a true Bulgarian national feeling grew more and more, especially in the army and amongst the officers. What had hitherto kept the Bulgarians together was religion and the bonds of race, whilst the actual meaning of a 'Fatherland' was more distant from their minds, and was simply non-existent during the Turkish rule. With the booming of the guns at Slivnitza this idea seems first to have burst upon them, and that throughout the entire people of Bulgaria, Bulgarians and Turks. The reconciliation of the Christian and the Moslem faith, or more properly the recognition of the equal rights of the Mahomedans, has always been one of my pet theories, and during eight years I have fought for it with very wretched results, for the intolerant spirit that once led to the craze of the crusades is still rampant today. But now, after the battles of Slivnitza, and ... throughout the war, it seemed to me as if this idea had taken a rapid stride forward, and had for the first time made a commencement towards realisation. I saw Turks and Bulgarians fighting side by side, and if the absence of the cross on the front of their busbies had not distinguished the Turks from the Bulgarians, no one would have thought that the representatives of two races were here standing together who but a few years ago had waged a most cruel war on each other. Though the Turks who were incorporated in the troops of the line always remained in a large minority compared to the Bulgarians, still in the Breslaw, [Preslav] Plevna, and Varna regiments they formed 10 to 15 per cent of the whole. According to the opinion of all the officers, these Mahomedan soldiers fought quite splendidly, were in nothing behind their Bulgarian comrades, and frequently set them a good example. For this the fullest recognition was not wanting both from their superiors, and, what is still more important for a subsequent peaceful existence, from their comrades, who though in the majority, often voluntarily resigned their places and allowed the minority to take precedence of them. This requires a short explanation. The Bulgarian army has taken over from the Russian the custom that when honours and rewards are given for conspicuous services in the field, they are not awarded to individuals, but given in a lump to the regiment, which distributes them amongst the different companies. In the companies, however, the men elect those from their number who are to be the recipients of these honours. Now, when the first crosses for valour were distributed, it was a singular circumstance that the Mahomedans, who formed an insignificant minority, received nearly as many crosses in some regiments as the Christians, and that by the choice of their comrades. The very first cross for valor of the first class adorned the breast of a Mahomedan. Does not this justify one in hoping that the same spirit of good fellowship and friendly tolerance may be ultimately introduced into everyday life?

Unlike the Turks, the Greeks did nothing towards defending the country, and even the victories made at the most a painful impression on them. With too little energy to stand up against the Bulgarian movement, they waited for some one else to be their catspaw, and to save the heroic

Greek people the trouble of proving their heroism themselves. And they are waiting still.[59]

Although comaradeship in arms was to be found again in the First World War, von Huhn's optimistic expectations proved hopelessly exaggerated, and the political cohesion of even the Bulgarians themselves did not survive a year beyond the great victory at Slivnitsa.[60] Rather than finding a greater unity, the Bulgarian and Turkish communities drifted further apart as Bulgarian domination was entrenched in the now-unified state of Bulgaria and in Eastern Rumelia. The Turks also tended to drift away physically after the war, departing Bulgaria largely by their own choice: they were not driven out, their emigration being as much the result of the attractions of the Ottoman Empire as of the perceived disadvantages of remaining in Bulgaria. This was particularly so up until the turn of the century, as the Porte continued to entice Turks and Pomaks from Bulgaria with offers of land in Thrace or Asia Minor.

The war years, 1912-1918, brought further demographic changes. After the second Balkan war a convention signed in Constantinople provided for the exchange of population in a fifteen-kilometer band on either side of the Bulgarian-Ottoman border, and the exchange which preceded and followed this agreement further reduced the Turkish population in southern Bulgaria.[61] Population also were exchanged with Greece, which proved beneficial to the Turks remaining in Bulgaria.

The Greeks in Bulgaria had faced increasing hostility ever since Bulgarian and Greek claims in Macedonia had begun seriously to compete in the late 1890s. Pogroms in 1906 caused an egress of some 35,000 Greeks, and the bitternesses of the second Balkan and the First World wars brought more population movements.[62] By 1919 both Sofia and Athens were keen to exchange populations, a desire gratified through the Convention Respecting Mutual Emigration signed on the same day as the treaty of Neuilly in November 1919.[63] Some 46,000 Greeks took advantage of the Convention, and by the end of the 1920s only a few thousand were left in Bulgaria. These changes benefited the Turks in that the departure of the Greeks, with whom relations had been steadily deteriorating since 1900, made it easier for Bulgaria to enact and comply with the minority protection laws upon which the victors in the First World War had insisted. To grant minority rights would no longer be a question of giving gifts to Greeks but, rather, one of favoring Turks, who had been compliant citizens and loyal allies in the recent conflict.[64]

---

[59]*The Struggle of the Bulgarians for National Independence under Prince Alexander. A Military and Political History of the War between Bulgaria and Servia in 1885* (London, 1886), pp. 181-83.

[60]Crampton, *Bulgaria, 1878-1918*, pp. 105ff.

[61]S. P. Ladas, *The Exchange of Minorities. Bulgaria, Greece and Turkey* (New York, 1932), pp. 10-20.

[62]Ibid., pp. 121-23.

[63]Ibid., pp. 27-41.

[64]In fact, during the Greek-Turkish war in Asia Minor the Greeks so feared a recrudescence of the Bulgaro-Turkish alliance that they moved many Bulgarian families in the lower Maritsa valley to the Greek islands and to Thessaly, lest the Bulgarian army march down the valley; ibid, pp. 212-23.

There were, of course, occasional outbursts against the Turks, as for example in Rusé in 1910 when twenty-eight people died in disturbances following disagreements over a projected Christian-Muslim marriage;[65] and the late nineteenth century saw in Bulgaria, as elsewhere, a certain amount of basically racist literature.[66] In the 1920s a deep-seated cultural chauvinism could still be detected in some Bulgarian writing; one Bulgarian in 1926 wrote, "Our songs, our early poems, our whole life was simply saturated with the habits and customs of our conquerors, the Turks. It will be a long time before we can free ourselves of all these things."[67] There was no complete Bulgarian-language edition of the Koran until 1930.[68] Despite these feelings there was no anti-Turkish pogrom to compare with the anti-Greek outbursts which swept along Bulgaria's Black Sea coast in 1906.[69] As relations with the Ottoman Empire deteriorated and Bulgarian nationalism became sharper in the disputes over Macedonia before the outbreak of the Balkan wars, there was a growing defensiveness among the Muslims of Bulgaria—an insecurity reinforced by the Rusé incident and reflected in the formation in 1911 of the Muslim Alliance, the *Iftifak-i-Islâm*, the function of which was do defend the constitutional rights of Muslims, to intercede with the authorities on their behalf, and, where necessary, to give material aid to impoverished or suffering co-religionists.[70]

Despite the lack of official or even overt public hostility, the Turkish emigration began again in the inter-war period, even though it was a process made tedious and lengthy by the new formalities, which demanded passports and visas, certificates of health and of land sale, and evidence of a sponsor in Turkey. Between the signing of the 1925 Turco-Bulgarian agreement, and 1940 there was an average annual loss from Bulgaria of between ten and twelve thousand Turks, although from 1930 to 1935 the annual rate was under a thousand.[71] There were peaks of emigration in 1927 and 1935. The 1927 surge resulted from pent-up frustration, released by the new agreement of 1925. Before then some Turks had resented what they saw as discriminatory taxation policies, economic exploitation, poverty, and a further bout of geographic name-changing; the latter was believed by defenders of the Turks to be a campaign on the part of post-1923, right-wing governments in Sofia to make Bulgaria into an ethnically homogeneous society. There were further complaints about violence by the small proto-fascist organization, *Rodna Zashtita* (Defence of the Homeland), and also that land

---

[65]Crampton, *Bulgaria 1878-1918*, p. 318; Lory, *Le Sort de l'Heritage*, pp. 171-72.

[66]See, for example, Georgi G. Dimitrov, *Knyazhestvo Bŭlgariya v istorichesko, geografichesko i etnografichesko otnoshenie v tri chasti* (Sofia, 1894), This work is also quoted by Stefan Troebst in "Partei, Staat und türkische Minderheit in Bulgarien: Kontinuitat und Wandel '1956-1986)," *Europäische Rundschau*, no. 2 (1986): 158.

[67]Ivan Gantcheff, "Islam in Bulgaria," *The Moslem World* 16 (1926): 158.

[68]Natanail Nazifoff, "The Bulgarian Koran," *The Moslem World* 23 (1933): 187-90.

[69]Crampton, *Bulgaria, 1878-1918*, pp. 296-98. I also discussed this problem in "The Second Stambolovist Ministry, Public Order and Internal Unrest," *Bulgarian Historical Review*, 10, no. 1 (1982): 37-49; Before publication of this article, with no notice to or consultation with me, all references to the anti-Greek incidents were very carefully removed and subsequent footnote numbers altered to disguise the exclusion.

[70]Popović, "Les Turcs" p. 388: and idem, *L'Islam*, p. 77.

[71]H. L. Kostanick, "Turkish Resettlement of Bulgarian Turks, 1950-1953," *University of California Publications in Geography* 8, no. 2 (1957): 68.

legislation of 1921 was unfair. The latter dispute echoed that of the post-liberation years, for the government ruled that all land left untilled since 1912 would be taken into state ownership if its owners had not recommenced work upon it by 27 July 1925. The agreement of 1925 did little to help in this matter because the contracting parties put differing interpretations upon those clauses regulating the reversion of land to the state.[72] The wave of emigration in 1935 was prompted partly by a series of minor issues, such as the desecration of a Muslim cemetery in April 1933;[73] but the main impetus came as a result of the political changes of 1934, which brought to power the centralizing and rationalizing Zveno (Link) faction.[74] For reasons of administrative tidiness and to garner popular support, the Zvenari insisted upon wholesale changes in place names; 1,971 (94.26 percent) of the 2,091 changes between 1920 and 1935 took place in 1934. Names imposed during Ottoman rule, or those that were dialectal or archaic in form were deemed inappropriate to the nationalist, centralizing, dynamic, modernizing Bulgaria of the Zvenari.[75] Not all the émigrés of 1935, however, left entirely because of displeasure at Bulgarian official policies. The Sofia correspondent of the *New York Times* reported in February 1935,

> People have been wondering why so many Turks, who have lived happily in Bulgaria for many years, have been selling their homes lately and emigrating to Turkey with large consignments of sugar bought with the proceeds of their sales and any other capital they could rake together.
>
> Now it is revealed that about eight months ago the Turkish government decreed that any Turks living abroad who would return to settle in their homeland might import goods duty free to the value of 350,000 leva, about $3,800. As sugar for export can be bought in Bulgaria at 5 leva a kilogram, and sold in Turkey at 38 leva, many poor Turks in Bulgaria were delighted to take advantage of an opportunity to make a small fortune by returning home.[76]

The egress of 1935 was the last major exodus before the Second World War. After the treaty of Craiova and Bulgaria's re-acquisition of southern Dobrudja in August 1940, some 130,000 more Turks were added to the Bulgarian population. This prompted another bout of name-changing, with 357 (82.64 percent) of the 432 recorded changes between 1935 and 1944 coming about because of the re-acquisition of southern Dobrudja.[77]

---

[72]Popović, *L'Islam*, pp. 82-83; idem, "Les Turcs," pp. 390-92.

[73]Popović, "Les Turcs," p. 392.

[74]For a summary of this faction and its brief but energetic few months in office, see R. J. Crampton, *A Short History of Modern Bulgaria* (Cambridge, 1987), pp. 111-14.

[75]Koledarov and Michev, *Promenite* p. 8.

[76]I found a small cutting of this article among the papers of the reporter concerned, Joseph Swire; the papers are in my possession. I have not had the opportunity to consult the files of the *New York Times*, but the article is date-lined February 15 and must refer to 1935. Presumably it was published shortly after February 15.

[77]Kostanick, "Turkish Resettlement," p. 68.

Minority Rights in Bulgaria, 1878-1944

A series of treaty provisions enjoined the Bulgarian state to tolerate religious and other minorities. The treaty of Berlin contained clauses requiring equality of opportunity and freedom of worship (Article IV and V), and the question of Muslim rights was extensively treated in the Turco-Bulgarian Convention of 6/19 April 1909, which settled the disputes arising from Bulgaria's declaration of complete independence in 1908.

The treaty of Neuilly in 1919, without in reality making any new demands, spelled out Bulgaria's obligations in great detail. Bulgaria was required to "assure full and complete protection of life and liberty to all inhabitants of Bulgaria without distinction of birth, nationality, language, race or religion" and to ensure that "all inhabitants of Bulgaria shall be entitled to the free exercise, whether public or private, of any creed, religion or belief, whose practices are not inconsistent with public order or public morals" (Article 50).[78] All those residing in Bulgaria when the treaty became effective were to be Bulgarian nationals and all Bulgarian nationals were guaranteed equality before the law and were to enjoy "the same civil and political rights without distinction as to race, language or religion"; nor was religious affiliation or ethnic origin to prejudice a Bulgarian citizen's chances of employment, promotion, or public honors; nor was there to be any restriction "on the free use by any Bulgarian national of any language in private intercourse, in commerce, in religion, in the press or in publications of any kind, or at public meetings"; and "adequate facilities" were to be given to Bulgarian nationals who did not speak Bulgarian for the use of their language, either in speech or in writing, before the courts (Article 53). Members of the national or religious minorities were to be guaranteed "the same treatment and security in law and in fact as the other Bulgarian nationals"; "In particular they shall have an equal right to establish, manage, and control at their own expense charitable, religious and social institutions, schools and other educational establishments, with the right to use ther own language and to exercise their religion freely therein" (Article 54). In areas where a "considerable proportion" of the population were from minority groups the government was to provide primary education in the local language, although this was not to prevent the government from making Bulgarian a compulsory subject in such schools; and the minority groups were also to benefit in due proportion from the sums expended in other social sectors. (Article 55). Finally, Bulgaria agreed that these clauses of the treaty were to be guaranteed by the League of Nations. (Article 57).

Bulgaria, like other states which had seen co-nationals alienated by the new frontiers, had every reason to wish to see all minority protection treaties honored. Before signing the treaty, however, the Bulgarian delegates in Paris had argued that their country did not need to have such clauses forced upon it because it had a long tradition,

---

[78]The minority protection provisions are to be found in Section IV of the treaty, Articles 49-57 inclusive; see United Kingdom, Parliament. *Treaty of Peace between the Allied and Associated Powers and Bulgaria and Protocol signed at Neuilly-sur-Seine, November 27, 1919*, Treaty Series, no. 5. Cmd. 522. 1920. For a detailed examination of the various treaties and other documents spelling out Bulgaria's legal obligations to its minorities, see "The Rights of Minorities in International Law and Treaties: The Case of the Turkish Minority in the People's Republic of Bulgaria" by A. Mete Tuncoko, in this issue of *IJTS*.

reaching as far back as the foundation of the first Bulgarian state in 681 A.D., of tolerance and respect for minorities.[79] There was some substance to this claim. In the years before the war Bulgaria had accepted a number of Jews from Russia and Romania, and, although there were occasional outbursts of anti-semitic activity, these Jews lived in Bulgaria with greater security than they could have hoped for in the countries they had recently left. As a result of the outrages of 1895, 1913, and 1915 some 25,000 Armenians also found refuge with the Bulgarians, who accepted this influx "avec une générosité dont ils ont rendu témoignage."[80]

Foreign observers of Bulgaria both before and after the First World War tend in general to support the Bulgarian case and indicate that the minority protection articles of the treaty were observed and that Bulgarian and non-Bulgarian, Christian and Muslim, lived together in reasonable harmony, with neither side showing a great desire to dominate or restrict the other. In 1914 a correspondent for an American missionary journal could report in glowing terms on the behaviour of Bulgarian troops during the Balkan wars: "One Pastor, who had been in the army, told of repeated cases he had personally met of people migrating so that they might come under Bulgarian authority; and it is known that Jews in Salonika offered Bulgarian soldiers money to live in their houses and protect them from the other soldiery."[81] However, as Bernard Lory has noted, this could have reflected ignorance and indifference as much as a positive sense of tolerance.[82] There were bungled and short-lived attempts to convert some Pomaks after the first Balkan war;[83] and during the First World War such attempts were again made.[84] Later, in the 1920s, an American observer could write that "The Muslims of Bulgaria enjoy civil and religious liberty";[85] and in 1931 the distinguished scholar Irwin T. Sanders noted that comradeship in arms during the First World War had helped dispel what hostility remained between Bulgarian and Turk in Bulgaria, supporting the contention of the Italian expert, Professor Baldacci of Bologna, that centuries of co-existence had made the two communities compatible.[86] A book published in Britain a few years later noted that "the Bulgarians seem to bear no malice against the considerable Turkish population living in their midst," and the author went on to give a down-to-earth example of racial tolerance by recalling how in the Valley of the Roses he had been in a bus where a bottle of rose-water was passed around until it reached a young Turk who, smiling upon us all, filled his mouth full and squirted it out again like a fountain over the passengers. For one minute I imagined that another Bulgarian

---

[79]See Girard, *Les minorités*, pp. 159-203 for these arguments and some of the more important documents used to support them.

[80]Ibid., p. 31. After the Russian civil war, at least as many White Russians found safety in Bulgaria, even though their political beliefs and bellicose past were unwelcome in Stamboliiski's Bulgaria; see John D. Bell, *Peasants in Power, Alexander Stamboliski and the Bulgarian Agrarian National Union, 1899-1923* (Princeton, New Jersey, 1977), pp. 195-96.

[81]Robert Thomson, "Conditions in Bulgaria," *The Moslem World* 4 (1914: 74, 75.)

[82]*Le Sort de l'Héritage*, p. 61.

[83]Thomson, "Conditions," pp. 76-77.

[84]G. Pedersen, untitled article in *The Moslem World* 13 (1923): 85.

[85]Zwemer, "Islam," p. 340.

[86]"The Moslem Minority," p. 358.

revolution might result, and feared for the Turk, but I need not have worried, for the company shrieked with mirth."[87] At the end of the decade another visitor noted that "the Bulgarian Moslems, an ethnical and a religious minority, enjoy an unusually liberal treatment in legal matters. They are citizens on a par with Orthodox Bulgarians ... Bulgarian Islam... enjoys the greatest tolerance on the part of the majority."[88] A closer examination of the record concerning religious, legal, cultural, educational, and political rights tends in general to confirm the positive judgements of these observers.

The obligations dictated at Berlin with regard to the freedom of conscience and worship were fulfilled in Articles 40 and 42 of the Tŭrnovo Constitution of 1879.[89] These gave the non-Orthodox community the right to administer their own internal affairs—which meant, for example, that Muslim villages were not required to observe Sunday as a day of rest nor to honor Christian holidays (though they did have to respect the three national holidays).[90] For the keeping of religious law there were, even before First World War, *muftis* in Sofia, Vidin, Vratsa, Pleven, Tŭrnovo, Varna, Shumen, Rusé, Plovdiv, Sliven, Stara Zagora and Burgas: that is, one for each provincial capital except Kiustendil (with an extra one at Sliven). There were also thirty-two assistant *muftis*. The *muftis* were responsible for mosques, Muslim educational institutions, the *vakŭfs*, and for administering justice inside the Muslim community. They were nominated and paid by the Bulgarian government, although the Porte contributed to the salary of the *mufti* in Plovdiv. The *muftis* and their assistants were Turks rather than Pomaks.[91] Under the terms of the Turco-Bulgarian convention of 6/19 April 1909 the *muftis* were to be elected by the local Muslim communities; their election was to be vetted by a grand *mufti* in Sofia and, if all were in order, confirmed by the Sheik-ul-Islam in Constantinople. At the communal level the *kadis* continued to decide on detailed disputes within families on issues of marriage, divorce, inheritance, etc.[92] The Convention also allowed that, although Bulgaria was to exercise the rights of a fully independent state, its Muslims could continue to offer public prayers for the *khalif*, notwithstanding the fact that the latter, as sultan, was the head of a foreign state. The 1909 convention also made the grand *mufti* the intermediary between the other *muftis* and their assistants, on the one side, and the Sheik-ul-Islam, on the other.[93]

The questions raised in 1909 over the rights and status of Muslims and their institutions in Bulgaria were many and complicated and demanded detailed changes in Bulgarian law. These took years to prepare, and the enormity of the task, together with the emergencies of the war years, meant that the final codifying act, the Law Concerning the Establishment and Administration of the Mohamedan Religious Community in the

---

[87]H. Hessell Tiltman, *Peasant Europe* (London, 1934), p. 99.

[88]G. H. Bosquet, "Islam in the Balkans," *The Moslem World* 27 (1937): 68-69.

[89]These articles are among those printed in Stephen Fischer-Galati, *Man, State and Society in East European History* (New York, 1970), pp. 211-17; see also, C. E. Black, *The Establishment of Constitutional Government in Bulgaria*, Princeton Studies in History, vol. 1 (Princeton, New Jersey, 1943), pp. 291-309.

[90]Girard, *Les minorités*, pp. 105-107.

[91]Popović, "Les Turcs," pp. 386-87, 394-95.

[92]Lory, *Le sort de l'Héritage*, p. 60.

[93]Girard, *Les minorités*, pp. 133-37.

Kingdom of Bulgaria, did not reach the statute book until 23 May 1919. The act gave the Muslim communities considerable autonomy in their internal affairs, and it was to remain the basis of Muslim communal rights until after the Second World War. Under the terms of the 1919 act the Ministry of Foreign Affairs and Cults in Sofia agreed that a council of the Muslim religious community could be established in any settlement which had forty or more Muslim families. Such councils would be recognized as legal entities that could own property, such as mosques and schools, and could receive benefactions. The councils would administer the *vakūf*s and employ the *muftis*—who had to be Bulgarian subjects and literate in Bulgarian as well as in their own minority language. Each council would consist of from five to nine members elected by the males of the community. The law also allowed for the appointment of a grand *mufti*, who would reside in the Banya-Bashi mosque in Sofia. With regard to internal affairs, the Muslim councils enjoyed an autonomy much greater than that of their Christian equivalents and more extensive than that previously allowed to Muslims. They could now regulate matrimonial disputes, disagreements between parents and children, divorces, paternity cases, and disputes over wills and testaments.[94] One of the first expressions of the extended rights of the Muslim communities was the decision of a commission of *mufti*s to set the minimum age for marriage at eighteen for boys and seventeen for girls, rather than twenty and eighteen as enacted by the Bulgarian government in 1879.[95] After the Kemalist revolution the Muslims of Bulgaria were free to follow a traditional Islam, while their co-religionists in Turkey had to adopt the secularist policies of the new regime. Muslim women in Bulgaria were free to continue wearing the veil, and the Arabic script could be retained in the writing of Turkish. The Bulgarian Muslims had in the region of 2,300 mosques in which to worship and some four thousand *hodja*s to lead them in prayer.[96]

The 1919 act also established Muslim religious courts. The court of first instance was the local tribunal, or *sheriyat* court, set up by the *mufti* of the province, and above this were religious courts of appeal in Sofia, Ruse, and Plovdiv, whose members were nominated by royal decree. The final court of religious appeal was to be the Supreme Tribunal in Sofia, headed by the grand *mufti*. By 1935 there were twenty-two *sheriyat* courts;[97] but the situation was less satisfactory with regard to the three courts of appeal, none of which in reality existed. This, however, was not due to any malfeasance on the part of the Bulgarian authorities but rather to the fact that there were no qualified candidates; and, although there was a Muslim supreme tribunal in Sofia, there were almost no Muslims in that city and, according to one contemporary, the president of the supreme tribunal, the Grand Mufti Hussein Ahmedov, did not know a word of Bulgarian.[98]

In the earliest days of liberated Bulgaria, a French observer feared that Bulgarian national passions were so fierce that "On ne peut pas dire que la justice existe pour d'autres que

---

[94]Ibid., pp. 127-48; Kostanick, "Turkish Resettlement," p. 80; Popović, *L'Islam,* pp. 90-91.

[95]Bosquet, "Islam in the Balkans," p. 69.

[96]Girard, *Les minorités,* pp. 133-37.

[97]Popović, "Les Turcs," p. 395.

[98]Bosquet, "Islam in the Balkans," p. 69.

pour les Bulgares."[99] Such fears were exaggerated. The Tŭrnovo constitution guaranteed that minority languages could be used in courts of law, although written records would in Bulgarian. In areas with high proportions of minority groups legal officials with a knowledge of local languages were the norm rather than the exception, and, after the First World War, all magistrates in the Razgrad and Shumen districts, for example, could speak Turkish.[100]

The use of minority languages outside the law courts was also widespread. According to Girard, Bulgarians more frequently spoke a minority language than vice versa, and, he added, "Nul n'a jamais été inquiété en Bulgarie du fait de l'usage d'une langue maternelle."[101] On the quaysides of Varna in the early 1920s Turkish was still a widely used, if not the predominant, tongue.[102] A law of 1902 had required elected mayors and their deputies to be literate in the official language, Bulgarian, but had gone on to allow such officials in communities where the dominant language was not Bulgarian to be literate in that other language; in mixed communities the mayor had to know Bulgarian. As a result of this law, Greek mayors were elected in Anhialo, Sosopol, Messemvria, and elsewhere, while a number of Muslim settlements chose Turkish-speaking officials.[103]

Education is always a critical issue for minority groups, and in Bulgaria there was widespread provision of this vital facility. A law of 1885 on communal and private schools provided that all settlements, whatever their size, should have at least one school. The first major piece of educational legislation enacted in Bulgaria, the act of 1891, allowed only non-Christian children to be educated in their mother tongue, although the schools which they attended were to be private and not financed by the local community. The object of the 1891 legislation was, in fact, to weaken Greek influence, particularly among the Gagauzes; of the twelve Greek-speaking private schools extant in 1881-82, eight were to be found in purely Gagauze villages, and the Greek bishop of Plovdiv regularly toured his diocese urging Greek and Gagauze families to send their children to Greek patriarchist rather Bulgarian exarchist schools.[104] The Bulgarian authorities interfered little, on the other hand, in the Turkish primary schools, which by 1904 numbered 1,293 with 64,422 pupils. These cost 283,000 *leva* to run, of which the government in Sofia contributed 24,000, the remainder coming from the income from the *vakŭfs* and from the donations of parents. There were schools for girls in Plovdiv, Rusé, Sofia, and other large towns.[105] The administration of education was centralized in 1909, but the Turco-Bulgarian convention of that year and, later, the 1919 Law on Muslim Communities did much to shield Muslim educational institutions from increased interference from the now powerful central ministry in Sofia.

---

[99]Lory, *Le Sort de l'Héritage*, pp. 54-58.

[100]Girard, *Les minorités*, p. 69.

[101]Ibid., p. 67.

[102]Max Hoppe, "Islam in Bulgaria," *The Moslem World* 14 (1924): 160.

[103]Girard, *Les minorités*, pp. 58-62, 71.

[104]Yordan Parushev, "Pŭrvata Prosvetna Reforma v Bŭlgariya prez 1891," *Istoricheski Pregled* 43, no. 6 (1987): 39-44.

[105]Popović, *L'Islam*, p. 77.

The major problem in Muslim and Turkish education was not the hostility of the authorities but the backwardness, the remoteness, and the cultural exclusiveness of many Turkish communities. Put simply, the Turks did not attend school in sufficient numbers. In 1905, 47 percent of adult Bulgarian-speakers could read and write, but only 6 percent of Turks; and for the Pomaks, the literacy figure was 4 percent; for gypsies, 3 percent. There had been some improvement by the time of the census of 1926, which recorded adult literacy rates of 54.36 percent for Bulgarians, 12 percent for Turks, 6.5 percent for Pomaks, and 8 percent for gypsies.[106] Contemporaries insisted that much higher literacy rates prevailed amongst the young of the Turkish communities: "All the younger generation know how to read and write. The material and intellectual progress of Bulgaria is evident in many ways."[107] Some of this improvement was due to the increased autonomy granted to Muslim communities under the act of 1919 and to the establishment, in 1920, within the Ministry of Education, of a Turkish Inspectorate. The Inspectorate was to be headed by the inspector-general for Sofia, who was to have two assistants, one for Plovdiv and the other for Shumen. The first inspector-general was Mustafa Djepoun, until then director of the Turkish gymnasium at Suhindol.[108] By 1926 there were 1,329 Turkish schools with 58,000 pupils.[109] By the second half of the 1930s the number of pupils in Turkish-speaking schools had dropped to an estimated 50,000, a decline that was primarily the result of continued Turkish emigration.[110] The Turkish-speaking schools were jointly funded by the state, the provinces, the *vakufs*, the Muslim Councils and by individual donations.[111]

Higher education was not unknown amongst the Turks of Bulgaria. A lectureship in Turkish had been established at Sofia University in 1907, but in that same year the entire faculty was sacked and replaced following political disturbances by the students and some of their teachers.[112] By the late 1930s Sofia University had a considerable number of Turkish students (earlier in the decade there had even been a female Muslim student). Turks, with or without degrees, were to be found in a number of professions—including journalism, medicine, university teaching, and engineering—as well as in industry. There was also provision for higher religious education for Muslims. The most important institution was the Grand Medresse, *Medresse-i Nuvvab*, established in Shumen in 1922, which taught the Arabic and Turkish languages as well as Islamic

[106]Girard, *Les minorités*, p. 43.
[107]Zwemer, "Islam," p. 340.
[108]*The Near East* 17, no. 459 (19 February 1920): 243.
[109]Kostanick, "Turkish Resettlement," p. 68. A lower estimate of 1,294 schools teaching in Turkish is given by Ivan Gantcheff in "The Bible and Islam in Bulgaria," *The Moslem World* 17 (1927): pp. 391-93. The figure given by Bachmaier of 832 schools in 1931 for minority ethnic groups would seem to be an underestimate, see Peter Bachmaier, "Assimilation oder Kulturautonomie. Das Schulwesen der Nationalen Minderheiten in Bulgarien nach dem 9 September 1944," *Oesterreichische Osthefte* 26, no. 2 (1984): 391-92.
[110]Bosquet, "Islam in the Balkans," pp. 68-69.
[111]Popović, "Les Turcs," pp. 395-96.
[112]Lory, *Le sort de l'Héritage*, p. 182. On the disturbances, see Crampton, *Bulgaria, 1878-1918*, pp. 300-303, and idem, "Public Order," pp. 43-47. The University is treated fully in M. Arnaudov, *Istoriya na Sofiiskiya Universitet sv. Kliment Ohridski prez pŭrvata mu polustoletie* (Sofia, 1939); see pp. 238-63 for the events of 1907.

theology and attracted students from Romania as well as from Bulgaria. There was also a special higher institute in Sofia for training *hodjas*.[113]

The Turkish-language press suffered no more constraint than its Bulgarian counterpart, the restrictions of the 1903, 1923, and 1934 laws, for example, being felt by both. Between 1878 and 1944 there were over a hundred Turkish newspapers or journals, with at least sixty appearing in the inter-war period. Some were published by Bulgarians, some by Bulgarian Turks, some by émigré opponents of Atatürk, and other by Christian missionaries. The publications of the Bulgarian Turks were intended for Turks rather than for Muslims; there never was in Bulgaria, as there was in Yugoslavia and Albania, an official publication of the Muslim community. There was a Turkish Communist paper between 1920 and 1923.[114] The large Turkish population in Shumen had a choice of three newspapers.[115] There was also a Turkish printing press in Shumen, which in 1926 printed some forty thousand items, including books and pamphlets in addition to newspapers; most of the former were primers, Turkish-Bulgarian conversation manuals, and religious works. A second printing house in Shumen produced Turkish-language tracts attacking freemasonry and rationalism but also turned out a Bulgarian-Turkish reader, illustrated Turkish primers as well as reading manuals, devotional works, and a synopsis of Muslim law. In Plovdiv another press specialized in Turkish novels and illustrated grammars. Also in Plovdiv was a bookshop, which, in the second half of the 1920s, was reported as stocking five different Turkish editions of the Koran as well as other books in Turkish and Arabic.[116]

The Turks and Muslims of Bulgaria were granted political as well cultural rights. There was at least one Muslim in the constituent assembly that drew up the constitution of 1879, a constitution that, in theory at least, remained in force until December 1947.[117] There were Turks in every parliament thereafter, although their numbers varied: in 1891 there were twenty-five Muslims in the Sŭbranie, in 1908 fifteen, in 1920 nine, in 1923 ten, in 1925 five, and in 1933 four.[118]

Although they enjoyed political rights, the Turks and the Muslims were a passive element, the Muslim deputies being known as "the government dowry" because they could be relied upon always to support the incumbent ministry. In 1914 the Radoslavov cabinet, in serious danger of losing a general election, rapidly and illegally enfranchised the Muslims of the newly-acquired territories as the easiest and quickest

[113]Bosquet, "Islam in the Balkans," p. 68; Girard, *Les minorités,* p. 62; Popović, "Les Turcs," pp. 395, 397; Kostanick, "Turkish Resettlement," p. 80.
[114]Popović is the best source on Turkish publications in Bulgaria; see *L'Islam,* pp. 85-88, 93, "Problèmes," p. 247, and "Les Turcs," pp. 388-89, 393, 396-97. In *L'Islam* (pp. 73, 78-79, 85-87) he lists the many journals he has identified, indicating which were dailies, which weeklies, etc. For a further discussion of the Turkish press and Turkish literary activity in Bulgaria and of the fate of these endeavors under recent regimes, see Bilâl N. Şimşir, "The Turkish Minority in Bulgaria: History and Culture" in this issue of *IJTS.*
[115]Hoppe, "Islam in Bulgaria," p. 160.
[116]Zwemer, "Islam," pp. 340, 349-50, 351.
[117]Girard, *Les minorités,* pp. 58-62; Black, *The Establishment,* p. 69.
[118]G. Shaw Lefevre, "Sofia Revisited," *Contemporary Review* 59 (January-June 1891): 551-52; Popović, *L'Islam,* pp. 78, 94; Zwemer, "Islam," p. 341.

means of picking up dependable seats.[119] When, during the radical Agrarian administration of Stamboliiski, the gypsies petitioned the Ministry of Justice for the restoration of political rights taken from them early in the century, the Turks did not join them.[120]

Political opinion in the Turkish communities seemed to be overwhelmingly conservative, the publication of a Communist newspaper notwithstanding. After the Kemalist revolution the press in Turkey attacked the traditionalist aspects of Bulgarian Islam with its *sheriyat* courts and *medresse*, as well as its continued use of the veil and the Arabic script. The Kemalist Turkish newspaper in Bulgaria had two columns in the Latin script, but this met with scant favor because if Bulgarian Turks knew a script other than Arabic it was Cyrillic rather than Latin. Some Bulgarians, attempting to exploit the Kemalist view of Islam to weaken the communal rights of the Bulgarian Muslims, introduced into the Subranie a bill to abolish the religious tribunals—the *sheriyat* courts; but the government sensed that Muslim opinion was against such a move, and the bill was quashed.[121]

The Turks of Bulgaria, between 1878 and 1944, had thus been allowed communal and civil rights that would have been the envy of the many other minority groups. After 1878 many Turks, particularly in Eastern Rumelia, had hoped that something of their former social and political ascendancy could be restored; when it was not—and by 1882 it was clear it would not be—the remaining groups, the large Turkish landowners, joined the urban intelligentsia in exile, and the Turks in Bulgaria were deprived of any leadership element. After 1885 the united principality became more and more Bulgarian in character, the Greeks now being the only minority with economic, social, and cultural power. When they in turn had been cowed or had departed, Bulgaria was free of any troublesome ethnic minority (with the possible exception of the White Russians, who settled there in the early 1920s). By then, the dangerous element in Bulgarian politics was not an ethnic minority different from the Bulgarians but a group whose national consciousness was intensely, even dangerously, Bulgarian: the Macedonians.

The minorities in Bulgaria, as elsewhere, were affected directly and indirectly by external events. In the late 1880s and early 1890s—the years after liberation and the great military victory of 1885—when the ruling cadres of the young state could easily have fallen prey to national arrogance, Bulgaria found itself isolated and in need of political friends if its new prince, Ferdinand, were to be recognized. The principality's strongest political personality, Stefan Stambolov, looked first to Constantinople, hoping there to gain concessions in Macedonia which would consolidate the régime at home and therefore encourage the great powers to recognize the prince.[122] No concessions would be granted if Bulgaria persecuted its Turkish population. When, after Stambolov had been removed and Ferdinand had secured international recognition, Bulgarian claims in Macedonia could be pursued, it became apparent that the Bulgarians'

---

[119]Crampton, *Bulgaria 1878-1918*, pp. 430-31.

[120]*The Near East* 17, no. 459 (20 May 1920).

[121]Girard, *Les minorités*, pp. 136-37, 146-48.

[122]For the Bulgarian-Turkish symbiosis, see Crampton, *Bulgaria, 1878-1918*, pp. 136-39.

real foes were not the enfeebled and generally indulgent Turks but the culturally aggressive and expansionist Serbs and Greeks. The critical point in Bulgarian-Ottoman relations was 1908, when Bulgaria, fearing the implications of Young Turk nationalism, declared full independence. That crisis was contained, not least because of Russian negotiating skills, and from it came the 1909 Convention and, a decade later, the legislation of 1919 that made the minority protection clauses of the treaty of Neuilly otiose. Finally, the Kemalist revolution meant that Turkey itself was now employing the modernizing, secularizing policies which had so offended many Bulgarian Turks in the post-liberation years; this did not however deter many Turks from leaving Bulgaria for a new life in their neighboring nation-state.

University of Kent at Canterbury, United Kingdom

Table 1. Bulgarians, Turks, and Greeks as Proportions of the Bulgarian Population, 1880-1934 (Statistics according to Mother Tongue)

Year	Total Number	Prent	Bulgarians Number	Prent	Turks Numbe	Prent	Greeks Number	Prent
1880/4	2,932,949	100.00	2,037,241	69.46	727,772	24.81	53,028	1.80
1887	3,118,375	100.00	2,326,250	74.60	607,331	19.48	58,326	1.87
1892	3,310,713	100.00	2,505,326	75.67	569,728	17.21	58,518	1.77
1900	3,744,283	100.00	2,887,860	77.13	539,656	14.41	70,887	1.89
1905	4,035,646	100.00	3,205,019	79.41	497,820	12.35	69,761	1.73
1910	4,337,513	100.00	3,523,311	81.23	504,560	11.63	50,886	1.17
1920	4,846,971	100.00	4,041,276	83.38	542,904	11.29	46,759	0.96
1926	5,478,741	100.00	4,455,355	81.32	577,552	10.54	10,564	0.19
1934	6,077,939	100.00	5,274,854	86.78	618,268	10.17	9,601	0.16

This figure is for Eastern Rumelia only.

SOURCES: The 1880/4 figures are from Franz Joseph Prinz von Battenberg, *Die Volkswirtschafliche Entwicklung Bulgariens von 1879 bis Gegenwart* (Leipzig, 1891), p.6, which relies on official publications. The 1887, 1892, and 1900 figures are from Statistichesko Biuro, *Naselenieto v Bŭlgariya spored preobroyavaniyata na 1 Yanuarii 1888, 1 Yanurarii 1893 i 31 Dekemvrii 1900* (Sofia, 1907); the date on which the data was recorded was 31 December, and when cited the year of the census varies from 1887 to 1888, etc. The 1905 figures are taken from Statistichesko Biuro, *Obsht Resultat ot Preobroyavanieto na Naselieto v Tsarstvo Bŭlgariya na 31 Dekemvrii 1905* (Sofia, 1911); the 1910 data from ibid., *Obsht Resultat ot Preobroyavanieto na Naselieto v Tsarstvo Bŭlgariya na 31 Dekemvrii 1910* (Sofia, 1911); the 1920 figures from ibid, *Obsht Resultat ot Preobroyavanieto na Naselieto v Tsarstvo Bulgariya na 31 Dekemvrii 1920* (Sofia, 1927); for 1926, see ibid., *Obsht Resultat ot Preobroyavanieto na Naselieto v Tsarstvo Bulgariya na 31 Dekemvrii 1926* (Sofia, 1931). In all these cases the figures are taken from Table III of the census. The 1934 figures were taken from Joseph Rothschild, *East Central Europe between the Two World Wars: A History of East Central Europe*, vol. 9 (Seattle and London, 1979), p. 328. Rothschild's data is taken directly from the offical census figures.

Table 2. Ethnic Composition of Bulgarian Towns, 1880/4-1910

Town	Date	Total	Bulgarians		Pomaks		Turks		Tatars		Gagauzes	Greeks		Jews		Gypsies	
Burgas	1884	5,865	2,083	35.52%	0	0.00%	1,268	21.62%	0	0.00%	0.00%	1,993	33.98%	213	3.63%	15	0.26%
	1887	5,749	2,137	37.17%	0	0.00%	1,149	19.99%	0	0.00%	0.00%	1,937	33.69%	251	4.54%	0	0.00%
	1892	8,426	3,171	37.63%	0	0.00%	1,617	19.19%	0	0.00%	0.00%	2,669	31.68%	448	5.32%	5	0.06%
	1900	11,738	4,727	40.27%	0	0.00%	1,291	11.00%	48	0.41%	0.03%	3,674	31.30%	648	5.52%	32	0.27%
	1905	12,946	6,096	47.09%	0	0.00%	1,359	10.50%	79	0.61%	0.01%	3,564	27.53%	706	5.45%	117	0.90%
	1910	14,897	9,160	61.49%	1	0.01%	1,287	8.65%	74	0.50%	0.09%	2,473	16.60%	767	5.15%	258	1.73%
Chirpan	1884	11,573	9,399	81.21%	0	0.00%	1,790	15.47%	0	0.00%	0.00%	6	0.05%	199	1.72%	169	1.46%
	1887	11,024	10,095	91.57%	0	0.00%	790	6.71%	0	0.00%	0.00%	8	0.07%	156	1.42%	11	0.10%
	1892	11,069	10,133	91.54%	0	0.00%	691	6.24%	0	0.00%	0.00%	5	0.05%	217	1.96%	14	0.13%
	1900	11,760	10,973	93.31%	0	0.00%	423	3.60%	0	0.00%	0.00%	12	0.10%	254	2.16%	87	0.74%
	1905	11,863	11,147	93.96%	0	0.00%	425	3.58%	0	0.00%	0.00%	3	0.03%	236	1.99%	37	0.31%
	1910	11,675	11,026	94.44%	0	0.00%	170	1.46%	0	0.00%	0.00%	1	0.01%	230	1.97%	243	2.08%
Kavlaklii	1884	7,064	84	1.19%	0	0.00%	14	0.20%	0	0.00%	0.00%	6,824	96.60%	2	0.03%	134	1.90%
	1887	7,282	55	0.76%	0	0.00%	11	0.15%	0	0.00%	0.00%	7,144	98.10%	0	0.00%	68	0.93%
	1892	7,456	127	1.70%	0	0.00%	17	0.23%	0	0.00%	0.00%	7,205	96.63%	0	0.00%	56	0.75%
	1900	8,163	203	2.49%	0	0.00%	8	0.10%	0	0.00%	0.00%	7,853	96.20%	1	0.01%	82	1.00%
	1905	8,416	320	3.80%	0	0.00%	0	0.00%	1	0.00%	0.01%	7,949	94.45%	0	0.00%	130	1.54%
	1910	6,330	384	5.91%	0	0.00%	0	0.00%	0	0.00%	0.00%	5,846	92.35%	0	0.00%	81	1.28%
Kiustendil	1880	9,590	6,520	67.99%	0	0.00%	1,572	16.39%	0	0.00%	0.00%	17	0.18%	959	10.00%	0	0.00%
	1887	10,689	8,612	80.57%	0	0.00%	581	5.44%	0	0.00%	0.00%	19	0.18%	940	8.79%	391	3.66%
	1892	11,383	9,205	80.87%	0	0.00%	462	4.06%	0	0.00%	0.00%	27	0.24%	1,086	9.54%	473	4.16%
	1900	12,042	9,896	82.18%	0	0.00%	225	1.87%	0	0.00%	0.00%	38	0.32%	1,226	10.18%	551	4.58%
	1905	12,334	10,259	83.81%	0	0.00%	121	0.98%	0	0.00%	0.00%	22	0.18%	1,271	10.30%	591	4.79%
	1910	13,748	11,574	84.29%	0	0.00%	104	0.76%	0	0.00%	0.00%	24	0.17%	1,250	9.09%	725	5.27%
Haskovo	1884	13,797	8,558	62.03%	0	0.00%	3,951	28.64%	0	0.00%	0.00%	434	3.15%	393	2.85%	379	2.75%
	1887	14,191	9,572	67.45%	0	0.00%	3,799	26.77%	0	0.00%	0.00%	196	1.38%	424	2.99%	9	0.06%
	1892	14,392	10,259	66.51%	0	0.00%	3,166	22.00%	0	0.00%	0.00%	86	0.67%	446	3.10%	305	2.12%
	1900	14,966	11,574	75.66%	1	0.01%	2,445	16.34%	1	0.00%	0.01%	148	0.99%	446	2.98%	471	3.15%

Town	Date	Total	Bulgarians		Pomaks		Turks		Tatars		Gagauzes		Greeks		Jews		Gypsies	
	1905	15,105	11,761	77.86%	5	0.03%	1,760	11.65%	0	0.00%	1	0.01%	137	0.91%	562	3.72%	748	4.95%
	1910	15,067	12,076	80.15%	0.	0.00%	1,295	8.59%	0	0.00%	1	0.01%	82	0.54%	606	4.02%	905	6.01%
Pleven	1880	11,774	9,319	81.22%	0	0.00%	1,589	13.85%	0	0.00%	0	0.00%	8	0.07%	203	1.77%	0	0.00%
	1887	14,307	11,638	81.34%	0	0.00%	1,908	13.34%	0	0.00%	0	0.00%	16	0.11%	340	2.38%	249	1.74%
	1892	15,546	12,915	83.06%	0	0.00%	1,823	11.73%	0	0.00%	0	0.00%	8	0.05%	383	2.46%	276	1.78%
	1900	18,761	15,677	83.56%	19	0.01%	2,030	10.82%	0	0.00%	0	0.00%	12	0.06%	451	2.40%	366	1.95%
	1905	21,145	18,131	85.75%	3	0.01%	1,924	9.10%	0	0.00%	0	0.00%	25	0.12%	455	2.15%	369	1.75%
	1910	23,049	19,760	85.73%	1	0.00%	1,901	8.25%	0	0.00%	0	0.00%	16	0.07%	477	2.07%	563	2.44%
Plovdiv	1884	33,442	16.75	50.09%	0	0.00%	7,144	21.36%	0	0.00%	0	0.00%	5,497	16.44%	2,168	6.48%	112	0.33%
	1887	33,032	19,542	59.16%	0	0.00%	5,615	17.00%	0	0.00%	0	0.00%	3,930	11.90%	2,202	6.67%	348	1.05%
	1892	36,033	20,834	57.82%	0	0.00%	6,381	17.71%	0	0.00%	0	0.00%	3,906	10.84%	2,696	7.48%	237	0.66%
	1900	43,033	26,070	60.58%	77	0.00%	4,706	10.94%	30	0.00%	0	0.00%	3,908	9.08%	3,602	8.37%	1,934	4.49%
	1905	45,707	28,276	61.86%	60	0.00%	4,852	10.62%	4	0.01%	0	0.00%	3,497	7.65%	4,325	9.46%	1,701	3.72%
	1910	48	32,726	68.21%	44	0.09%	2,946	6.14%	12	0.03%	0	0.00%	1,571	3.27%	4,436	9.25%	3,534	7.34%
Razgrad	1880	11,625	4,898	42.13%	0	0.00%	6,371	54.80%	0	0.00%	0	0.00%	7	0.06%	224	1.93%	0	0.00%
	1887	11,840	5,324	44.97%	0	0.00%	6,034	50.96%	0	0.00%	0	0.00%	34	0.29%	279	2.36%	75	0.63%
	1892	13,295	7,070	53.18%	0	0.00%	5,793	43.57%	0	0.00%	0	0.00%	25	0.19%	251	1.89%	73	0.59%
	1900	13,829	7,140	51.63%	1	0.01%	5,918	42.79%	32	0.23%	0	0.00%	23	0.17%	336	2.43%	251	1.82%
	1905	13,799	7,655	55.48%	1	0.01%	5,612	40.67%	35	0.25%	2	0.01%	22	0.02%	230	1.67%	148	1.079
	1910	13,975	8,188	58.59%	0	0.00%	4,974	35.59%	40	0.29%	0	0.00%	5	0.04%	178	1.27%	515	3.69%
Rusé	1880	26,163	11,349	43.38%	0	0.00%	10,252	39.19%	0	0.00%	0	0.00%	291	1.11%	1,943	7.43%	0	0.00%
	1887	27,194	14,229	52.32%	0	0.00%	8,177	30.07%	0	0.00%	0	0.00%	338	1.24%	1,975	7.26%	37	0.14%
	1892	28,121	15,730	55.94%	0	0.00%	7,484	26.61%	0	0.00%	0	0.00%	367	1.31%	2,196	7.81%	16	0.06%
	1900	32,712	18,921	57.84%	9	0.03%	6,545	20.01%	15	0.05%	1	0.00%	406	1.24%	3,101	9.48%	35	0.11%
	1905	33,632	20,317	60.41%	0	0.00%	5,913	17.58%	28	0.08%	2	0.01%	292	0.87%	3,450	10.26%	225	0.67%
	1910	36,255	22,733	62.70%	8	0.02%	5,790	15.97%	20	0.06%	5	0.01%	197	0.54%	3,851	10.62%	268	0.74%
Samokov	1880	9,970	7,996	80.20%	0	0.00%	608	6.10%	0	0.00%	0	0.00%	6	0.06%	833	8.36%	0	0.00%
	1887	9,658	7,935	82.16%	0	0.00%	187	1.94%	0	0.00%	0	0.00%	10	0.10%	962	9.96%	404	4.18%
	1892	9,568	7,878	82.34%	0	0.00%	151	1.58	0	0.00%	0	0.00%	10	0.10%	1,020	10.66%	392	4.10%
	1900	9,642	7,925	82.19%	0	0.00%	117	1.21%	0	0.00%	0	0.00%	17	0.18%	1,078	10.18%	357	3.70%

Town	Date	Total	Bulgarians		Pomaks		Turks		Tatars		Gagauzes		Greeks		Jews		Gypsies	
Town	1905	10,205	8,795	86.18%	0	0.00%	79	0.77%	0	0.00%	0	0.00%	3	0.03%	876	8.58%	349	3.42%
	1910	10,440	9,068	86.86%	0	0.00%	73	0.70%	0	0.00%	0	0.00%	2	0.02%	787	7.54%	409	3.92%
Shumen	1880	23,093	10,943	47.39%	0	0.00%	9,844	42.63%	0	0.00%	0	0.00%	45	0.10%	738	3.20%	0	0.00%
	1887	23,161	12,287	53.05%	0	0.00%	8,528	36.82%	0	0.00%	0	0.00%	45	0.19%	1,153	4.98%	60	0.26%
	1892	22,517	12,470	55.38%	0	0.00%	7,324	32.52%	0	0.00%	0	0.00%	71	0.32%	1,117	4.96%	223	0.99%
	1900	23,102	13,622	58.96%	0	0.00%	6,384	27.63%	420	1.82%	3	0.01%	114	0.49%	1,088	4.71%	386	1.67%
	1905	22,275	13,686	61.44%	2	0.01%	5,757	25.85%	226	1.01%	6	0.03%	118	0.53%	1,184	5.32%	391	1.76%
	1910	22,225	14,123	63.55%	4	0.02%	5,480	24.66%	224	1.01%	2	0.01%	65	0.29%	1,063	4.78%	445	2.00%
Silistra	1880	10,642	3,341	31.39%	0	0.00%	5,303	49.83%	0	0.00%	0	0.00%	264	2.48%	314	2.95%	0	0.00%
	1887	11,414	4,090	35.83%	0	0.00%	5,308	46.50%	0	0.00%	0	0.00%	214	1.87%	360	3.15%	37	0.32%
	1892	11,710	4,612	39.39%	0	0.00%	5,072	43.31%	0	0.00%	0	0.00%	184	1.57%	395	3.37%	25	0.21%
	1900	12,130	5,709	47.07%	0	0.00%	4,278	35.27%	334	2.75%	1	0.01%	141	1.16%	473	3.90%	189	1.56%
	1905	12,055	6,142	50.95%	1	0.01%	4,126	34.23%	270	2.24%	0	0.00%	88	0.73%	397	3.29%	149	1.24%
	1910	11,646	6,312	54.20%	2	0.02%	3,820	32.80%	169	1.45%	0	0.00%	52	0.45%	320	2.75%	225	1.93%
Sliven	1884	20,248	15,184	74.99%	0	0.00%	2,877	14.21%	0	0.00%	0	0.00%	68	0.34%	401	1.98%	1,399	6.91%
	1887	20,893	16,408	78.52%	0	0.00%	2,321	11.11%	0	0.00%	0	0.00%	90	0.43%	403	1.93%	1,367	6.54%
	1892	23,210	18,188	78.36%	0	0.00%	2,661	11.46%	0	0.00%	0	0.00%	119	0.51%	626	2.70%	1,193	5.14%
	1900	24,548	19,237	78.36%	0	0.00%	2,216	9.03%	0	0.00%	1	0.01%	170	0.69%	584	2.38%	1,884	7.67%
	1905	25,011	20,147	80.55%	0	0.00%	1,768	7.07%	0	0.00%	1	0.00%	148	0.59%	561	2.24%	1,998	7.99%
	1910	25,142	20,107	79.97%	1	0.00%	1,367	5.44%	0	0.00%	2	0.01%	71	0.28%	606	2.41%	2,618	10.41%
Sofia	1880	20,501	13,195	64.36%	0	0.00%	535	2.61%	0	0.00%	0	0.00%	246	1.20%	4,146	20.22%	0	0.00%
	1887	30,482	20,257	66.46%	0	0.00%	335	1.10%	0	0.00%	0	0.00%	326	1.07%	5,102	16.74%	1,231	4.04%
	1892	46,593	33,586	72.08%	0	0.00%	514	1.10%	0	0.00%	0	0.00%	492	1.06%	6,409	13.76%	1,242	2.67%
	1900	67,789	51,341	75.74%	0	0.00%	475	0.70%	1	0.00%	0	0.00%	709	1.05%	8,725	12.87%	1,642	2.42%
	1905	82,621	63,954	77.41%	1	0.00%	208	0.25%	1	0.00%	2	0.00%	599	0.72%	10,713	12.97%	1,875	2.27%
	1910	102,812	81,051	78.82%	5	0.00%	193	0.19%	6	0.01%	0	0.00%	523	0.51%	12,880	12.53%	2,360	2.30%
Stanimaka	1884	11,784	2,506	21.27%	0	0.00%	490	4.16%	0	0.00%	0	0.00%	8,583	72.84%	111	0.74%	80	0.60%
	1887	12,191	4,584	37.60%	0	0.00%	488	4.00%	0	0.00%	0	0.00%	6,834	56.06%	150	1.23%	105	0.86%
	1892	13,089	6,071	46.30%	0	0.00%	685	5.23%	0	0.00%	0	0.00%	6,149	46.98%	126	0.96%	25	0.19%
	1900	14,054	5,886	41.00%	11	0.08%	436	3.10%	0	0.00%	0	0.00%	7,292	51.09%	128	0.91%	238	1.69%

Town	Date	Total	Bulgarians		Pomaks		Turks		Tatars		Gagauzes		Greeks		Jews		Gypsies	
Stara Zagor	1905	14,157	6,258	44.20%	5	0.05%	503	3.55%	0	0.00%	0	0.00%	7,139	50.43%	106	0.75%	90	0.64%
	1910	12,969	7,685	59.26%	3	0.02%	591	4.56%	0	0.00%	0	0.00%	4,440	34.24%	145	1.12%	51	0.39%
	1884	15,258	11,912	78.07%	0	0.00%	2,599	17.03%	0	0.00%	0	0.00%	44	0.29%	332	2.18%	309	2.03%
	1887	16,039	13,133	81.88%	0	0.00%	2,071	12.91%	0	0.00%	0	0.00%	91	0.57%	415	2.59%	254	1.58%
	1892	17,357	14,487	82.99%	0	0.00%	2,056	11.78%	0	0.00%	0	0.00%	36	0.21%	480	2.75%	299	1.71%
	1900	19,516	16,680	85.47%	0	0.00%	1,641	8.41%	0	0.00%	1	0.01%	74	0.38%	576	2.95%	377	1.93%
	1905	20,788	18,370	88.37%	0	0.00%	1,240	5.96%	0	0.00%	0	0.00%	70	0.34%	580	2.79%	324	1.56%
	1910	22,003	19,533	88.77%	0	0.00%	1,039	4.72%	0	0.00%	0	0.00%	41	0.19%	562	2.55%	655	2.98%
Tatar Pazardjik	1884	15,425	10,018	64.95%	0	0.00%	2,600	16.86%	0	0.00%	0	0.00%	388	2.52%	1,259	8.16%	918	5.95%
	1887	15,659	11,511	73.51%	0	0.00%	1,587	10.13%	0	0.00%	0	0.00%	240	1.53%	1,277	8.16%	803	1.54%
	1892	16,343	11,331	69.33%	0	0.00%	2,071	12.67%	0	0.00%	0	0.00%	253	1.55%	1,394	8.53%	1,022	6.25%
	1900	17,175	12,262	71.39%	30	0.17%	1,981	11.53%	0	0.00%	0	0.00%	232	1.35%	1,404	8.17%	939	5.47%
	1905	17,554	13,150	74.91%	22	0.13%	1,206	6.87%	1	0.01%	0	0.00%	198	1.13%	1,458	8.31%	1,228	7.00%
	1910	18,098	14,145	78.16%	15	0.08%	708	3.91%	0	0.00%	1	0.01%	153	0.85%	1,375	7.60%	1,436	7.94%
Türnovo	1880	11,247	9,738	86.58%	0	0.00%	1,362	12.11%	0	0.00%	0	0.00%	16	0.14%	19	0.17%	0	0.00%
	1887	11,314	10,482	92.65%	0	0.00%	688	6.08%	0	0.00%	0	0.00%	22	0.19%	13	0.11%	11	0.10%
	1892	12,559	11,551	91.97%	0	0.00%	760	6.05%	0	0.00%	0	0.00%	25	0.20%	28	0.22%	4	0.03%
	1900	12,665	11,628	91.81%	0	0.00%	748	5.91%	0	0.00%	0	0.00%	29	0.23%	17	0.13%	23	0.18%
	1905	12,185	11,206	91.97%	2	0.02%	690	5.66%	0	0.00%	0	0.00%	23	0.19%	18	0.15%	82	0.67%
	1910	12,649	11,566	91.53%	0	0.00%	835	6.60%	4	0.03%	1	0.01%	10	0.08%	12	0.09%	45	0.36%
Varna	1880	24,555	6,714	27.34%	0	0.00%	8,904	36.26%	0	0.00%	0	0.00%	5,367	21.86%	541	2.20%	0	0.00%
	1887	25,256	8,449	33.45%	0	0.00%	7,569	29.97%	0	0.00%	0	0.00%	5,423	21.47%	585	2.32%	618	2.45%
	1892	28,174	10,580	37.55%	0	0.00%	8,314	29.51%	0	0.00%	0	0.00%	4,270	16.58%	782	2.78%	396	1.41%
	1900	34,922	15,590	44.64%	0	0.00%	4,544	13.01%	949	2.72%	1,490	4.27	5,616	16.08%	1,308	3.75%	512	1.47%
	1905	37,417	19,722	52.71%	1	0.00%	4,490	12.00%	811	2.17%	1,119	2.99	4,522	12.09%	1,474	3.94%	381	102%
	1910	41,419	24,446	59.02%	3	0.01%	4,430	10.70%	769	1.86%	1,100	2.66	3,561	8.60%	1,687	4.07%	916	2.21%
Vidin	1880	13,714	6,021	43.90%	0	0.00%	4,482	32.68%	0	0.00%	0	0.00%	38	0.28%	1,427	10.41%	0	0.00%
	1887	14,772	8,020	54.29%	0	0.00%	3,487	23.61%	0	0.00%	0	0.00%	36	0.24%	1,323	8.96%	329	2.23%
	1892	14,551	8,560	58.83%	0	0.00%	2,729	18.75%	0	0.00%	0	0.00%	44	0.30%	1,546	10.62%	445	3.06%
	1900	15,791	9,421	59.66%	14	0.09%	2,184	13.83%	6	0.04%	2	0.01%	41	0.26%	1,780	11.27%	765	4.84%

Town	Date	Total	Bulgarians		Pomaks		Turks		Tatars		Gagauzes		Greeks		Jews		Gypsies	
	1905	16,387	10,216	62.34%	0	0.00%	1,883	11.49%	4	0.02%	1	0.01%	43	0.26%	1,873	11.43%	737	4.50%
	1910	16,450	10,796	65.63%	0	0.00%	1,527	9.28%	4	0.02%	0	0.00%	32	0.19%	1,727	10.50%	900	5.47%
Vratsa	1880	11,190	9,766	87.27%	0	0.00%	1,085	9.70%	0	0.00%	0	0.00%	2	0.02%	202	1.81%	0	0.00%
	1887	11,323	10,245	90.48%	0	0.00%	736	6.59%	0	0.00%	0	0.00%	3	0.03%	196	1.73%	123	1.09%
	1892	12,279	11,385	92.72%	0	0.00%	570	4.64%	0	0.00%	0	0.00%	2	0.02%	115	0.94%	139	1.13%
	1900	13,965	13,019	93.23%	3	0.02%	578	4.14%	2	0.01%	0	0.00%	7	0.05%	123	0.88%	126	0.90%
	1905	14,916	13,978	93.71%	0	0.00%	498	3.34%	4	0.03%	0	0.00%	2	0.01%	79	0.53%	205	1.37%
	1910	15,230	14,209	93.30%	1	0.01%	523	3.43%	0	0.00%	0	0.00%	9	0.06%	75	0.49%	203	1.33%
Yambol	1884	10,771	8,290	76.97%	0	0.00%	1,507	13.99%	0	0.00%	0	0.00%	120	1.11%	745	6.92%	48	0.45%
	1887		8,825	78.51%	0	0.00%	1,252	11.14%	0	0.00%	0	0.00%	181	1.61%	783	6.97%	116	1.03%
	1892	13,588	10,528	77.48%	0	0.00%	1,558	11.47%	0	0.00%	0	0.00%	247	2.55%	1,011	7.44%	118	0.87%
	1900	14,916	11,805	80.97%	0	0.00%	1,012	6.94%	0	0.00%	1	0.01%	246	1.69%	1,183	8.11%	165	1.13%
	1905	15,230	12,944	82.23%	0	0.00%	926	5.88%	0	0.00%	2	0.01%	238	1.51%	1,335	8.48%	175	1.11%
	1910	15,956	13,168	82.53%	0	0.00%	953	5.97%	0	0.00%	2	0.01%	161	1.01%	1,248	7.82%	310	1.94%

SOURCE: Glavna Direktsiya na Statistika, "Liste des Localités, 1879-1910, aperçu comparative, historique, ethnographique" (Sofia, 1920).

NOTE: Included in the source is a category also of "Others." These were west and central Europeans such as French, British, Germans, Austrians, and Hungarians as well as other Slavs—Russians, Serbs, Poles, etc.—and local non-Slavs such as Armenians, Vlachs, and Romanians. For the most part there were not significant numbers of "others" in any of the towns. Those falling outside the eight main categories amounted to less than 2% in most of the towns for most of the years surveyed. The most notable exception is Varna, which in 1910 had "others" totalling just over 35% of the population. Varna is also the exception in that the percentage of "others" there shows an increase in each of the years from 1880 (when it was a mere 1.23%) on. There were several reasons for this. As the major seaport of Bulgaria, Varna attracted more foreign merchants and traders than any other center. It also had the largest concentration of Gagauzes, many of whom ended up listed as "others" because both the Greeks and the Bulgarians wanted to claim them and the Greeks, in the early years of the principality, at least, refused to provide the authorities with complete statistics (see Jireček, Pătuvane, p. 887). In later years the continued increase in the number of "others" was attributable to the developing foreign trade and to the influx of refugees: Armenians (who in 1881 already amounted to 10% of the foreign population of the city) in the 1890s, Greeks in 1906, and Russians and Romanians after the upheavals of 1905 and 1907, respectively (among the Russians were many sailors from the Potëmkin). In all other localities the percentages of "others" decreased steadily from 1880 on or showed an up-and-down variation. Besides Varna, there were only five towns that had more than 10% (but less than 15) of "others" in any year surveyed. These were Burgas (11.20% in 1900, 10.12% in 1905); Rusé (11.25% in 1900, 10.12% in 1905); Silistra (13.34% in 1880, 12.31% in 1887, 12.14% in 1892); Sofia (11.60% in 1880, 10.42% in 1887) and Vidin (12.73% in 1880, 10.68% in 1887). Of these, Vidin had a sizeable Serbian population, while Silistra and Rusé were home to many Romanians, largely for reasons of geographic propinquity. Sofia was growing rapidly in the 1880s and attracted many foreign subjects as temporary residents: engineers from Germany, stone masons from Vienna, and whores from Macedonia, for example. Burgas and Rusé had rather large foreign mercantile communities, as they, like Varna, were centers for external trade. Burgas also had an established Russian community.

Table 3. Population Change in Bulgarian Towns, 1880/4-1910.

TOWN	DATES	TOTAL	BULGARIANS		TURKS		GREEKS		JEWS	
			Percent change	Percentile change	Percent change	Percentile change	Percent change	Percentile change	Percent change	Percentile change
Burgas	1884-1900	+100.14	+126.93	+13.37	1.81	-49.12	84.35	-7.89		
	1884-1910	+154.00	+339.75	+73.11	1.5	-60.04	24.08	-51.15		
Chirpan	1884-1900	+1.62	+16.75	+14.90	-76.37	-76.73				
	1884-1910	+0.88	+17.31	+16.45	-90.5	-90.56				
Haskovo	1884-1900	+8.47	+32.31	+21.97	-38.12					
	1884-1910	+9.20	+41.11	+29.21	-67.22					
Kavlaklii	1884-1900	+15.56	+141.67	+109.24	-42.86	+15.08	-0.41			
	1884-1910	-+10.39	+354.24	+396.64	All Turk	-14.33	-4.40			
					departed					
Kiustendil	1880-1900	+25.57	+51.78	+20.87	-85.66	-88.59			+27.84	+1.80
	1880-1910	+43.36	+77.52	+23.83	-93.38	-95.36			+30.34	-0.1
Pleven	1880-1900	+63.51	68.23	+2.88	+27.75	-21.88				
	1880-1910	+100.88	112.04	+5.55	+19.63	-40.43				
Plovdiv	1884-1900	+28.68	+55.62	+20.94	-34.13	-48.78	-28.91	-44.77	+66.14	+29.17
	1884-1910	43.48	+95.36	+36.17	-58.76	-71.25	-71.42	-80.11	+104.61	+42.75
Razgrad	1880-1900	+18.96	+45.77	+22.55	-7.11	-21.91				
	1880-1910	+20.22	+67.17	+39.07	-21.93	-35.05				
Rusé	1880-1900	+25.03	+66.72	+33.33	-36.96	-48.94			+59.60	+27.59
	1880-1910	+38.57	+100.31	+44.54	-43.52	-59.25			+98.20	+42.93
Samokov	1884-1900	-3.29	-+0.89	+2.48	-80.76				+29.41	+33.73
	1884-1910	+4.71	+13.41	+8.30	-87.99				-5.52	-9.81
Shumen	1880-1900	+0.04	+24.48	+24.41	-35.15	-35.19	-35.19			
	1880-1910	-3.76	+29.06	+34.10	-44.33	-42.15	-42.15			
Silistra	1880-1900	+13.98	+70.88	+49.95	-19.33	-19.33	-29.22			
	1880-1910	+9.43	+88.83	+72.67	-27.97	-27.97	-34.18			
Sliven	1884-1900	+21.24	+26.69	+4.49	-22.98	-36.45				
	1884-1910	+24.17	+34.42	+6.64	-52.49	-61.71				
Sofia	1880-1900	+230.66	+289.09	+17.68	-11.21	-73.18			+110.44	-36.35
	1880-1910	+401.40	+514.26	+22.48	-63.93	-92.72			+210.66	38.03
Stanimaka	1884-1900	+19.26	+134.00	+92.76	-11.02	-25.48	-14.47	-29.61	+15.32	-3.19
	1884-1910	+10.06	+206.66	+178.61	20.61	+9.62	-48.09	-52.82	+30.63	19.15
Stara Zagora	1884-1900	+27.91	+40.03	+9.48	-36.86	-50.62				
	1884-1910	+44.21	+63.98	+13.71	-60.02	-72.28				
Tatar Pazardjik	1884-1900	+11.35	+22.40	+9.92	-23.81	-31.61			+11.52	+0.12
	1884-1910	+17.33	+41.20	+20.34	-72.77	-76.81			+9.21	-6.86
Turnuvo	1880-1900	+12.61	+19.41	+6.04	-45.08	-51.2				
	1880-1910	+12.47	+18.88	+5.72	-38.69	-45.5				
Varna	1880-1900	+42.22	+132.20	+63.28	-48.97	-64.12	4.64	-26.44		
	1880-1910	+68.68	+264.10	+21.59	-50.25	-70.49	-33.65	-60.66		
Vidin	1880-1900	+15.15	+56.46	+35.90	-51.27	-57.68			+24.74	+8.26
	1880-1910	+19.95	+79.31	+49.50	-65.93	-71.7			+21.02	+0.86
Vratsa	1880-1900	+24.80	+33.31	+6.83	-46.73	-57.32				
	1880-1910	+36.10	+45.59	+6.91	-51.8	-64.64				
Yambol	1884-1900	+35.36	+42.40	+5.20	-32.85	-50.39			+58.79	+17.17
	1884-1910	48.14	58.84	+7.22	-36.76	-57.33			+67.52	+13.01

SOURCE: Glavna Direktsiya nak Statistika, "Liste des Localités, 1879-1910, aperçu comparative, historique, ethnographique" (Sofia, 1920).

TABLE   4. Population Change in the Ten Most Rapidly Expanding Bulgarian Towns, 1900/4-1910.

TOWN	TOTAL	BULGARIANS		TURKS	
	Percent change	Percent change	Percentile change	Percent change	Percentile change
Sofia	+401.50	+514.26	+22.48	-63.93	-92.72
Burgas	+154.00	+338.75	+73.11	+1.50	-60.04
Pleven	+100.88	+112.04	+5.55	19.63	-40.43
Varna	+68.68	+264.10	+21.59	-50.25	-70.49
Yambol	+48.14	+58.84	+7.22	-36.76	-57.33
Stara Zagora	+44.21	+63.98	+13.71	-60.02	-72.28
Plovdiv	+43.48	+95.36	36.17	-58.76	-71.25
Kiustendil	+43.46	+77.52	+23.83	-93.38	-95.36
Rusé	+38.57	+100.31	+44.54	-43.52	-59.25
Vratsa	+36.10	+45.49	6.91	-51.80	-64.64

SOURCE: Glavna Direktsiya na Statistika, *Liste des Localités, 1879-1910, aperçu comparative, historique, éthnographique* Sofia, 1920).

Machiel Kiel

URBAN DEVELOPMENT IN BULGARIA IN THE TURKISH PERIOD: THE PLACE OF TURKISH ARCHITECTURE IN THE PROCESS*

For half a millennium the lands now constituting the Socialist Republic of Bulgaria were an integral part of the empire of the Ottoman Turks and had a full share in the political, economic, and cultural life of those days. A number of cities in today's Bulgaria were in the past among the largest and most important in the Turkish Empire, having an exclusively or predominantly Muslim Turkish population or actually founded by the Turks themselves. Some of these cities played a role of first importance as centers of Ottoman education, literature, and architecture. In no way were the Bulgarian lands a provincial backwater, as some of the surviving Turkish monuments show in an eloquent way. In this article we confine ourselves to the discussion of some salient aspects of urban development in the long Turkish centuries of Bulgaria and try to show how Ottoman Turkish architecture fit into this development. We shall focus on the origin and demographic composition of the population of the towns, in order to find out how Turkish the Ottoman Bulgarian towns were and for whom the numerous buildings of that period were erected. The scope and quality of the monuments of architecture erected by the Turks in Bulgaria will be shown by photographs and drawings accompanied by descriptive notes. Being intended as a general overview, this article does not deal with the theoretical aspects of the use of the principal sources. The famous Ottoman census and taxation records are not analyzed, as the figures given here are intended as general indications of the size and proportion of the population, not as exact counts (although the Ottoman bureaucrats of the fifteenth and sixteenth centuries certainly strove to be as correct as possible).[1]

* The bulk of the documentation used in this article was collected during a number of journeys through the Balkans and in the course of archival work in Istanbul, Ankara, and Sofia made possible by scholarships of the Netherlands Organization for Scientific Research, Z.W.O, The Hague, and the Prince Bernhard Fund, Amsterdam. The author wishes to thank the Turkish and the Bulgarian authorities for allowing him access to their archives.

[1] On the nature, the possibilities, and the shortcomings of the Ottoman sources on population and taxation, see, e.g., Ö.L. Barkan, "Türkiye'de Imperatorluk Devirlerinin büyük nüfus ve arazi tahrirleri..." in *Istanbul Üniversitesi İktisat Mecmuası* 2 no. 1 (1940): 20-59, and 2 no. 2 (1941): 214-47; idem, "Tarih Demografi Araştırmaları ve Osmanlı Tarihi," *Türkiyat Mecmuası* 10 (1953): 1-26; idem, "Essai sur les données statistiques des registres de recencement dans l'Empire Ottoman aux XVIe et XVIe siècle," *Journal of the Economic and Social History of the Orient* 2 (1957) 103-129: 9-36; Halil İnalcık, "Ottoman Methods of Conquest," *Studia Islamica* 1 (1954) 103-129: idem, *Suret-i Defter-i Sancak-i Arvanid* (Ankara, 1954), introduction; idem, the article "Daftar-i Khakânî" in *Encyclopaedia of Islam*, New Edition hereafter E.I. 2); Heath Lowry, "The Ottoman Tahrir Defters as a Source for Urban Demographic History: The Case of Trabzon (ca. 1486-1583)," (Ph. D. diss.,

It is not commonly known that many buildings erected by the Ottoman Turks in Bulgaria belong among the oldest examples of Ottoman architecture extant: the Eski Cami of Yambol and of Hasköy (Haskovo), the Imaret Camii of Ihtiman, and the *türbe* (mausoleum) of Lala Şahin in Kazanlık are all three-quarters of a century older than the oldest Turkish building in Istanbul. In the Bulgarian lands we also find examples of Ottoman architecture that rank among the largest and most monumental of buildings in the entire Balkans: the Cumaya Camii of Filibe (Plovdiv), the Büyük Cami of Sofia, the *bedesten* (covered market) of Yambol, the bridge of Cisr-i Mustafa Paşa (Svilengrad), the caravan station of Harmanlı, and the dervish lodge of Akyazılı Baba near Varna, for example. Ottoman Turkish architecture in Bulgaria participated in all the stages of development of this art, from the Early Ottoman style to Classical Ottoman to the weak elegance of the Lale Devri, and ending with the structures of the age of reform (Tanzimat). The products of impulses from Asia Minor, these various architectural styles soon took root deeply and contributed to the cultural milieu through their creative development of the transplanted forms and types. Buildings in the prevailing style were commissioned by Turkish governors and administrators, designed by Turkish architects, and molded also by the aesthetic feeling and taste of the Turkish population, from among whom a large proportion of the stonemasons and master builders were recruited (as is evident from the paylists of numerous fifteenth- and sixteenth-century building projects). When the actual constructors were local Bulgarians, the result can clearly be seen to be different from that achieved in accordance with Turkish taste and by Turkish hands. Only in the eighteenth, and particularly in the nineteenth, century did building activity in Ottoman Bulgaria come to be concentrated largely in Bulgarian hands. Therefore, it is of real importance to establish what the population was like in the centuries when Ottoman art was at its prime.

Turkish Islamic architecture, in Bulgarian lands and elsewhere, is basically urban, as is Islamic civilization as a whole (even the word "civilization"— *medeniyet*—derives from the word for "town"—*medina*). In all the villages of the Ottoman realm, no matter where located, the mosques were mostly of simple construction, and few have survived to the present. Those that were of a more monumental, durable quality were often built for the purpose of securing the promotion of the village in question to a town, for which the possession of a mosque (and a market) was the principal prerequisite. (See Plate 1, following this article) As is known, towns with independent municipalities, as in Western Europe, did not exist in the Ottoman context.

Ottoman architecture encompassed mosques, schools, market halls (*bedestens*) or stone-vaulted market streets (*arastas*), mausolea (*türbes*), dervish lodges (*tekkes*),

University of Michigan, 1977); Bruce MacGowan, "Food Production and Taxation on the Middle Danube (1568/69)," *Archivum Ottomanicum* 1 (1969): 139-96; Irène Beldiceanu and N. Beldiceanu, "Règlement ottoman concernant le récencement (première moitié du XVIe siècle)," *Südost-Forschungen* 37 (1978); 1-40, with translation and facsimile of original Ottoman census instructions, including a list of names of census-takers. Cf. also the critical analysis of Heath Lowry, "The Ottoman Tahrir Defterleri as a Source for Social and Economic History: Pitfalls and Limitations," in *Proceedings of the IVth International Congress on Turkish Social and Economic History, Munich, August 1986* (forthcoming), and the survey of Suraiya Farouqhi, "Agriculture and Rural Life in the Ottoman empire ca. 1500-1878 (A Report on the Scholarly Literature Published between 1970-1985)," in the same *Proceedings*.

kitchens for the poor and for travelers (*imarets*), bridges, caravanserais, urban merchant depots (*khans*), baths (*hamams*), and various kinds of waterworks, fountains, basins, and, of course, water supply systems, including tunnels and aqueducts. (There are various references to the latter kinds of works in Bulgaria, but examples have apparently not been preserved.) Lastly, the Ottomans constructed a number of fortresses along almost all the Danube frontier, beginning with simple repairs made to existing castles and ending with sophisticated nineteenth-century construction.[2]

In this paper we shall concentrate on towns and their development. However, we do not mean to say that Ottoman architecture did not reach the villages: bridges over minor rivers could be situated in or near remote villages, as could the lodges of some dervish orders. The latter sometimes preferred to be outside the towns, either because of their heterodox inclination or simply because their principal adherents were tribal or rural groups—as, for example, the numerous Alevi and proto-Bektashi, or Bedreddiniye, groups of the Deli Orman in the northeast of the country or similar tribal groups in Bulgarian Thrace. In both these areas, far away from any urban center, monumental dervish lodges, or their ruins, survive.[3] Ö. L. Barkan has published vast documentation on this kind of dervish lodge in the open countryside, which played a large role in the internal colonization of the land—a function clearly appreciated by the central authorities.[4] Because of the practical difficulties of traveling in the villages, hitherto unknown good examples of Ottoman architecture far away from the towns might possibly still be found.

The Ottoman Urbanization Policy: Varying Views

If there was an "Ottoman policy of urbanization," what it was like is debatable. We have at least the "Barkan Thesis" and the "Todorov Thesis";[5] but both seem to be,

---

[2]On Ottoman architecture in general, see, e.g., Oktay Aslanapa, *Turkish Art and Architecture* (London, 1971); Ekrem Hakki Ayverdı, *Osmanlı Mimarisinin İlk Devri* (Istanbul, 1966); idem, *Çelebi ve II. Sultan Murad Devri* (Istanbul, 1972); idem. *Fatih Devri*, vols. 3 and 4 (Istanbul, 1973 and 1974); Mustafa Cezar, *Typical Commercial Buildings of the Ottoman Classical Period, and the Ottoman Construction System* (Istanbul, 1983); Ernst Eğli, *Sinan, Baumeister osmanischer Glanzzeit* (Zurich and Stuttgart, 1976); Godfrey Goodwin, *A History of Ottoman Architecture* (London, 1971); Aptullah Kuran, *The Mosque in Early Ottoman Architecture* (Chicago and London, 1968); Behçet Ünsal et al., eds., *Turkish Architecture, Seljuk and Ottoman Periods* (London, 1959); and Ulya Vogt-Göknil, *Living Architecture: Ottoman* (Freiburg, 1965).

[3]On the largest of all these, the Akyazılı Baba, see Semavi Eyice, "Varna ile Balçık arasında Akyazılı Sultan Tekkesi," *Belleten* 21, no. 124 (1967): 551-600; for a description of a second example of type, see M. Kiel, "A Monument of Early Ottoman Architecture in Bulgaria: The Bektaşi Tekke of Kıdemli Baba Sultan at Kalugerovo—Nova Zagora," *Belleten* 25 no. 137 (1971): 45-60. Other important *tekkes* of this kind—Demir Baba and Otman Baba—have not been adequately publicized Some *tekkes* of minor importance but still with fine *türbes* in the classical Ottoman style are Ali Baba and, especially, Kadır Baba near Topolovgrad; these have remained practically unknown but testify eloquently to the Turkish spiritual life once concentrated there.

[4]"Istilâ Devirlerinin Kolonizatör Türk Dervişleri" *Vakıflar Dergisi* 2 (1942): 278-286.

[5]Nikolaj Torodov, "Sur quelques aspects du passage de féodalisme au capitalisme dans les territoires Balkaniques de l'Empire Ottoman," *Revue des Etudes Sud-Est Européennes,* 1, nos. 1 and 2 (1963): 103-136; O. L. Barkan, "Quelques observations sur l'organisation Economiques et sociale des Villes Ottomanes des XVIᵉ et XVIIᵉ siècles," in *Recueil de la Société Jean Bodin* (Brussels, 1956), pp. 289-

like most models of development, too rigid. Reality was far more diversified. Besides these two views, we have the Bulgarian theory of the "bourgeois period," the pre-war view that the Ottoman conquest had turned Bulgaria into a desert and that destroyed towns were rebuilt and repopulated exclusively by Turkish colonists. It is very interesting to see, in this particular case, the champion of Turkish historiography taking a "Bulgarian" point of view and the leading Bulgarian historian opting for a "Turkish" view. The view that the Ottoman conquest meant a catastrophic end for the old Bulgarian culture is particularly dear to Bulgarian historiography; and, on the popular level, in publications intended for foreign readers or in histories commissioned by the present leadership, it can be found expressed in terms of varying degrees of horror and intensity.[6] Speaking about the development of Balkan towns, Barkan states:

> It involves mostly towns that were, so to speak, recreated along the strategic roads and commercial arteries of the Empire where they, because of that situation, developed rapidly. They were settled and colonized by the state in a systematic manner... Contrary to [the case of] a very large number of western cities, it does not deal with spontaneous formation but with products of the will of the emperors, who had at their disposal all the resources of the Empire, constructing all installations a city would need by the money they had accumulated in their treasury.[7]

Opposed both to this view and to the pre-war Bulgarian view, Todorov sees a much greater continuity in the life of the Bulgarian towns: they were not totally new elements, the products of Ottoman colonization and deportation, but were, rather, the continuation of urban settlements with much older foundations.[8]

Most recently, some Bulgarian scholars have expressed the view, eagerly accepted by the politicians, that the Muslim population of the towns was for the most part, if not entirely, composed of converted native Bulgarians. This view is based on Ottoman sources material and has been vigorously defended by prominent Bulgarian historians at occasions such as the Second International Congress of Bulgarian Studies in Sofia in May 1986. The validity of this view will be questioned further on. As to the work of

---

311. Cf. also H. J. Kissling, "Die türkische Stadt auf dem Balkan," *Südosteuropa Jahrbuch* vol. 8 (1968), pp. 72-83, and Adem Handžić, "Ein Aspect der Entstehungsgeschichte osmanischer Städte im Bosnien des 16. Jahrhundert," *Südost Forschungen* 37 (1978): 41-47 (this stresses the role of the government in the process).

[6]"Classical" examples of these views are to be found in N. Todorov, L. Melnishki, and L. Dinov, *Bulgaria, Historical and Geographical Outline* (Sofia, 1965) and Hristo Hristov, *Bulgaria, 1300 Years* (Sofia, 1980). These works are replete with references to "brutal oppression" and "Asian exploitation" and to the "inhumanity," "bloodthirstiness," and "religious fanaticism" of the "Ottoman hordes." The crowning touch was provided by the Bulgarian head of state himself, Todor Zhivkov, in his "Peace, Democracy, and Socialism" (this appeared in many western languages, but I used the Dutch edition [Amsterdam, 1981], p. 19). Zhivkov uses terms such as "forced levelling," "total" and "spiritual" subjection, and "factual extermination." For a different version, see my *Art and Society in Bulgaria in the Ottoman period* (Assen, 1985).

[7]"Quelques observations," pp. 290-291. See also idem, "Deportations comme Methode de Peuplement et de Colonisation dans l'Empire Ottoman," *Revue de la Faculté des Sciences Économiques de l'Université d'Istanbul* 11, no. 4 (1953):1-65 (this article is continued in succeeding issues).

[8]"Sur quelques aspects," p. 110.

the two pioneers, Barkan and Todorov—and of model-builders in general—we can say that there is much over-simplification and generalization, even as the map we offer here must, by its very nature, be also a simplified version of a much richer reality. In truth, all four views are equally valid in a restricted number of cases: There really were newly-founded towns with Turkish populations of colonists directed thither by government action; there were also towns that survived because they were added to the Ottoman dominions without fighting and consequent destruction; and there were towns that sprang up spontaneously, or grew into towns under the protection of a castle in the pre-Ottoman period. It is best to discuss the urbanization process district by district, because the historical conditions and local circumstances were rather varied. There was no uniform pattern in Bulgarian history, and the need for new urban centers was very different from province to province.

Very different from area to area also is the state of preservation of the surviving Ottoman monuments in Bulgaria and, especially, the number of surviving buildings, some provinces having many, others none at all. With a bit of unavoidable simplification, the towns of Ottoman Bulgaria may be divided into five groups according to the way they emerged. (Plate 2.)

1) Towns surviving from the Byzantino-Bulgarian period, further developed by the Ottomans and having a mixed population since the beginning of the Ottoman period: Silistra, Niğbolu (Nikopol), Vidin, Lofça (Loveč), Tărnovo, Varna, Misivri (Mesemvria), Ahyolı (Anchialos), Sizebolu (Sozopolis), and Melnik. (These may be called "Todorov-thesis" towns.)

2) Towns developing near a Bulgaro-Byzantine castle (which may or may not have been maintained by the Ottomans after the conquest) and having a mixed population, the development of which was promoted by the construction of some Turkish buildings of importance: Pravadi (Provadia), Aydos, Karınabad (Karnobat), Rusçuk (Russe), Plevne (Pleven), İvraca (Vratsa), Kutlofça (Kutlovitsa—now Mihailovgrad), Belgradcık, Samokov, Ihtiman, and Petrič (also "Todorov-thesis" towns).

3. Pre-Ottoman towns, largely recreated and repopulated by the Turks, the development of which was promoted by building activity on a great scale, directed by the state: Sofia, Filibe (Plovdiv), Eski Zağra (Stara Zagora), Yambol, Şumla (Shoumen), and Köstendil. (These may be called "Barkan-thesis" towns, having mostly a minimum of continuity.)

4. Original Turkish towns, new foundations growing around important government-sponsored buildings: Hezargrad (Razgrad), Tatar Pazarcık (Pazardžik), Cisr-i Mustafa Paşa (Svilengrad), Harmanlı, and, to some extent, also Kazanlık and Zağra Yenicesi (Nova Zagora) (also "Barkan-thesis" towns).

5) Towns developing, more or less spontaneously from villages—some, expanding slowly in a long drawn-out process, others growing quickly—with mostly modest Turkish building activity but populations that were mostly Turkish: Hacıoğlı Pazarcık (Dobrič—today Tolbuhin), Osman Pazar (Omurtag), Eski Cuma (Tărgovište), Yenice-i Çirpan (Čirpan), Dupnitsa (Stanke Dimitrov), Yeni Pazar (Novi Pazar), and Selvi (Sevlievo).

In the Ottoman period a substantial number or Bulgarian towns also developed from villages created in the fifteenth and sixteenth centuries with exclusively Bulgarian populations and with privileged status (this should be Group 6). In the course of time, but especially in the seventeenth and eighteenth centuries, these settlements developed into exclusively Bulgarian towns living from crafts, home industry, and trade. They were mostly situated on both sides of the Balkan mountains, with some on the slopes of the Sredna Gora, just south of the Balkans. The towns of Drjanovo, Elena, Etropole, Gabrovo, Kalofer, Koprivštitsa (Avret Alan in Turkish), Kotel, Panagjurište, Teteven, Trjavna, and Žeravna, to mention the most important of them, came into being in this way. For the preservation of the Bulgarian national life, for Bulgarian post-Byzantine architecture, painting, literature, and ecclesiastical life these towns, with their enterprising population, monasteries, churches, scriptoria, and schools, were of prime importance. For the subject of Ottoman architecture and urban development they need not concern us any longer, but their emergence was part and parcel of the Ottoman policy of internal colonization and urbanization, and thus they require mention here.

Why Turkish Buildings in Bulgaria?

Before surveying the towns architecturally, we should remark that there is also a specific view about the reason why the Turkish conquerors constructed the buildings they did. Indeed, immediately after the conquest, after the situation had calmed down in the last decades of the fourteenth century, the Ottomans constructed scores of new buildings in Ottoman style to serve the needs of the newly established Muslim communities. In Bulgarian historiography this activity is usually explained as being part of a deliberate policy to de-bulgarize the towns and to turkify them. This was seen as a part of the method employed to subdue the conquered Bulgarian nation. (The other part of this supposed method was the deliberate destruction of the monuments of the old Bulgarian culture: palaces, castles, churches, and magnificent monasteries that reminded the people of the former glory of the vanished state. This is certainly an interpretation that can be supported circumstantially. Indeed, in no other country of the Balkans are so few pre-Ottoman buildings still standing.[9] How dangerous such a view is for the Ottoman cultural heritage of Bulgaria—for architecture, first of all—is clear if we examine the fate of the Turkish monuments in the last few years: the supposed destruction in the remote past is used as an excuse for what is done to Turkish buildings today.) The other interpretation of the presence of Turkish buildings in the Bulgarian towns is the obvious one. Was it not mainly the result of the course of events? Of the necessity of repopulating war-torn areas with the human material then available? And if this human material was of Muslim Turkish origin, Muslim buildings were needed.

There was a great difference in the repopulation policy of the Ottomans from area to area. In the southeast of the country, close to Anatolia and Turkish Thrace, the new settlers were basically Turks; but in the previously uninhabited woods of the Sredna Gora between Filibe/Plovdiv and Sofia, in the middle of the country, large groups of Bulgarians were used to settle the new villages. When a network of villages to guard the

---

[9] For other reasons for the disappearance of most of Bulgaria's mediaeval monuments than the usual Bulgarian view provides, see my *Art and Society,* ch. 4.

Balkan passes was set up, Bulgarians were installed there; and in the fertile plain of Sofia, along the most stragetic highway of the Balkans, hardly any Turkish village was founded, because this plain had not suffered depopulation from the endless Bulgaro-Byzantine border wars of the pre-Ottoman period and was well inhabited by Bulgarian Christians, who were not evicted from the land to make place for the Turkish newcomers.

Once an urban Muslim community had come into being, the simple need arose to have places of prayer for them and baths for the religiously-prescribed bodily cleanliness. In a few limited cases they could at first make do with a confiscated church, to which a minaret, *mihrab,* and *minbar* were added. Yet, this solution could be applied only in towns taken by storm, where the Muslim law assigned all property to the victor. In places that surrendered voluntarily this could not be done, so the Muslims had to provide their own places of worship. Many Bulgarian cities had surrendered voluntarily, so many new structures were required. Moreover, the Bulgarian churches of the thirteenth and fourteenth centuries were mostly very small, accommodating a limited number of people. Thus they were not entirely satisfactory even when confiscation was regarded as justified. They were so small because of the lack of funds in those centuries full of war and destruction and because of the fact the old Bulgarian towns were very small themselves.[10] As to other types of buildings, they were unknown to local tradition. The great bath culture of antiquity had died out in the Middle Ages. The Turks had to introduce their *hamam*s from Anatolia to the Balkans and did so on a massive scale. The same was true for such building types as *khan*s, caravanserais, or *bedesten*s. The institution of the *khan* was completely unknown in the Byzantino-Slavic culture of the Balkans, as was the *bedesten.* The types of buildings the local architectural vocabulary knew were churches, monasteries, stone-built houses, and, of course, fortress walls of pre-artillery type. All other varieties of public buildings had to be transplanted to Bulgaria, and to the Balkans in general. If we see the matter this way, there can be no room for theories about a deliberate policy to de-bulgarize the towns based on the lack of Bulgarian buildings. One must also keep in mind the plain fact that the most important Ottoman buildings were built in places where there had been no Bulgarian towns before as, for example, in the original Turkish towns of Harmanlı, Tatar Pazarcik, or Cisr-i Mustafa Paşa/Svilengrad.

Finally, it must be remembered that an important stretch of the country was, in medieval times, before the Turks came, a part of the Byzantine Empire, and its population was largely, or in sizeable part, Greek or Greek-speaking.[11] This was true of

---

[10]For details and plans of numerous buildings, see my *Art and Society,* ch. 7; other plans and details are to be found in Kr. Mijatev, *Mittelalterliche Baukunst in Bulgarien* (Sofia, 1974), and Assen Tschilingirov, *Die Kunst des christlichen Mittelalters in Bulgarien* (Munich, 1979)..

[11]For example, Harmanlı, Tatar Pazarcık, and Cisr-i Mustafa Paşa / Svilengrad. The German churchman Stephan Gerlach, who was in Filibe in 1573 and 1578, noted that the city was inhabited by "Turks and Greeks," visiting all the eight churches of the city, mentioning them by name, and adding details on the habits of the Greek inhabitants; see *Stephan Gerlachs des Aelteren Tage-Buch...* (Frankfurt am Main, 1674), pp. 515-16. The oldest preserved Ottoman register on Filibe, Tahrir Defter no. 26 from 1489, mentions among the Christion inhabtiants of this city many Yorgos, Christos, Yanis, Kostas, Theodors, etc. but hardly any specifically Slavic names (an exception seems to be the Widow Dragane). A rather long list of western travelers who mentioned Greeks in Filibe might be

the second most important town of Bulgaria, Filibe/Plovdiv. (Both forms of this name are corruptions of Philipopolis, the foundation of Philip of Macedonia, father of Alexander the Great.) The other important Thracian towns, Yambol and, especially, the Black Sea towns of Varna, Mesembria, Anchialos, Achtopol, and Sozopol(is), also had been Greek since the dawn of history, during the medieval as well as the Ottoman period, although temporarily occupied by Bulgarian forces. In Bulgarian historiography, as well as in the writings about the history of art, this fact is usually forgotten. We will now proceed to the examination of the individual provinces and towns that are the subject of this study.

Developments in Bulgarian Thrace

The first major division of modern day Bulgaria is Bulgarian Thrace. Architecturally it is the most important, containing the greatest number of Ottoman monuments that are, moreover, the oldest and, from the typological point of view, the most important. The area encompasses principally the great Thracian plain from the Black Sea coast and Edirne in the east to the little town of Saruhan Beyli (Septemvri) in the west where the Balkan mountains to the north of the plain and the Rhodope mountains in the south are connected by a range of lower mountains, the Ihtimanska Sredna Gora ("The Middle Mountains of Ihtiman"). The rivers Maritsa (Meriç) and Tundza (Tunca) flow through this plain before they join each other at Edirne. Only in the southeast is there a mountainous region, the Strandža, which extends deep into Turkish Thrace and which is, and always was, very thinly populated. Before the Ottoman conquest (1360-1370) the land between Edirne and Filibe/Plovdiv had been a largely deserted no-man's-land, a wide border zone between Bulgaria and Byzance, its towns and castles changing hands repeatedly.[12] During the conquest the Ottomans had most of the castles razed and the town walls destroyed. This was the case with Zağra-i Eskihisar (or Eski Zağra today Stara Zagora), Yambol, Karınabad/Karnobat, and Aydos. For some of these towns the situation remains unclear: the Ottoman chroniclers (Oruç, Aşıkpaşazāde, Neşri) simply mention their capture, usually attributing it to Lala Şahin Paşa, the leader of the conquest and first beylerbey, but give no further comments.

---

might be compiled. "Tuercken und Griechen" in "Filipolis" are also mentioned in 1499 by Arnold van Harff, *Die Pilgerfahrt des Ritters Arnold van Harff von Colln,* ed. E. von Groote (Cologne, 1860), p. 211. Gerlach, it should be added, was a very good observer, noting immediately the presence of Bulgarians and of Bulgarian books in the churches of Vetren, the first village at the western end of the Thracian plain, which, according to him, did not belong to the Greek patriarchate of Constantinople but to the Serbian patriarchate of Peć, together with all the land west of Vetren. Bulgarian authors usually stress the Bulgarianness of the Christian inhabitants of Filibe/Plovdiv, with the tendency to know better than their sources. On the Greeks of the Black Sea area, see also Constantin Jireček, *Das Fürstenthum Bulgarian* (Prague, Vienna, and Leipzig, 1891); this work is a veritable goldmine of information, written by a scholar free of any national bias. For some older accounts of the history and the historical monuments of the city, see Stefan Šiškov, *Grad Plovdiv, svojeto minalo i nastojašča* (Plovdiv, 1926) (text also partially in French), and Otto and Gertrud Radloff-Rille, "Grad Plovdiv i njegovite sgradi," *Izvestija Bălg. Arheol. Družestva* 7 (1935).

[12]See Jireček, *Fürstenthum,* pp. 48-49, or my "Vakifnāme of Rakkas Sinan Beg in Karnobat and the Ottoman Colonization of Bulgarian Thrace," *Journal of Ottoman Studies* 1 (1980): 15-32, and the literature mentioned therein.

Yambol was allegedly taken after a fierce struggle, and it is logical that its walls were also destroyed. Yet, during the Ottoman civil war—in February 1410—that city was besieged by Prince Musa, with help of the Valachian troups of Mircea the Old of Valachia.[13] It eventually was conquered, but the simple fact that it had to be besieged before it could be taken tells us that the supposed destructions of *circa* 1370 were rather limited, if they took place at all. The same is true for Filibe/Plovdiv. The Ottoman sources say that it was conquered by Lala Şahin Paşa in 1360/61, together with Eski Zağra. Konstantin of Kostenets, the Bulgarian chronicler of the Serbian Prince Stephan Lazarević, writing shortly after the event, noted that Musa Çelebi captured Filibe/Plovdiv and had its walls torn down.[14] However, when in 1433 the Burgundian knight Bertrandon de la Broquière passed through Bulgaria he called Filibe a "very beautiful castle on mountain, which has been built in the shape of a long crescent."[15] From these notes it may perhaps be concluded that the destruction of the walls of the most important towns of Bulgarian Thrace was a gradual process rather than a total leveling caused by a particularly violent Ghazi warfare.

Besides the fact that there are aspects of the conquest about which we have only the vaguest information, we should bear in mind also that we have to do here with border towns in a heavily contested area. Filibe/Plovdiv was destroyed on a number of occasions and was always, during this period, in the position of a border town at the far edge of either Bulgaria (1205-1241 and 1344-1360/61) or of the Byzantine realm (1241-1344). Concerning the open land we have less information, but the simple fact that almost the entire toponymy is Turkish points to the existence of only a very limited local population on the ground to pass on existing place names at the time the Ottoman arrived.

FILIBE. When we can first determine the population of Filibe with any degree of certainly is 1489/90; this is with help of the detailed (*mufassal*) register T.D. 26 as preserved in the Prime Minister's Archives in Istanbul (Başbakanlik Arşivi, hereafter to be cited as BBA). This register provides some important data. The town then had 26 Muslim quarters (*mahalle*), 4 Christian *mahalles,* and one group of gypsies, Muslim and Christian. The number of households was as follows: Muslim, 796; Christian, 78; gypsy, 33.

The Muslim quarters were arranged around their mosques and *mescids* (small mosques). The largest Christian quarter, with 33 households, was called Hisar İçi ("The Castle's Inside"). In the "castle"—i.e., the old walled town—no Muslims lived. The fact that inside this oldest part of Plovdiv today a number of churches are still standing and that throughout time the Christians contined to reside there, the Muslims remaining below the castle in newly founded quarters around mosques built in the fifteenth or sixteenth century, tells us that, while Bulgaro-Byzantine Plovdiv must have suffered badly from the conquest and the Ottoman civil war, there was a considerable degree of

---

[13]For information about this little known event, see Peter Schreiner, "Die byzantinischen Kleinchroniken," pt. 2, *Historisches Kommentar* (Vienna, 1977), pp. 395-96, 72a/16, 96-92.

[14]See Maximilian van Braun, *Lebensbeschreibung des Despoten Stefan Lazarević von Konstantin dem Philosophen* (The Hague and Wiesbaden, 1956), pp. 39-41.

[15]*Voyage d'Outremer, de Bertrandon de la Broquière,* ed. C. H. Schefer (Paris, 1892), p. 200.

continuity.[16] The one note about Musa's siege of Yambol and Plovdiv and the remark of Bertrandon give grounds to conclude that it was not violent Ottoman conquest but, rather, developments later on that led to the decay of the pre-Ottoman urban structure and the decline of the populations of at least these two towns in Bulgarian Thrace. The 1489/90 register also gives us an idea of what kind of people the Muslims were. The bulk of them must have been craftsmen, as many bore epithets such as Tanner, Mason, Tailor, Weaver, Goldsmith, Perfumer, etc.; some were members of other significant groups in urban society with names like Broker, Learned, Imam, etc. Most important, only 20 household chiefs bore the patronym "Son of Abdullah," which meant that they were converts to Islam. This number is very low, only 2.5 percent. In the sixteenth century we encounter far more of them. The supposition that the Sons of Abdullah were indeed recent converts is generally accepted among Balkan historians as well as among their western and Turkish colleagues. It means that in the case of Filibe we really have to do with a population of Muslim Turkish colonists from Asia Minor.

Filibe is a good example of a Barkan-thesis town of our third category. It is one of the oldest towns of the Balkans and survived all the ups and downs of the tormented history of this part of the world. One of its ups was the Ottoman reconstruction after the 1410s. A part of this work was the construction, on the order of Sultan Murad II, of the Great Friday Mosque, one of the largest mosques of the Balkans and particularly well staffed. It was erected in the heart of the old town, in a depression between two hills. On one of the hills, divided in three separate parts, lay the medieval fortified town, which was the citadel of the much larger antique city. Deep below the mosque lay the foundations of a huge Hellenistic stadium, recently uncovered. (This buildings is still mentioned by Anna Commena in the first half twelfth century. It disappeared most probably during the thorough destruction of Byzantine Philippopolis by Tsar Kaloyan in 1206). A huge urban *khan* was later built next to the mosque, as well as a six-domed *bedesten* and more mosques. A kilometer down the hill, at the bridgehead of the Maritsa bridge of Lala Şahin Paşa, lay another focal point of the town, the monumental Zaviye-Mosque of Sihabuddin Paşa, constructed a decade or more after the completion of the Cumaya Mosque of Murad II. The Zaviye-Mosque was inspired by the famous Green Mosque of Bursa. Next to it arose a large *medrese* (religious college), a bath, and a *khan*, as well as a kitchen for the poor. This complex of buildings, of which the mosque still survives in good condition, was completed in 1444, as was stated by an inscription in Arabic that was situated above the entrance of the mosque (with the restoration of the building in the 1970s, this inscription was removed). The Ottoman town of Filibe developed between these two urban foci. The street linking the Great Mosque with the Imaret Mosque became the main shopping street, and a number of additional mosques and *khans* were built along it over the course of time. In the 1460s the Ottoman gover-

---

[16]This is an indication that the city was initially conquered not by force but by treaty; otherwise the churches would have been confiscated and the inhabitants carried off. In 1578 Gerlach (no. 12) described these churches, and those he mentioned still stand today, mostly having been reconstructed in the nineteenth century. The Ottoman historians Sa'adeddin and Müneccimbaşı (whose work is largely based on the unpublished accounts of Ruhi-i Edirnevi) both give the story of a voluntary surrender of Filibe, with the commander and his family leaving for Serbia; see *Tacü't-Tevärih*, vol. 1, ed. İsmet Parmaksızoğlu (Istanbul, 1974), pp. 121-122, and *Müneccimbaşı Tarihi*, vol. 1, Turk. trans. İsmail Erünsal (Istanbul, H. 1001), pp. 105-106.

nor of Filibe, the deposed ruler of Kastamonu, Ismail Beg, took care of the water supply for the city.[17] The Sālnāme of the Edirne Vilayet of 1291 (1874) mentions 24 great mosques in this town as well as 9 *mescids*, 13 churches, 1 synagogue, and 12 *hamams*. In 1986, of the mosques and *mescids* only 2 were still standing; of the *hamams* also only 2 remained (Čifte Banja and Orta Mezar Banja), both in a state of dire neglect. Yet the churches are all preserved and in a good state. (See Plates 3, 4, 5, and 6.)

YAMBOL. The second town of Thrace, Yambol (formerly Diampolis), comes into view as early as 1457 in a summary (*icmal*) register made in the first years of the reign of Sultan Mehmed II (1451-1481) and dated by a large number of marginal notes with detailed changes. The register is No. 89 in the Cedvet Yazmaları collection in the former Belediye Library of Istanbul. The population figures (p. 222) give Yambol/Yanbolı as having in 1457 a total of 711 Muslim households and 57 Christian households, 14 of which were Voynuk, i.e., in the Ottoman military service. Thus the town was 94 percent Muslim, 6 percent Christian. Totals for the entire *kaza* (administrative district) of Yambol are found in BBA register T.D. 370, p. 460, dated 1526-28. The register shows that in the district there were 95 villages and 1 town, with a total of 1,424 Muslim households and 75 Christian households, for a grand total of 1,499. Thus the district as a whole was 95 percent Muslim and 5 percent Christian.

Neither the register from 1457 nor that from 1526-28 gives names of the heads of households. For that we have to wait until 1595 for the Mufassal Defter Kuyudu Kadime 86, preserved in the Tapu ve Kadastro Genel Müdürlüğü in Ankara (hereafter Kuk). This register records the population of *liva* (subdivision of a province —*sancak*) of Silistra, in which Yambol was then situated. This census shows that the town shared the tendency observable in many towns of Thrace: it did not grow, but slightly declined. This is very much against the general tendency of demographic development in the Ottoman Balkans, where the entire sixteenth century is characterized by an explosive growth. Did the population of Ottoman Thrace move on to the newly conquered provinces of the western Balkans? Or were there other forces at work? This question must be left for a special study. In 1595 the population of Yambol was as follows: Muslim households, 407 (including those in the suburb of Karguna); Christian households, 110; gypsy households, 7; Jewish households, 5. This is a total of 529 households, or a population of possibly 2,800 to 3,000 inhabitants. If we express this in percentages, we must come to the remarkable conclusion that, in spite of supposed massive conversions to Islam, it was the Muslim part of the Yambol population that was losing ground: from 94 percent of the total in 1457 the Muslims had declined to only 77 percent in 1595, with 20 percent being Christian and 3 percent gypsies and Jews.

---

[17]See Yılmaz Öztüna, *Türkiye Tarihi*, vol. 2 (İstanbul, 1964), p. 210. Unfortunately Öztüna does not mention his sources. In the Imaret Camii of Filibe a number of inscriptions are preserved which were once inscribed on 40 different fountains in this city, repaired in the nineteenth century on order of the .sultan (documentation in my private collection); this can hardly be other than Ismail Beg's water supply system. For Ismail Beg's other buildings in his former residence of Kastamonu (mosque, *zaviye*, kitchen, caravanserai, *medrese*, bath, primary school, and *türbe*, all very well preserved), see Oktay Aslanapa, *Türk Sanatı*, vol. 2 (Istanbul, 1973), pp. 212-17.

Conversion of Christians certainly had taken place in Yambol. We have, therefore, to presume some influx of Christians from the neighboring districts, especially from the Balkan mountain area with its predominant Bulgarian Christian population that had little soil to plow but a healthy climate—circumstances that soon produce population pressure resulting in emigration. It is hardly likely that the towns' Bulgarians converted, because of their expanding numbers. (The name "Bulgarian" should be used with care anyway, because the chances of their being mixed with Greeks was fairly good in this area). Most significant is the fact that among the Muslims only 17 percent were Sons of Abdullah, which is rather below the average for other Bulgarian towns. What these numbers suggest is that, in fact, the opposite happened from what is supposed in the current Bulgarian theories: the Muslims did not increase at the expense of the Christians; it was, rather, the other way around, with the Christians slowly gaining in number throughout the entire sixteenth century. We will point out a number of other examples later on.

Yambol was taken by the Ottomans in about 1370, allegedly after prolonged resistance.[18] The attack was under the command of Timurtaş Beg, later beylerbey of Rumeli, succeeding Lala Şahin Paşa. The town must have suffered from the conquest by by the Ottoman Ghazis, but the fact that the fortifications were still defendable during the civil war among the sons of Yıldcrım Bayezid tells us that no categorical statement may be made. The old Diampolis was situated on a long tongue of land thrust out into the river Tunca. The site is roughly four hectares in area, which would mean a maximum population of 1,200 to 1,400 people.[19] Whether there were open suburbs is difficult to say, but the great insecurity of this specific border area between Bulgaria and Byzance makes it hardly likely that people would have lived outside the walls. When a lasting peace was established the town walls became superfluous. Very probably the stones were used to build the Ottoman town. In the oldest part of the Eski Cami of Yambol a large amount of the spoils of the conquest was used. This building is from the period of about 1375-1385 and was the focal point of the new Ottoman town, built outside the old castle on the northern bank of the river. When this mosque was enlarged over the course of the fifteenth century, no more war spoils were used.

The new Ottoman city spread out fanwise over the open land. Sultan Murad II added to its development by the construction of a bridge between the old and the new part of the town and by the building of a *hamam*. Both buildings are mentioned in the *vakıf* (pious foundation) records published by Barkan. Toward the end of the fifteenth

---

[18]Sa'adeddin, *Tacü't-Tevarih*, vol. 1, p. 135. The account of the long siege of Diampolis is given by the contemporary Byzantine historian Ioannes Cantacuzenus, who remarked that the town was besieged by the armies of Timurtaş Paşa from early spring to midsummer and that the shortage of supplies and the outbreak of epidemics eventually forced it to surrender on terms; see J. Cantacuzenos, *Historia*, ed. J. Schopen, vol. I, Bonn 1828, p. 179. This may be the reason why the town walls were not destroyed immediately after the conquest.

[19]This calculation implies a density of 300 inhabitants per hectare, which is very high; for a discussion of this question, see Anthony Bryer, "The Structure of the Late Byzantine Town," in Bryer and Lowry, eds., *Continuity and Change in Late Byzantine and Early Ottoman Society* (Birmingham and Washington, 1986), pp. 263-79. Some fourteenth-century Bulgarian towns (Shoumen, Cerven) had a concentration of houses far higher than the known average for that time, which was 150 to 200 per hectare.

century the town received more buildings of the first order: the so-called Sofular Mosque and the enormous *bedesten* of Grand Vizier Hadım Ali Paşa. The great Eski Cami and the market hall belong among the largest and most important Ottoman buildings in the Balkans. The Sofular Mosque was a rare type; but, alas, this construction disappeared long ago, and the only trace that remains of it are some notes in the Ottoman registers, a description by the traveler Evliya Çelebi, and some old photographs, preserved in private collections. The *bedesten* and the Old Mosque have recently been restored in a most exemplary manner. They are the sole historical buildings in Yambol district, and this is why such a great interest has been taken in them. Today Yambol is a Bulgarian city with just under 100,000 inhabitants, among whom there are left only a few Turks. (See Plates 7,8, 9, and 10.)

Let us next examine the general situation in the Thracian lands on the basis of the 1526-28 BBA register T.D. 370.

ESKI ZAĞRA. The register shows (p. 77) that in the district of Eski-Zağra there were 123 villages and 1 town, having a total of 2,332 Muslim households, 61 gypsy households, and 57 Christian households, for a grand total of 2,450 households. Thus the district was 95 percent Muslim, 2 percent local Christian. Even if we presume a certain degree of inexactitude in this kind of general statistic, the overall picture is striking.

The town itself was composed of 18 *mahalles* with 513 Muslim households. Not a single Christian lived there, according to the register. This suggests that we are here confronted with a really new town recreated on the foundations of the older one, the walls of which dated from the Antique period, when it was under the rule of the Emperor Trajan and was called Beroe. Idrisi, compiling his information in the twelfth century, called it a rich trading center.[20] About the size of the town in the thirteenth and fourteenth centuries when it was predominantly a frontier fortress, we have not the slightest bit of information. Constantin Jireček, working in the last decades of the nineteenth century, noted an old tradition that the original population of the town was deported after the Ottoman conquest.[21] This would indeed fit with what we know of Ghazi warfare and of Ottoman policy in important areas where their hold was still insecure. The town was soon rebuilt, but it was some decades before important buildings appeared; this was in 1408, when the so-called Eski Cami was built by the Ottoman commander Hamza Beg. It was the largest single-domed structure in Bulgaria and a great feat of early Ottoman engineering. In 1528 the town had 2 Friday mosques, 9 *imarets*—of Veled-i Gümlü, a commander under Yıldcrım Bayezid (1389-1402)—2 *zaviyes* and 5 *hamams*.

If we take a look at Eski Zağra forty years later we can see a process similar to that in Yambol. The town had increased in size from 513 to 802 households, but it had lost its exclusive Muslim character. The detailed register Kuk 65 from 1568/69 (pp. 1r -

---

[20]Idrisi's *Geography*, written in the twelfth century. I used the Bulgarian translation of B. Nedkof, Sofia, 1960.
[21]*Fürstenthum*, p. 389-90

5r) gives the following totals: Muslim households, 728 (in 18 *mahalles*); Christian households, 53; and gypsy households, 21. Thus the city was at that time 90 percent Muslim.

The Christian part of population kept gaining over the course of time. The BBA register TD 729, dating from circa 1603-1617, i.e., from the time of Ahmed I (on the historical evidence, probably 1610 or a year or two later) mentions 120 Christian households, among which were some Armenian newcomers. It is interesting to note that this general tendency for the Christians to increase in number went on through the centuries. The Sālnāme (Yearbook) of the Edirne Vilayet of 1291 (1874/75), about the last Ottoman source to give details on the population of Thrace before independent Bulgaria came into being, lists 4,327 male Muslim inhabitants as against 7,481 male non-Muslim inhabitants. Thus the wholly Muslim Turkish town of the early sixteenth century had developed into a town in which the Muslims were only 36 percent of the population. The same situation is observable in the entire district of Eski Zağra (Zağra-i Atik in the Sālnāme): there were 127 villages with 22,685 inhabitants of which only 4,891 were Muslims, or 21 percent, compared with the 95 percent Muslim population 1528. Even if we allow for some changes in the borders of the kaza, the difference is striking. This school example of the "Barkan Thesis" thus very much brings into question the modern Bulgarian view of the turkification of Bulgaria. (See Plates 11 and 12.)

KAZANLIK. The next district of which we want to show general numbers is that of Kazanlık. In 1526-28, according to register TD 370 (p. 334), the district had 20 villages and 1 town. The latter, a mini-town of 150 households, all Muslim, was the new town of (Akçe) Kazanlık itself, which contained 1 mosque, 2 *mescids,* and a *hamam.* Kazanlık lies to the northwest of Eski Zağra at the foot of the Balkan mountains and at the very end of the border zone between medieval Bulgaria and Byzance. The population structure reflected its border town status: there were more autochthons and fewer colonists. For the entire district of Kazanlık, including the town, there were listed 849 Muslim households (including 38 Tartar households) and 360 Christian households, for a total of 1,209, of which 70 percent were Muslim and 30 percent Christian. (See Plate 13.)

To the northeast of Yambol we are again at the limit of the old Byzantino-Bulgarian no-man's-land, and here again more of the original population survived.

KARNOBAT. This is the town and the kaza of Karınabad. The learned Hoca Sa'adeddion tells us that in 1368 the castle of Karınabad surrendered voluntarily to the Ottomans, following the example of the nearby stronghold of Aydos, which also surrendered without any trouble or disturbances.[22] Perhaps the name the Ottomans gave to this castle, "Castle of the Companion (or ally)," should suggest to us what happened there in 1368. (Or is this idea too romantiç?)

In 1526-28 the town had 205 households, all Muslim. Among them are mentioned the household of one *hatib,* or preacher at the Friday sermon, and of seven

---

[22]*Tacü'l-Tevarih*, vol. 1, p. 135.

imams, from which we may conclude that there were one Friday Mosque and seven *mescids* in this town. This mosque was the foundation of Rakkas Sinan Beg, a commander from the time of Bayezid II (1481-1512). His *vakifhane* (deed of trust) was dated 893 (1488).[23] Sinan Beg's foundations in Karınabad included a Friday Mosque, a bath, a school (*muallimhane*), an *imaret*, and a *mescid* in the nearby village of Köpeklü, which was a part of the foundation and from which tax revenue was used in upkeep of the buildings and the payment of the salaries of the staff. There was, as well, another bath in the town of Anchialos on the Black Sea coast (today called Pomoric). Only the *hamam* in Karnobat is preserved today; it is a single bath used alternately by men and women. Its stalactite decoration of the interior is so rich and elaborate that it exceeds all bounds of "provincial" architecture, and it is an officially recognized "Monument of Culture."

In 1528 the district of Karnobat included 1 town and 44 villages with 688 Muslim households and 108 Christian households, for a total of 796. Thus it was 86 percent Muslim. It is interesting to note that in the *vakıfname* of Rakkas Sinan not only the general toponymy but also the microtoponymy—i.e., the names of meadows, streams, conspicuous rocks, paths, etc.—is Turkish. There is no need to theorize that the Muslim inhabitants of this kaza were Turkish colonists, for the names of the villages show us clearly that they were. We find, for example, Saruhanlu, Ahlatlı, Saruhanlu-i Küçük, Geredeli, and Germiyanlü, all named after districts or towns in Anatolia. The same holds true for the other districts of Bulgarian Thrace as well. In Anchialos (Ahyolı) we find another Germiyanlü; near Aydos are a Geredeli and a Germiyanlü; near Yambol we find villages such as Germiyanlü, Karamanlu, and Saruhanlu, or Tatarlar; near Zağra-i Eskihisar are Avşarlu (tribal name), Karamanlu, or Alayuntlu, (Apolyont, west of Bursa); near Kazanlık we find Hamidlü; near Filibe, Menteşelü; and and so on. The Ottoman sources explicitly mention the settlement of Turks from Saruhan under Bayezid I (the little town of Saruhanbegli near Tatar Pazarcık gives evidence of that event) and of Tatars from the Iskilip region (Tokat-Amasya) who were deported under Mehmed II (1491) and went to Konuš near Filibe.[24]

To summarize the characteristics of Thrace—the first area to be examined—we may say that it provides examples of deportation and colonization as well as of continuity; of recreated towns and surviving old ones alongside wholly new foundations. It is interesting also to observe that the recreated old towns received the largest Ottoman buildings: foundations of the ruler himself or of his most important governors (Filibe, Eski Zağra, Yambol). Continuity seems very limited, probably because of the ruined state of the land and the towns immediately prior to the Ottoman conquest (this is a personal interpretation). It is at least notable that in the open plain the local Christian population is at its lowest, while at the edges of the area, where was shelter in the nearby mountains, a much higher percentage survived. What we do not find—and this is the most interesting facet of this area—is any extensive conversion of the surviving local population to Islam and gradual assimilation into the Turkish community.

---

[23] See my English translation of this document in the *Journal of Ottoman Studies* 1 (1980): 15-32.

[24] For example, Aşikpaşazäde, see the German translation of this chronicle by R.F. Kreutel, *Vom Hirtenzelt zur Hohen Pforte* (Graz, Vienna, and Cologne, 1959), pp. 108, 128.

In Bulgarian Thrace more Turkish colonists were settled than elsewhere in Bulgaria, including peasants and cattle breeders as well as craftsmen in the towns. There being in Thrace the largest concentration of Muslims from the very beginning, numerous Islamic buildings were needed, and in Thrace the most important and largest number of Ottoman Turkish works of architecture were constructed. There also the largest number of them remained preserved. A factor contributing greatly to this state of affairs is that never after the conquest in the period 1360-1370 and the civil war under Musa and Mehmed Çelebi (1410-1413) was the peace of the area disturbed; no foreign army entered the territory until the nineteenth century. Only after 1800 did everything change fundamentally.

Southern Bulgaria: The Rhodope Mountain Area

The second area that needs our attention briefly is the stretch of mountainous land, often of Alpine character, all along the southern border of today's Bulgaria. It was a land without towns but with a relatively large number of castles at the foot of which clusters of houses were built, forming an agglomeration of semi-urban character. The area was predominantly under Byzantine control throughout the Middle Ages.[25] In the last part of the nineteenth century Jireček noted that the population of such small "towns" was for the most part Greek, while the villagers of the mountain valleys were Bulgarian.[26] Perhaps they were Bulgarian-speaking, there being a view particularly dear to a number of Greek writers, that the inhabitants of the Rhodopes—on both sides of the early-twentieth-century frontier between Greece and Bulgaria—are the descendants of the autochtonous Thracians, who accepted the Bulgarian language during the period from the eighth to the tenth century.[27]

The Ottomans annexed the Rhodope district in a slow process, the garrisons of the scattered Byzantino-Bulgarian castles surrendering one by one to the Ottomans, usually in exchange for privileges. Jireček reports the local traditions concerning this point.[28] From the 1360s on today's Greek Thrace, the wide coastal plain of the Aegean, was part of the Ottoman state. This area had been largely depopulated in the course of the Byzantine-Bulgarian wars of the thirteenth and fourteenth centuries and, especially, by the Catalans and the two long Byzantine civil wars under the various Palaeologi. What population was left was further diminished during the Ghazi warfare of the years of the conquest, when Ottoman troops partly entered the territory as mercenaries in Byzantine service. The area was finally conquered by Ghazi Evrenos Beg, who made Komotini/Gümülcine his base and brought over settlers from his native district of Karasi in northwestern Anatolia. Many of these settlers were actually nomads who spent

---

[25]For the mediaevel history of this area, see Catharine Asdracha, *La Region des Rhodopes aux XIIIe XIVe Siècles, Etude de Geographie Historique* (Athens, 1976).

[26]*Fürstenthum*, pp. 135-40.

[27]For a balanced account of the Pomaks in Greece, giving the various views, see Emmanuel Sarides, "An Ethnic Minority between Scylla and Charibdis, The Pomaks of Greece," in Centre National de Recherches Scientifiques, Jeune Equipe No. 420004, *Lettre d'Information*, no. 5 (April 1986), 17-27.

[28]C. Jireček, *Geschichte der Bulgaren*, Prag 1876, p. 322.

the summer on the mountain pastures of the Rhodope above the Bulgarian-speaking villages in the valleys. Jiriček notes three strata of toponyms: the lowest zone, in the bottom of the valleys, having river and place names of Greek origin; the second zone, with Slavic names for the villages, higher in the valleys and on the slopes; and a third zone, having Turkish names for mountain tops, alpine pastures, etc. which points to the presence, long ago, of roaming Yürüks. It is possible that some of the Yürüks came from the north, from the Thracian plain around Filibe/Plovdiv, to spend the summer on the Yayla of the Rhodopes. The Ottoman administrative divisions listed in the census registers of the fifteenth and sixteenth centuries did not include special kazas in the Rhodopes; the northern half of these mountains were in kazas of Filibe and Tatar Pazarcık, while the southern half was included in Gümülcine and Yenice-i Karasu (today both in Greece).[29] The oldest preserved register for this part of the Balkans, the previously mentioned number 89 of the Cevdet collection in Istanbul that dates from 1457 or a few years earlier, lists a large number of villages with Turkish names and Muslim inhabitants, but the work of identifying these has only begun and will take years. The 1526-28 BBA register T.D. 370 gives for the whole of Filibe/Plovdiv Kaza the figure of 5,200 Muslim households, 5,873 Christian households, and 283 gypsy households (90 of these Muslim, 193 Christian), for a total of 11,356 households, of which 46 percent were Muslim. The total, then was about 55,000 to 60,000 people who partly lived in the plain of Bulgarian Thrace, partly in the Rhodope mountains. In Tatar Pazarcık, a kaza which comprised a large stretch of the Rhodopes but also some lowlands, the picture was as follows: there were 1 town and 79 villages, having 1,634 Muslim and 1,736 Christian households, for a total of 3,370. The Muslim households were 48 percent of the total.

As for the southern Rhodopes, the register 89 of the Cevdet collection gives for the district of Gümülcine (which then, in 1452-57, comprised the area of the bay of Porto Lago in the west to the Maritsa in the east and, very probably, the watershed of the Rhodopes to the north) a total of 2,020 households, of which 1,513, or 75 percent, were Muslim and 507 Christian. It is important to point out that this *defter* mentions that 334 of the Muslim households were Yürük, i.e., Turkish-cattle breeders, nomads. This is 22 percent of the total Muslim population; of the others, 28 percent were city dwellers, and 50 percent were peasants.

The number of Yürüks in the neighboring kaza of Karasu Yenicesi, near the modern town of Xanthi, was even greater; but the total number of inhabitants of this district was greater than of Gümülcine. This situation of Karasu can also be used to illustrate where and which districts were most throughly destroyed at the eve of the Ottoman conquest. It is interesting to remark that here, as in Gümülcine and all other kazas of Thrace mentioned previously, the Christians lived in the towns or in the once-walled settlements:[30] in Gümülcine, these included the town itself and Enoz, Maroneia,

---

[29]Xanthi/Isketçe has always remained the largest urban settlement of the kaza of Karasu, the town of Karasu remaining small. In the nineteenth century the administration moved to Isketçe, and Karasu declined to a mere village, which it still is today, with two mosques and a *tekke* and a mixed Greek-Turkish population (its modern "Greek" name is Genisea).

[30]For a description of these settlements, see Asdracha, *La Region des Rhodopes,* pp. 93-179. The overall conclusion of Asdracha is that in this part of Thrace, at least, in the fourteenth century, before

and Makri; in Karasu it was, first of all, the town of Iskeçe/Xanthi where almost half of all Christians of this kaza lived, and elsewhere in the district they lived together in a few large villages. This is the settlement pattern in times of insecurity and can be seen in all ages and all places where human beings live. The pattern continued well into the sixteenth century, but it can be seen that in the time of peace the Christians began to disperse and to settle partly in formerly exclusive Muslim villages and partly in newly founded villages. On the other hand, the Turkish colonists of the Gümülcine district and as well, of Karasu, Filibe, and Tatar Pazarcık, lived in a large number of small to very small villages spread out over the entire open land. It is the opposite of the settlement pattern of the native Christian population. As settlement patterns do not change overnight, we can be sure that the 1452-57 register, and the 1526-28 register as well, still show to a large extent the true situation of the years of the conquest and colonization. These settlement patterns and their interaction and changing forms over time deserve closer study within another framework. As for Karasu, it showed the following, in 1526-28: Muslim households, 3,290; Christian households, 2,029, for a total of 5,319 (62 percent Muslim). Of the Muslims, 695 households, or 21 percent, are registered as Yürük.

We now have the numbers for the four kazas in which the greater part of the Rhodope area was included and can be sure of the presence of at least a thousand Yürük households (perhaps 6,000 souls) who wintered to the south of the mountains. To the north of it there must have have been other groups of importance. The total Muslim-Turkish population of the districts of Filibe and Pazarcık was 6,834 households, or roughly 37,000 souls. If we assume that, as in the southern kazas, 20 percent of them were Yürük and largely roamed the Rhodope mountains, we get a figure of at least 7,500 Yürüks. The estimate that some 10,000 Yürüks were wandering through the Rhodope Yayla or later were settled there seems to be a fair one. We have no numbers as to the Christian inhabitants of the mountains; these are included in the total of the Christian population for the four kazas together, namely: 10,928 households, or roughly 60,000 souls. If we assume that about half lived in the very extensive mountain zone, we are at once able to understand how strong the Yürük impact on the mountains was. No less than a quarter, or perhaps even one-third, of the population of the mountains in the good season was Turkish cattle-breeders.[31]

It is known that an important part of the Bulgarian-speaking mountaineers accepted Islam at an unknown date. Bulgarian historiograpy, of the past and of the present, associates this with a single event: a supposed forced islamization under Grand

---

the Ottoman conquest, the local population was concentrated in the walled settlements, having deserted the open land as a result of the invasions, civil war, and social conflicts of that time. It would be very interesting if someone would do the same detailed research for the Bulgarian part of Thrace, before the Ottomans came.

[31] Barkan, in his much cited map in "Déportation comme méthode," gives 25 symbols for Yürüks in the area, each symbol standing for 250 households. This is 6,250 households of Yürüks, and where such masses came from is not clear, unless the general registers badly underrepresent the Yürüks (as various authors have warned; see, e.g., Farouqhi, "Agriculture"). However, even if there actually were more Yürüks, that does not change the general picture painted here but makes it truer to life. As to Barkan's map, it should be said that the historical toponymy of the Rhodope and of much of Thrace is still insufficiently known; therefore, we ought to regard his symbols as truly symbolic.

Vizier Köprülü Mehmed Paşa between 1666 and 1670 (although he in fact died in 1661!) This "forced conversion" was mentioned in two highly suspicious sources that, moreover, disappeared immediately after they were "discovered" and published at the end of the nineteenth century.[32] These accounts, especially that of "Pope Metodije Draginov," were popularized and are common knowledge for Bulgarians from the level of school child upward, doubtless because of their political usefulness. A more enlightened current in Bulgarian historiography, however, represents islamization as a gradual, stretched-out process, which can be followed step by step with the aid of the rich collection of Ottoman *ciziye* registers preserved in the Sofia National Library. (The *ciziye* was a Poll tax levied on Christians in lieu of military service.) Working with these registers, the eminent historian Strašimir Dimitrov could show that the islamization process was largely finished at the time the "sources" described it as just starting.[33] Jireček noted that "from Pomak [Bulgarian-speaking Muslims] tradition, it is visible that long ago the strong groups of Yürüks in the Rhodope had an impact on the change [of religion]."[34] Besides the influence of associations at village level for a period of at least as long as two centuries, other factors influenced the change. Neither the Yürüks nor the Bulgarian-speaking villagers were of the most orthodox in their religion. The Yürüks had Alevi-Bektashi inclinations. The Christians were partly affected by the heterodox Bogomil doctrine: its adherents hated the cross and icons and called the Orthodox Christians idolaters.[35] The Christians, furthermore, were under Greek ecclesiastical control, which was not popular and therefore not very intensive. All these factors combined must be held responsible for the slow conversion of the Bulgarian-speaking mountaineers of the Rhodope. After conversion they intermarried with Turkish settlers from the eastern part of the Rhodope (Kırcalı district) and with the Yürüks to such an extent that at present it is impossible to say to which ethnos these people belong. (The subject is, in fact, of interest only for the racist, because religion is, and was, the determining factor.[36] To which group the Bulgarian-speaking Muslims of the Rhodope *want* to belong is clear from their stubborn resistance to the process of Bulgarization.)

It will be clear, we hope, that the Rhodope district is not one where large numbers of magnificent works of Turkish architecture can be expected to be present. At the time that Ottoman Turkish architecture was at its prime there was no need for them, as there were no urban centers of any size in the area. By the time Ottoman architecture slowly emerged in the Rhodope, this art had entered the stage of decay. What was built

---

[32]For details and further references, see my "Art and Society," pp. 5-6.

[33]"Demografski otnošenija i pronikvane na isljama v Zapadnite Rodopi i dolinata na Mesta prez XV-XVII v.," *Rodopski Sbornik*, I, (1965): 63-114.

[34]*Fürstenthum*, p. 104.

[35]Ibid., pp. 108-112. Jireček's principal sources are the letters of the Catholic bishops Bulgaria in the seventeenth century, edited by Eusebius Fermendžiu, *Acta Bulgariae Ecclesiastica ab 1565 usque AD 1799, Monumenta Spectantia Historiam Slavorum Meridionalium* (Zagreb, 1887), a very rich source.

[36]The Greek researcher Xirotiris went so far as to analyze the blood of a thousand Greek Pomaks and concluded that these people had no relationship with the Pomaks on the Bulgarian side of the border, although he did not study the blood of the latter; see N. Xirotiris, "Exploration into the distribution of blood-groups among the Pomaks" (in Greek) (Ph. D. diss., University of Thessalonika, 1971).

were simple village mosques and *tekke*s of the dervish orders (which are reported to have been influential there) and, of course, some fine examples of domestic architecture. Only the latter have been studied in some detail. (See Plate 14.)

About the size and composition of the population of the Rhodope and the quantitative aspects of Ottoman buildings in the last decades of Ottoman rule in the area we find some detailed information in sources such as the Sālnāme of the Edirne Vilayet for the year 1310 (1892/93). This particularly rich official yearbook gives, in its description of the sancak of Gümülcine/Komotini, figures for the four kazas exclusively situated in the territory today forming the Bulgarian Rhodope. These are Sultanyeri, Ahi Çelebi, Eğri Dere, and Darı Dere. It can be see that the population of the area had soared; there were many new villages, nonexistent in the sixteenth century, and, hence, a more diversified local administration had emerged. The town of Gümülcine had moved upward in status from central village of a kaza to capital of a sancak; its province, once undivided, now was split in into a number of administrative sub-units. The description of Sultanyeri Kaza contains the remark that all the mosques there were built by the villagers, but it gives no numbers. For Ahi Çelebi, it is written that in this district of 40 villages there were 36 mosques and 37 *mescid*s but that the villagers did not know when they were built or by whom. Eğri Dere had together 44 mosques and *mescid*s, 6 *medrese*s, 106 primary schools (*mektep*) and only 2 *hamam*s. In Darı Dere there were 49 mosques and *mescid*s and 86 *mektep*s. If we count the population of all four kazas (283 villages) together, we arrive at the following figures for 1892/93: Muslim inhabitants (male and female), 116,909; Greek Orthodox, 1,223; Bulgarian Orthodox (Exarchist), 11,696. Of the total of 129,828 inhabitants, therefore, 90 percent were Muslim, 9 percent Bulgarian Christian, and 1 percent Greek Christian.

As for architectural evidence of the Muslim preponderance, we may conclude that in the Rhodope there were in existence perhaps 300 village mosques at the end of the nineteenth century. Since then the number has gone down drastically, especially after World War II when the new regime was installed with its stubborn de-islamization policy. However, painful as this may have been for the people concerned, from the point of view of art history the loss was not too serious, as may be understood from the materials presented above. It must be added that no comprehensive study was ever made of the Muslim buildings in the Rhodope. Large parts of the district are closed to foreigners: because the area borders the NATO country Greece; in order "to stop epidemics from coming from across the border;" and for other reasons. Thus the possibility is not excluded that the area may have housed a few valuable works, perhaps in the field of *tekke* buildings.

Danubian Bulgaria

The third of the zones into which Bulgaria can be divided is the land to the north of the Balkan chain, for the most part an undulating plateau sloping from the mountains to the Danube, with its tributary rivers running down from the mountains, often through deep canyons cut in the plateau. This land is uncontestably Bulgarian. It formed the nucleus of both the First and the Second Bulgarian Empire and was politically under almost unbroken Bulgarian control for as long as independent Bulgarian states existed. It is the land where the modest civilization of medieval Bulgaria unfolded itself, with castles and small towns built on unassailable plateaus, on all sides surrounded by steep cliffs, canyons, and the loops or rivers. These were typical *"Fluchtstädte,"* illustrating vividly the insecurity of that time (twelfth to fourteenth centuries).

Historically and demographically Danubian Bulgaria can be divided into three parts: the Dobruja and Deli Orman in the east; the former kingdom of the last Şişmanids, by far the largest and most important part, in the middle; and the old principality of Vidin in the west. All three areas became Ottoman sancaks: Silistra, Nikopol, and Vidin, respectively. The time and the manner of their incorporation into the Ottoman Empire differed, but all three remained border districts throughout five centuries of Ottoman rule and were subjected to numerous invasions from the north that brought mass destruction of Ottoman buildings.

The principality of Dobruja had a predominantly Turkish-Christian population as early as the thirteenth century. The least we can say is that the population of the area was rather mixed, with Greeks in the coastal settlements, with some Bulgarians inland, and with a very prominent group of descendants of the Seljuk colonists of Sultan Izzeddin Kaykaus who came in 1261. Some of the Seljuks moved elsewhere, as is known, while others remained behind and accepted Christianity around the year 1300.[37] Shortly afterwards they formed a semi-independent principality, which lasted until subjection by the Ottomans under Mehmed I around 1415. Besides the Seljuk Turkish colonists there must have been also a stratum of Peçenegs or other groups of formerly pagan Turks from the northern steppes.

King Ivan Şişman and the two semi-independent princes of the area were vassals of Murad I. In the crisis of 1388/89 (the defeat of Pločnik, victory of Kosovo) only Sratsimir of Vidin remained loyal, and in the winter of 1388/89 an army was sent against the two disloyal vassals, leading to the incorporation of most of Şişman's state. Ivanko/Yanko, son of Dobrotić, more or less succeeded in holding his ground. However, after the battle of Kosovo, while the new Sultan Bayezid was busy in Anatolia, the prince of Valachia, Mircea the Old, supported by King Sigismund of Hungary, invaded the land south of the Danube and penetrated as far as Karınabad/Karnobat, killing or taking prisoner a large number of Muslims, according to accounts by Mevlana Neşri and Ruhi Edirnevi. Both of these accounts were based on a previous account by a well-informed eyewitness, the original of which is lost. This source provides the only details of the conquest of northern Bulgaria.[38] In 1393 the kingdom of Şişman was fully

---

[37] The story of the Seljuk colonists of the Dobruja has been told in detail by Paul Wittek in "Les Gagaouzes = Les Gens de Kaykaus," *Rocznik Orientalistyczny* 17 (1952): 12-24; in this article the older views (of Mutafčiev in "Die angebliche Einwanderung von Seljuk-Türken in die Dobrudja in 13. Jahr-hundert," *Spisani na Bǎlgarskata Akademija na Nauka i Izkustva* 66 [1943]: 1-129, and Herbert Duda, "Zeitgenössische Islamische Quellen und das Oguzname...," ibid., pp. 131-45) are shown to be untenable. See also Yazijioğlu Ali on the Christian Turks of the Dobruja in *Bulletin of the British School of Oriental and African Studies* 14 (1952): 639-88. Elisabeth Zahariadou found further evidence supporting Wittek's story of the Seljuks in the archives of Mount Athos; see "Oi Hristianoi apogonoi tou Izzeddin Kaikaous II sti Verroia," *Makedonika* 6 (1964/65): 62-74.

[38] There are no local or any other sources (except Neşri and Ruhi) concerning the end of the Bulgarian state in 1393 except an old Bulgarian hagiography on the last patriarch of the country, Euthymius of

annexed. Almost all cities and castles of Şişman surrendered voluntarily. Neşri gives a list of them, and eighteen of the twenty-four strongholds mentioned can easily be identified. Kosova and Venčan offered stubborn resistance but were taken. Venčan was destroyed, its walls leveled and its population made slaves. In all other places the people came to offer the keys of their castles voluntarily and remained where they were.

In the Dobruja the situation was more diversified. Its most important town, Varna, was very probably incorporated by Dobrotić shortly after 1371. The Ottomans failed to take it in 1388/89. Subsequently Mircea took the other important town in the area, Silistra, and kept it for some years. In 1399 the Tatars took Varna. In 1403 Varna returned to Byzantium as a part of the treaty between Bayezid's son, Süleyman, and the Byzantines, but the Byzantine position on the Black Sea coast remained very weak. After more fighting with Mircea, Dobruja was finally incorporated into the Empire by Mehmed I (1416).[39]

Prior to the Ottoman conquest Dobruja had been very thinly populated. Politically, it was fragmentated and unstable, and for centuries it had been regularly devastated by the Tatars and the Noghay from the north, assuming the status of Tatar protectorate in the last decades of the thirteenth century. Ibn-i Battutah, who passed through the area in 1332/33, saw nothing but wasteland from the Tatar border near Babadag all the way south to Yambol, then a Byzantine frontier castle.[40] The frequent raids by the Ottomans, by Mircea and his ally, the Ottoman Prince Musa, and by the Tatars, all acting on their own account, can have done little good for the general situation. There was, therefore, plenty of open land, and this was one of the main reasons the Ottomans chose to settle masses of Turks from Anatolia there—in addition to the factor of the area's strategic importance.[41] Part of the land, in particular the forests of the Deli Orman (the "Wild Forest") to the west of the plains of the Dobruja proper, became at a very early date the refuge of a number of heterodox groups led by dervishes. It is very probable that a part of the surviving Christian Turkish population (the Gagauz) re-converted to Islam under the guidance of the dervishes. Others remained Turkish-speaking Christians, as they still are. (The well known historian Michael Guboğlu was a Gagauz.) In the Deli Orman the famous Sheikh Bedreddin was able to stage a revolt against the central authorities, having large popular support among the heterodox Turkish population.

Tărnovo, who was banished by the Turks to a monastery in the south of the country. This source was written long after the conquest of 1393, not by an eye witness, and is highly legendary. For an edition of this text, see R. Rumšev and Iv. Gălăbov, *Pohvalno Slovo za Evtimi ot Grigorij Tsamblak* (Sofia, 1971); also valuable is Emil Kalužniacki, *Aus der panegyrischen Litteratur der Südslaven* (Vienna, 1901).

[39] See Halil İnalcik's article, "Dobrudja," in *E.I.*[2].

[40] Ibn Battutah, *Travels in Asia and Africa, 1325-1354*, translated by H.A.R. Gibb, (London) 1929, p. 153.

[41] This settlement of Turks from Anatolia was connected with Bayezid I's conquest of the old *beyliks* of Aydin, Saruhan, and Menteş in the 1390s. The defter T.D. 370 from 1528/29 abounds in references about deported Turkish groups "from Anatolia to the Dobrudja". They are mentioned especially in the districts of Provadija and Varna-Balčık (pp. 434-446, Provadija; 418-434, Varna).

SILISTRA. We first get a comprehensive account of the size and the composition of the population of this area from the register T.D. 370. For Silistra sancak which also included a large piece of land today belonging to Rumania but in 1528 having a population that was negligible, we find the following (p. 470): the population resided in 15 towns, 7 castles, and 1,068 villages, having 8,587 Muslim households and 5,188 Christian households, for a total of 13,775 households, 62 percent of which were Muslim. In contrast, the figures for Nikopol are as follows (p. 563): towns, 13; castles, 5; villages, 995; Muslim households, 6,845 (including *sipahis* and garrison troops); Christian households, 29,616 (including 2,616 privileged, para-military households); Jewish households, 206; total 36,667, 18 percent Muslim.

VIDIN. Vidin sancak presents a very different picture. Nikopol, we can clearly see, had been less affected by the devastating Tatar and Peçeneg raids and Ottoman-Valachian strife than Silistra. The further west we go the less the destruction and the less the need to settle Turkish colonists. Vidin was annexed after the Crusade of Nikopol, when the previously loyal Sratsimir had become compromised (1396). A large part of his army, accustomed to serve in the Ottoman ranks, went over to direct service of the Ottomans.[42] More or less the same had happened in Nikopol, where a large part of the military was composed of local Bulgarian Christians. The western half of Vidin Sancak now belongs to Yugoslavia; in the past it had a partly Bulgarian population but was perhaps predominantly Valachian. In 1528 the picture was as follows (T.D. 370, p. 608): in the 4 towns, 6 castles, and 987 villages of Vidin there were 1,138 Muslim households (including *sipahis* and garrison troops) and 19,038 Christian households, for a total of 20,176. Thus the sancak was only 6 percent Muslim. In this part of Danubian Bulgaria the Ottoman presence was restricted to the strong town of Vidin itself and some inland castles. Unlike the situation in Silistra, or even Nikopol, the bulk of the Muslim population was military: *sipahis* (225 men), members of the garrison with their families (251 men), and others having a para-military status (107 *azabs* in the countryside and 436 privileged households, mainly in the town itself). Vidin was made an important Ottoman military and administrative center, which is reflected in the number of Ottoman buildings: 5 Friday Mosques, 15 *mescids*, 4 *hamams,* and 5 *zaviyes* for dervishes. Three quarters of these buildings were in Vidin itself. Here is clearly a case of government action, of the recreation of a town with a very important section of the local population retained, thus assuring continuity.

Most of the towns in all parts of Danubian Bulgaria received important groups of Turkish settlers immediately after the conquest. All of them except the old Bulgarian capital expanded greatly in the course of the following two centuries. Only after 1480 can this exansion be charted in any numerical detail. The case of Vidin, where the military constituted the bulk of the Muslim population, stands out as an isolated

---

[42] A good survey of the military situation in the Vidin district seventy-two years after the Ottoman conquest is given in the *defter* Maliyeden Müdevver no. 18 of August 1468. The total number of Christians in Ottoman military or para-military service in that year was 478, or 56 percent of the total military personnel of this frontier province! This was twenty-four years after the Varna crisis, when the reliability of the Sultan's Christian soldiers was put to the test.

instance. In the other towns civilians formed the large majority. The turning point in the development of the Danubian towns was the Crusade of Varna. The Christian armies moving along the great river captured or destroyed all in their path. There are several eyewitness accounts of this event, from parties on both sides. Vidin, Lom, Nikopol, Shoumen, Provadia/Pravadi, Madara, Măglis, Petrič, and Kalliakra (once capital of Dobrotić principality) were looted and burned, the Muslim inhabitants killed. The Bulgarian inhabitants of Vidin were spared, as were the Greek inhabitants of Varna. Tărnovo, deep inland, could be held by the Ottoman garrison. Loveč, Pleven, and Vratsa, also in the interior, seem to have been bypassed. The important towns of Vidin and Nikopol were soon to revive, but Kalliakra remained deserted forever, while Madara, Červen, Petrić, and Măglis vegetated as mere villages. The destroyed mountain stronghold of Shoumen was rebuilt in the plain; the old town remained deserted and was only brought to light by extensive excavation in the last decades. Červen, which was a small but particularly well-built town, more or less recovered but declined substantially in the seventeenth century. (See Plate 15.)

RUSÇUK. Very probably the comet-like rise of Rusçuk on the Danube, which was far better situated, caused the decline of the lonely hill-top town of Červen, 30 killometers inland. In the aftermath of the Crusade of Varna a fleet of Burgundian ships under command of Walerand de Wavrin roamed the lower Danube. The knights captured and then destroyed the Ottoman castles of Yergöğü (Giurgiu, opposite Rusçuk) and Tutrakan, killing their Turkish garrisons. To escape the same fate, the Turks of Rusçuk themselves destroyed the castle before the Burgundians landed and burned down the "village" around it.[43] Rusçuk was soon rebuilt, but this action is not recorded. In 1461 the terrible Valachian ruler, Vlad the Impaler, the historical prototype of Count Dracula, captured Rusçuk and wreaked havoc in the Nikopol area; but after this the eastern half of Danubian Bulgaria was calm until the end of the sixteenth century, when the troops of the Rumanian ruler Michael the Brave crossed the Danube and brought ruin with them. (Vidin suffered an Hungarian attack in 1502 and was again destroyed. Its castle still bears traces of the reconstruction under Bayezid II.) The development of Rusçuk, overshadowing the medieval Červen, is clearly shown in the following table.

---

[43]For un account of the actions of 1445, see D. Angelov, "Une source peu utilisée sur l'histoire de la Bulgarie au 15ᵉ siècle," *Byzantine-Bulgarica* 2 (1966):169-79, with reference to the sources.

Year Of Register	Ruşçuk Households			Çerven Households[44]		
	Muslim	Christian	Total	Muslim	Christian	Total
1480	------	239	239	32	107	167
1528	50	350	400	37	142	300
1550/52	467	628	1,095	34	217	251
1580	525	532	1,057	33	272	313
1640	-------	-------	3,400	------	-------	------

By 1640 Červen, was described as "a paltry Christian village";[45] and although sixteenth-century Ottoman Červen, perhaps had more inhabitants than the Bulgarian town, of the late fourteenth century, the place was no longer urban. The garrison and the administration had moved to Ruşçuk. The Orthodox bishop must have followed after 1659 (at which time he was still residing in Červen, as mentioned by Philip Stanislavov).[46] The 1550-52 register mentions explicitly that the largest part of the Muslim settlers, 21 families, were *müsellem*s who lived in the castle and had to perform the duty of garrison soldiers in case of an enemy attack and that this had always been the arrangement.[47] Besides them there was a group of Muslim settlers who did no military service and had therefore to pay the normal taxes. This was a group of 13 households and 8 bachelors, people who very probably had come on their own initiative. Among the 21 para-military households were no Sons of Abdullah, while among the others were 4 converts. It has been shown that the rate of conversion to Islam was greatest in the time of Sultan Süleyman and was very probably linked to victories by the armies of Islam, which made an enormous impact on the minds of the people. This seems to have been particularly true for the towns, where socio-economic factors also played a role.[48] In the villages, islamization was very limited; in the semi-rural Červen it stood at 9

---

[44] The figure for Červen in 1480 is from the fragment of an Ottoman *defter* preserved in Sofia and published in *Turski Izvori za Bălgarskata Istorija,* vol. 2 (Sofia, 1966), pp. 325-27. The Muslim households of Červen are given as *nefer* in the registers (adult males, married *and* unmarried). The household numbers shown on the table are our estimates, based on the number of *nefers*. The reconstructed numbers have been placed in brackets.

[45] Hadschi Chalfa (Katip Çelebi), *Rumeli und Bosna,* trans. J. von Hammer (Vienna, 1812), p. 44.

[46] Cited in Fermendzin, *Acta Bulgariae,* p. 263. Stanislavov also mentions two churches still in Červen, at that time.

[47] In 1480, according to the register fragment published in *Turski Izvori* (see n44) the military presence in Červen, included a Dizdar, a porter, and only 1 soldier; but 57 Muslim *nefer* in the settlement below the castle hill were headed by men with the status of auxiliary troops. Thus the arrangement had *not* always been according to the same formula.

[48] See, for example, John Thirkell, "Islamization in Macedonia as a Social Process," in *Islam in the Balkans, Papers of a Symposium in Edinburgh, 1976* (The Royal Scottish Museum: Edinburg, 1979), pp. 43-48. According to T.D. 382 (p. 78), in 1550 Červen still had two monasteries. One of these was dedicted to the Holy Archangels and owned vineyards, on which it paid some tithe; the other is not named. The presence of these two institutions, hitherto not known of, is evidence of a process of slow decay rather than a violent end through conquest; see also n46.

percent, which was lower than the percentage in the towns (20 to 25 percent) and higher than that of the villages (5 percent or less).

The rapid development of Rusçuk into a Muslim Turkish town was a bit outside the general pattern. We have to assume that numerous new settlers moved there: Turks from the Balkan interior, looking for better job opportunities, and Bulgarian Christians from the countryside. In the 25 years between 1526-28 and 1552, the Christian population grew by a yearly percentage of 2.34, which is above rate of growth (around 1 per cent) generally accepted as that prevailing in many places in the Balkans and elsewhere in Europe in the sixteenth century. For the Muslims of Rusçuk the rate was even higher—as much as 9 percent! Bulgarian settlers must have moved to the booming town, but even more did Turkish settlers find their way there. The 1552 list of inhabitants shows people coming from far away; e.g., 3 families "from Anatolia," 1 from Akkirman on the Dnjestr, 4 Tatar families, and 1 particularly ethnologically interesting immigrant, a "son of the Kuman" (Kipçak Turk). Besides the influx of new Muslim settlers, there was some effect from the limited islamization of the local Christian population and its slow assimilation into the Turkish civilization. Current Bulgarian theories now represent *all* the Turks of the Bulgarian cities of the past as Bulgarians who lost their nationality; but it is clear that, for the successful assimilation of one set of language, manners, and culture into another, a large majority group into which the minorities can sink is needed. Large majorities cannot be assimilated by small groups of soldiers and administrators especially not as a spontaneous process rather than a determined educational policy (and it must be remembered that schools to educate the masses were nonexistent in those days). For 1552, the heyday of the process of islamization in the Balkan towns, we find among the 467 Muslim households of Rusçuk 109 Sons of Abdullah, or 23 percent only.

Rusçuk continued to grow rapidly into the seventeenth century, for which there are a number of accounts giving estimates of household numbers, all wildly at variance with each other.[49] The only thing the figures do show is that the small fortress and the village beneath it (as it was in 1480) had developed into one of the largest towns of Danubian Bulgaria. It remained large and important until the end of the Ottoman period and remained a place of mixed inhabitants. Felix Kanitz, using Ottoman statistics from shortly before 1877, mentions 10,800 Turkish inhabitants, 7,700 Bulgarians, 1,000 Jews, 800 Armenians, 500 gypsies, 1,000 Turkish soldiers, 800 Valachians, and 400 Europeans.[50] At the time it was the capital of the Danube Vilayet and one of the most progressive cities of the Empire. The expansion of the city was also reflected in the number of mosques: the 1552 register mentions 1 mosque and 6 *mescids*. Bishop Bakšič mentions 10 mosques in 1640, while his colleague, Philipp Stanislavov, gives the

---

[49]Bishop Bakšič (cited in Fermendžiu, *Acta Bulgariae*, p. 75) lists 3,400 houses in 1640; Hadschi Chalfa, *Rumeli und Bosna,* for about the same year gives a figure of 6,000 houses; Evliya Çelebi, in *Seyyahatname*, vol. 3 (Ücdal ed.), p. 934, lists 2,200 houses in 1666; and Bishop Stanislavov (cited in Fermendžiu, *Acta Bulgariae*, p. 263) give 6,300 houses in 1659.

[50]*Donau-Bulgarien und der Balkan,* 2nd ed. (Leipzig, 1882), vol. 2, p. 15. Thus it remained about half-and-half Muslim and non-Muslim, as it had been in the sixteenth century. No great changes seem to have occurred in the intervening period.

number as 16.[51] In the yearbooks of the Danube province we find listed 30 mosques. In 1974 only 4 of these were still standing.[52] It is characteristic for towns like Rusçuk that no monumental Ottoman buildings were erected there. Most of the mosques about which we have information were simple wooden structures. The mosque of Grand Vizier Rüstem Paşa, supposed to have been built in Rusçuk by the great architect Sinan, is the product of a notorious misreading of the sources, which has been followed blindly by almost all who wrote about this town. The real Rüstem Paşa Mosque stands in Rodosçuk (Today: Tekirdağ) and not in Rusçuk. In the Arabic alphabeth the difference between the two names is just one letter (the d̲). In conclusion, it may be said that Rusçuk is a very typical example of spontaneous urban development, proceeding without much government intervention.

RAZGRAD. Rather different was the case of Razgrad, the new town in Danubian Bulgaria, 70 kilometers inland from Rusçuk. The 1528 register, which contains the figures from the census made under Süleyman in 1524, does not yet list this town. The first source, as far as I am able to tell, that mentions "Yenice, also known as Hezargrad-i Cedîd" is a fragment of a register of *vakif* property in the sancak of Nikopol.[53] The fragment is undated but was placed, on internal evidence, somewhere between 1544 and 1561, most likey close to the first of these dates. We can, however, be sure that it actually is at least a decade older than this, dating from shortly after 1535, because the number of inhabitants is far lower than that given in another register of the Nikopol district preserved in the Başbakanlik Arşivi in Istanbul (T.D. 382, pp. 847-49). The latter has to be dated shortly before 1551 but after the year 1542 when the important mosque of Ahmed Beg, which still stands today, was built—as is clearly stated by its inscription in the Persian language.) This important epigraphic document was not used by the Bulgarian orientalists in dating the register fragment. The population picture that emerges shows that in about 1535 Razgrad had 104 households, all Muslim, located in a single *mahalle*; by about 1550 there were 195 households, again all Muslim, in 4 *mahalles*.

In this case we have to do with a town of the Barkan-thesis type, an urban center founded on government order and equipped with the buildings necessary for its functioning as a Muslim center. (See Plate 16.) Why Grand Vizier Ibrahim Paşa decided

---

[51]Cited in Fermendžiu, *Acta Bulgariae*, pp. 75, 263.

[52]For a report on the situation of the Turkish monuments of Rusçuk in 1897, see Eşref Eşrefoğlu, "Bulgaristan' Türklerine ve Rusçuk'taki Türk eserlerine dair 1897 tarihli bir rapor," in *Güney-Doğu Avrupa Araştırmaları Dergisi* 1 (1972): 19-37. In 1908 the number of mosques had gone down to twelve; see *Revue de Monde Muselman* 5 (1908): 492. In the mid 1980's the most important of the mentioned 4 mosques, the Tombul Cami, was demolished together with its historical graveyard, containing the tombstones of such famous men as the Şazeliye Sheykh and poet Zarifi Ömer Efendi and Tirsniklizâde Ismail Ağa, the well known early 19th century ayan of Rusçuk.

[53]This fragment is preserved in the National Library of Sofia and has been published in *Turski Izvori*, vol. 3 (Sofia, 1972), pp. 441-42; the editor of this fragment (Bistra Cvetkova) believed that the list of Christian households, following that of the Muslims of Razgrad after a break in the register, also pertained to that town, and she reported this in the article "Hezargrad" in E.I.[2]; however, the subsequent Ottoman *defters* concerning Hezargrad, preserved in Istanbul, show that the Christians lived in separate villages elsewhere in the district.

to build a Muslim town precisely at that spot is not known. Perhaps there was the need for an urban center in this area, where towns were far apart. The district had a mixed Bulgarian and Turkish population, the former being in a comfortable majority. Among the earliest population of the town we find some converts to Islam, very probably attracted by the jobs to found in the new place. Among the 104 households were 21 households of Sons of Abdullah, or 20 percent of the total.

The 1535 register contains a note on how Razgrad came into being. The grand vizier had possessed villages in the area of Istanbul; they were his *mülk*, or full property. These villages he exchanged for some others in the kaza of Červen. Subsequently, on a flat plot near a small river, about one kilometer from the site of the ruined and deserted Roman town of Abrittus,[54] Ibrahim Paşa constructed a large domed mosque, a *medrese*, a *hamam*, a *khan* and an *imaret*, and very probably also a number of shops.[55] The functionaries of this socio-religious compound numbered at least 16 heads of households, mentioned in the register. With their fixed salaries the members of this relatively large group formed the nucleus of the town and its economic backbone. This new settlement developed quickly, attracting more settlers. The 1550 register mentions four *mahalles*, called after the founders of the new places of worship: the Mahalle of the Friday Mosque, the Mahalle of the Mescid of Ahmed Beg, the Mahalle of the Mescid of Iskender Beg, and the Mahalle of the Mescid of Bahram Beg. We should not imagine these *mescid*s to be humble prayer chapels. In the early part of Ottoman history a *mescid* could be a sizeable, monumental structure, such as that of Ahmed Beg. At a later stage many *mescid*s were upgraded to Friday Mosques, about which there is considerable, though scattered, written evidence; those of Bahram Beg and Iskender Beg in Razgrad were domed buildings and had become known as "mosques" before they were demolished (shortly after World War II.)[56]

It is interesting to note that the number of converts had gone down from 20 percent in 1530 to 17 percent in 1550, contrary to the Bulgarian theory. In the enumeration of the individual inhabitants we find indications why this was so. No fewer than 5 heads of households have the epithet "Anadolu"; 1 came from Karaman (southern Anatolia); 1 had the name Selçuk: others came from Turkish centers elsewhere in Bulgaria, as, for example, Filibe/Plovdiv. The list also shows that by 1550 the town was no longer a religious center alone. Many craftsmen are mentioned, among them 12 tanners, 3 wool carders, 3 *halva* makers, 3 tailors, and saddlemakers, smiths, a stonecutter, etc. The list is far from complete. That the names of the professions were very probably noted to facilitate identification of newcomers and were not needed for old, established citizens is a hypothesis put forward by Heath Lowry.[57]

---

[54]On the ruins of Abrittus, see R. F. Hoddinott, *Bulgaria in Antiquity* (London, 1975). The popular name of these ruins was the Turco-Bulgarian "Thousand Castles" (Hezargrad) from which comes the modern name of the town.

[55]The *medrese* is mentioned in T.D. 382, pp. 847-49. For information about teachers at the *medrese* and their careers, see Câhit Baltacı, *XV-XVI. Asırlarda Osmanlı Medreseleri* (Istanbul, 1976), pp. 257-58.

[56]On these mosques and other details, see Ivan Javašov, *Razgrad, Njegovo Arheologičesko i Istoričesko Minalo* (Sofia, 1930); unfortunately, his dates for the mosques are based on bad miscalculations of the chronograms.

[57]"Ottoman Tahrir Defters," p. 71

Soon the new town became a separate administrative unit. In the 1530 fragment it is still listed as part of the kaza of Červen; in 1550 it is mentioned as the seat of a kaza itself. The large district of Červen must have been split. The town must have come into being in the last years of İbrahim Paşa's (Pargali, Makbul) grand viziership (1523-1536). Razgrad continued to grow, and Bishop Bakšic' described it in 1640 as a town with 1,600 Turkish households and 150 Bulgarian households. The Turks possessed three "bellisima" mosques and a number of less conspicuous ones, while the Bulgarian Christians had two churches.[58] The existence of the latter buildings spotlights one facet of actual Ottoman policy in governing a multinational empire. According to the strict rules of Islamic law such churches were forbidden, for Razgrad was a new town where there had been no Christian places of worship dating from before the conquest. Doubtless the Bulgarian settlers of the seventeenth century needed their churches in order to function properly as a community, and this was recognized by the local Muslim authorities.

The case of Razgrad is also of interest as an example of how such towns developed, and it provides a counterexample to the recent Bulgarian theories: there was not further islamization and turkification at the expense of the Bulgarians but, rather, the opposite. At the end of the development process we see a town of 10,000 inhabitants of whom only 66 percent were Muslim-Turkish, not 91 percent as in 1550. The Sālnāme of the Danube Vilayet of 1290 (1873/74) gives details, as do some western travelers. The Sālnāme (p. 141) numbers 1,244 Muslim households and 563 Christian households and a population of 3,430 male Muslims and 1,770 male non-Muslims. Using the multiplier 5, we arrive at a figure of 6,220 Muslim inhabitants and 2,815 non-Muslim (only Christian Bulgarian, in this case); or, if we simply assume that males and females were equal in number, we arrive at a total of 6,860 Muslim inhabitants and 3,540 Christians. (It should be noted here that in the nineteenth century the Bulgarian Christian households contained as a rule more people than the average Turkish household. In the case of Razgrad it was 6.29 against 5.5; thus, were this article about the demography of the area, some correction would be necessary. However, I have used the convenient multiplier of 5 throughout for areas and periods of time when no sure knowledge of household size is available. For uniformity's sake, then, I use it here also.) The Sālnāme gives also some statistics about buildings: there were 11 mosques, 2 churches, 1 *hamam*, and 618 shops. A single *hamam* seems inadequate for a town the size of Razgrad, but the building was a very large one. It was in existence until the 1970s, so we could study it; but soon after that it was destroyed on order of the city council, much against the wishes of the Sofiot Institute for the Preservation of Monuments of Culture. The mosque of Ibrahim Paşa is preserved, but not in its initial from. It was completely rebuilt in 1615, as is stated on the inscription above the entrance. Some years ago it was in restoration, its monumental portico being rebuilt and the whole building adapted for cultural purposes. Except for the previously mentioned mosque of Ahmed Beg, there are no other buildings for Islamic worship standing. (See Plate 16.)

---

[58]Fermendžiu, *Acta Bulgariae*, p. 75.

PLEVNE. An example of a different kind of successful town development is provided by Plevne/Pleven, which has been famous since the stubborn Turkish resistance against the Russian army in the war of 1877/78.[59] It is a typical example of a recreated town, built and settled by a provincial Turkish commander, not by the central government. The city is said to have developed in the course of the fourteenth century near the site of the early medieval town of Storgosia (today known as Kailâk, from the Ottoman Kayalık). This late medieval settlement was a small castle, the ruins of which were still to be seen by Evliya Çelebi in the mid-seventeenth century. While the Ottoman chronicles are silent about conquest of this castle, Evliya attributes it to "Ghazi Mihal" under Murad I,[60] this which perhaps connects it to the campaign of 1388/89 against the kingdom of Şişman, in which Pleven was situated. (The conqueror was of course not the famous companion of Osman I but a later member of this important family, hereditary leaders of the Ottoman vanguard, the Akıncıs.) It is possible that the castle was destroyed on that occasion and the inhabitants killed or carried off. It is also possible that is was destroyed during the Crusade of Varna in 1444. The earliest Ottoman record of the area, the oldest written source, as far as I am aware, is found in a fragment of an İcmal Register dating from 1479/80, preserved in Sofia and published in *Turksi Izvori* (vol. 2, p. 245). In various places in this register we find the remark that this or that village has remained uninhabited since the times of the mentioned crusade.

The "town" of Plevne in 1480 had 9 Muslim households and 10 Christian ones (perhaps 100 inhabitants). Despite its small size it was the seat of the *nahiye* of Plevne, to which frequent reference is made in the register. It was also part of a *ziamet*. Sometime towards the end of the fifteenth century the situation changed fundamentally. This was due to the action of the famous frontier warrior of the time of Bayezid II and Selim I, Mihaloğlu Ghazi Ali Beg. In a long note in the detailed register of the Nikopol Sancak of about 1550 (T.D. 382, p. 675), it is stated that the town of Plevne and a number of villages near it were given to Mihaloğlu Ali as *mülk* property. This was done in the time of Sultan Bayezid II (1481-1512). After having received the necessary written statements and laid down that all the rights and taxes of the town and the villages were from now on the full property of Ali Beg, the new owner had assembled people without fixed residence and persons not registered in the head tax registers and made them settle in the town and the villages. After this Ali Beg acquired a new imperial order of confirmation and then made the town and villages the *vakf* property of the mosque, the *imaret*, the *zaviye*, etc. that he had constructed in Plevne.[61] He made other villages the property of his sons and servants. This status was reconfirmed three times, during new registrations, which must have been in 1516 under Selim I (1512-1520); in about 1535, for which we have the preserved fragment we used for Razgrad;

---

[59]This is splendidly described by Ruppert Furneaux in *The Siege of Plevna* (London, 1958). This book also appeared in Bulgarian translation.

[60]For Evliya's account of Plevne I have not relied on the printed edition of the *Seyyahatname* (vol. 4) but on the autograph of this famous traveler preserved in Istanbul, Topkapı Sarayı, Revan Kösk No. 1457, fol. 59r; this differs considerably from the printed version and is much richer.

[61]A. S. Levent, in *Gazavât-Nâmeler ve Mihaloğlu Ali Beg'in Gazavât-Nâmesi* (Ankara, 1956), published an extract of the *vakfiye* of Ali Beg; it was dated 901 (1495/96), the year the construction of the buildings of Ali Beg in Plevne was largely completed.

and again in 1555. The 1516 and 1550 registers are well preserved, and as the later one contains information on the latest development of the towns and villages, we worked from that text.

Ali Beg must have attracted settlers by promising tax advantages. The summary register T.D. 370 in Istanbul, which contains the data of the 1516 registration, shows, for example, that the head tax for the non-Muslims was 30 *akçe* per year instead of the usual 50 to 60 *akçe*. A note in the same register states that the town of Plevne was free of the legal and the customary taxes. The development of Plevne over the years is shown in the following table, drawn from data in registers dating from 1480 to 1874.[62]

Year of Register	Muslim households	Christian households	Jewish households	Gypsy households	Total households
1480	9	10	--------	---------	19
1516	200	99	69	11	370
1550	472	185	104	36	797
1579	558	180	209	44	991
1873	1:241	1,477	(75)	(65)	2.858

The effect of the settlement policy of Ali Beg is evident. The later expansion of the town is due to various reasons. More Turkish settlers came from elsewhere: among the heads of households listed in the 1550 register we find 4 from Anatolia, 1 Karamanlı, 1 Tatar, and 2 from the nearby town of Loveč. (Such indications of origin are rare in the registers.) There was also growth attributable to births. Through a careful inspection of the registers and a comparison of the yearly percentages of growth in the three main religious communities of the town with that in the 15 *vakif* villages around it, as listed in 1516 and 1579, we are able to conclude that the Muslims grew at a faster rate than the other groups. The Jews were second in growth rate, while the Bulgarian group grew the slowest, very markedly so in the villages. Polygamy may have played a role in the more rapid increase of the Muslim population, but it seems the main factor may have been the different marriage pattern of the Turks. Since the nineteenth century at least it has been the case that in western Bulgaria women marry rather late—at 25 to 28 years of age. This seriously reduces the number of births of children because seven to ten strong childbearing years are lost. For the sixteenth-century Bulgarians the pattern may well have been similar, although there is no direct evidence on this point. However, in the

[62]The source for 1579 is a register preserved in Ankara, KuK 559, Tapu Kadastro Gen. Müd., "Defter-i Evkaf-i Livä-i Niğbolu," pp. 79-84; for that year the number of Christians must actually have been greater than the number of households (180) would suggest, as there was a relatively large number of unmarried Christian males there. The figures for Muslim and Christian households for 1873 are from the sälnäme of that year, (H. 1290) combined with the data reproduced by H. J. Komrumpf in his rich, informative work which has much secondary literature, *Die Territorialverwaltung im östlichen Teil der europäischen Türkei, 1864-1878* (Freiburg, 1976), p. 319. For Jewish and gypsy households the estimated figures, shown in parentheses, were arrived at by dividing the known populations of these inhabitants by five, the theoretical number per household.

large and almost purely Bulgarian district of Sofia, with over 200 villages, the population growth was also very slow, whereas in most of the Empire the population in the sixteenth century doubled or in some cases even trebbled, as also occurred in most of Europe. The Muslim population was increased to some extent by the assimilation of local Bulgarian Christians. The 1550 register shows us that in Plevne 21 percent of the Muslims (103 of the 772 households) were converts. However, even if we add the figure for the converts to the total Christian population, subtracting it from the Muslim total, the yearly percentage of growth in the Christian community was still below that of the Muslim and the Jews.

The relatively large Jewish community also reflects the settlement policy of the Mihaloğlu. In 1516 there were communities of Jews from Germany and one from the Frankish lands in Plevne. The latter must have come via Thessaloniki/Selanik, where they had arrived in large numbers after their expulsion from Spain by the "Catholic Kings." From Selanik, and after about 1500, they began to spread out over the Balkans, as a number of Ottoman registers show. The Plevne Jews must have been invited by Ali Beg, who was looking for able settlers. A third community of Jews, about 25 households, appeared, in the years between 1516 and 1550, coming from Buda(pest). This migration was very probably connected with the first Turkish conquest of Buda, in 1528, after which event the Buda Jews found their way to the Ottoman dominions.[63] Some of these must have been invited by the Mihaloğlu to Plevne.

· The nucleus of the architectural development of Plevne was the buildings of Ali Beg: a Friday mosque, an *imaret* distributing food to the staff of the mosque and to the poor and to travelers, a *medrese* for higher Islamic learning, a *zaviye* for dervishes, and a *hamam*. The latter is mentioned in the registers of the sixteenth century as a source of revenue for the pious foundations. Much of the information provided by Evliya Çelibi's detailed description of the town as it was in 1073 (1662/63) is corroborated by details given in the 1516 and 1550 registers. These show that the principal income of Ali Beg's foundation came from 15 neighboring villages and from Plevne itself, and the expansion of the town is reflected in the the increasing revenues of the *vakif*. In 1516 the income recorded included 11,686 *akçe* from the town, 3,000 from the *hamam*, 390 *akçe* from 13 mills, and 1,272 from shops; in 1550 these amounts had increased to 35,137 *akçe* from the town, 8,000 from the *hamam,* 880 from 29 mills, and 1,770 from the shops. Evliya specifically mentioned a *bedesten,* built from the stones of the demolished castle, as being among the *vakif* property of Ghazi Ali ; after the destruction of Plevne by the Valachians in 1006 (1597/98), the Mihaloğlu had had the structure repaired and had added to it a mighty khan—a castle-like building with 70 fireplaces. Ali Beg and his exploits became a legend, one that was sung by the poet Suzi Çelebi of Prizren.[64] All in all, we can regard the actions of this warlord as a reflection of the general concern of the

---

[63]See Mark A. Epstein, *The Ottoman Jewish Communities and Their Role in the 15th and 16th Centuries* (Frieburg, 1980), p. 24.

[64]On Suzi and his work, see Aleksandar Olešnički, "Suzi Celebi iz Prizrena, Turski pesnik-istorik, *Glasnik Skopskog Naučnog Društva*, no. 7 (1934): 69-82. For the great *mecenas* of Plevne, compare also Olga Zirojević, "Mihaloğlu Ali Bey, Der Sandjakbey von Smederevo," in *VII Turk Tarihi Kongreye sunulan bildiriler*, vol. 2 (Ankara, 1973), pp. 567-77. For the source of Evliya's description of Plevne, see n 60.

government with the reconstruction and internal colonization of the land. When Ali Beg died in 1521 he was buried in the *türbe* next to his mosque.

The architectural development of Plevne did not come to an end with Ali's death. His sons continued his work, sponsoring further building in "their" town. His son Mehmed succeeded him as leader of the Ghazis; and from the work of another sixteenth-century poet, Za'ifi, who worked as a professor there, we know that a *medrese* was built in Plevne by another son of Ali, Hızır Beg.[65] Thus Plevne became an important provincial center of Islamic learning. The 1550 register mentions a *mahalle* of Hızır Beg and a *mescid,* as well as *mescid*s of the mother of Hızır Beg, of Hacı Budak, and of the Tanners (an indication of the importance of this craft). The 1579 register mentions all these buildings and *mahalle*s and adds new ones: a mosque of Hadice Sultan, a mosque of Süleyman Beg, a *mescid* of Katip Nasuh, and a *mescid* of Halil Voyvode. Evliya Çelebi mentions a primary school built by Mihaloğlu Süleyman Beg, one of seven schools of this type in the town. The *imaret* of Ghazi Ali Beg was still fully active when Evliya wrote. He noted that "in the morning and the evening an abundance of food is lavished upon all coming and going guests. Every time there is rice soup, and on Fridays boiled rice with butter, meat and fat, sweet rice with saffron, and stew with onions is given to them."[66] Three years before Evliya, the Sofiot Catholic bishop Philipp Stanislavov visited "*Pleven civitas*" and remarked that the town numbered "500 Bulgarians of the schismatic rite (Orthodox) with 2 churches, and 5,000 Turks with 7 mosques.[67] The number of Turks must be an exaggeration, as are a number of Stanislavov's other totals for Turks in Bulgarian towns. Evliya, who was usually eager to depict cities as big as possible, mentioned 2,000 houses, double the number of 1579, which was a sizeable increase for this time when at many places the population was in decline rather than growing.

The Danube Vilayet Sālnāme of 1873/74 shows the ultimate outcome of the process of development of Plevne: in the sixteenth century the town had been roughly two-thirds Muslim Turkish, but by the last quarter of the nineteenth century the Turkish element had decreased to about 47 percent. The Sālnāme of 1286 (1869/70) mentions 18 mosques in Plevne, 2 churches and 1 synagogue. The Sālnāme of 1285 lists also 3 *medrese*s and 5 *tekke*s. After the gallant defense of the town in 1877, the Turkish population suffered an eclipse. Almost all fled before the Russians moved in, and most did not return. The place was taken over by a mass of Bulgarian settlers. At the time of the Bulgarian census of 1888 there were 14,000 inhabitants, far less than shown by the last Turkish figures.

In 1973 there was still a minuscule Turkish community in Plevne, having only 1 miserable mosque of wood and beaten earth. By then the town had passed the 100,000 mark in population. It has been wholly rebuilt, and literally nothing remains of its rich Turkish past. This brief review of the development of Plevne as a Turkish town with

---

[65]On Za'ifi and his work, see Robert Anhegger, "16. Asır şairlerinden Za'ifi" in *Istanbul Üniversitesi Edebiyat Fakültesi Türk Dili ve Edebiyatı Dergisi* 4, no. 1-2 (1950): 133-66; on other professors at this *medrese*, see Baltacı, *Osmanlı Medreseleri*, pp. 85-86.

[66]See n60.

[67]Fermendžiu, *Acta Bulgariae*, p. 262.

important buildings shows, however, that the opinion of some that the Turkish period cannot have been important because so little is preserved of it is totally invalid![68]

ESKI CUMA. As one last example of urbn development in the important sancak of Nikopol, I mention the town of Eski Cuma (or Cum'a-i Atık in the Ottoman sources). It originated as a town with an important market on Friday; hence its modern Bulgarian name, Tărgovište (Market Place). This town is a typical example from the category of urban settlements that sprang up neither because of acts of government or of important provincial grandees nor because of the proximity of a castle. Eski Cuma /Tărgovište (and towns such as Selvi/Sevlievo) developed from a centrally located village where, in the course of the sixteenth century, a weekly market was set up into a town with craftsmen and a seat of local administration. The oldest reference I found to this town is in the detailed 1579 register of the Nikopol Sancak (Kuk 42 in Ankara). There it is described as a village having 85 Muslim households and 7 Christian households. It was already the seat of a *nahiye*. In the seventeenth century it must have developed rapidly. A detailed head tax register from 1692, preserved in Sofia, mentions it as a *kasaba* (town) and seat of the kaza of Eski Cuma, having 86 *cizye hane* (poll tax units) of Christians.[69] Being a tax only paid by Christians and Jews the Muslims of Eski Cuma are not mentioned in this register. The rise in the number of Christians, from roughly 35 to 40 in 1579 to about 430 to 460 in 1692 is extraordinary. What little other data we have concerning this town also suggest that the Christian Bulgarian element was not submerged into the Turkish population but grew considerably over the course of time. The Sālnāme of 1291 (1874/75) mentions 3,026 male Muslim inhabitants and 1,671 male Bulgarians (and 114 male gypsies). Kanitz states that in 1872 there were 8 Turkish *mahalles* and 3 Bulgarian *mahalles* with, respectively, 1,400 and 400 houses.[70] The 1286 Sālnāme of Tuna Vilayet mentions 17 mosques, 1 *hamam*, and 3 churches. Throughout the nineteenth century Eski Cuma was the place where one of the largest fairs of the Balkans was held yearly.

In the eighteenth century Eski Cuma was an agricultural center of importance and the seat of some wealthy notables (*ayans*). One of these, Mollazāde, was responsible for the construction of the largest and architecturally most important mosque of this town, the Sa'at Camii, or Mosque of the Clock Tower. In 1987 this mosque was still standing, the only one surviving. The 16 others had all been destroyed previously; however, their value as works of architecture had been very limited, as they were simple rectangles of wood and mud brick, typical for the type of town they served. Besides the Sa'at Camii there was the Clock Tower itself, built on order of Midhat Paşa, while this great reformer served as governor of the Danube Vilayet. Kanitz, shortly before 1874, noted that the district of Eski Cuma had 45 Turkish villages of which only 8 were partly

---

[68]For more details on Plevne before 1878, see the rich work of Jordan Trifonov, *Istorija na grad Pleven de Osvoboditelnata Vojna* (Sofia, 1933); unfortunately, this work is not reliable for the first centuries of the Ottoman period because the Ottoman registers were unknown when Trifonov wrote.
[69]This is the register O.A.K. 13/60, p. 13v.
[70]*Donau-Bulgarien und der Balkan*, vol. 3 (Leipzig, 1879), p. 52.

inhabited by Bulgarians, 5 partly Turkish-Çerkes, and 3 others mixed Turkish-Tatar.[71] On the hills to the west of the town there was in 1987 still standing and active the large Bektashi *tekke* of Kızane, the nearby village being entirely Bektashi. The vast village graveyard on the slope below the *tekke* testified to the size and antiquity of this Turkish settlement. (See Plates 18 and 19.) Today Tărgovište is overwhelmingly Bulgarian; it is said to have only 60 Turkish families remaining.

In sum, if we review the development of the various towns of Danubian Bulgaria as a whole, it can be seen that Turkish architecture was an important facet of the emergence and life of these towns but that is was of lesser importance there than in Thrace, south of the Balkan mountains. It seems that, as time went on, less was invested in monumental structures because the district was overrun too many times by invading armies. Judging by what is left of the Turkish buildings in Danubia, especially mosques, and from looking at old photographs, we can say that in this vast district a special type of mosque seems to have come into being: a spacious rectangle with a flat wooden ceiling or, at most, a wooden inset dome, covered by a gently sloping tiled roof. Such a structure was much lighter than a mosque covered by stone dome, so the walls could be much thinner and the cost of erection was two-thirds or one-half that for a domed structure. If rubble masonry was used, the cost was even less than when the fine white limestone, which abounds in Danubian Bulgaria, was the building material. The preserved remains suggest that stone mosques were preferred by *paşas* and *ayans*. Rubble masonry was used by wealthy craftsmen and wood and mud brick by sponsors from the less wealthy groups of society. The latter types of mosques were found especially in the towns that sprang up spontaneously (Eski Cuma, Selvi, Osman Pazar, etc.). This was in the greatest possible contrast to the situation in Thrace, Macedonia, Albania, or Kosovo, where monumental domed structures were preferred right into the nineteenth century. There are some exceptions, such as the *külliye* (compound) of Şerif Halil Paşa in Şumla/Shoumen; but Şumla was never destroyed during the numerous wars in Danubia, protected as it was by its natural setting and very strong fortifications. (See Plates 20, 21, 22, and 23.)

To illustrate this point about repeated destruction, I give some details. In the time when Thrace and Macedonia enjoyed an unbroken peace, the Ottoman provincial capital of Silistra, one of the largest cities along the Danube, witnessed the following events: in 1425 the Bulgarian pretender to the throne of Tărnovo, Fruzin, with help of a large army of Valachians of Voyvode Dan, plundered and destroyed the town; in 1445 the Burgundians of Walerand de Wavrin, together with the Valachians, captured and destroyed the town; in 1462 Vlad the Impaler boasted of having burnt and destroyed a large number of Turkish settlements to the south of the Danube, among which was Silistra, where his troops had killed 6,840 people, Turks and Bulgarians; in 1594 the Valachians crossed the frozen Danube and plundered Silistra; in 1595 Michael the Brave burned the town and destroyed the castle; in the war of 1768-1774 the Russians attacked Silistra (they destroyed a number of towns in the northeastern part of the Empire, but of the towns in today's Bulgarian territory only Hacioğlu Pazarcik [Dobric/Tolbuhin] was capture and razed); the Russo-Turkish War of 1787-1792 again brought destruction in

---

[71]Ibid., p. 52

Silestra; in the war of 1806-1812 the town was taken and mostly destroyed and the fortress works were blown up by Kutuzov; in the war of 1828/29 the half-rebuilt town was captured after a long seige and bombardment and was again destroyed; and during the Crimean War Silestra suffered enormous damage, although it held out valiantly and was not captured.

The same sort of periodic destruction occurred in most of the Danube frontier towns. In the 1806-1812 war Kutuzov ordered the entire population of the great city of Rusçuk to evacuate within three days, after which he blew up the castle and other fortifications; the city was turned to rubble by the ensuing fires.[72] During the war of 1828/29 the important Black Sea town of Varna was captured after a protracted siege by Tsar Nicolas I.[73] Before the Russians retreated in 1830, after the Treaty of Adrianople (1829), they blew up all the fortifications of Varna, and much of the town suffered heavily. The same was done to the town walls of Mesembria, which dated from the Greco-Roman times; their ruins, washed by the waves of the Black Sea, can still be seen as the explosions left them. Svištov/Ziştova was destroyed in 1462, 1595, and again in 1811. Vidin, on the upper end of the Danube, was destroyed in 1444, 1502, and 1689; it suffered heavily from months of bombardment in 1828/29, 1853/54 and, last, in 1877/78, when it held out until the very end, capitulating only after the Treaty of San Stefano, marking the end of Ottoman control over Bulgaria, was signed. After each of these wars the Ottomans immediately set out to rebuild and modernize the destroyed fortifications, and these works were perhaps the most important pieces of a Turkish architecture in Danubian Bulgaria, being both characteristic of the troubled history of the area and illustrative of the place of Turkish architecture in the district. (See Plate 24.)

Western and Southwestern Bulgaria

The last part of Bulgaria we discuss briefly is the west and southwest of the country. In contrast to Danubia or Thrace, this is a particularly mountainous area in which there are only a few plateaus of importance, surrounded by mountains and sealed off from each other. Through this area ran two very important roads: the Istanbul-Belgrade highway and the road from Thrace to Macedonia and Albania; the latter branched off from the Belgrad highway west of Tatar Pazarcık and passed through Samokov, Dupnitsa, and the sancak capital of Köstendil to the important Turkish center of Üsküp/Skopje. (See Plate 25.) The focal point of the district was Sofia, from which another important road led down along the river Struma to Selanik/Thessaloniki. During the greater part of the Ottoman period this part of the country was divided in two sancaks, Sofia and Küstendil. The Sofia area and the town were taken by the Ottomans

---

[72]For the fate of the Rusçuk fortifications and Kutuzov's actions, as well as his destruction of a number of other old Bulgarian castles, see the work of Aleksander Kuzev, "Prinos kăm istorijata na srednovekovnite kreposti po dolnaja Dunav," *Izvestija na Narodenija Muzej Varna* 2 (1966), 3 and 5 (1969); this article gives references to Russian sources inaccessible to me.

[73]This siege is described in detail by the famous Prussian commander, Helmut von Moltke, *Der russisch-Türkische Feldzug in der europäischen Türkei, 1828-1829, dargestellt im Jahre 1845*, 2d. ed. (Berlin, 1877).

around 1385, the town, which had been one of the principal towns of Tsar Ivan Şişman, allegedly falling through a surprise attack. It was added to the Paşa Livası, but in the administration scheme some sort of separate status was given to Sofia. The Sofia distict included the minor towns of Samokov, Berkovitsa/Berkofçe, and Sehirköy/Pirot. The last became a part of Serbia after 1878, of Yugoslavia after 1918. The western half of the Küstendil Sancak also belongs today to Yugoslavia. This district was composed of the former principality of Velbužd, established by Konstantin Dejanović, a Serbian nobleman who set up his own rule after the death of the Serbian Tsar Dushan (1355). Konstantin was an Ottoman vassal from 1371 on and served his suzereign until his death on the battlefield of Rovine in 1395.[74] After that his principality was incorporated into the Empire without major disturbance.[75] Both of these districts were very Bulgarian and relatively well inhabited.

Although some minor urban settlement developed throughout these districts in the course of time, each was dominated by its main town. In each, groups of Turkish adminisitrators and military men came to settle, followed soon by craftsmen. On the plateaus of Sofia and Küstendil small groups of Turks settled, at what date is not known exactly. Perhaps we may conclude that they came shortly after the conquest, or partly as an overflow of the settlers in the western part of the Thracian plain (the deportation of Turkish nomads from Saruhan under the son of Yılderım Bayezid took place shortly before 1400). The oldest registration of the population of Sofia district of which something is preserved is one which very probably took place under Mehmed II's brief first rule (1444-45). This is a fragment of an İcmal Defter dating from 1445 at the latest, preserved in Sofia.[76] In this fragment we find an enumeration of 90 villages, 5 of which had Turkish names and were inhabited by Muslims.

The first complete registration, a detailed one, is T.D. 130 in the BBA, Istanbul, dated 930 (1524/25). It describes 186 villages in the Sofia district, among them the 5 villages mentioned in the earlier fragment. The total number of Muslim-Turkish villages mentioned was 16. The BBA register T.D. 236 from 951 (1544-45) lists 211 villages in the area, while the register KuK 61 in Ankara, dating from about 1585, lists 212 villages. The number of Muslim villages mentioned in each of these was the same (16) as in the 1524/25 register. Among them were places with very specifically Turkish names, such as Ak Danişmend, Kırk Poladlü, Deli Ahmedlü, Mansur, and Ormanlü; these were exclusively Muslim and numbered almost no converts among their inhabitants. Besides these few Turkish villages, there were 10 villages with Bulgarian names, inhabited by Christians but with a few Muslims living among them. One village had a Muslim population and a Turkish name but had a considerable group of Bulgarian Christian inhabitants. The population in this highland plain grew very slowly. In 1524 there were 7,091 Christian households and 490 Muslim households; in

---

[74]See Jireček, *Fürstenthum*, pp. 470-75. On the reliability of the princes of Vidin and Köstendil, see also A. Kuzev, "Die Beziehungen des Königs von Vidin, Ivan Sratsimir zu den osmanischen Herrscher," *Etudes Balkaniques* 7, no. 3 (1971):121-24.

[75]Constantin Jireček, *Geschichte der Serben* (Gotha, 1911), vol. 2, p. 102. Many details also are to be found in the still useful work of Jordan Ivanov, *Severna Makedonia* (Sofia, 1906), ch. 4.

[76]National Library Cyril and Methodius, Oriental Department, D. 707, 1/1959 published in *Turski Izvori*, vol. 2, pp. 8-51; it includes a list of 50 *timars*, describing 123 villages.

1585 the Muslim households had doubled to 1,012 and Christians had gone up to 7,562. In both cases the rate of growth is low, but the Muslims increased more quickly.

SOFIA. If we now turn to the town of Sofia, we see that its population grew at a much higher rate than the villages and that the number of Christian households expanded vigorously after an initial setback. The following table shows the development of Sofia in the sixteenth century.

Year of Register	Muslim households	Christian households	Jewish households	Total households
1524/25	848	280	------------	1128
1544/45	1146	168	88	1402
1570/71	1276	323	208	1801

The history of early Ottoman Sofia is very obscure. The fact that the Christian community kept its old churches seems to confirm the story that it surrendered instead of being taken by storm. What happened during the troubled period of the civil war among the sons of Bayezid is not known. In 1433 the Burgundian knight Bertrandon de la Broquière passed through the plain of Sofia and the town, remarking that the plain was well inhabited, strewn with Bulgarian villages with very few Turks among them. The town was also predominantly Bulgarian, although with walls torn down. The Bulgarian population was at that time fostering anti-Ottoman sentiments.[77] The chance to act against the Ottomans came during the "Long Campaign" of King Vladislav of Poland-Hungary in 1443, when the local Bulgarians joined the crusader army. However, the crusade ended in failure, and the army fell back on Sofia; but when the king saw that he could not winter his army there, he ordered that the town be burned, as is related by the "Serbian Janissary."[78] After this event a new start had to be made. It seems that by their revolt the Christians had forfeited their right to continue in possession of their churches. The largest of these, the early-Christian basilica of St. Sophia, to which the city owes its name, was confiscated. It also appears that this led to a thorough shake up of the town's population. Crucial was the transfer of the seat of the beylerbey of Rumeli from Filibe/Plovdiv to Sofia. This is clearly connected to the events of 1443/44. Between 1420 and 1444 some of the largest Ottoman buildings of the Balkans had been erected in Filibe, by Sultan Murad II and Beylerbey Şihabuddin Paşa. The latter's huge Imaret Camii was finished in the year of the crusade. Then building activity suddenly moved to Sofia, with the erection of Büyük Cami—the Great Mosque (still standing in

---

[77]*Voyage d'Outremer*, pp. 201-203.

[78]I used the excellent German translation and commentary on this work by Renate Lachmann, *Memoiren eines Janitscharen oder Türkische Chronik*, Slavische Geschichtschreiber, no. 8 (Graz, Vienna and Cologne, 1975), p. 91.

the center of town just outside the demolished walls on the old road to Istanbul) by Mahmud Paşa, who succeeded Şihabuddin as beylerbey.[79] The construction of the mosque marks the new function of the town. Hordes of administrators and army personnel, with their retainers and auxiliaries, appeared. This created new job opportunities for craftsmen, who soon moved in from the hinterland. The subsequent Ottoman registers show a great number of all kinds of craftsmen among the Sofiot Muslim population.

The year 1444 thus appears to have been for Sofia the breakpoint in its development, after which it was rebuilt as a Turkish town with the help and encouragement of the highest Ottoman government officials. Thus it provides an example of Barkan-thesis town development. As, however, the villages of the plain and, even more so, of the mountains remained well inhabited, there was no room for Turkish colonization on a scale comparable with that in Thrace. Thus the small Sofiot Christian community could easily be reinforced by Christians coming in from the district around it. The Muslim population, on the other hand, seems to have grown largely by natural increase, at a rate of less than 1 percent per year between 1544 and 1571, which is slightly below the normal rate for the century. In the same years the Sofiot Christian population grew at a rate of 2.5 percent annually, which is indeed beyond all bounds and must have been the result of immigration from the villages to the town. As no great upheavals took place in the subsequent history of the town, we may perhaps assume that this trend continued.

The Ottoman yearbooks of the 1860s and 1870s make it clear that the majority of the population of Sofia was non-Muslim. The 1585 register seems to mark the highest point of the numerical expansion of the Muslim Turkish element, then 12 percent of the total rural population. The 1873/74 Sālnāme gives 2,883 Muslim households and 11,961 Christian households as the totals for the entire district. If we subtract from these the 1,369 Muslim and 1,737 Christian (and Jewish) households of the town, we arrive at a rural population that was again 12 percent Muslim. Thus, although the 1874 borders of the Sofia district were not exactly the same as in 1585 (containing only 163 villages to the 212 of 1585), the figures indicate that no major change in the Christian-Muslim ratio had taken place over the years.

Because of its function as the capital city of Rumeli and the seat of a vast administrative apparatus, Sofia received the attention of all branches of government. Beylerbeys, *defters*, (registrars), *kadis*, (judges), *katips* (secretaries), etc., assisted by merchants and craftsmen, filled the expanding town with a number of outstanding buildings. In 1506 Beylerbey Yahya Paşa, later vizier and son-in-law of Sultan Bayezid II, erected there the largest *bedesten* in the Balkans, as well as a famous mineral bath.[80]

---

[79]Mahmud served until 1456, when he became grand vizier. The construction of the Great Mosque has thus to be dated between 1444 and 1456; for the period when Mahmud Paşa was in charge, see Halil İnalcik, "Mehmed the Conqueror and His Time," in *Speculum, Journal of Mediaeval History* 25 (1960): 415.

[80]Both these buildings are mentioned in Yahya's *vakıifname*, dated 3 Receb 912/ 19 November 1506, published by Gliša Elezović in his *Turski Spomenici*, Knj. 1, sveska 1, Zbornik za Istočnjačku Istoriku i Književnu Gradje, vol. 1 (Belgrade 1940), pp. 420-524, esp. pp. 437, 439; this is the Serbo-Croat translation of the original, which was published by Elezovic in the second volume of the Zbornik.

The enormous *bedesten* had 44 shops inside its domed hall and 101 shops on the outside around it. The German traveler Hans Dernschwam, usually not very enthusiastic about what he saw in the Turkish Empire, compared the dome of the mineral bath with that of the famous Pantheon in Rome.[81] According to the foundation deed of trust of Yahya Paşa, the revenue of the market hall and the bath was tied to the beautiful buildings this man had erected is Üsküp/Skopje in Macedonia. These consisted of a mosque, a *medrese*, an *imaret*, etc. The deed reveals that Yahya also bought a great caravanserai in Sofia and added it to his foundation in Üsküp. He was responsible, in addition, for the construction of a large caravanserai in Nikopol and a *hamam* in Loveč. The bath still exists. All other buildings of Yahya in Bulgaria, including the fortress-like *bedesten*, were demolished at the turn of this century. The size of the *bedesten* alone is enough to tell us that after 1444 Sofia had developed from a military and administrative center into a trading metropolis. Another highlight of its urban development was the construction of the compound (*külliye*) of Sofu Mehmed Paşa. This *külliye* was designed by the great architect Mimar Sinan and was comprised of a monumental single-dome mosque—the dome being one of the largest ever erected in the Balkans—a *medrese* with 16 domed rooms for students, a library, a *hamam*, a caravanserai, a *mekteb*, a kitchen for the poor, fountains, washing basins, etc.[82] Of all these buildings nothing but the mutilated body of the great mosque is still standing today; it was transformed into a church between 1901 and 1903. The great *medrese* survived until 1928, then serving as a prison. Some accounts of travelers still give us an impression of the disappeared magnificence of this complex.[83] In 1587 Reinhold Lubenau wrote:

> In the evening we came to the beautiful, large and very ancient city of Sophia, in which we lodged in a fine new caravanserai, built of large blocks of stone and with finely cut pillars, covered over and over with lead. Opposite stands a very beautiful mosque, built in the style of Christian churches, in which there are Turkish monks.... The aforementioned caravanserai was built by a certain Mehmed Bassa... and every stranger in the caravanserai is given free food, such as boiled mutton, boiled rice in Czorba, a soup, and a portion of bread, and they brought each of us his share.[84]

In 1680 the Italian doctor Antonio Benetti noted:

> Mehmet Pasha of Rumelia constructed in this city a hospital or college for the benefit of the poor, sick people and as a seminary for students of law and the Mohammedan religion, and a good income is

---

[81]*Tagebuch einer Reise nach Konstantinopel und Kleinasien* (1553/55), ed. Franz Babinger (Munich, 1923), p. 15.

[82]These buildings are mentioned in lists of Sinan's works compiled by his friend Mustafa Sa'i; see Rıfki Melûl Meriç, *Mimar Sinan, Hayatı, Eseri,* (Ankara, 1965), pp. 25, 84. For Sinan's Sofia buildings, see also Ismail Eren, "Mimar Sinan'ın bilinmiyen Eseri," *Belgelerle Türk Tarihi Dergisi* 8 (1968): 66-70.

[83]See the detailed work of A. Iširkov, *Grad Sofija prez XVII vek* (Sofia, 1912), which contains, in Bulgarian translation, the bulk of the vast number of travelers' descriptions of Sofia.

[84]*Beschreibung der Reisen des Reinhold Lubenau*, ed. W. Sahm, Mitteilungen aus der Stadtbibliothek zu Königsberg i. Preussen no. 4 (Königsberg, 1912), pp. 107-108.

donated to it.... Next to this structure is its mosque, with a light architecture, with architraves of stone in the Roman fashion and a dome on top and around, firmly mounted on a circle, which is inserted in the quadrangle of the mosque. We lodged in a khan, marvelously built, divided into two apartments, all covered with lead, and a grand court with a beautiful fountain in the center.[85]

The registers of 1544 and 1571 also show us the rapid development of Sofia as a Turkish city. Both registers contain a synoptic page giving the numbers of the most important buildings in the town, which were as follows: in 1544, 4 mosques, 31 *mescids*, 3 *zaviyes*, 4 *hamams*, 3 caravanserais, and 1 *bedesten*; in 1571, 10 mosques, 34 *mescids*, 4 *zaviyes*, 7 *hamams*, caravanserais, and 1 *bedesten*.

A large number of Turkish writers, poets, and spiritual leaders were born in Ottoman Sofia or worked there for long periods, making the city one of the most important centers of Turkish culture in Europe. Ahmed Hādı, poet, was born in Sofia. Abdi Efendi worked and died there. Seyfi Efendi was for many years judge of the city and constructed there the monumental Banjabaşi Mosque, a work of the school of Sinan, which survives until today. Hekimzāde Subhi, son of Vizier Sinan, was likewise judge of this city and died there.[86] The greatest sixteenth-century figure is doubtless Sofiāvi Bali Efendi, a Halveti sheikh and poet who carried the Path of Seclusion (Ṭarīkatü-l Halvetiyye) to western Bulgaria and Macedonia, where his name is still remembered. Bali Efendi died in 960 (1553) in the city where he had worked so long and was buried outside it, on the slope of Mount Vitosha. A magnificent mausoleum was erected over his grave, becoming a place of pilgrimage; around it the Sofiot suburb Bali Efendi, today known as Knjaževo, sprang up.[87] Great figures from the seventeenth century were Ibrahim Efendi, scholar and judge, born in Sofia and buried there in 1669, and Parsa Mehmed Efendi, a native of Gallipoli, who wrote studies on law and translated Persian poetry and was a poet himself.[88] Another native of Sofia was Sofiavi Vahid Mehmed Çelebi, a forceful poet who died in 1094 (1683) in Bursa an was buried in the Pınarbaşı cemetery, where so many other great Ottomans were laid to rest.[89]

Ottoman Sofia, the metropolis of the Balkans, the importance and beauty of which is so well documented by the many travelers who passed through it, declined in

---

[85] Benetti's work, *Observationi fatte dal fu Dottor A.B....* was published in Venice in 1687, but the excerpt here is translated from the Bulgarian; see n.83.

[86] Joseph von Hammer, *Geschichte der Osmanischen Dichtkunst* (Pesth, 1836-1838), vol. 2, pp. 562 (on Hadi), 268 (on Abdi Efendi), 440 (on Seyfi Efendi), and 255 (on Suhbi). Abdi Efendi, the brother of Kaziasker Abdurrahman Çelebi and son-in-law of Grand Vizier Piri Mehmed Paşa, served as *kadi* in Serres and Üsküp in Macedonia before going to Sofia. Seyfi Efendi is mentioned as a poet and founder of the mosque in Sofia, where he was buried, by the two well-known sixteenth century biographers of poets, Aşık Çelebi and Kınalızāde Hasan Çelebi; see *Tezkiretü's-Su'ara,* ed. Ibrahim Kutluk (Ankara, 1978), vol. 1, pp. 497-98. Today's miniscule Turkish community in Sofia still carries the memory of Kadi Seyfuddin Efendi as the builder of the mosque.

[87] For details on the life of Bali Efendi, see, for example, H. J. Kissling, "Aus der Geschichte der Chalwetijje Ordens," *Der Islam* 28 (1953): 233-89; see also Bursalı Mehmed Tâhir Efendi, *Osmanlı Müellifleri,* in modern Turkish version by A. Fikri Yavuz and Ismail Özen (Istanbul, n.d.), vol. 1, p. 59.

[88] Hammer, *G.O.D.* vol. 3, pp. 484-85 (on Ibrahim Efendi), 523 (on Parsa Mehmed Efendi)..

[89] Mehmed Tâhir, *Osmanlı Müellifleri,* vol. 2, p. 427.

the nineteenth century. A terrible earthquake in 1818 destroyed many houses and mosques. In the war of 1828/29 the Russian army under General Geismar occupied the city for some days, which made a deep impression on its inhabitants. The Muslims started to emigrate to safer places. In 1832 Sofia was occupied and plundered by the combined forces of the rebellious paşa of Skutari, Mustafa Bushatli, and Ali Bey, son of Kara Feyz, the robber baron of Breznik. Soon afterwards the newly independent principality of Serbia erected a high tariff wall at the border near Alexinax and blocked Sofia's most important trade route, greatly contributing to the decay of the town. In 1836 the seat of the beylerbey of Rumeli was removed from the rapidly declining Sofia to Bitola in Macedonia, a city full of expansionist energy. Ami Boué, visiting Sofia in 1837, called it the most ruined city of the Ottoman empire and added:

> Its mosques and its twenty-two minarets announce a large population; nevertheless, this city hardly counts 5,000 houses or 20,000 to 22,000 inhabitants, the majority of whom are Bulgarians.[90]

The worst was still to come. In the autumn of 1858 a whole series of earthquakes, lasting two weeks, with thirty to fifty shocks daily, shook the city. Most of the houses were destroyed, as were the mosques and caravanserais. Nearly all minarets collapsed. The ancient monuments were beyond repair. There was some recovery in the city under the energetic rule of Rasin Paşa and Esad Paşa: new industries were set up, new boulevards were driven through the crooked old street pattern; a railway also was constructed to link Sofia with Filibe and the Ottoman capital and continue westward to Üsküp/Skopje, and the minarets were rebuilt.[91] The Bulgarian April Uprising of 1876 put an end to all this activity, but in the last decade of Ottoman rule there were still 44 mosques, 4 *medreses*, and no less than 18 *tekkes* in Sofia.[92]

In the Russo-Turkish war of 1877/78, the Russian army occupied Sofia. The Muslim population had fled to Macedonia immediately before the Russians entered and did not return after the war. The Russian soldiers used the wood of the abandoned Turkish houses for firewood in the extreme winter temperature then prevailing, and during the rains of the following spring these houses were reduced to piles of melting mud brick.[93] The great sixteenth-century Ottoman buildings had already been ruined by the earthquakes. In the years after 1878, when Sofia was proclaimed capital of the new Bulgarian state, the city was rebuilt on a totally different plan, as a modern city in which there was no room for relics of a past now regarded as undesirable. The "minaret forest", which had impressed the Russians in 1877, was dismantled or simply blown up with dynamite. All Ottoman buildings were demolished as soon as they could be dispensed with, even buildings that in their ruined state still impressed the visitors by their enormous size and strength. The ruthless destruction went on for decades. Protests

---

[90]*Recueil d'itinéraires dans la Turquie d'Europe* (Vienna, 1854), vol. 1, pp. 65-66.

[91]Reported by the otherwise anti-Turkish Felix Kanitz, who seems to have been impressed by all the work being done; see "Vilayetstadt Sofia," in *Österreichische Monatschrift für den Orient* 11 (1876).

[92]Komrumpf, *Territorialverwaltung*, pp. 335-36.

[93]Jireček, *Fürstenthum*, p. 369. Jireček heard the story directly from eyewitnesses a few years after the events.

of some Bulgarian intellectuals, urging the government to spare at least the most important Ottoman works, were ignored. At present Sofia is a city of a million population. Those ancient buildings—two early-Christian churches and three mosques—that escaped the wave of destruction lost all connection with their original architectural environment, which is now unrecognizable.

The case of Sofia is typical of the fate of the Turkish towns in Bulgaria and their monuments of architecture. For this reason we have devoted a bit more space to and provided a few more details on this particular place. The rest of the story is quickly told. Western Bulgaria had a few more towns, but none of the size and importance of Sofia, although there are two that are worth some discussion.

KÜSTENDIL. This was the capital of the sancak of the same name, which is the corruption of the Ottoman-Bulgarian Kostandil-ili, "The Land of Konstantin" (the last Christian ruler of the land in the pre-Ottoman times). In the troubled years of the Ottoman civil war, or at the ascension of Murad II (1421), the town must have suffered a similar fate to Sofia's, being destroyed and its population dispersed. There are only very vague local memories about a Bulgarian revolt in those years and that the town had to be retaken.[94] Küstendil is another example of a wholly re-created town of the Barkanthesis type. The cramped medieval fortress town high on Hisarlık hill was given up for an open settlement at the foot of the hill along the important Istanbul-Filibe-Üsküp/Skopje road and near a number of mineral springs where, in Roman times, the city of Pautalia had been situated. At this new site the oldest Ottoman structure still standing very probably dates from the time of Murad II. The oldest preserved Ottoman register containing reliable information on the new town is one dating from 1519 (detailed register Maliyeden Müdevver no. 170 preserved in Istanbul). It lists a civilian Muslim population of 293 households and a Christian population of 47 households. The bulk of the Muslims must have been Turkish colonists, the number of converts being only 45, or 15 percent. The register KuK. 85 gives us a picture of the situation in 1573: at that date the number of Muslim households had gone up to 623; of Christians, to 84. Thus population had doubled. While the 1519 register mentions the existence of one Friday Mosque, 7 *mescids*, 2 *hamams*, 1 mineral bath (*ılıca*), 2 *imarets*, a *tekke*, and a school (*muallimhane*), the 1573 register lists more than double the number of *mescids*—16. The numbers of the *imams* and *müezzins* as given in the two registers also demonstrates the rapid expansion of Islamic institutions in this town: in 1519 there were 7 *imams* and 8 *müezzins;* in 1573, the figures had risen to 17 *imams* and 15 *müezzins*. Also in 1573 a monumental mosque was added to the roster of places of prayer already existing: this was the Mosque of Ahmed Beg, the sancak beg of Küstendil. This mosque survives to the present, serving as the Archaeological Museum of the town. (See Plate 27.) Another monumental building, which has *not* survived, was

---

[94]For this little known story and many other details on ancient Küstendil, see the rich article of Jordan Ivanov," Kjustendilskijat Hisarlik i negovite starine," *Izvestija na Bălgarskoto Arheologičeski Družetvo* 7 (1919-1920): 66-123; see also idem., *Severna Makedonija*, ch. 4: "Posleden Velbuždski Voyvoda Iusuf i padanije na knjažestvoto prez XV v."
Maliyeden Müdevver No. 170, fol. 557v in the BBA, Istanbul; a facsimile, translation, and transcription of this was provided in my "Art and Society in Bulgaria," pp. 68, 354.

the *mescid* of Hoca Dundar, dating from the second half of the fifteenth century; old photographs show it to have been a huge domed edifice, the chief structure of a separate *mahalle* in Küstendil.

The Ottomans also cared for the mineral springs. They captured the sources and covered them over with separate disrobing rooms and domed bath houses with their own swimming pool of mineral water. Mehmed-i Aşık, in his geographical work *Menâzırü'l-Avâlım*, noted in 997 (1589) twelve mineral baths in Küstendil, all with stone-built domes over their disrobing section and over the bath room proper, some even with separate rooms. The most beautiful was the so-called Beg Ilıcası, the name suggesting that it was the work of a sancak beg.[95] One of these twelve baths, the so-called Dervish Banja still survives. (See Plate 28.)

No detailed overview of the population of the sancak of Küstendil can yet be given, as the research into the Ottoman *defters* has not advanced far enough. The 1519 register has a summary table showing that the total population—in 5 cities, 3 towns, and 1,508 villages—was 7,504 households. The military, the para-military, and the civilian Muslim population came to 5,758; the Christians, among whom was a large group with military status (Voynuk), totaled 53,571. Thus, just under 10 percent of the population was Muslim, and half of them were military or para-military, among whom were 300 Yürük auxiliaries.[96] Modern Macedonian research shows that in the first decades of the reign of Sultan Süleyman (1520-1566) important groups of Yürük colonists came to settle in the half of the sancak of Küstendil that today belongs to Yugoslavia and has turned to agriculture.[97] There is little reason to think that just across the present border, in the Bulgarian half of sancak of Küstendil, the process was different.

In 1071 (1660/61) Evliya Çelebi visited Küstendil and left a detailed description of the town. It seems the rapid development of the sixteenth century had come to a standstill. The heavy earthquakes of 1585 and 1641 had done the town no good, but as a whole the town seems to have suffered mainly from the general malaise of the seventeenth century. Evliya mentions 11 *mahalles* with 1,100 houses—a number which seems reasonable. He made some important notes on the mosques of the town and noted also the presence of 3 *medreses*, 5 *tekkes*, 6 schools, and 12 mineral baths "with lofty vaults and many basins."[98] On the wall of the Ahmed Bey Mosque we still can read the signature of this famous traveler, below a line of poetry he wrote.

The yearbooks of Danube Vilayet give us a picture of the Küstendil in the last years of the Ottoman period. The Sālnāme of 1285 (1868/69) mentions 16 mosques, 3 *medreses*, and 16 *tekkes* of various dervish orders. Turkish Islamic spiritual life was, then, well developed in this faraway outpost. The 1873/74 Sālnāme lists only 768 Muslim households and 570 households of non-Muslims. In spite of the slow and

---

[95] I used the manuscript Halet Efendi No. 616, I. fol. 212ᵃ preserved in the Süleymaniye Library, Istanbul.

[96] A facsimile, translation, and transcription of this summary table is provided in my "Art and Society," pp. 68 and 354.

[97] For details, see M. Sokoloski, "Kumanovo i Kumanovsko vo tekot na XVI vek," in *Makedonska Akademija na Naukite i Umetnostite, Prilozi* 7, no. 2 (1976): 57-81.

[98] *Seyyahatname*, Üçdal ed., vol. 6, pp. 1823-25.

steady influx of Bulgarian settlers the town was thus still 57 percent Turkish place (in 1573 it had been 88 percent!). In the 173 villages of the kaza of Küstendil were 8,049 households, of which 1,529, or 19 percent, were Muslim. If we compare this with the figures for the much larger sancak of Küstendil of 1519, of which the kaza was the central seat, we see no fundamental change. After the Turkish settlers had come to the newly founded town and the villages, and after being reinforced by an influx of Yürüks in the sixteenth century, the colonists multiplied themselves and perhaps assimilated a small group of locals but remained essentially the same. They left when Bulgaria became an independent state. In 1891 Küstendil counted 10,689 inhabitants, of which only 581 were Turks (5 percent).[99]

The Bulgarian half of the old Küstendil Sancak had some more towns of importance—Petrič, Melnik, Nevrokop (today Goče Delčev) and Dupnitsa (today Stanke Dimitrov). The first three are situated near the southern border of the country, where Bulgaria proper shades off into Macedonia. Melnik was a wholly Greek-speaking "island" in this area. In the Nevrokop district there were, or, better, there *are* numerous Pomaks; but concerning their conversion and their subsequent history very little is known.[100]

DUPNITSA. Dupnitsa is another example of a town emerging almost spontaneously at a point where the Filibe-Küstendil-Üsküp road crosses the Struma and the Bistritsa brook joins the main river. A wooden bridge was first built there, it being replaced in the seventeenth century by a mighty stone bridge. A *hamam* and a prominent mosque were built near this bridge, and the town developed around this nucleus. In a fragment of a detailed register of the Sofia-Samokov area from 1452-55, preserved in the National Library of Sofia, we find the remark that some imhabitants of the village of Kliselü originally came from "the village of Dupnitsa."[101] The oldest mention of Dupnitsa as a town is apparently that in the travel account by the Rhenish kinght Arnold van Harff,

---

[99]Jireček, *Fürstenthum*, pp. 470-72.

[100]Figures for the Muslim and Christian households of the towns of Nevrokop, Melnik, and Petrič, taken from the Ottoman registers dating from the fifteenth and sixteenth centuries, are given by Metodija Sokoloski, in "Le dévelopment de quelques villes dans le sud de Balkans au XVe et XVIe siècles," *Balkanica* 1 (1970), pp. 81-106, M. Sokoloski, "Nevrokop i Nevrokopsko vo XVI Vek," *Prilozi*, II, Makedonska Akademija Naukite i Umetnosti, Skopje 1975, pp. 5-30 and by Aleksandar Stojanovski, *Gradovite na Makedonija od krajot na XIV do XVII vek* (Skopje, 1981), esp. pp. 66-72 (tables). Lists of the head tax households in 29 villages of the district of Nevrokop for the years 1615, 1635, and 1660 are given in the study by Dimitrov, "Demografski otnošenija," p. 104; these show a sharp decline in the number of such households, which Dimitrov explains as clear sign of the islamization of the district. As the Muslims did not pay the head tax, they do not appear in *ciziye defters*, and Christian villagers who converted to Islam could thus have disappeared from the record. However, in other parts of the Balkans, where hardly any Muslims lived, the head tax records of the seventeenth century also show a marked decline in number of households. Whether this might reflect a different way of registration of these households (more people per tax unit?) is difficult to say. In any event, the whole seventeenth century stands out as a period of declining populations everywhere in Europe, including the Ottoman dominions. Thus, at least a part of Dimitrov's "converts" must have dropped out of the source simply through natural decline in numbers.

[101]See *Turski Izvori*, vol. 2, p. 73.

who saw it in 1499 and called it "Tobinitsa, a fine town."[102] The detailed register (T.D. No. 170) from 1519 mentions it as the center of a *nahiye,* with one group of 42 Muslim households clustered around its mosque and with 141 Christian households also—together perhaps 1,000 inhabitants. Of the Muslims, 24 percent were recent converts to Islam, a not unusual percentage in an area where Turkish settlers were rare. The 1573 register (KuK. No. 85) shows us a relatively rapid development, especially in the number of Muslims: instead of one community of Muslims there were in that year 4 Muslim *mahalles,* with the Friday Mosque of Ahmed Beg and *mescids* of Mehmed Çelebi, Dizdar Hasan, and Turhan Çelebi. The number of Muslim households had gone up to 141, of which only 16 percent were converts, indicating that the process of assimilation of local elements had passed its peak. The town was further developed as a Muslim Turkish place, a road station and centre of local crafts. The register mentions a school teacher as being one of the Muslim inhabitants. Most probably Ahmed Beg had provided for the construction of the school as well as the mosque. As for the Christian population, the 1573 register shows that this had increased slightly to 160 households. An account by the geographer Mehmed-i Aşik, who lived in Dupnitsa in 998 (1589/90) describes it as "a small town without walls, with a modest market place, a Friday mosque, and bath. In the days when I was there a wealthy man was about to build another bath there."[103] Thus we find Dupnitsa on its way to transforming itself from a well-situated village into a real urban Muslim center. The bath and marketplace were probably also provided by Ahmed Beg as the prerequisites for promotion to the rank of town.

The mosque of Ahmed Bey still exists. It must have been rebuilt in the seventeenth century, in a curious variant of provincial Ottoman architecture, showing local building methods. The minaret, left over from the older building, had an orientation slightly different from the main structure, a trait to be seen in many fourteenth- or fifteenth-century Ottoman mosques. When the building was reconstructed the direction of its orientation (toward Mecca) had been corrected.

In 1828 the traveler J. Hütz described the town as having 6,000 inhabitants, who lived especially from mining and iron work, with one mosque and many Greek churches and a *hamam.*[104] Hütz certainly must have meant one *great* mosque, for in 1836 Ami Boué noted that the town had "many small mosques."[105] In 1867 the local historian Biserov mentions 1,432 houses, 11 mosques, 494 shops, 3 *hamams,* 2 *imaret-medreses,* 7 schools, 9 *tekkes* and *türbes,* 2 churches, and 1 synagogue.[106] All in all Dupnitsa was a typical example of a Turkish Balkan town! As to its population trend, we see there a different tendency from Küstendil, where the Muslim population had held its ground against the mounting Bulgarian demographic pressure. In 1828 the 6,000 inhabitants of Dupnitsa were divided into two groups of equal size, but when the area was incorporated into the new Bulgarian state, the Turkish population fled to Macedonia. When Jireček

[102]*The Pilgrimage of Arnold van Harff,* Eng. tr. Malcolm Letts (London, 1949), p. 247.

[103]Codex Halet Efendi, No. 616, vol. II, fol. 22^r.

[104]*Beschreibung der europäische Türkei* (Munich, 1828), pp. 250-51.

[105]*Recueil d'itinéraires,* p. 291

[106]For Biserov's comments, see Ivanov, *Severna Makedonija,* pp. 188-89.

visited there in 1890 only 85 Turks were still living there.[107] The void left by the departure of the Turks was soon filled with Bulgarians from the mountain villages, where Islam had never taken root. (In the 1873/74 Sālnāme of the Danube Province there were listed 70 villages in the kaza of Dupnitsa, with 20,314 inhabitants, of which only 766, or 4 percent, were Muslim.,

The Turkish buildings disappeared along with the Turks. Only the great domed mosque of Ahmed Beg, which began the urban development of Dupnitsa, remained standing, used for various purposes. It was saved in the 1970s, when it was carefully restored by the Bulgarian Institute for Monuments of Culture, and it now serves as an art gallery.

The fate of the Turkish buildings throughout western Bulgaria is typified by what happened in Sofia, Küstendil, and Dupnitsa. In that area the Muslims largely disappeared and their buildings became relics and rare; thus, in the west there is a slightly more positive attitude towards these buildings than in the east, where Turks are still present in large numbers. Immediately after 1878 the presence of masses of Turks in the east guaranteed the survival of at least the most important mosques because they were still used; and, in the pre-war period, the violent anti-religious policy did not exist. The now, despised Tsar Ferdinant is even said to have built a mosque at his own expense. In the last 30 years, in the areas where there were no rapidly expanding Turkish minorities to pose a threat to the established order, mosques could receive attention and could even be restored. When the great *bedesten* of Yambol was restored the results were highly valued by the local Bulgarian inhabitants. In places like Şumla/Shoumen, on the other hand, where there are sizeable Turkish minorities, efforts have been made to eradicate the stamp of Turkish Islam. Dozens of mosques—no less than seven all at once in 1984-85—have been demolished. Thus the existence of monuments of Turkish architecture is linked with the composition of the population even as it was in the past but in reverse: Such structures were mainly in areas with a large Turkish population (Thrace and eastern Danubia), with only a few in some selected towns elsewhere; but, paradoxically, they were better cared for in areas where no, or hardly any, Turk still lives today.

How Turkish was Ottoman-Turkish-Architecture?

The question of how "Turkish" Ottoman-Turkish architecture actually was is not easy to answer, mainly because of the insufficient progress in the study of the Turkish archives. In my opinion the problem is closely linked with the Turkishness of the population of the towns where the buildings came into being. It is common knowledge that architects and some leading master builders can be dispatched from the capital centers but that the bulk of the workmen have to be recruited locally. In various towns of Ottoman Bulgaria trained Muslim Turkish master builders and stonecutters were available during the centuries when the great Ottoman buildings were constructed. The published accounts of the greatest of all Ottoman architectural undertakings, the building of the Süleymaniye mosque and compound in Istanbul, may serve as guide in this

---

[107]*Fürstenthum*, pp. 484-86.

matter. In the paylists of this huge project, in progress from 1550 to 1557, we find for example: 5 stonecutters from Nikopol on the Danube and 4 stonecutters and 5 bricklayers from Sofia, all Muslim Turkish; 1 stonecutter from Silistra, 1 from Filibe, and 1 from Samokov, also all Muslim Turks; and two bricklayers from Küstendil. These are not many when compared with the numbers of those from some important Turkish centers in Macedonia, such as Selanik (9 stonecutters), Serres (11 stonecutters) or Skopje/Üsküp (12 stonecutters). The Christian Bulgarians, on the other hand, are very under-represented on the lists: we find only 3 Christian Sofiots as bricklayers and 2 stonecutters from the same city, not more.[108] A more detailed picture is presented by some of the day-to-day paylists of construction work in the provinces and in Bulgaria.

1) A paylist for the repair in 896 (1490/91) of the castle of Kilia in Moldavia (today in USSR), which provides an overview of a job of three months' duration and a cost of nearly half a million *akçe* (the *akçe* was a small silver coin, 50 to 60 of which made up a gold ducat), shows that 61 Muslim bricklayers came from the important Turkish center of Edirne; 6 from Eski Zağra (which then was wholly Turkish, it may be recalled); 11 Muslim and 2 Christian bricklayers from Filibe; and 1 from Sofia. In addition, Filibe dispatched 353 unskilled Muslim-Turkish daily jobbers (*ırgad*); Zağra Yenicesi, 25; Yambol, 103; and Eski Zağra, 72. The job was carried out under the supervision of Yakub Beg, the sancak beg of Cingene (near Aydos), and Kadı Husam of Kilia. The administration was done by the Emin Ramazan and his secretary Kemal, *katib* of the *sipahis*. The state architect was Mimar Yakub Shah, an Armenian.[109]

2) The summary account of the construction of a bridge over the Kozlu Dere near Tatar Pazarcık in the very heart of Bulgaria in 964 (1556/57) shows us how the work was organized and paid for. The money for this state project—25,279 *akçe*—came from the annual revenue of the state rice fields near Tatar Pazarcık, with a small sum from another state monopoly in Samokov, the mining town nearby. A total of 8,060 *akçe* was spent for the salaries of the carpenters; 3,004, for the unskilled workmen; and 1,291, for the smiths and iron workers. Materials, mostly wood, accounted for the remainder of the expenditure. The work was supervised by the *kadı* of Filibe, Mevlana Şemşeddin.[110]

3) Also in 1557/57 a new warehouse for timber was built at the harbour of Sizebolu/Sozopol in the kaza of Ahyolı/Ahtopol, now called Pomorie. Here the work was under supervision of Mevlana Tayyib, *kadı* of Ahyoli. The money for the project—15,660 *akçe* all—came from the state saltpans of Ahyolı, which were farmed to Demetrius Kantakuzinos. The sum of 3,270 *akçe* was used for stone, caulk, and tiles for the roof; 5,064, for wood; 1,942, for iron. The total of the salaries paid for the job was

---

[108]These key figures are given in the excerpts from the paylists made by Ö. L. Barkan in "Türk Yapı ve Yapı Malzemesi Tarihi için Kaynakları," *İktisat Fakültesi Mecmuası* 17, nos. 1-4 (1955): 3-26. For the complete publication of this material, see idem, *Süleymaniye Cami ve İmaret inşaatı*, 2 vols. (Ankara 1972, 1979). For a survey of architectural practices, based on the records, see J. M. Rogers, "The State and the Arts in Ottoman Turkey," *International Journal of Middle East Studies* 14 (1982): 71-86, 283-313.

[109]Barkan, *Süleymaniye*, vol. 2, pp. 225-56 (appendix).

[110]Unpublished register of accounts of state building projects in European Turkey, mid-sixteenth century, Maliyeden Müdevver no. 55, fol. 310ʳ-311ᵛ, Istanbul, BBA.

5,348 *akçe*, a third of the entire sum, the greater part of which went to the carpenters.[111] These accounts indicate that Muslim Turks undoubtedly had the supervision of work also at minor provincial building projects.

4) Two years before the bridge of Tatar Pazarcık and the store in Ahyolı were built, some important works of repair were carried out at the mosque of Sultan Mehmed Khan in Köstendil ("Nefs-i Ilica-i Küstendil" in the source). The work was under supervision of Mevlana Abdurrahman, *kadı* of Dupnitsa, and Ali, *emin* of the Voynuks of Küstendil. The sum reserved for the job was 20,000 *akçe*, payed by the *emin* from the tax of the Voynuks of the Küstendil and Dupnitsa districts, money which they were due to pay to the capital but which in this case, as in the cases previously cited, remained in the province to be used there. The work lasted from the middle of July until the middle of December 1555, and the accounts were settled two and one-half months later in Istanbul as follows: 12,346 *akçe* went for the building materials; 5,069 *akçe* was used to pay the workmen. For the salaries on this project there is a detailed, day-to-day account. Listed as master masons we find Murad, with a wage of 9 *akçe* daily; Mustafa, with 8; Nikola, with 8, Mehmed, with 9, Hasan, with 9; another Nikola, with 4; Dimitri, with 4; and Todor, with 4. As carpenters we find listed Hasan with 11 *akçe* per day in wages; Pervane, with 11; Mustafa, with 8; and Michail, with 7.[112] If we recall that in the sixteenth century many *imams* did not receive more than 3 or 4 *akçe* daily and that in 1553/55 one could buy 20 eggs or 4 loaves of bread for 1 *akçe*, a sheep for 22 to 24 *akçe*, and 2 kilograms of rice for 8 or 9 akçe, we can see that these masters were not badly paid.[113] It is notable that salaries were paid for the quality of the work done: the more skilled the master, the more he earned. The Süleymaniye paylists in particular give a mass of this kind of information. Muslim and Christian worked side by side on the scaffold and there was no discrimination as to religion; nor does the paylist of Küstendil stand alone for Bulgaria. Masses of similar material are still awaiting the attention of the diligent researcher. The little bit given here may serve as a pointer toward further work.

The bulk of the work at Ottoman building projects was indeed performed by Muslim Turks. The Süleymaniye paybooks give a great deal of the information needed to reach this conclusion, including the names of the masters, their patronyms, and the places they came from. In places where the population was largely Christian, it is logical to assume that Christians did most of the work. In some buildings preserved in Bulgaria we can even see this from the character of the masonry (your author was for long years a master mason himself), as is very evident in the great mosque of Dupnitsa: local Bulgarian techniques are visible, which accounts for the curiously un-Ottoman impression this building makes. In fact, throughout the Struma area there are still a multitude of churches built in the sixteenth century, testifying not only to the Ottoman tolerance of that time but also to the existence of a local building tradition, and in

---

[111]Ibid., fol. 211-212.

[112]Ibid., fol. 580-586.

[113]These current prices for foodstuffs at the market are given by Hans Dernschwam, who was himself a merchant and bookkeeper with a keen interest in prices, in *Tagebuch*, pp. 45, 46, 47, 48, 248, and 249. It should be noted that the workmen listed in the account did not work every day, a phenomenon also to be observed from other paylists.

Bulgaria it is believed by many that the great Ottoman buildings were actually constructed by Bulgarian masters and not by Turks; but the sixteenth century sources tells us otherwise. More of these kind of sources, also giving names of many Turkish architects not recorded elsewhere, are preserved in a research defeating mass in the Istanbul archives.

Only in the last phase of the Empire, especially in the nineteenth century, did Bulgarians really begin to do these jobs and provide the architects too. Master Kolyo Fičev constructed not only the magnificent bridges at Loveč and Bjala over the Yantra but also the Ottoman government building (*konak*), of Tărnovo, and others. The Bayraklı Cami of Samokov, lastly rebuilt in the 1830s on order of the Vizier Hüsrev Paşa of Samokov, was reconstructed by Bulgarian masters, designed and painted by them. When the plaster of these paintings was taken off during the restoration of the mosque, a number of signatures of these Bulgarian masters, scratched in the soft lime of the first layer, became visible.[114] The nineteenth century was very different from the fifteenth to the seventeenth as to building work as well as to the size of the families. Bulgaria was emerging from a long sleep, while the Turks were retreating on many fronts. Yet is is a gross mistake to project these nineteenth century realities into a past which was very different.[115]

The surviving monuments of Turkish architecture in Bulgaria are the symbols of the Ottoman policy of urbanization, of which they were the major instruments. This

---

[114]The restoration and study of this curious structure, looking more like some sort of rich house than an Ottoman mosque, is the pride of the Sofiot Institute of Monuments of Culture; see the monograph of Anna Roschkowska, *Die Bajraklı Moschee* (Samokov and Sofia, 1977), in the series Restaurierte Kulturdenkmäler, which appeared in French, English, German, Bulgarian, and Russian versions. It should be added that on the occasion of many restorations of Turkish mosques in Bulgaria the minaret has been removed under all sorts of pretexts ("bad static condition", etc.). An example is the minaret of the mosque of Hamza Beg in Stara Zagora. The pressure to do such things usually stems from the local politicians. In Samokov, however, the beautiful minaret we see today is entirely the product of the modern restorers, a reconstruction. For an overview of all the monuments of Samokov—mosque, *çeşme,* churches, synagogue, and old houses, mostly with rich paintings and woodcarvings—see Anna Roschkowska, *Samokov, Kulturdenkmäler* (Sofia, 1977).
It is logical to assume that at all times, from the very beginning of Ottoman architecture onward, use has been made of craftman locally available. The 15th and 16th century paylists mention them in detail. Perhaps the oldest written reference to local craftsmen in Bulgaria was discovered in 1966, during excavations beneath the ruins of the mosque of Firuz Bey (from 1435) in Tărnovo. It is a brick in which a Bulgarian text is scratched stating that "Kosta, son-in-law of Yannaki, made 10,000 bricks ("keramidi") for the constructions of the masgit. The Bulgarian authors who published the find (in : *Archeologija* N° IX,2, Sofia, 1967, pp. 27-35) concluded that : "the inscription proves that the official buildings of the Turkish governors are from the very beginning of the Turkish Joke build by Bulgarian masters, who were well-educated people who could make use of the Bulgarian literary language and literature." The Ottoman archival material is of course wholly ignored by them. However important the role of local craftsmen in these first centuries might have been the sources clearly show that the planning, the supervision and the vital parts of the execution of the work was solidly in Ottoman-Turkish hands. Masons and bricklayers not trained and moulded by a specific style cannot suddenly erect a work of pure Ottoman style as was the Mosque of Firuz Bey. What the authors of the 1967 study did was precisely the projection of 19th century realities into centuries long ago.
[115]For numerous details, illustrations, city plans, etc. of nineteenth-century Ottoman towns in Bulgaria, see especially the two works of Todor Zlatev, architect and professor of the history of architecture from the pre-war generation trained in Germany, Bǎlgarskijat grad prez epohata na Vǎzraždaneto (Sofia, 1955) and *Bǎlgarskite gradove po r. Dunav prez epohata na Vǎzraždaneto* (Sofia, 1962).

process was a diversified one. Elements of the theories of Barkan and of Todorov, as well as the pre-war Bulgarian view, are valid for a few cases only. Even the modern Bulgarian view is valid for a few isolated cases. Centrally directed town planning did exist, as well as initiatives at the local level, side-by-side with cities surviving from the remote past and towns springing up spontaneously without much direction. The subsequent fate of many of the towns of Bulgaria in the later centuries, which we have tried to trace in a very cursory way, raises doubts about the modern Bulgarian view that the Muslim element in the cities grew at the expense of the Christian. In a number of places it was quite the other way around, as we have tried to show. We cannot be certain of how representative our examples are because an all-embracing evaluation of the Ottoman population and taxation registers, which is needed to make any kind of categorical statement at all, still needs to be done; and this can only be done through the teamwork of Ottomanists, Slavists, and geographers—not by single researchers, although until now this has very much been the fashion.[116]

For many Bulgarians, today and in the past, the surviving monuments of Ottoman architecture are the symbol of an undesired past, which they do not want to rememberd. For the better part of the Bulgarian intellectuals, however; for historians and art historians; and for the architects of the Sofiot Institute of Culture, they are valuable works of architecture on Bulgarian soil; and so they were considered by the late gifted minister of culture of the 1970s, the daughter of the head of state, Dr. Ljudmila Zhivkova. The joint action of these groups of people led to the rescue of many a building which otherwise would have been lost and, in some cases, led to spectacular restoration. It is to be hoped that, when the destructive current of the most recent years has run its course, the impressive campaign of restoration and adaptation of the 1970s and early 1980s will be resumed.

Utrecht State University, Utrecht, The Netherlands

---

[116]An exception is the excellent co-production, edited by Bryer and Lowry, *Continuity and Change in Late Byzantine and Early Ottoman Society* (Birgmingham and Washington, 1986).

SOURCE. Reconstructed by the author on the basis of his own
view of the preserved ruins, travelers' accounts, and a detailed
plan, section, and view by Hauptmann Schad dating from 1741;
see Karl Teply, "Das Han von Harmanli," *Südost-Forschungen*
33 (1974). Drawing by Gerd Schneider, Karlsruhe.

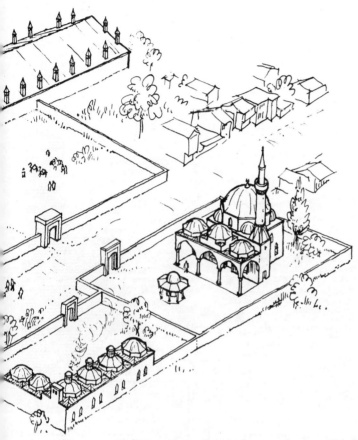

PLATE 1. CARAVANSERAI, BRIDGE, MOSQUE, AND IMARET
AT HARMANLI

Harmanlı, in Bulgarian Thrace, rose from a small mixed
Turkish-Bulgarian village to a substantial town serving the
Istanbul-Belgrade highway. These buildings are representative
for the largest of such road stations in the Balkans. The bridge,
which remains in good shape to the present, was built in 1584-
85, on the order of Grand Vizier Kaniyeli Damat Siyavuş Paşa.
The traveler Melchior Besold mentioned that it was under
construction when he passed through Harmanlı in 1584, and a
long inscription at the bridge, written in Ottoman Turkish
verse, relates the completion of the structure in 1585. The poet
of the inscription was the well-known Mustafa Sa'i, the friend
and biographer of the great architect Mimar Sinan. The mosque
and *imaret* and all but one wall of the caravanserai are
demolished. The caravanserai was of the type found in Bulgaria,
mostly along the Belgrade road, in Mustafa Paşa/Svilengrad,
Uzunça Ova, Tatar Pazarcık, and Novi Khan. The type probably
developed during the second half of the sixteenth century.

PLATE 2. SCHEMATIC MAP OF THE URBAN DEVELOPMENT OF BULGARIA IN THE TURKISH PERIOD

SOURCE: Research and drawing author

= Towns surviving from the Byz.-Bulg. period, further developed by the Ottomans. Mixed population. Continuity (Todorov).

= Turkish towns from the very beginning. New foundations growing around important government sponsored buildings (Barkan).

= Pre-Ottoman towns, largely re-created and re-peopled by the Turks (Barkan).

= Predominantly Turkish towns, developing spontaneously, assisted by some Turkish building activity.

= Towns developing near or below a Bulgaro-Byzantine castle. Mixed population. Developent assisted by some Turkish building activity.

PLATE 3. CITY CENTER OF FILIBE PLOVDIV IN ABOUT 1930.

The Turkish town of Filibe was still largely intact at the time this photograph was taken. In the foreground is the Cumaya Cami, one of the largest and most important mosques in the Balkans. In the background are the *bedesten* and the Kazancılar Camii, both no longer in existence. The date of the construction of the Great Mosque is uncertain, it having been attributed to both Murad I (1370-1380) and Murad II (1420-1430). The confusion between the two Murads is as old as Evliya Çelebi; but as early as the seventeenth century it was attributed to the Murad II period by the historian of Edirne, Abdurrahman Hibri Efendi in his *Enisü'l-Müsāmirīn* (still in unpublished manuscript form, of which I used the Vienna Codex M 189/78). Hibri was a very careful writer, a scholar upon whom one may rely. Also, the mosque is mentioned in Ottoman financial records as being one of the pious foundations of Murad II; see Ö. L. Barkan, "Edirne ve civarındaki bazı İmâret tesislerinin yıllık muhasebe bilânçoları," *Belgeler* 1, no. 2 (1965): 372-76, 377. The date of construction is thus brought to between 1421 and 1451. The somehow archaic features of the building seem to suggest the earlier date; very probably sometime in the late 1420s or early 1430s—a period of peace when Filibe was recovering from the damages of the civil war among the sons of Bayezid I and was the seat of the beylerbeyi of all Rumeli (as it was until 1444). The paylist published by Barkan shows that the mosque had a staff of real sultanic size—26 in all.

SOURCE. Photograph courtesy of the German Archeological Institute, Istanbul, Topogr. T. 4701.

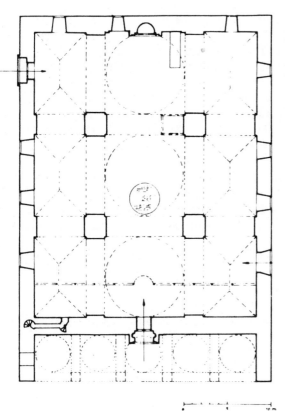

Plovdiv Djumaya Camii
reconstruction

PLATE 4. THE FRIDAY MOSQUE AT
FILIBE / PLOVDIV, INTERIOR AND
PLAN

The Djumaja, or Friday Mosque, was
built in Filibe between 1422 and
1430 by Sultan Murad II as a focal
point for this refounded old city,
destroyed through conquest and civil
strife. The building is one of two
examples in Bulgaria of the "Ulu
Cami" type. Its prototype was
developed in the architecture of Seljuk
Asia Minor in the twelfth and
thirteenth centuries. The oldest
Ottoman mosques of this type are the
Şehadet Camii in Bursa (1365) and the
Ulu Cami of Bergama (1391); a link
between them and the thirteenth-
century Seljuk buildings is the mosque
of the Mongol governor Sungur Beg
in Niğde in central Anatolia, built
shortly after 1335.

SOURCE: Photo and Plan by author

PLATE 5. BEDESTEN AND KAZANCILAR MOSQUE AT FILIBE/PLOVDIV

Both of these buildings, which dated from the fifteenth century, were destroyed before World War II. The *bedesten* was of the standard type with six domes. That of Sofia was much larger, but it also is no longer in existence, having been destroyed at the begining of the present century. The only example of this type of *bedesten* still standing in Bulgaria is at Yambol; others are reported to have existed at Balçık, Eski Zağra, Hacıoğlı Pazarı, Plevne, Pravadi, Rusçuk Silistra, and Uzunca Ova (see K. Kreiser, "Bedesten-Bauten in osmanischen Reich," *Istanbuler Mitteilungen* 29 (1979): pt. 1, pp. 367-400.

SOURCE. Reconstructed by the author on the basis of old photographs and designs. Drawing by Gerd Schneider.

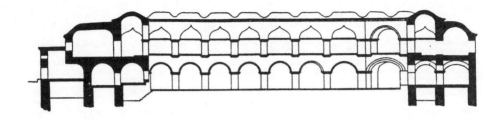

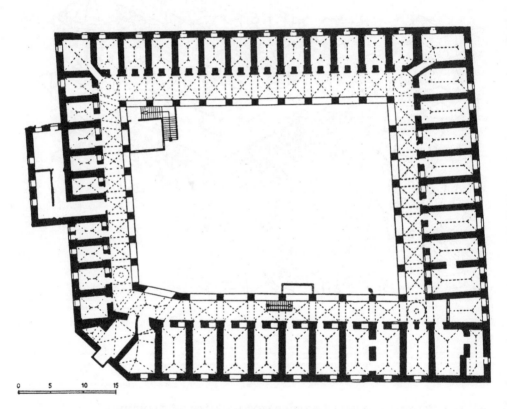

PLATE 6. PLAN OF KURŞUNLU KHAN AT FILIBE/PLOVDIV

This was a fully developed and perfectly preserved example of an Ottoma urban *khan* of the early seventeenth century. The building survived until the beginning of W.W. II, but is was then razed and replaced by a tasteless modern shopping center. In Bulgaria today no examples of urban *khans* remain.

SOURCE. *Kratka Istorija na Bălgarskata Arhitektura* (Sofia, 1965), p. 179 (hereafter *Kratka Istorija*).

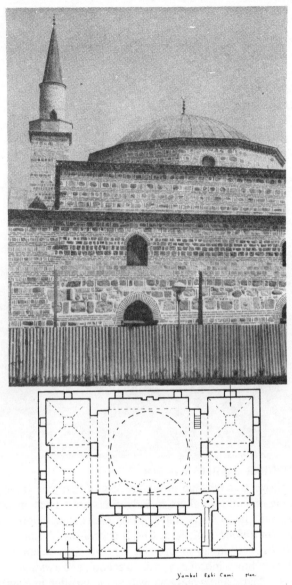

Yambol Eski Cami Plan.

PLATE 7. PHOTOGRAPH AND PLAN OF ESKİ CAMİ AT YAMBOL

The central part of this building dates from the period 1375-1385, the lateral additions from the mid-15th century. The domed central hall with engaged piers, creating a cross-shaped interior space, is inspired by the (30 years) older mosque of Orhan Ghazi in Old Bilecik, the cradle of the Ottoman state. The lateral enlargements are very probably due to the influence of the great Üç Şerefeli Mosque in the Ottoman capital of that time, Edirne, only a hundred kilometers to the south of Yambol and situated on the same river (Tunca). The mosque was recently restored by the Sofiot Institute and will be used for cultural purposes.

SOURCE. Plan by the author. Photograph courtesy Prof. F. de Jong, 1984.

PLATE 8. THE SOFULAR CAMII IN YAMBOL, 1908

The photograph shows this mosque in the process of being destroyed, demonstrating that the dismantling of Turkish culture in Bulgaria is not a phenomenon of today only. The mosque was built in 1481. A transcription of its inscription is given by Evliya Çelebi in his *Seyyahatname* (vol. 8, p. 61). It shows that the building was part of a much more extensive foundation created by the Sufi scholar Sheikh Mehmet Noktacızāde and including a mosque, a *tekke,* a school, and a *mescid* in Edirne; a school and a *tekke* in Eski Zağra; and a *tekke* as well as the mosque in Yambol. A part of the expenditure of the Yambol foundations was defrayed by the annual rent of some shops and the income from a public bath. The mosque was built on the site of the castle of Diampolis, destroyed during the Ottoman conquest. The new Turkish town spread out fanwise on the opposite side of the river Tunca and around the Eski Cami, the *hamam* of Murad II, and the huge *bedesten* of Hadım Ali Paşa, all three of which are preserved. The Yambol mosque housed an important collection of books on mystic philosophy, exegesis, biography of Sufi saints, and poetry; among the last were classics such as the *Mesnevi* of Celaleddin Rumi and the *Gulistan* of Saadi. As a work of architecture the mosque is characteristic of the time of Sultan Bayezid II (1485-1512), i.e., a dome on pendatives; but it is special because of its double porch—a closed interior one and open outer ones—which relates it to the mosque of Djandarlızade Halil Paşa in Iznik near Bursa. The latter dates from 100 years earlier, and why this archaic type reoccured is difficult to say. On the foundations of Sheikh Noktacızāde, see M.T. Gökbilgin, *Edirne ve pasa livasi* (Istanbul, 1952), pp. 468-69.

SOURCE. Private Collection

PLATE 9. THE BEDESTEN AT YAMBOL

This building, dating from the beginning of the sixteenth century, was for a long time a neglected, mutilated ruin. In the 1970s it was saved by an inspired restoration and partial reconstruction by the able architect Nikola Muschanov of the Sofiot Institute for Monuments of Culture.

SOURCE. Photograph by author.

PLATE 10. PLAN OF THE BEDESTEN AT YAMBOL

Grand Vizier Hadım Ali Paşa (1506-1511) was the builder of this *bedesten*. From the architectural point of view it is unique, being one elongated hall covered with a succession of domes but without the usual central pillars (compare it with the *bedesten* of Filibe, which is of the standard type). The annual revenue of the shops in this market hall went to support the vizier's numerous pious foundations, which also included mosques, schools, baths, kitchens for the poor, dervish lodges, etc. throughout the Empire (the most important of these being the mosque in the center of old Istanbul—Cemberlitaş). The Yambol *bedesten* is mentioned in the *vakıfnāme* of Ali Paşa, dated May 1509 (see Gökbilgin, *Edirne*, pp. 394-403; Barkan, "Edirne"; and E.H. Ayverdi, *Istanbul Vakıfları Tahrir Defteri, 1546 tarihli* [Istanbul, 1979], pp. 67-70). On the career of Ali Paşa, see Hedda Reindl, *Männer um Bayezid* (Berlin, 1983), pp. 147-61.

SOURCE. Plan by author.

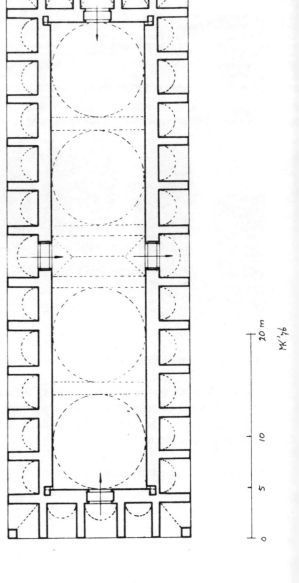

PLATE 11. THE OLD MOSQUE AT ESKI ZAĞRA/STARA ZAGORA

This mosque was built in 811 (1409) by "Emir Hamza Beg," who in the Arabic inscription above the entrance to the prayer hall titled himself in a manner typical of an independent Muslim ruler: "Shadow of God on Earth, Glory of the State and the Religion." There were several Hamza Begs known to the early fifteenth century, but most probably the founder of the Eski Zağra mosque was Izmiroğlu Cüneyd Beg, a descendant of the Anatolian beylik dynasty of Aydınoğlu, who served first under Emir Süleyman, then under Musa Çelebi, and then went over to the service of Mehmed I in 1413, immediately before the battle between Musa and Mehmed that ended the Ottoman civil war. The inscription testifies about Hamza's pride at being a son of an illustrious house. The mosque itself is also a testament to Hamza's pride: the dome measures 17.[47] meters in diameter—a great feat of engineering for a time when the Byzantio-Bulgarian style of architecture ran to domes that did not surpass 6 or 7 meters in diameter. The plan of the Eski Zağra structure is inspired by that of the mosque of Yılderım Bayezid in the Anatolian town of Murdurnu (built before the prince mounted the Ottoman throne in 1389). An even more remote ancestor was the Great Mosque of Eski Çine in the territory of the Menteşe beylik, built in 1308 by Ahmed Ghazi. The Eski Cami has been restored in the last few years and will serve cultural purposes. Alas, its tall minaret, a reconstruction dating from after 1878, was torn down. (The condition of the mosque before restoration is shown in my article, "Early Ottoman Monuments in Bulgarian Thrace," *Belleten* 37, no. 152 (1974).

SOURCE. Photograph courtesy of Prof. Fred de Jong, 1984.

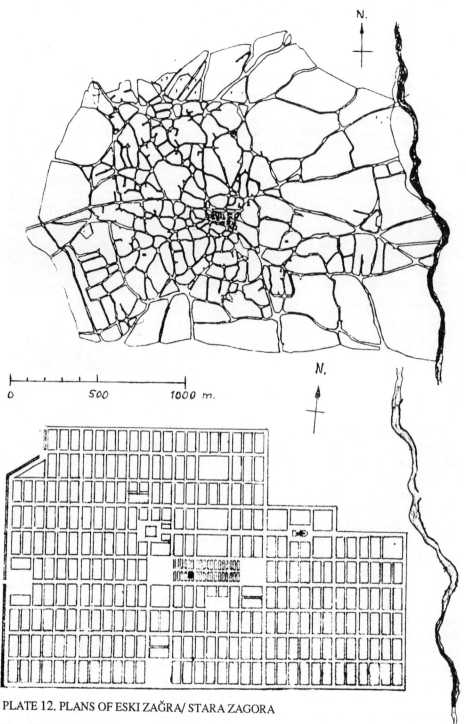

PLATE 12. PLANS OF ESKI ZAĞRA/ STARA ZAGORA

Top: This plan shows the late Ottoman city before 1878 in the form resulting from its spontaneous growth.

Bottom: This shows the plan for the reconstruction of the city after 1878 (Stara Zagora was burned during the war of 1877/78). In few Balkan cities was the break with the Turkish past so radical.

SOURCE. Redrawn by the author on the basis of plans in *Kratka Istrija*.

PLATE 13. THE MAUSOLEUM OF LALA ŞAHIN PAŞA IN KAZANLIK

This *türbe* of the first Turkish governor of Rumeli was one of the very first buildings erected by the Turks in the newly-conquered territory. This type of open, or canopy, *türbe* was very common in the early phase of Ottoman architecture, especially in the fourteenth and fifteenth centuries, and a number of examples have been preserved in the Balkans as well as in Anatolia, where the type originaly came from. The Ottoman chroniclers mention Şahin Paşa as the conquerer of Filibe and Eski Zağra. He died shortly after 1383, and his body was laid to rest in a fine *türbe* in the old Kirmasti (Mustafa Kemal Paşa) near Bursa, next to his mosque and *medrese*; see E.H. Ayverdi, *Osmanlı Mimarisinin ilk Devri* (Istanbul, 1966), pp. 189-97. The Kazanlık mausoleum marks the place where the famous commander died and where, in conformance with the old Ottoman practice, his bowels were buried.

SOURCE. Photograph by author

PLATE 14. OTTOMAN DOMESTIC ARCHITECTURE IN THE RHODOPE

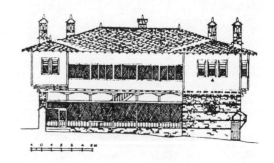

Top: House (with plan below) of Emin Bey in the village of Smiljan, district of Smoljan, first half of the nineteenth century.

Bottom: The *konak* of Agušev in the village of Čerešovo, district of Smoljan, first half of the nineteenth century. This building was the focal point of an important *čiftlik*.

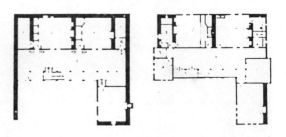

Both of these buildings show a close affinity to the houses of Bursa, Kutahya, Safranbolu, Göynük, and other places in Anatolia, as well as those of several old towns in Greece and Yugoslavia that still retain their Ottoman appearance (Verria, Ambelakia, Kastoria, Siatista, Ohrid, Prizren, Novi Pazar)— although in most places some local peculiarities can be detected.

SOURCE. Drawings by the author on the basis of information provided in *Kratka Istorija*.

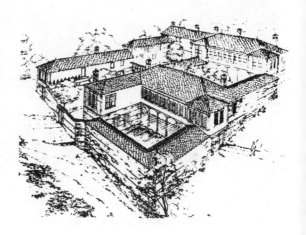

PLATE 15. THE ESKI CAMI OF ŞUMLA/SHOUMEN

This mosque is in all probability a foundation of Yahya Paşa, vizier and son-in-law of Sultan Bayezid II. The fortified mediaeval town of Şumla was destroyed by crusaders during the Varna campaign of 1444 and was subsequently deserted. A new settlement, predominantly Turkish, emerged in the course of the second half of the fifteenth century. The detailed register no. 42 of the *liva* of Niğbolu, dating from 1578, mentions (pp. 165-67) a total of 226 Muslim households in the town, 141 Christian households. (Şumla became an important town only in the eighteenth century.) The nucleus of the new settlement was formed by the mosque, built a few years after 1500, and a *hamam* (the Eski Hamam), built by Kadı Sinan Çelebi circa 1480-90 and purchased by Yahya Paşa to add to his foundation properties in Üsküp in Macedonia. Around the two buildings a market district sprang up, which among the elderly inhabitants of the town today is still remembered as the Eski Çarşı, although the shops have long since disappeared. The ruins of the bath were still visible some decades ago. The Old Mosque was restored in 1253 (1837/38) on order of Sultan Mahmud II, who visited Şumla during his famous tour of his European provinces. (A long inscription in Ottoman Turkish recorded this event. The text of the inscription was by the court poet, Seyyid Mustafa Ta'lib Efendi.) This mosque was demolished in 1984 as part of the Bulgarian campaign to wipe out the memory of the Turkish period in the town. In the background of the photograph may be discerned the stump of the minaret of the Saat Camii, an eighteenth-century monument; this relic was also torn down by the Bulgarians (in 1984). On Yahya Paşa as founder of the mosque, see Osman Keskinoğlu, "Bulgaristan'daki bazı Türk vakıfları ve Abideleri," *Vakıflar Dergisi* 7 (1968), and on his life, see Reindl, *Männer um Bayezid,* pp. 336-45; on Yahya's *vakıfname* itself, see Gliša Elezović,*Turski Spomenici* (Belgrade, 1983), pp. 420-55, esp. p. 444 (Şumla); and on the poet Ta'lib, see Daut Fatin Efendi, *Tezkere-i Hatimeti'l-Asar* (Istanbul, H. 1270), p. 250.

SOURCE. Author

PLATE 16. THE MOSQUE AND BATH OF IBRAHIM PAŞA AT HEZARGRAD /RAZGRAD

This mosque (photo, *top*) and bath (plan, *bottom*) were originally constructed in the period 1530-36 as the focal point for a newly established town with an exclusively Turkish-Muslim population. Later the buildings were entirely reconstructed. In its present form the mosque dates from 1616. It is the largest single-domed mosque in Bulgaria and still dominates the town center. The bath was demolished in the 1970s. Both the mosque and the *hamam* showed pronounced seventeenth-century features. There were originally other buildings also in this compound—a *medrese* a primary school, shops, a large *khan,* and fountains—but all of these disappeared during the nineteenth century.

SOURCE. Photograph and plan by author.

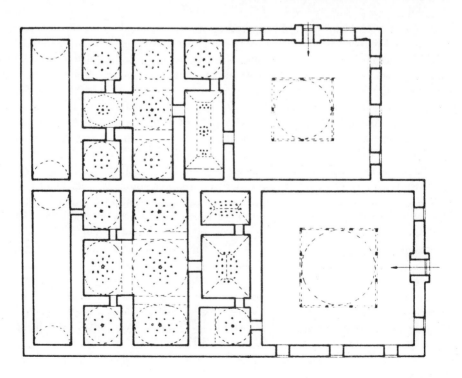

PLATE 17. THE CLOCK TOWER AT ZIŞTOVA/SVIŠTOV

This is a characteristic example of a late-Ottoman building type. Clock towers were constructed all over the Empire in the eighteenth and, particularly, the nineteenth centuries. The tower of Ziştova is situated in the center of town, in the former bazaar area. It bears two inscriptions relating to its construction: one is a three-line text in Ottoman Turkish stating that the tower was the pious foundation of the Voyvode Hüseyin Ağa ben Ali of Ziştova in 1179 (1765/66); and the other is a long poem, also in Ottoman Turkish, telling that the tower was rebuilt on the bequest of Haci Abdullah Ağa, a rich native of Ziştova, who died just before 1276 (1859/60) when the work was finished. Clock towers are preserved in many Bulgarian towns, but in most cases the Turkish inscriptions have been removed. The Ziştova tower is held locally to be Bulgarian in origin because of grafitti carved into the soft limestone in Cyrillic script. The largest of these carvings is by one Manol, whom the local people consider the builder. The two Turkish inscriptions are ignored.

SOURCE. Photography by author

PLATE 18. KIZANE TEKKESI
DERVISH LODGE NEAR ESKI
CUMA/ TARGOVIŠTE

This *tekke* is characteristic of
the great lodges of the Bektaşi
order in the sixteenth century.
The complex includes a
kitchen, guesthouse, assembly
hall, and mausoleum of the
saint venerated at that place.
The official name of the villege
around the *tekke* is Momino.
According to the official
statistics of 1972 this village
had 458 inhabitants; locally I
was told that it had 60
households, all Turks. Kizane
Tekkesi is said to be centuries
old. A long inscription over the
main entrance tells of the
reconstruction in 1272 (1855
/56) of a previous lodge. The
buildings are of wood and mud
brick. This complex overlooks
the plain of Eski Cuma, and in
the background of the top
photograph the town of Eski
Cuma is just visible on the horizon. The bottom photo is of
the interior of the mausoleum.
SOURCE. Both photographs
taken by the author.

PLATE 19. VILLAGE GRAVEYARD AT KIZANE TEKKESI

The upright, uncut lumps of stone shown here mark the graves of the villagers of Kızane Tekkesi (now: Momino) in the same manner as in the graveyards of Asia Minor. On the horizon is the town of Eski Cuma/Tărgovište. Momino itself was still, in 1975, inhabited exclusively by Turks of heterodox Muslim creed.

SOURCE. Photograph taken by author.

PLATE 20. MOSQUES AT VIDIN ON THE DANUBE

Top: The mosque of Mustafa Paşa, dating from the early eighteenth century, was built of broken stone, wood, and mud brick and covered by a inset wooden and plaster dome. This mosque was once the focal point for the large suburb (Varoş) outside the town walls.

Bottom: The Ak Cami, the White Mosque, was a foundation of the famous governor of Vidin, Osman Pasvantoğlu (1800/1801). It is made of rubble masonry and covered with a flat wooden ceiling under a tiled roof.

These mosques were very characterisatic of the Turkish architecture of northern Bulgaria, where monumental domed structures built of excellent ashlar masonry were rare. Both buildings were demolished within the last fifteen years on order of the Vidin city council—Mustafa Paşa's mosque in 1974, the Ak Cami more recently.

SOURCE. Photographs taken by author

PLATE 21. MOSQUE AND LIBRARY AT VIDIN. CEILING CARVING AT BELGRADCIK

Above: The mosque of Osman Pasvantoğlu was built, according to well-preserved inscriptions in Ottoman Turkish, in 1801/1802, and the library was built one year later. The poet who wrote the inscriptions was the Pasvantoğlu's librarian. Ibrahim Mahir Efendi. (He is also known for his Turkish adaptation of the famous tales of Kalila and Dimna.) The library contained the greater part of the works on history and geography printed at the famous Müteferrika Press, as well as numerous manuscripts of works of history, anatomy, medecine, and other sciences; see the article of Michaila P. Stajnova in *Etudes Balkaniques*, no. 2 (1979), and her book *Osmanskite Biblioteki ve Bǎlgarskite zemi, XV-XIX vek* (Sofia, 1982).

Left: The mosque of Hacı Hüseyin Ağa at Belgradcik was built in 1756/57 on the site of an older mosque. The wood carving of the ceiling is a curious blend of local Bulgarian and Turkish styles. It is one of the oldest preserved examples of this type of decoration, which was used in profusion in the houses of the newly rich Bulgarian bourgeoisie of the mountain towns—Koprivštitsa, Žeravna, Kotel, Trjavna, etc.— where many other examples remain.

SOURCE. Author

PLATE 22. MOSQUE AND COMPOUND AT ŞUMLA /SHOUMEN

The Tombul Cami—the mosque and compound of Şerif Halil Paşa, deputy grand vizier and native of Şumla, were constructed in 1744/75. These buildings were inspired by the art of the Tulip Period in the capital of the Empire. The exterior is still very Ottoman looking, but the interior, especially in the decorative elements, show the influence of the Baroque that radiated out from Istanbul. The compound (plan *below*) includes, besides the mosque, a *medrese*, a library, and a primary school. It is the only well preserved example of an Ottoman *külliye* in Bulgaria. During the large-scale campaign of destruction of Turkish buildings in Şumla (1984-85), this group of buildings was the only one to be spared, other than more "neutral" structures such as the caravansarai of 1806/1807 (which was actually restored and transformed into a restaurant).

SOURCE. Photograph and plan by author.

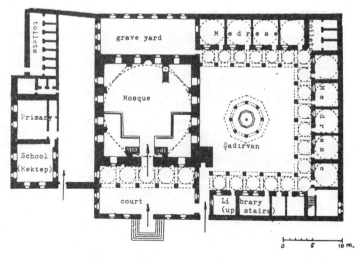

PLATE 23. THE COMPOUND OF ŞERIF HALIL PAŞA AT ŞUMLA/SHOUMEN
In this photograph is shown the place of ablution (a unique example of its kind in Bulgaria) and the library that were included in Halil Paşa's *külliye*. A number of distinguished calligraphers, whose work is preserved in inscriptions at Rusçuk, Eski Cuma, and Nikopol (on the castle gate, now housed in the Sofia Archaeological Museum), were trained at the *medrese* here. The published *vakıfname* lists a calligraphy teacher as a member of the college staff. The library is said to have housed 5,000 works on religion, medicine, mathematics, the Arabic and Persian languages, and geography. Among the last was a fine copy of the twelfth-century *Geography* of Idrisi, written in 963 (1555/56) in Cairo and containing 70 maps now in the Sofia National Library. On the library, see Stajnova, *Osmanskite Biblioteki;* on the foundation deed of trust, see Herbert Duda, *Balkantürkische Studien,* Sitzungsberichte Österreiche Akademische Wissenschaft Philosophie-Historie Klasse, no. 226 (Vienna, 1949), pp. 63-89.
SOURCE. Photograph by author.

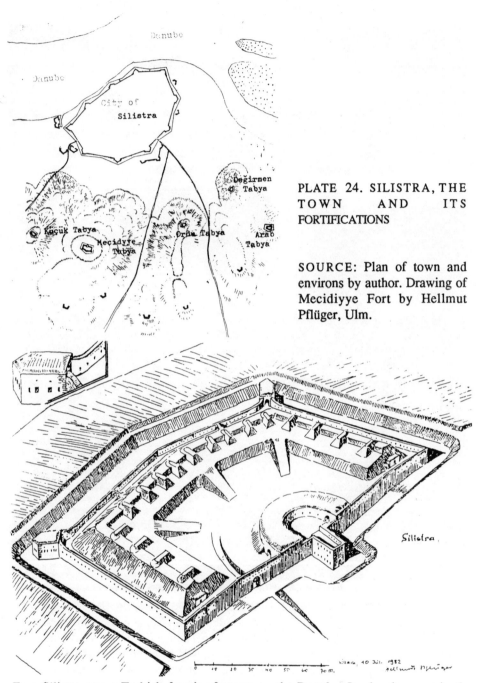

PLATE 24. SILISTRA, THE TOWN AND ITS FORTIFICATIONS

SOURCE: Plan of town and environs by author. Drawing of Mecidiyye Fort by Hellmut Pflüger, Ulm.

Top: Silistra was a Turkish frontier fortress on the Danube. Its development in the nineteenth century proceeded as follows: the enceinte of the town, 1811; the detached forts of Sultan Abdülmecid I, 1852/53; and the outer line of redoubts, 1877.

Bottom: The Medidiyye Fort was a typical example of a polygonal fort of mid-nineteenth-century type, with caponiers instead of bastions, a Carnot wall instead of a stone-revetted escarp wall, and "bomb-proof" semicircular barracks. This fort was up to date with the best contemporaneous European forts.

PLATE 25. BRIDGE OVER THE STRUMA RIVER AT KÜSTENDIL

This bridge was built in 874 (1469/70) on order of Inegöllü Ishak Paşa, the well-known Turkish statesman of the time of Sultan Mehmed the Conquerer. The date of construction and the names of the ruler and his vizier are given in the Arabic inscription on the bridge, still preserved. The bridge is one of the oldest and largest Turkish stone bridges of Bulgaria. It served the once important road from Istanbul to Üsküp and Albania via Filibe, Samokov, and Küstendil. Its name, Kadın Most—"Woman's Bridge"—derives from the local legend that the architect had to sacrifice his wife before the main arch, which was 21.65 meters wide, could be closed. (Such a motif is a common one in Balkan folklore.) The bridge was built partly from the spoils of the antique city of Pautalia, and the name Pautalia appears on an inscription (in ancient Greek) found on its stones. Other great Turkish bridges in Bulgaria are at Svilengrad/ Cisr-i Mustafa Paşa (from 1528/29) and Harmanlı (from 1585; see Plate 1).

SOURCE. Photography by author.

PLATE 26. CARVED GRAVESTONE AT SAMAKO/SAMOKOV

This tombstone of Lady Seyide, the mother of Governor Mehmed Hüsrev Paşa, is situated in the yard of the Bayraklı Cami, which was reconstructed by Hüsrev Paşa. The stone is typical of Turkish grave markers found in urban centers. The calligraphy and carving of the inscription are of superb quality, on a level with the best contemporaneous works in Istanbul, Bursa, or Edirne. The stone is dated 12 Zilkade 1261/ (12 November 1845). Hüsrev Paşa was a protector of Bulgarian painters and sculptors; and, a native of Samokov himself, he sent talented young artists from the town to Western Europe to complete their educations. (See Anna Roschkowška, "Kǎm Kulturnata istorija na grad Samokov pres Vǎzraždaneto, Godišnik na Obstestvenata Prosvetno-Kulturna Organizatsija na Evreite b NPB, vol. 10 [Sofia, 1975], pp. 109-216). Hüsrev Paşa constructed a number of fountains in his native town and encouraged urban development and the work of craftsmen. The public library founded by him was one of the richest in Ottoman Bulgaria. The library was built in 1256 (1840/41), according to a beautiful Turkish inscription on a large slab of marble, now housed in the Samokov Museum. (The text of the inscription is by Mehmed Rif'at Mısrī.) A handwritten catalog of the library's holdings is preserved in the National Library at Sofia (Cod. Or. No. 1121), as are most of its books; for details about these books, see Stajnova, *Osmanskite Biblioteki*, pp. 38-80.   SOURCE. Photograph by author.

PLATE 27. THE AHMED BEG
CAMII AT KÜSTENDIL

Constructed in 1573, this
mosque is a good example of
the Classical style of the
sixteenth century, of the single-
domed mosque enriched by a
half dome, then very much the
fashion in the capital, Istanbul.
The mosque is today serving as
local museum.

SOURCE. Plan and photograph
by author.

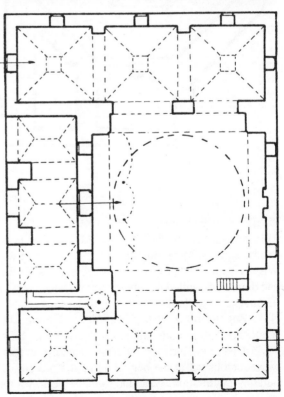

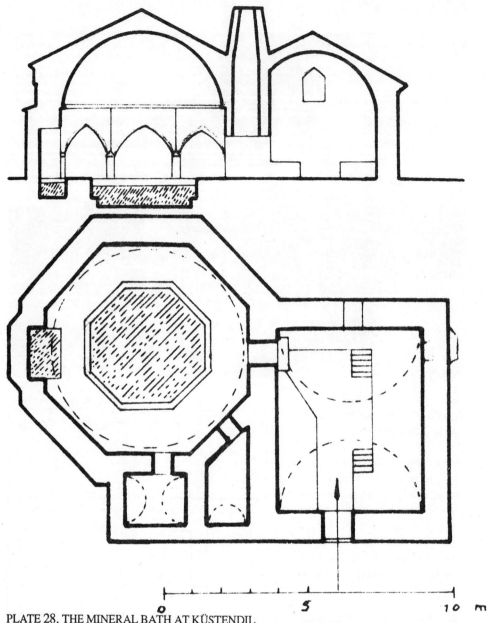

0   5   10 m.

PLATE 28. THE MINERAL BATH AT KÜSTENDIL

This mineral bath (called Dervish Banja) constructed in 1566 is the single survivor of
twelve such buildings in Küstendil. It is a good example of a modest provincial spa.
Wherever mineral springs were discovered, the Turks built over them domed bath rooms
and domed or vaulted disrobing rooms. (Such baths are not to be confused with ordinary
hamams). Intact mineral baths or their ruins are to be found at places such as Aydos,
Nova Zagora/Baraki, Eski Zağra/Stara Zagora, Čepino/Velingrad, Sliven, and Banja
Razloško. The famous mineral baths of Sofia, built in the shape of the better-known
Turkish baths of Budapest (octagon shaped, with four separate rooms and four "eyvans")
were demolished at the beginning of the present century and replaced by the present
building in imitation Byzantine style. In the 1980s the foundations of another polygonal
mineral bath were uncovered in the center of Sofia.

SOURCE. Redrawn by the author from plans in Kratka Istorija.

Bilâl N. Şimşir

THE TURKISH MINORITY IN BULGARIA: HISTORY AND CULTURE

There is a large Turkish minority in the People's Republic of Bulgaria today, a remnant of the rule of the Ottomans over the Balkan territory. The Ottomans conquered the area in the fourteenth century, and it remained a part of the Empire for five centuries. Because of its proximity to Istanbul and its position astride the main way to the West, the Bulgarian land became populated by large numbers of Turkish migrants from Anatolia who crossed the Balkan peninsula close on the heels of the Ottoman armies and settled in various parts of Bulgaria.[1] When the Empire collapsed, many Turkish people chose to remain.

Bulgarian historians have written in detail about this migration of Turks. For example, Professor Christo Christov, director of the Institute of History of the Bulgarian Academy of Science states that

> When the Bulgarian land was conquered by the Turks, the native population retreated to the mountainous regions... [and] the Turkish population brought over from Anatolia was settled in the land vacated by them. The fertile valleys of Thrace, Macedonia, and the Rhodopes were settled by the animal-rearing masses of Yörüks. The Turkish people settled in the cities also. Thus, in the fifteenth century the towns of Bulgaria assumed the identity of Turkish cities where the majority of the population was Muslim.[2]

Strashimir Dimitrov and Christo Manchev, furnish the following information on the subject:

> During the settlement of the Balkans by the Ottomans, considerable numbers of Oğuz Turks were resettled there. Because of the Mongol invasions coming from the east, large masses of nomadic and semi-nomadic Oğuz Turks concentrated in eastern Anatolia towards the beginning of the fourteenth cintury. These masses were looking for new places for settlement and grazing land for their herds. The onslaught of

---

[1]See Bilâl N. Şimşir, *Glimpses of the Turkish Minority in Bulgaria* (Ankara, 1986), p. 1,

[2]Dimitar Kosev, Christo Christov, and Dimitar Angelov, *Kratka Istoriya na Bulgaria* [Short history of Bulgaria] (Sofia, 1969), p. 83.

these Turkish masses toward the west changed the ethnic outlook of Anatolia.... When the Balkan Peninsula was conquered, these Turkish masses marched once again towards the west and served as a reserve source of settlers to populate the newly-conquered land.

This colonization took place partly naturally and spontaneously and partly within the framework of a State program having definite purpose. At a time as early as 1352, when Simpe Castle on the Gallipoli Peninsula was conquered by the Turks, Suleyman Pasha had settled the area with Oğuz Turks transported from Anatolia. Sultan Murad I (1325-1389) resettled in the Sar region of Macedonia large groups of Turkish nomads from the Saruhan region of Anatolia, where they were creating turmoil.

But the colonization of certain parts of the Balkans cannot be explained only by the Ottoman Sultans' efforts towards a certain goal. We see the most important Turkish colonization taking place in the area conquered in the initial stage of Ottoman expansion.... These areas were flooded by Yörük masses in the first half of the sixteenth century. As early as between 1520 and 1635 the Muslims amounted to more than half of the overall population in the Gallipoli, Vize, Cirmen, and Silistra districts.[3]

On the eve of the Turkish-Russian War of 1877-1878, the number of Muslim-Turks living in the territory that is now Bulgaria exceeded the Bulgarian population.[4] Just before the establishment of the Bulgarian state—that is, in 1876—the Turks and Bulgarians living in the Danube (Tuna) Province of the Ottoman Empire, which is now northern Bulgaria, were practically equal in number, as M. Aubaret, the French consul in Ruschuk (Ruse), the capital of the Danube Provice, informed his chief:

Il n'est pas inutile à ce propos de rectifier l'opinion éronnée partagée par beaucoup de publicistes qui supposent dans la Turquie d'Europe une infime minorité de Musulmans. Dans le seul Vilayet du Danube, l'un des plus peuplés de l'Empire, on compte d'après les meilleurs renseignements 1,120,000 Musulmans... contre 1,233,500 non-musulmans parmi lesquels 1,130,000 Bulgares... L'égalité numérique est donc presque complète.[5]

In the territory south of the Balkan mountains the Bulgarian population was in the minority. According to the Ottoman official statistics of 1876, the non-Bulgarian population outnumbered the Bulgarians by ratios of from nearly one-and-one-half to over

---

[3]*Istoriya na Balkanskite Narodi XV-XIX vek.* [History of Balkan Nations, XV-XIXth centuries] (Sofia, 1971), pp. 73-74.

[4]Şimşir, *Oppression and Discrimination in Bulgaria (The Case of the Muslim Turkish Minority). Facts and Documents.* Preface by Kenneth Mackenzie. (London, Nicosia, and Istanbul 1986), p. 1.

[5]*Archives des Affaires Etrangères. Correspondance Politique des Consuls. Turquie. Roustchok, 1876-1879,* vol. 3, Report of 6 October 1876, Political direction no. 29, pp. 118-19, Aubaret to M. Decazes, French Minister of Foreign Affairs.

three-and-three-quarters to one in seven southern sandjaks (see Table 1 following this article).

When the Bulgarian national state was founded in 1878 the piece of land on which it was established had a population with a multi-racial and multi-national character. In order to create a unitarian Bulgarian state in an area where half of the population was Turkish, an operation to cut away the non-Bulgarian portion of that population was performed. The 1877-78 Turco-Russian war destroyed the demographic structure in the Balkans, especially in Tuna and Edirne Provinces. During the seven-month war, some one-and-a-half million Muslim Turks were forced to emigrate from the Balkans.[6] Some 500,000 of them died "like flies" from hunger, exposure, and epidemics, while others were massacred. In the central and western parts of the newly-established Principality of Bulgaria, the Turkish population remained a majority because that region had not been invaded by the Russians and Bulgarians during the war and its Turkish inhabitants had not been much affected by the forced emigration and massacres. According to the results of the first official census taken by the Bulgarian government in January of 1881, the Turkish/Muslim element of the population of the various districts of eastern Bulgaria amounted to from 43.7 to 79.3 percent of the total (see Table 2). The census indicates that despite the 1877-78 Turco-Russian war, the multinational character of the Ottoman Danube Province was retained even after it became part of the newly-constituted Bulgarian state.

Since then, hundreds of thousands more Turks have emigrated from Bulgaria to Turkey, but the Turkish minority has remained sizeable nevertheless. The reasons for this are two: natural population growth and the expansion of Bulgaria. While emigrations drained the Turkish population in Bulgaria, its growth rate of 2 to 2.5 percent worked in the other direction. Even more important were Bulgaria's repeated expansions. When it moved against its neighbors and seized new territory it gained areas densely populated by Turks. In 1885 Bulgaria annexed Eastern Rumelia, which included the Filibe (Plovdiv) and Islimye (Sliven) *sandjaks* where a considerable number of Turks lived. In the Balkan War of 1912-1913 Bulgaria annexed nine Ottoman districts, all of them Turkish-Muslim strongholds. The official Bulgarian census taken in 1920 gave the Turkish-Muslim population percentages of these districts as follows:

District (kaza)	Percent of Turkish-Muslims	District (kaza)	Percent of Turkish-Muslims
Kircaali	95.7	Dövlen	92.9
Koşukavak (Krumovgrad)	94.0	Pashmakli	54.1
Egridere (Ardina)	98.3	Nevrokop	43.0
Mestanli (Momchilgrad)	98.7	Ortaköy (Ivailovgrad)	13.1
Daridere (Zlatogra)	35.1		

---

[6]See Bilâl N. Şimşir, *Turkish Emigrations from the Balkans. Documents.* Vol. 1, *A Turkish Exodus (1877-1878)* and vol. 2, *A Year of Transition* (Ankara, 1968-1970).

In the last three of these districts, Muslim Pomaks were in the majority. The first six districts were all pure ethnic Turkish centers where, as can be seen, the ratio of the Turkish population compared to the overall population ranged between 92.9 and 98.7 percent. Thus, the annexation by Bulgaria of these overwhelmingly Turkish regions further increased the Turkish population within the state. Finally, Bulgaria annexed southern Dobroudja under an agreement signed with Romania in September of 1940 and gained an additional 65,000 Turkish and 3,958 Tatar subjects.[7]

When the Principality of Bulgaria was created in 1878, it covered some 63,000 square kilometers. By 1885 its territories had reached 96,000 square kilometers; in 1913, 103,000; and still later, 111,000. The stage-by-stage Bulgarian expansion resulted at each stage in an increase in the number of Turks within the boundaries of the state. According to Bulgarian statistics, the Turkish and Muslim population in Bulgaria was as follows in census years from 1887 to 1965:[8]

Census Year	Turkish Population	Muslim Population
1887	602,331	676,212
1892	569,728	643,258
1900	539,656	643,000
1905	505,439	603,867
1910	504,560	603,084
1926	577,555	825,774
1934	618,268	821,298
1956	656,025	676,025
1965	746,755	

As the table above shows, while the Turkish population declined by about 98,000 (the Muslim population by about 73,000) during the years from 1887 through 1910, it began to increase again after that, reaching 746,755 in 1965, a figure about 144,500 above that of 1887, despite emigration. The Muslim total shows an abrupt decline in 1956 because in that census the Muslim Pomaks began to be counted as Bulgarians. Although the Bulgarian government no longer published the statistics on its Turkish and Muslim populations, the Turkish segment is estimated today at 1,200,000, while the Muslim population is believed to be around 1,500,000.[9] There is one Turk for every ten Bulgarians, and the Turks are, thus, the largest ethnic minority in the country.

---

[7] Georgi T. Danailov, *Izsledvaniya Virhu Demografiyata na Bulgariya* [A study on Bulgarian demography] (Sophia, 1931), p. 388. According to another source, with the annexation of southern Dobrudja some 150,000 Turks were added to Bulgaria's Muslim-Turkish population; see *Oppression and Discrimination*, p. 1. See also Mustecip H. Fazil (Ülküsal), *Dobruca ve Türkler* [Dobdudja and the Turks] (Köstence, 1940), p. 125.

[8] Bilâl N. Şimşir, *Bulgaristan Türkleri (1878-1985)* (Ankara, 1986), p. 19.

[9] Şimşir, *Bulgaristan Türkleri*, p. 20, and the English translation of that work, *The Turks of Bulgaria (1878-1985)* (London, 1988), p. 6 ; idem, *Glimpses*, p. 11, and *Oppression and Discrimination*, p. 1.

The Turks of Bulgaria have official status as a minority group protected under international law by virtue of various treaties and bilateral and multilateral agreements signed by the Bulgarian government. The Treaty of Berlin (1878), which established Bulgaria as a tributary principality recognized the differences—in religion, language, culture, and ethnic origin—between the Bulgarians themselves and the ethnic minorities that were included within the boundaries of the new national state and included provisions designed to protect the right of these minorities to preserve their different languages and ways of life. Bilateral agreements between Turkey and Bulgaria specifically protected the rights of the Turks. Finally, the United Nations charter and declarations and the Helsinki Final Act of 1975 made general pronouncements about the protection of human rights that also benefitted the minority Turks of Bulgaria. For over a century, therefore, the Turks in Bulgaria were able, under the protection of international law, to maintain and develop their own institutions: educational institutions, religious organizations, pious foundations, and cultural associations. A local Turkish press and a literature were also developed.

The Education of the Bulgarian Turks

Turkish education in Bulgaria can trace its roots to the Ottoman era. The region was one of the most educationally developed in the Ottoman Empire. The *Tanzimat* reforms were first tested in Tuna (Danube) Vilayet, the north part of today's Bulgaria. In this part of the Empire modern secondary schools, called *rüşdiye,* were created in the mid-nineteenth century. Especially during the *Islahat* (Reform) period (1856-1876) many schools were opened in the region. In 1875 there were in Tuna Vilayet 2,700 Turkish primary schools, 150 *medresse*s, and 40 *rüşdiye.* In the part of Edirne Vilayet that is now inside Bulgarian borders there were approximately 2,500 Turkish schools.[10]

The Turco-Russian War of 1877-1878 was a major setback for the Turkish education in Bulgaria. During this war about 1,500 Turkish schools were destroyed in the Balkans, hundreds of Turkish teachers were dispersed or forced to emigrate to Anatolia, and the revenues of the Turkish schools were diminished. Many school properties were plundered or seized by the Bulgarians. After 1885 the Turkish educational system in Bulgaria began to revive. School buildings were partly repaired, teaching posts were filled, and education was adapted to the new conditions, which placed the Turkish minority in Bulgaria under the protection of the Berlin Treaty of 1878 and of a Bulgarian constitution and laws drafted in conformity with treaty provisions.[11] According to official Bulgarian statistics, the number of Turkish schools

[10]Şimşir, *Bulgaristan Türkleri,* p. 23, and *The Turks of Bulgaria,* p. 9.

[11]Şimşir, *Bulgaristan Türkleri,* p. 29, and idem, *Turkish Minority Education and Literature in Bulgaria,* (Ankara, 1986), p. 3. See also B. Sakarbalkan, "Prenslik Devrinde Bulgaristan'da Türk Eğitimi," *Türk Kültürü,* no. 26 (December 1964): 80-89; no. 27 (January 1965): 185-96; and no. 28 (February 1965): 252-67.

extant in various years from 1895 to 1950, and the number of teachers and pupils in the schools, were as follows:[12]

Academic Year	Schools	Teachers	Pupils
1895/96	1,341	1,549	75,160
1907/08	1,234	1,566	63,516
1909/10	1,222	1,522	63,033
1921/22	1,713	2,113	60,540
1923/24	1,688	2,350	77,559
1949/50	1,199	3.037	100,276

In conformity with old Ottoman practice, Turkish schools in Bulgaria were organized as private bodies; their administration, the appointment of teachers, and the preparation of the curriculum were the responsibility of the Turkish community. All the Turkish minority schools in Bulgaria were managed by school councils elected from the community. Bulgarian officials only inspected and controlled them at the ultimate level. Education was in Turkish, although later on Bulgarian language instruction was introduced in higher classes.[13]

Up until the First World War, Turkish schools in Bulgaria were regularly assisted by the Turkish government. Some of their teachers were graduates from the schools in Turkey, textbooks were printed in Turkey, and the salaries of the *rüşdiye* teachers were paid by the Ottoman Ministry of Education. Immediately after the First World War the Agrarian government of Alexander Stambuliyski undertook to provide necessary facilities so that minority children could receive education in their own languages. According to Section IV of the Neuilly Peace Treaty of 27 November 1919, Bulgaria was to recognize the full equality of all minorities irrespective of differences of religion, language, race, or nationality. No restrictions were to be imposed on the minorities' use of their own languages. Article 54 of the Neuilly Treaty reads:

> Bulgarian nationals who belong to racial, religious, or linguistic minorities shall enjoy the same treatment and security in law and in fact as the other Bulgarian nationals. In particular they shall have an equal right to establish, manage, and control, at their expense, charitable, religious, and social institutions, schools and other educational

---

[12]Direction Générale de la Statistique (de Bulgarie), *Statistique de l'Enseignement dans le Royaume de Bulgarie, Année scolaire 1907/1908, 1909/1910, 1923/1924* (Sofia, 1911, 1919, 1928), and idem, *Statistiques des Ecoles en Bulgarie, Année scolaire 1894/1895, 1895/1896, 1896/1897, 1898/1899, 1899/1900, 1901/1902, 1902/1903, 1903/1904...* (Sofia, 1897, 1897, 1898, 1899, 1900, 1902, 1903, 1908).

[13]For further information on Turkish minority education in Bulgaria, see Osman Keskioğlu, *Bulgaristan'da Türkler* (Ankara, 1985), pp. 57-100; and B. Sakarbalkan, "Krallık Devrinde Bulgaristan'da Türk Eğitimi, 1908-1944," *Türk Kültürü,* no. 29 (March 1965): 325-29, no. 30 (April 1965): 377-90, and no. 32 (June 1965): 521-28.

establishments with the right to use their own language and to exercise their religion freely therein.

On 18 October 1925 a treaty of friendship was signed between Turkey and Bulgaria. By the annexed Protocol to the treaty, Bulgaria undertook specifically to ensure that all Muslims living as a minority in Bulgaria would benefit from all the provisions of the Neuilly Treaty. The Turkish-Bulgarian Treaty of Frienship of 1925 is still in force.

In the 1920s Turkish minority education in Bulgaria was flourishing. In 1921 the number of Turkish schools had reached 1,713. In Shumen, a pedagogical school was created for the training of Turkish teachers within Bulgaria. In 1923 another higher Turkish school, called *Nüvvab,* was opened in the same town. In 1928 the Turks in Bulgaria adopted, immediately after Turkey itself had done so, the new Turkish Latin alphabet. The alphabet reform facilitated the education of Turkish children and thus speeded the development of the system of Turkish minority education in Bulgaria. This upward trend came to an abrupt end in 1934. On 19 May of that year a military junta took the power. According to Bulgarian historians, it was a fascist government. The policy followed by the new regime towards the Turks in Bulgaria was to keep them ignorant, to oppress and exploit them, or to force them to emigrate.[14]

An era of "terror and darkness" thus began for the Turkish minority in Bulgaria. During the first year of rule by the Bulgarian fascist junta, ten Turkish newspapers were closed, and Turkish writers, teachers, and intellectuals of all sorts were forced to emigrate. School buildings and lands were expropriated by the government. During the decade (1934-1944) of Bulgarian facist rule that followed, a total of about 1,300 Turkish schools were closed down, leaving only 400 in operation by 1944, those being in the urban centers only. The community school councils were abolished, and the property of the foundations that provided revenue to operate the Turkish schools was seized. All of the Turkish language newspapers were eventually closed, so there was no longer any press organ to provide information of specific interest to or to reflect the views of the Turkish minority. Turkish associations and social clubs were banned also. There came to be no security in Bulgaria for Turkish property or life, and the entire community was exhausted and depressed.

Such was the atmosphere when the Bulgarian Communists came to power on 9 September 1944. The new regime presented itself to the Turkish minority as a "savior." On 14 May 1945 a Turkish newspaper *Işık* (Light), began to be published in Sofia. It was an organ of the new regime, and it lauded the new government in order in gain the support of the Turkish minority. According to this paper, there was a bright future ahead for the Turks in Bulgaria.[15]

On 27-28 December 1944, about 200 Turkish delegates met at the Bulgarian capital and put together a list of demands for the restoration of their human rights. These demands were for policy changes under to two main headings: education and *wakfs*

---

[14]Bilâl N. Şimşir, "Türk Harf Devriminin Türkiye Dışına Yayılması: Bulgaristan Türkleri Örneği," *Harf Devriminin 50. yılı Semposyumu* (Ankara, 1981), pp. 187-206.

[15]Bilâl N. Şimşir, "The Fate of the Turkish Minority in the People's Republic of Bulgaria, *Foreign Policy,* 12, nos. 3-4 (February 1986): 20-66.

(foundations) and other religious matters. On this occasion a Turkish editorialist of long experience, Hüseyn Cahit Yalçın, wrote in an Istanbul paper:

It is a fact that the Turks who were so unfortunate as to live in Bulgaria until this date were deprived of their most inalienable human rights. But now the Turks in Bulgaria have raised their voices. They demand the new Turkish alphabet. They want a gymnasium for Turks. They want teacher training colleges. They want the religious head of the Muslims not to be appointed by Bulgarians of a different religion but elected by the Muslim people.

It is an established fact that Turks today live the life of pariahs in the Bulgaria of the Bulgarians. Now they claim their rights; but will these rights be granted to them? What if the Bulgarians say, we will respect your rights in the future? How shall we be sure that Turkish rights will not remain only on paper and will indeed be implemented? The past practice suggests no confidence but suspicion for the future implementations.[16]

Yalçın's suspicious attitude toward the new Bulgarian government's promises was the attitude that prevailed also within the Bulgarian Turkish community—and, as it turned out, quite rightly.

In 1946, two years after coming to power, the communist regime nationalized the Turkish educational system. During the Ottoman era the Turkish community in Bulgaria had operated its own schools as private institutions. This arrangement had been continued when the Bulgarian national state was created and was supported by the various international treaties pertaining to Bulgaria. However, the communist regime, like the facist government before it, chose to disregard the treaties, albeit by transforming the Turkish schools into state schools rather than by simply destroying them and seizing their property. The law nationalizing the Turkish schools was adopted by the Bulgarian parliament on 27 September 1946. This law, which carried the name "The Appendix to the Bulgarian National Education Law," entered into force on 12 October 1946. The relevant article was as follows:

Article 154. For the purpose of meeting the educational needs of the minority people in Bulgaria and to ensure education in their own language, the State and the Municipalities may open minority schools of any grade according to the needs observed. The material expenses of these schools are met by the Municipalities while the salaries of teachers and administrative staff are paid by the State.[15]

Thus Turkish schools were to continue for a while under the name "minority schools" but they would cease to be private schools and would be run by the state. The Turkish community in Bulgaria would no longer have the right to open new schools of its own, and the existing ones were required to be turned over lock, stock, and barrel to

[16] "Bulgaristan Türklerinin Hakları," *Tanin*, 1 January 1945, and *Ayın Tarihi*, no. 134 (January 1945), pp. 428-29.

the state. The relevant provision of the law (Article 164f) stated that "the private schools ... as well as school funds and real estate are transferred to the [state] school fund; and the buildings, the school inventories, tools, and equipment are to be turned over to the municipalities." With the implementation of this clause all the school buildings and other properties and the school funds built up by the Turkish minority through the centuries since the time of Ottoman Empire became the property of the Bulgarian state.

This was revolution in its full sense, and to be deprived of their most precious property, namely, their schools by parlimentary fiat did not seem greatly different from the "illegal" destruction and seizure of school property by the facist government. For the time being, however, the Turkish children went to their Turkish schools as before, and the teachers were the same. There was no sudden change in the teaching staff or the school curricula, and Turkish remained in language of instruction.

Article 79 of the Bulgarian constitution stated that the minorities had the right to receive education in their mother languages and also the right to develop their own cultures. However, through its enactment of the "Appendix to the Bulgarian National Education Law" the communist government was preparing the ground for its future drive to completely bulgarize its Turkish population. To begin with, the provision of the previously quoted Article 154 for minority schools within the state system was "according to the needs observed." If no "need was observed" the government was under no obligation to provide special schools for its minorities—who were also prevented by the law from providing them for themselves. Furthermore, Article 155, paragraph 22 of the "Appendix" contained language permitting the government to decide not to accord minority rights to some groups (despite the fact that the status of minorities within Bulgaria had been determined by treaty and international agreement):

> Upon the motion of the National Education Minister, the Bulgarian Council of Ministers decides which minority people in Bulgaria will benefit from minority rights and will receive education in their mother tongues in their schools.

Still another weapon for the fight to bulgarize the Turks was provided by Article 156 of the "Appendix," which stated that minority children would be entitled to be educated in Bulgarian schools on petition by their parents.[17]

For nearly twenty years following enactment of the new education law, Article 156 was the provision principally used against the Turks, as many Turkish parents were compeled by threats and force of arms to sign petitions for their children to attend Bulgarian schools. The nationalization of their schools and the employment of force to get them to transfer their children to Bulgarian schools caused increasing numbers of Turks to abandon their homes in Bulgaria and to emigrate to Turkey. In the years 1950-51 some 154,393 of them—about 12 percent of the total in Bulgaria at that time—left

---

[17]For the full text of the "Appendix to the Bulgarian National Education Law," see *Darjaven Vestnik* [Bulgarian Official Gazette], no. 234 (12 October 1946).

the country. On 30 November 1951, however, the Bulgarian government prohibited further emigration.[18]

For a time those Turks who had not left Bulgaria seemed to benefit from a flourishing minority education system. According to Bulgarian sources, the number of Turkish schools steadily increased under the communist regime: from the 400 that remained at the end of facist rule to 673 in 1946, to 987 in 1948, and to 1,199 in 1950.[19] Meanwhile textbooks for the Turkish schools began to be printed in Sofia, using the new Latin Turkish alphabet. New schools continued to be opened, and by 1960 the number of pupils being educated in them had reached about 150,000. However, that year saw the end of any separate education for Turkish minority children in Bulgaria. By a decree of 16 June 1960 the Ministry of Culture and Education "unified" the Bulgarian and Turkish schools, requiring the Turkish children to receive their training in schools with Bulgarian children. For a few years classes in Turkish language and literature were included in the curricula of the "unified" schools, although these were offered for only two to four hours per week. Still, at least some limited opportunity to study their native language was available to the estimated 152,000 Turkish school children in Bulgaria in 1964.[20] Even this small gesture toward the educational rights of the Turkish minority was soon eliminated, however. Today it is estimated that there are some 200,000 Turkish children in Bulgaria who, despite all the treaties and agreements signed by the Bulgarian government over the years and despite the fact that in their 500 years of rule over the territory the Ottoman Turks permitted the Bulgarians freely to open their own modern schools, are being deprived of any opportunity to receive education in their mother tongue.

In 1964, when the learning of their mother tongue had been made as difficult as possible for Turks to accomplish, Todor Zivkov, the head of state spoke fulsomely of the importance of their education in the Turkish tongue:

All necessary conditions have been created for our country's Turks to improve their own language ....

Turkish children should learn their mother tongue well and they should also speak it perfectly. This creates the need for the improvement of Turkish education. The Turks will speak their mother language, they will improve their progressive customs with their mother language, they will create contemporary works in literature and they will sing their beautiful "Türküs" in the future as well as today.

Turkish language should be enriched even more with the publication of works related to the Turks. More Turkish books should be written in our country.[21]

[18]Bilâl N. Şimşir, "The Turks of Bulgaria and the Immigration Question," *The Turkish Presence in Bulgaria* (Ankara, 1986), pp. 39-58, and idem, "Migrations from Bulgaria to Turkey. The 1950-51 Exodus," *Foreign Policy* 12, nos 3-4 (February 1986): 67-92.

[19]*Otechestven Front,* 27 June 1948, and Direction de la Presse (de Bulgarie), *La Minorité turque en République Populaire de Bulgarie* (Sofia, 1951).

[20]*Yeni Işık* (New Light), 28 April 1964.

[21]"T. Jivkof yoldaşın 'Yeni Hayat' dergisi redaksiyasina selamlama mektubu," *Yeni Işık,* no. 29 (5 March 1964).

Today, however, there is no more pretence in Bulgaria of respect for the language of the Turkish minority or for the provisions of the treaties that guaranteed their rights to be educated in their own language and culture. Bulgarization of the Turkish minority is the goal, and no appeal to international law has been able to stop the Bulgarian government's drive toward that goal.

The Turkish Press in Bulgaria

The history of the Turkish press in Bulgaria also goes back to the Ottoman period. The well-known Turkish statesman, Midhat Pasha, who was governor general of the old Tuna Province, established a printing house in 1865 in the provincial administrative center of Rusçuk (Russe). In that same year the first Turkish newspaper, called *Tuna* (Danube), was published in Rusçuk. (This paper was closed the day of the Russian occupation, 13 June 1877.)[22] In Russe in 1867 a Turkish magazine titled *Mecra-i Efkâr* [Stream of Opinions] began publication, and in 1875 the bilingual newspaper *Güneş* [Sun] was inaugurated. Under Bulgarian rule many Turkish papers and magazines appeared. In 1880 two newspapers in Turkish were published in Sofia, the capital of the newly-established Bulgarian principality: one was named *Tarla* (Field) and the other was the Turkish edition of the Bulgarian Official Gazette. Two more Turkish newspapers, *Dikkat* (Attention) and *Çaylak* (Raven), began to be published in 1884, and in the following years others, were started in Sofia, Plovdiv, Russe, and Varna. During the three decades of the principality (1878-1908), more than forty newspapers in the Turkish language were published in Bulgaria: one in Sliven, eight in Russe, eleven in Sofia, and twenty-two in Plovdiv.

After 1908, during the period of the Bulgarian monarchy (1908-1944), Turkish publications in Bulgaria increased in volume. New Turkish papers of good quality appeared in different Bulgarian towns: twenty-eight were published in Sophia, sixteen in Plovdiv, ten in Kurdjal, and nine in Shumen. In the towns densely populated by the Turks, such as Razgrad, Turgovishte, Kazanlik, Vidin, Pleven, Yanbolu, and Rusçuk, new Turkish papers and magazines kept being started. Also under the Bulgarian monarchy several Turkish printing houses were founded: in Sofia there were the "Balkan," "Rehber," "Umit," "Nüvvab," and "Deliorman" printing firms, in Plovdiv, "Emniyet," "Hurşit," "Kocabalkan," "Hilal," "Tefeyyüz," and "Zerafet"; in Shumen, "Intibah" and "Terakki"; and in Varna, "Ileri." All of those printing houses contributed greatly to the burgeoning of the Turkish press and literature in Bulgaria. As well as several textbooks, sixty-seven newspapers and thirteen magazines in Turkish language were published in Bulgaria between 1908 and 1941.

Then, on 19 May 1934, came the coup that spelled disaster for the Turks of Bulgaria: the civil government was overthrown by a facist military group. During its first year of rule the fascist junta closed down ten Turkish newspapers: *Halk Sesi,*

---

[22]See Adem Ruhi Karagöz, *Bulgaristan'da Türk Basını 1879-1945* (Istanbul, 1945); İsmail Hakkı Tevfik Okday, *Bulgaristan'da Türk Basını* (Ankara, 1980), Bilâl N. Şimşir, *The Turkish Minority Press in Bulgaria: Its History and Tragedy, 1865-1985* (Ankara, 1986), and Keskioğlu, *Bulgaristan'da Türkler,* pp. 149-63.

Deliorman, İstikbal, Karadeniz, Rehber, Turan, Çiftçi Kurtuluşu, Yarın, and *Yenigün.* In the following years six others were closed, and by 1939 there was left only one Turkish newspaper in all of Bulgaria. On 28 February 1941, this last press organ of the Turkish minority, *Havadis* (The News), was abruptly shut down also.

When the Communists took power in 1944, they strongly condemned the previous regime as a regime of "terror and darkness." Under the Communists a new Turkish minority press was born. In 1945 two newspapers, *Vatan* (Fatherland) and *Işık* (Light), began to be published in Sofia. Both of these were under the aegis of the "Turkish Minority Commission of the Fatherland Front"—i.e., of the new regime. In 1946 a third Turkish newspaper called *Eylülcü Çocuk* (The Septembrist child) began publication in Sofia. It was the Turkish organ of the youth organization "Septemvriyche," or Bulgarian Pioneers. In the following year two more Turkish newspapers, *Halk Gençliği* (Popular Youth) and *Yeni Işık* (New Light), appeared in the Bulgarian capital. Finally, a monthly magazine titled *Yeni Hayat* (New Life) began publication in Sophia in 1953, completing the list.

For about two decades these five Turkish newspapers and one magazine continued publication under the communist regime. Then the government's attitude toward the Turkish minority changed, and, one by one, these publications were shut down. In 1980 only *Yeni Hayat* and *Yeni Işık* were still being published. The former was closed in 1981. As to the latter, it continued its existence for a few years longer, being published in both Turkish and Bulgarian. However, on 28 January 1985 the final issue of *Yeni Işık/Nova Swetlina* was published, and the Turkish minority press of Bulgarian went out of existence, as had the Turkish schools twenty years earlier. The tabulation below shows just how vigorous the the Turkish press had been in Bulgaria and how much was taken away from the Turkish citizens in the years after the fall of the monarch.[23]

Years (Gov't)	News papers	Maga- zines	Total	Years (Gov't)	News papers	Maga- zines	Total
1865-77 (Ottoman)	2	1	3	1908-34 (Monarchy)	67	13	80
1878-1908 (Principality)	44	0	44	1944-85 (People's Rep.)	5	1	6
TOTAL	46	1	47	TOTAL	72	14	86

Altogether a grand total of 133 Turkish periodical publications, including 118 newspapers and 15 magazines, had been made available over the years to the minority Turks of Bulgaria. The trend was clearly toward more and more such publication up until the end of the monarchy, but this continuing growth was cut off by the facist government and the press destroyed. Only limited regrowth was allowed by the communist regime, and only for a period of about twenty years was the new, smaller-sized Turkish press allowed to exist. "Everyone has the right to freedom... of

[23] Şimşir, *The Turkish Minority Press,* p. 6; idem, *Glimpses,* p. 22.

expression," states the Universal Declaration of Human Rights; but the Bulgarian government denies this rights to its Turkish citizens.

Turkish Literature and Art in Bulgaria

The literary and artistic output of the Turks in Bulgaria was, until recent years, at a significant level. This ethnic minority created, indeed, an original Turkish literature and art. (We do not include the old traditional literature of Rumelian or Balkan Turks.) In the early twentieth century there were several Turkish poets and writers in Bulgaria, but most of them emigrated to Turkey in 1930 when the Fascists seized power. They included Samim Rıfat, Muharrem Yumuk, and others. However, a few still remained in Bulgaria, such as the poets Aliosman Ayrantok, Mehmet Muzekka Con, and Hafız İslam Ergin, and this generation of 1920s poets was joined by others: Mulâzim Çavuşoğlu, Bilelaof, etc.[24] The 1950s witnessed the rise of a new generation of Turkish poets, short story writers, social novelists, humorists, and satirists, all native of Bulgaria. In the early 1950s they began to publish their work in local Turkish papers. The pages of *Işık, Yeni Işık, Halk Gençliği, Eylülcü Çocuk,* and, later, of the monthly review *Yeni Hayat* were open to them. Then, in the early 1960s, they began to publish their literary work in book format.

Poetry was the most developed form of original Turkish literature in Bulgaria, and there were numerous well-known young Turkish poets writing there. These included Latif Alief, Mehmet Çavuşev, Hasan Karahuseyinof, Ahmet Şerifof, Sabahattin Bayramof, Şahin Mustafof, Mustafa Mutkof, Naci Ferhadof, and others. Between 1959 and 1968 there were 34 books of verse, written by 24 Turkish poets, issued by the Narodna Prosveta publishing house in Sofia. The annual "1965 in Bıraktığı Şiirler" (Poems from 1965) printed 95 poems by 31 different poets. In the 1966 edition of this yearbook there were 105 poems from 40 poets; and the following year 109 poems by 36 poets appeared in this publication. There were also a number of female Turkish poets in Bulgaria, including Mefküre Mollova, Emenaz Islamova, Hava Pehlivanova, Nebiye Ibrahimova, Necmiye Mehmedova, Muzaffer Niyazieva, Şaziye Handiyeva, and others. During the 1960s there were over 50 Turkish poets active in Bulgaria. In their works one finds some words from the Azerbaijani dialect of Turkish and even a few Bulgarian words, but, generally speaking, they were skillful users of the Turkish poetic idiom, despite the fact that they were working in an environment with many non-Turkish cultural pressures.

Besides poetry, novel and short story writing was also developed among the ethnic Turks in Bulgaria. From 1959 on, new short stories were collected in yearly anthologies. An eight volume short story annual was published between 1959 and 1968, and in these same years the works of some 50 Turkish short story writers began to be printed in separate books. Between 1961 and 1968 there were 30 books containing the works of 23 writers published in Sofia. Many other Turkish stories were also published

---

[24]See Şimşir, *Bulgaristan Türkleri*, pp. 285-306; *Glimpses*, pp. 23-27, *Turkish Minority*, pp. 39-55; and Keskioğlu, *Bulgaristan'da Türkler*, pp. 127-48.

in newspapers during these years. The first novel of this new Turkish generation was *Gün Doğarken* (At Sunrise) by Sabri Tatov, published in 1963. The same author also wrote, in 1967, *Köyün Haymansi* (Wandering Peasant) — which was a long short story— and *İki Arada* (In between). Two other novels, *Saçılan Kıvılcımlar* (The flying sparkles) by Halit Aliosmanof, and *Ayrılırken* (While parting) by Ishak Raşidof, appeared in 1965 and 1968. (A list of poetic and prose works by Turkish authors in Bulgaria in the period 1957-1969 follows this article as an appendix.)

In 1952 and 1953 Turkish theaters were established in Shumen, Razgrad, and Kurdjali, and they developed many Turkish actors, who also performed on Bulgarian TV programs for the Turkish minority. Besides the three professional Turkish theater groups, there were also several amateur groups called "*Heveskârlar Kollektifi*" (Collectives of Amateurs). In order to provide materials for these acting groups many dramatic works were translated into Turkish and published in Sofia. In addition, original dramatic works were also created by the ethnic Turks in Bulgaria. Among these Bulgarian Turkish playwrights, İsmail Bekir (Ağlagül) was the most popular. He wrote seven original plays in Turkish, and they were all staged. (Bekir emigrated to Turkey in the 1970s and now works in the Ankara State Theater.)

In March of 1964, at the time when Turkish artists and writers in Bulgaria were flourishing vigorously and developing rapidly, Todor Zivkov declared that "more assistance should be provided for young Turkish writers, poets, playwrights, and journalists to better serve the people and socialism."[25] In the early 1970s, however, all of the 100 Turkish poets, playwrights, journalists, etc. were summarily silenced by Zivkov's government. Only six of them were able to emigrate to Turkey—Ali Mustafof, Ishak Raşidof, Mehmet A. Çavuşef, Mehmet Davudof, Şahin Mustafof, and, as noted above, Ismail Bekirof (Ağlagül). The fate of those forced to remain in Bulgaria but no longer permitted to create works in their own Turkish language is today unknown.

Native Turkish poets in Bulgaria tried to raise their voices against oppression and discrimination and to appeal to world public opinion. One of them, Mehmet Muzekka Con wrote:

> Time takes lives away
> Who will dry tears away?
> None to remedy woes
> Don't you see, don't you hear?
>> Human life is like a fake coin,
>> Friends of obscure fate,
>> Facing hung, hears bleeding
>> Don't you hear, don't you see?

Does the outside world hear the outcry of the Turkish minority in Bulgaria?

---

[25]See n. 21.

The poem "The Call" (*Çağrı*) written in November 1984 by Raif Recebof, another ethnic Turkish poet in Bulgaria, is an outcry of people who are afraid to live:

We are the Turks of Bulgaria
A nation deprived of her name, language, and religion.
Whatever you look at,
You will see a bleeding wound,
Flowing out of a crying heart,
In our blood tearing eyes.
....
....
How we are drowned, left alone,
In the pool of our sweat and tear,
In the pool of our outpouring blood.
We need the help of a meager hand,
The light of a candle,
Just a word.
Turks we are, oppressed, tormented, cursed.[26]

Conclusion

Bulgaria's push to assimilate its Turkish population has been labeled by one independent observer "cultural genocide." The phrase is completely apt, as the Turkish minority that is being inexorably forced to abandon its own special identity and to merge with the majority Bulgarians would attest. Once the Communist government decided to cease any pretence of abiding by international law in its treatment of its Turkish minority, it mounted a full scale, ruthless attack on the most important cultural asset of its Turkish citizens—namely, their language—as the most efficient way to cut them off from their ethnic-cultural roots. First, it made it extremely difficult for the language to be passed on to the children by eliminating all Turkish instruction in the schools. Next, it shut down all Turkish language periodicals published in Bulgaria, making it impossible for the Turks to keep themselves informed about current events through any but Bulgarian press organs or to view the world through any but Bulgarian journalists' eyes. Then it turned its attention to the Turkish literary and artistic scene and forbade the community's writers of poetry, prose, and drama to continue to create works in the Turkish language; this action blocked still another avenue through which those who managed, despite the difficulties, to learn their language might extend or strengthen their cultural roots. Turkish literary works already published were removed from the shelves and destroyed. (Naturally, it is prohibited to import any publications in Turkish). Now it has even become a crime to speak Turkish in public.

---

[26]For the full original text in Turkish of this poem, see *Türk Kültürü. Bulgaristan Türkleri Sayısı*, no. 263 (March 1985): 1522.

In addition to these direct assaults on all use of the Turkish language in Bulgaria, the government has decreed that the one last vestige of that language left to the Turks shall be obliterated—i.e., their Turkish names. By forcing the Turks to take on Bulgarian names the government anticipates that their identity as Turks will thus be completely destroyed. Once it is no longer obvious to the world that there is a large Turkish minority in the country, Bulgaria will feel free to say: "We are not violating any treaty obligations toward our Turkish minority. There are no Turks in Bulgaria."

Turkish Historical Society, Ankara, Turkey

TABLE 1. Population of the Territories South of the Balkan Mountains, 1876

Sandjak	Ethnic Origin		Total
	Bulgarians	Non-Bulgarians	
Islimye (Sliven)	100,500	186,400	286,000
Filibe (Plovdiv)	382,500	564,600	946,600
Edirne (Andrinople)	124,100	331,300	455,700
Selanik (Salonika)	152,600	275,000	427,600
Drama	26,500	91,100	117,600
Gelibolu (Gallipoli)	42,200	160,000	202,200
Tekirdağ (Rodosto)	40,100	133,200	173,300

SOURCE Archives of the Ambassador of Turkey to Paris, confidential circular of 2 May 1876, no. 51062/40, Safvet Pasha to Aarifi Pasha, annex: "Travail sur la Bulgarie." See also Bilâl N. Şimşir, *Turkish Emigrations from the Balkans. Documents,* vol. 2, *A Year of Transition 1879* (Ankara, 1970), p. CLXVIII.

TABLE 2. Population of Eastern Bulgaria in 1884

District	Religious Composition				Ethnic Composition			
	Ortho-dox	Per-cent	Maho-metan	Per-cent	Bulga-rians	Per-cent	Turks	Per-cent
Varna	55,594	52.5	47,531	44.9	40,885	38.6	46,304	43.7
Eski-Djuma	13,290	18.0	60,752	82.0	13,018	17.6	48,684	79.3
Pravadi	23,528	37.2	39,324	62.3	23,238	37.8	36,507	57.8
Razgrad	37,975	31.0	84,104	68.8	37,630	30.8	81,548	66.6
Raschuk	59,172	44.8	69,184	52.4	54,754	41.5	65,965	50.0
Silistra	28,514	28.2	71,864	71.1	26,156	25.9	65,087	64.4
Choumla	33,524	30.5	74,579	67.9	32,392	29.5	71,113	64.7
TOTAL	251,606		447,242		228,073		425,208	

SOURCE: Bulgarian Bureau of Statistics, *Résultats Généraux de Recensement de la Population du 1/13 Janvier 1881* (Sophia, 1884).

APPENDIX : List of Turkish Literary Works Published by Ethnic Turks in Bulgaria in the Period 1957-1969

Poets and Poetry :

1. Ahmed Şerifof, *Müjde* (Good news), 1960
2.   — *Azin Çoğu* (The most of the less), 1963
3.   — *Üçüncü Adım* (The third step), 1969
4. Ahmet Eminof, *Sensizliginle Beraber* (Without you), 1968
5. Ališ Saidof, *Bulutsuz Günler* (Cloudless days), 1966
6. Durhan Hasanof, *Insan Kardeşlerim* (My human brothers), 1965
7. Faik Ismailof, *Ağarınca Tan* (When it dawns), 1966
8. Hasan Karahuseyinof, *Sarhoş Gönül* (The drunk heart), 1961
9.   — *İç İçe* (Within each other), 1967.
10.   — *Bir Günün Romanı* (The Story of a day), 1966
11. Ishak Raşidof, *Dostlar ve Düşmanlar* (Friends and enemies), 1967
12. Ismail A. Çavuşef, *Dilek* (Wish), 1967.
13. Latif Aliyef, *Bir Bahçeden Bir Bahçeye* (From one garden to another), 1961
14.   —, *Bir Yeşil Seviyorum* (I love a green), 1968.
15. Lütfi Demirof, *Şafak* (Dawn), 1963.
16. Mefküre Mollova, *Şiirler* (Poems), 1964.
17. Mehmet A. Çavuşef, *Yılların Seranad* (The Concert of the years), 1964.
18. Mehmet Davudof, *Demette Bir Çiçek* (One flower in a bunch of flowers), 1966
19. Mehmet Muzekka Con, *Alın Terim* (My efforts), 1964
20. Mustafa Mutkof, *Sabah Yolcusu* (Morning passenger), 1965
21. Naci Ferhadof, *Dağli ve Deniz* (Mountain and sea), 1966
22. Nevzat Mehmedof, *Ayı Dayı* (Uncle bear), 1966
23.   —, *Deniz* (Sea), 1966
24.   —, *Üç Beygir* (Three horses), 1967
25. Niyazi M. Huseyinof, *Köy Yankıları* (The echoes of village), 1964
26. Osman Azizof, *Büyük Ateş* (The Fire), 1965
27. Recep Küpçü, *Ötesi Var* (Its beyond exist), : 1962
28.   — *Ötesi Düş Değil* (The other side is not a dream), 1967
29. Sabahattin Bayramof, *Adresim Şudur* (This is my address), 1962
30.   — *Ahmet*, 1964
31.   — *Sokaklarım Çağrışımlar içinde* (My streets remembered), 1966
32. Süleyman Yusufof, *Bir Uctan Bir Uca memleket* (The country from one end to the other), 1966
33. Şaban Mahmudof, *Gerginlik* (Stress), 1966
34. Şahin Mustafof, *Vatan Toprağı* (Fatherland), 1965
35. Ibrahim Tatarlief (Ed.), *Antalogiya: 9.9.1944'ten sonra Bulgaristan Türklerinin Edebiyatı—28 şair ve yazarı içine alır.* (Anthology: Literature of Bulgarian Turks since September 9, 1944- 28 poets and writers included), 1960

36.   —   *Antaloji: Bulgaristan Türklerinin 1944-1954 arası edebiyatı 38 şair ve yazarı içine alır.* (Anthology. Literature of the Turks in Bulgaria between 1944-1964, containing 38 poets and writers), 1964
37. B. Çakirof and H. Karahuseyinof (Eds.), Kaynak (Sources), 1957
38. Akif Solakof (Ed.), *Çağlıyan* (Waterfall), 1958
39. Ahmet Şerifof (Ed.), *Şiirler* : 1958 (Poems of 1958), 1959
40. Sabahattin Bayramof (Ed.), *Şiirler: 1959-1960* (Poems of 1959-1960), 1961
41.   —   (Ed.), *Şiirler: 1961* (Poems of 1961), 1962
42.   —   (Ed.), *1964'un Bıraktığı Şiirler* (Poems of 1964), 1964
43.   —   (Ed.) *1965'in Bıraktığı Şiirler* (Poems of 1965), 1966
44. S. Tahirof, I. Çavuşef and I. Beytullof (Eds.) *1966'nin Bıraktığı Şiirler* (Poems of 1966), 1967
45. N. Ferhadof - A. Eminof (Ed.), *1967'nin Bıraktığı Şiirler* (Poems of 1967), 1969

Writers, Stories and Novels:

47. Ahmet Şerifof, *Şirin* (Beautiful), 1966
47.   —   *Adım Adım Memleket* (The country step by step), 1967
48. Ahmet Timisef, *Aydınlık* (Light), 1965
49. Ali Kadirof, *Eserleri* (His works), 1965
50. Ali Murtazof, *Dostluk* (Friendship), 1961
51. Halit Aliosmanof, *Dağlının Oğlu* (The son of a montaineer), 1963
52.   —   *Yediveren Gülü* (Rose), 1966
53.   —   *Saçılan Kıvılcımlar — Roman* (The sparkies—ovel), 1965
54. Hüsmen Ismailof, *Bekleyiş* (Expectation), 1965
55. Ishak Rasidof, *Yeşil Kuşak* (Green Belt), 1966
56. Ishak Raşidof, *Ayrılırken—Roman* (While parting—novel), 1968
57. Karaoğlan (Karahuseyin), *Yiğitlik Özüdür Yiğidin* (Heroism is the essence of the hero), 1968
58. Kemal Bunarciyef, *Yıllardan Sonra* (After the years), 1968
59. Kazim Memisof, *Kalbimin Sesi* (The Voice of my heart), 1961
60. Mehmet Bekirof, *Yel Değirmeni* (Windmill), 1968
61. Mehmet Beytullah, *Aramızdakiler* (Those who are among us), 1966
62. Muharrem Tahsinof, *Ayak Sesleri* (The sound of footsteps), 1966
63.   —   *Carıklı Filozof* (Peasant Philosopher), 1969
64. Muhittin Mehmedeminof, *Zaman Zaman içinde* (Once upon a time), 1965
65. Mustafa Kahveciyef, *Hayat yolcusu* (Passenger of life), 1968
66. Nadiye Ahmedova, *Mavi Kordeleli Güvercin* (The dove with the blue ribbon), 1964
67. Nadiye Ahmedova, *Güldalı* (Rose branch), 1965
68.   —   *Solmayan Karanfil* (Everlasting carnation), 1966
69. Osman Salief, *Hayat Yollarında* (On the roads of life), 1966
70. Ömer Osmanof, *Yaralı Güvercin* (Wounded dove), 1965
71.   —   *Bırak Kocamı* (Leave my husband alone), 1967
72. Riza Mollof, *Olan Şeyleri* (Things that happen), 1965

73. Sabahattion Bayramof, *Türk Atasözleri* (Turkish proverbs), 1965
74. Sabri Tatof, *Gün Doğarken - Roman* (Sunrise—ovel), 1963
75.   —   *Köyün Haymanası* (Wandering Peasant), 1963
76.   —   *İki Arada—Roman* (Between two—novel), 1967
77. Salih Baklaciyef, *Çay Boyunda* (Alongside the river), 1961
78.   —   *Arda Dile Gelse* (If Arda could speak), 1964
79. Selim Bilalof, *Gerçekleşen Emel* (Realized dream), 1965
80. Süleyman Gavazof, *Tanıdığım İnsanlar* (People that I know), 1961
81.   —   *Yol* (Road), 1968
82. M. Ivanova (Ed.), *Hikâyeler 1959-1960* (Short stories of 1959-1960), 1960
83. Sabri Tatof (Ed.), *Hikâyeler 1960-1961* (Short stories of 1960-1961), 1961
84. S. Bayramof (Ed.) *Hikâyeler 1961-1962* (Short stories of 1961-1962). 1962
85. S. Bayramof (Ed.), *1964'un Bıraktığı Hikâyeler* (Short stories of 1964). 1965
86.   —   *1965'in Bıraktığı Hikâyeler* (Short stories of 1965), 1966
87. T. Deliorman (Ed.), *Hikâyeler 1962-1963* (Short stories of 1962-1963). 1963
88. I. Beytullof, K. M. Tahsinof, F. Saliyef and S. Tatof (Eds.), *1966'nin Bıraktığı Hikâyeler* (Short stories of 1966), 1967
89. M. Tahsinof, K. Memisef and H. Aliosmanof (Eds.), *1967'nin Bıraktığı Hikâyeler* (Short stories of 1967), 1968

NOTES : All of the above-listed works were published by Narodna Prosveta Publishing House in Sofia. Out of the 51 different poets and writers in this list, five had already emigrated to Turkey in the period 1969-1978. They are Ali Mustafof, Ishak Rasidof, Mehmet A. Cavusef, Mehmet Davudof, and Şahin Mustafof.

Bernard Lory

AHMED AGA TĂMRAŠLIJATA:
THE LAST DEREBEY OF THE RHODOPES

Few regions in Bulgaria have as strong a feeling of their own specificity as the Rhodopes. This is, of course, due first to the region's physical characteristics, crowded as it is with chaotic mountain ranges, covered with thick forests, and isolated for want of a communications system; but the main attribute of the Rhodopes is that it is "the oldest and most mysterious part of Bulgaria." This is not a reference to the area's geological age and shadowed forests but to a kind of historical depth: the country perpetually looks into its remotest past, into its Thracian origins.

This romantic view of the Rhodopes surfaced in the nineteenth century, exalting the figure of Orpheus, the Thracien poet inspired by nature. It found expression in a work of literary forgery known as "Veda Slovena," mythological folk songs, published in 1874 and 1881, in which ancient names, such as Orfen, were to be found complete with Sanskrit roots. (Some Bulgarian scholars still assume this work to be authentic.) At that time the Rhodopes were almost *terra incognita* for western scholars and for the young Bulgarian intelligentsia as well. With the exception of a few Christian villages, such as Čepelare, Široka Lăka, Rajkovo and Ustovo (the latter two now united, forming the town of Smoljan), the Rhodopes did not participate in the general Bulgarian national revival of the nineteenth century. The reason for this was not only the natural difficulty of communication in the region, but also the fact that the majority of the population was Muslim Turkish-speaking in the east (Arda valley), Bulgarian-speaking in the west.

The Bulgarian-speaking Muslims, the Pomaks, seemed especially mysterious, and it is no wonder that the apocryphal "Veda Slovena" was ascribed to them. The leaders of the Bulgarian revival ignored the Pomaks for a long time. This should not surprise us, as the Bulgarian renaissance was, in its first phase, a religious and cultural movement of reaction against the dominating Hellenism of the Orthodox church. As it progressed, this renaissance became more national and less religious, so that community of language little by little came to seem more important than differences of religion; but this evolution was only embryonic under the *millet*-system of Ottoman rule, becoming more definitive after independence in 1878.

The first Bulgarian to consider the existence of the Pomaks as a group (and not as a mere series of individual conversions to Islam) was, apparently, Vasil Aprilov, who in 1841 estimated their number to be approximately 50,000. Georgi Rakovski mentioned them in 1856 and deplored their lack of national feeling, as they were not interested in independence. Ljuben Karavelov in 1867 put their population at 500,000. Statements about the Pomaks in the Bulgarian press (*Carigradski Vestnik, Dunavska Zora*) during those years were very vague and confused.[1]

The first real concern about integrating the Pomak population into the general movement of Bulgarian revival appeared in 1869 in the correspondence of Najden Gerov, the Bulgarian-born Russian vice-consul in Plovdiv. The initiative for the concern, however, seems to have been that of the Russian embassy in Istanbul, which was worried about possible Polish propaganda among the Pomaks (on the basis of the phonetic similarity between Poljak and Pomak!). In a letter dated 8 October 1869, Gerov reassures Count Ignatiev on this point, but suggests that some action is needed:

> But the idea of nationality is spreading so quickly, that it may soon catch on among the Pomaks too. This is why, if it is necessary to prevent the undesirable development of the above-mentioned idea [Polish propaganda] among them and to give it the appropriate direction, indispensable measures must be taken soon.[2]

In order to have a direct effect on the "*kulturträger*" among the Pomaks, he suggests, some of their literate people ought to be employed as *kjatibs* (Turkish secretaries) at the vice-consulate or as teachers of Turkish—if not in schools, then for individuals, who would be able to convert them to the national cause. It is paradoxical that the first attempt to integrate the Pomaks proposed to use their (very relative) knowledge of Turkish as a bridge. In another letter, dated 15 December 1869, Gerov makes the following suggestions:

> In the places and villages inhabited both by Pomaks and Bulgarians, one might send to the latter, schoolteachers to spread propaganda among the Pomaks. But the municipalities of these places and villages are not able to pay the teachers' fees, which they are liable to ask for in return for the responsibility they are taking. So they will have to be subsidized.
> In conclusion, I am forced to add that, considering the impression which I made on the Pomaks during my short stay among them in Čepino, where I went last years to bathe, it would be very useful if I were to be allowed from time to time to travel through those places inhabited by the Pomaks under different pretexts such as, for example, hunting, collecting antiques, etc. One might object that my travels will provoke the suspicion of the Turkish government. Indeed, the Turkish government cannot but consider with suspicion the rounds of Russian agents, but in my experience this suspicion will be completely overcome if each time I borrow from the local authorities one or two zapties, the presence of whom, if one is clever enough, will not be the least disturbing.[3]

Thus, even though a real concern for the future of the Pomaks was expressed, nothing was really done at that time to integrate them into the Bulgarian national

---

[1] Kiril Vasilev, *Rodopskite bălgari mohamedani* (Plovdiv, 1961), pp. 232-45.
[2] Petăr Petrov, *Po sledite na nasilieto* (Sofia, 1972), pp. 396-97.
[3] Ibid., p. 396.

revival movement. With the Oriental crisis of 1875-1879 the pace of events suddenly accelerated, and the Pomaks, as well as the Orthodox Bulgarians, had to make fateful decisions, for which they were absolutely not prepared. Many tragic and bloody incidents occurred at a time when the Bulgarians had no clear idea of the place they occupied within the Ottoman Empire or of the place they might occupy in an independent Bulgarian state. The contradictions of that period, which many historians today still find confusing, can be seen reflected in the personality of one prominent Pomak leader, Ahmed aga Tămrašlijata (Ahmed aga of Tàmraš).

In this article, we shall explore the relationship between the Pomaks and the Christian Bulgarians during the period 1876-1886, as demonstrated not only by the historical facts but also by the interpretations these facts have received in historical works. After a brief discussion of the *nahija* of Rupčos and of Karahodžov family who ruled it in the nineteenth century, we shall analyze the events of the April Uprising of 1876 in relation to the Rhodopes and, in particular, the siege and destruction of Peruštica. The historical polemic concerning the participation of Ahmed aga Tămrašlijata in the massacres that occurred at this time reveals the ambiguity and contradictoriness of the relationship between the Pomaks and the Christian Bulgarians. This ambiguity was strengthened by Ahmed aga's rebellious attitude towards the Bulgarian government of Eastern Rumelia (1879-1886), demonstrated by his annexation of twenty-unsubordinate villages to the so-called "Pomak Republic."[4]

Rupčos and Its Rulers

The *nahija* of Rupčos, a dependency of the *kaza* of Plovdiv, was a part of the central Rhodopes, which comprised the Čaja River basin (now Čepelarska) and the right bank of the River Văča. It extended from the foothills of the Rhodopes, some ten kilometers south of Plovdiv and immediately south of Stanimaka (now Asenovgrad), to the watershed of the Arda basin, where the *kaza* of Ahă-Čelebi began. It included some fifty or sixty villages, and its main seat was in Čepelare until 1832, at which time, with the promotion of Hasan Karahodžov to the post of administrator of Rupčos, it was moved to Tămraš in the north. Hasan aga married a cousin of the influential Salih aga, ruler of the *kaza* of Ahă-Čelebi, and ruled the Rupcŏs district as his own, maintaining

---

[4]The most complete work on Ahmed aga Tămrašlijata is that by Angel Vălčev, *Tămraš* (Sofia, 1973). One of the oldest sources of information—but not always reliable—is Hristo pop Konstantinov, *Nepokornite sela*, 2 vols. (Tărnovo, 1887). See also "Iz Rodopite—Rupčos," *Periodičesko spisanie*, nos. 58, 59, and 60 (1899). Three authors reported on visits to the insubordinate villages: the Czech Vaclav Dobruski, *Bălgarija prez pogleda na česki pătešestvenici* (Sofia, 1894), pp. 64-94; the Bulgarian revolutionary Zahari Stojanov, *Săčinenija*, vol. 3 (Sofia, 1983); and the Englishman Burchier (orthography uncertain) in *Mišal*, nos. 6 and 7 (1894). The historiographers of the Rhodopes, often using accounts passed down orally, give interesting information: see Vasil Dečov, *Minaloto na Čepelare* (Plovdiv, 1978); and Nikolaj Hajtov, *Minaloto na Javrovo, Devin, Manastir* (Plovdiv, 1985), this edition containing also Hajtov's polemical articles on Ahmed aga. On the April Uprising, see Dimităr Strašimirov, *Istorija na aprilskoto văstanie*, 3 vols. (Plovdiv, 1907), and Hristo Gandev, *Aprilskoto Văstanie* (Sofia, 1976).

independence from the central administration (in Plovdiv or Istanbul).[5] He died in 1855 and was succeeded by his eldest son, Ahmed aga.

The wealth of the Karahodžov family came from its large sheep flocks, which moved between the rich Rhodopean summer pastures and the warmer Aegean winter pastures. This wealth and authority of the family was demonstrated by the size of their *konaks*. Hasan aga possessed three estates (*čifliks*), which were divided between his four sons at his death. The first one, south of Tămraš on the southern slopes of Mount Modăr, was inherited by Ahmed aga; the second, inherited by Smail aga, was situated some fifteen kilometers north of Tămraš, in a place called Sredne (the major part of it fell within Bulgaria after the territorial agreement of 1886). The third *čiflik*, attributed in common to Mustafa aga (who soon died) and Adil aga, was in Tikla, also north of Tămraš; Zahari Stojanov saw this estate in ruins in 1885:

> It is not just an ordinary *čiflik* of the kind we are used to: it is a palace, a summer residence, a fortress; it reminds us at first sight of the palaces of the feudal rulers which we never saw with our own eyes, but have only read about. Where are the *čifliks* of our *čorbadzi* and civil servants? All these gathered, together in one place might form but one wall of the aga's palace. This palace may have burnt down, but with its crenellated walls, its white chimneys still standing erect above the ruins, high walls decorated with many shooting-windows, two fountains still flowing with the same speed in its courtyard, it bears clear an undisputable witness to the fact that slavery reigned here, that its owner was powerful.[6]

This description should not mislead the reader. The Karahodžov family led the frugal life of all mountain dwellers. Their wives (Pomaks were with few exceptions monogamous) were active housewives, with very little domestic help. Their flocks could probably be counted by the thousands, not by the tens of thousands as was thought by some authors who were misled by the magnifying effect of the oral tradition. However, the prestige of the rulers of Tămraš was indeed immense, and the memory of Ahmed aga is still alive today in the Rhodopes.

Ahmed aga's prestige stemmed not only from his wealth (considerable by Rhodopean standards), but also from his independent attitude towards official authority, which he maintained under Ottoman as well as Rumeliot rule. Ahmed aga was an absolute ruler whose personal decisions were law in Rupčos; but he had also an intuitive feeling for justice, which was appreciated by the local population, Christian and Muslim alike. Many anecdotes about his expeditious decisions have been collected.[7] Human life did not count for much in his eyes, but honor and order did, and as a result—the fact was noted by the Russian consul in Plovdiv—robbery was unknown within the borders of Rupčos. This did not mean, however, that Ahmed aga had moral scruples about robbery, an activity deeply rooted in the poor mountain dweller's lifestyle—as was revealed during the 1876 events, to the detriment of the neighboring villages. This relationship

---

[5] Vălčev, *Tămraš*, p. 88.

[6] *Săčinenija*, p. 400.

[7] Hajtov, *Minaloto na Javrovo*, pp. 44-52; Vălčev, *Tămraš*, pp. 111,113.

between Ahmed aga and his people was picturesquely described by Stojanov, who in 1883, five full years after Bulgaria's liberation, witnessed the reaction to Ahmed's attendance at a dedication ceremony for the monastery of Bjala Cerkva (located on the northern slopes of the Rhodopes in a territory ruled by Eastern Rumelia) at a time when the man was leading twenty-one villages in open rebellion against the Plovdiv government:

> The news "Ahmedaa is coming" disrupted the calm and passed from mouth to mouth. Even the horo-dancing stopped, the bagpipes grew silent, everybody turned toward the fountain, many thought that a scandal was inevitable and that the crowd would assert its own will.
>
> But Ahmedaa was approaching, mounted on a black horse, in his Juzbaši-uniform, with saber, revolver and some decorations on his chest. His escort was composed of fifteen to twenty Pomaks, who accompanied him from the village. They were armed to the teeth, each with two revolvers, a Winchester held in the left hand, while the other hand rested on the handle of a long yatagan. This escort seemed to have been specially chosen: all handsome young Pomaks, tall as the fir trees of their mountains, with shirts open to the waist like *pehlivans*, with enormous moustaches, the tips of which reached to their eyes. I think that at the least sign of an attack from the Bulgarian side, they were prepared to take position, the yatagan's sharp edge would flicker in the air, the Winchesters would fire and all this despite the fact that the Bulgarians numbered three thousand and the Pomaks fifteen.
>
> But what a wonder. Instead of attack and offense, the Bulgarian peasants, men and women alike, welcomed the aga as if he were master there, as if he were not a rebel but still their *kǎrserdar*. While he was offering one hand, so that white-haired old men and old grandmothers mights kiss it, he was forced to abandon his second hand as well. "welcome, Ahmedaa," "Hoš geldin, aga," "While you were deciding whether to visit us or not, we grew old and you are still young!" Such voices were heard from the crowd, which gathered to welcome its Emperor of forty years. And it is ridiculous to suppose that the Bulgarians did this out of fear, as everybody knew that Ahmedaa was no more their master. Predominant here were feelings of a past grandeur, of present ceremony, of relationship between former slaves, now free people, on the one hand, and, on the other, these now destitute and humiliated.
>
> After a while, the Bulgarian *kabadaiti* reacted. These were rural policemen and *pandurs*, who in the Turkish era had had the ill fate to tremble before Ahmedaa's people, humiliating themselves as servants. In order to demonstrate that they were no longer raja, they began to undulate in a horo before the others. Not just an ordinary horo, but one with a display of knives and pistols, whose handles were protruding. Ahmedaa's people, leaning on each other's shoulders, began to criticize the Bulgarians for still not knowing how to wear knives and ammunition bags. The latter could not stand it any longer. They told the Pomaks, half seriously, half in jest, that God willing Ahmedaa would join them in a pilgrimage to Plovdiv. "Oho, you have thought about this very late in the day, komsular," answered the Pomaks, seizing the handles of their knives.

"Like many people gathered here, you'll have to pass over our dead bodies before you see Plovdiv."
        And all such arrogance, on Rumeliot territory, in the presence of 3,000 Bulgarians, in the presence of gendarmes and soldiers! The Bulgarian *kabadaii* hung their heads.[8]

But we have anticipated our story, showing Ahmed aga's very unique position during the Rumeliot period. Let us go back to the last years of Ottoman rule, to the fateful year of 1876, during which Ahmed aga Tămrašlijata achieved his sinister, world wide reputation.

The April Uprising of 1876: The Events in Peruštica.

The April Uprising of 1876 was an important event in Bulgarian history, but not as important in geographical or military terms as certain nationalistic Bulgarian historians would lead us to believe. It was, in fact, only effective in the region of Sredna Gora (with Panagjurište as center) and, to a lesser degree, in central Stara Planina (Balkan range) and the northern fringe of the Rhodopes. From a strategic point of view, it betrayed very poor, amateurish planning. It was a turning point in Bulgarian political attitude, however. For the first time the Bulgarians seriously envisaged taking their fate into their own hands and playing an active role on the international political chessboard. The uprising had been prepared for more by the spread of national enthusiasm among the population than by any true organization (planned coordination between the various committees abroad and in Bulgaria did not function well when the decisive moment came), and it demonstrated more romanticism than real political thinking. Its main effect was, in fact, indirect, shocking Russian public opinion by the ferocity of the repression and provoking a bellicose response.
        The Bulgarian Central Revolutionary Committee had been founded in December 1869 in Bucharest. Its most active member was Vasil Levski, who had the dangerous task of organizing local committees on Bulgarian (i.e., Ottoman) territory and, thus bridging the gap between the country's residents and its emigres. After Levski's capture and execution (February 1873), the Bulgarian committee was disorganized for some time, but the new Oriental crisis that flared up in 1875 in Herzegovina gave it new hope and decided it to act. A first, very localized, attempt at insurrection took place in Stara Zagora (Eski Zağra) in September 1875. For organizational purposes, Bulgarian territory was divided into four operational districts: Tărnovo, Sliven, Vraca, and Plovdiv. As the last was a security risk to the conspiracy—its population being part Turkish and part Greek—the seat of the fourth district was moved to Panagjurište. The main organizers (or "apostles") there were Panajot Volov, Georgi Benkovski, Zahari Stojanov, and Georgi Ikonomov. They encouraged patriotic and revolutionary activity in the Bulgarian villages of the northern slopes of the Rhodopes: Batak, Peštera, Bracigovo, Peruštica,

---

[8]*Săčinenija*, p. 398-99.

etc. We shall focus our attention on the last named village, as Ahmed aga Tămrašlijata was bound up with the bloody events that took place there.[9]

The insurrection had been set for 12 May 1876, but the plans were betrayed, and it broke out prematurely in Koprivštica on 2 May (20 April according to the Julian calendar, hence the name "April Uprising"). The news that the national uprising had begun reached Peruštica the following day. From the hills the inhabitants could see villages burning in the plain, not yet knowing whether they were Bulgarian or Turkish. The Ottoman authorities in Plovdiv (Aziz paša), confronted with what seemed to be a general uprising, called on Istanbul for help and decided in the meantime to use the local Muslim population against the rebels. The ill-renowed *bašibozuk*s (irregular auxiliary troops) included mainly Turks from the Thracian plain (Plovdiv, Tatar Pažardik, Karlovo, etc.), but also Tcherkess, Muslim gypsies, and (it will be painful for Bulgarian historians to acknowledge this) Pomaks from the Rhodopes.

The Bulgarian population of Peruštica, as in most places during the April events, was not unanimous as to what attitude should be adopted. On one side, the revolutionaries, led by the schoolteacher Petăr Bonev, decided to dig trenches around the villages in order to defend it. On the other side, the more conservative *čorbadži*s (djado Rangel Gačev, etc.) decided to call on the Ottoman authorities in Plovdiv for help. Both sides acknowledged that the main danger was from the roaming *bašibozuk* bands, but there was disagreement between them as to how an attack on Peruštica should be prevented. On 6 May, three Pomaks arrived, sent by Adil aga (some authors assert that they were sent directly by his brother, Ahmed aga) and asking for two cartloads of bread for the *bašibozuk*s from the Rhodopes, who were gathering at his *čiflik* at Sredne. At this point the committee members "seized power" in Peruštica and arrested the Pomaks. They were executed the same day, allegedly in retaliation for the murder near the village of a Bulgarian by an Albanian. Peruštica's position in the insurrection was thus established by the shedding of blood. The next day Ahmed aga sent a Bulgarian Christian to enquire about his men, whom the officials of Peruštica denied having seen. They were warned that an attack was being prepared against them, and they could see the flames from the neighboring villages of Bojkovo and Dedovo, set on fire by the Pomak *başibozuk*s of Tămraš, led by Smail aga. They continued to organize the fortification of the village, which counted 648 guns. On the following evening, djado Rangel Gačev arrived from Plovdiv, leading two zapties that had orders to defend Peruštica from attack. They did not stay, however, but left for the neighboring Turkish village of Ustina. (It should be noted that two mounted zapties were sufficient to protect the Bulgarian village of Brestovica from destruction, even though some of its inhabitants had participated in the insurrection.)

On 9 May the *bašibozuk*s from Tămraš appeared above Peruštica, burning down the monastery of Sveti Todor. They did not attack immediately because a special commission came from Plovdiv to negotiate with the *čorbadži*s from Peruštica and the

---

[9] Our description of the events in Peruštica generally follows the accounts given by Strašimirov, *Istorija,* and by Georgi Natev in his memoire, *Spomeni* (Sofia, 1976); unfortunately, Natev's complete memoire, published in Plovdiv in 1901, is unavailable, and we have used a reprint edition of a shorter version (about three-quarters of the length of the whole work). Included also among the sources are Vălčev, *Tǎmrǎš;* Hajtov, *Minaloto na Javrovo;* and Marija and Manol Manolov, "Ahmed aga Tamraslijata i za edno tălkuvane na negovata rolja v potušavaneto na Aprilšavoto Văstanie," *Istoričeski Pregled,* no. 1 (1972), pp. 97-109.

Turkish notables from neighboring Ustina. The Bulgarians categorically refused the idea that any of the irregular troops should enter their village, even with the official mission of "protecting" them. The Turkish authorities considered that this was open rebellion, although still not sending any regular army troops to crush it. As the commission was retiring to Ustina, part of the Bulgarian population decided to surrender. When this crowd of notables, women, and children, led by the priests, had come to within fifty steps of the *bašibozuks*, some shots were fired from Peruštica, causing the troops, who had seemed friendly up until that time, to massacre this harmless population.[10] So the fight began, and it was to last five full days, as the inhabitants of Peruštica defended themselves passionately.

The regular army, led by Rašid paša, arrived on the evening of 10 May and began to bombard the village on the following day, demolishing the upper church (Sv. Atanas), so that the population had to seek shelter in the lower church (Sv. Arhangel). During that night and the next some hundreds of people managed to escape from the village. The bombardment continued on 13 May, with an interruption for negotiations at about midday. The three Bulgarian negotiators were, however, shot in the back while returning to the still resisting church. The desperate defense was finally crushed on 14 May and ended in a blood bath.

The uprising cost Peruštica all its 30 houses, burned during the fighting. Shortly after the massacre there there were estimates of 1,000 or 1,500 dead.[11] Strašimirov gives a list of 208 inhabitants (47 women among them) killed.[12] Being one of the villages destroyed closest to Plovdiv, Peruštica's ruins were visited by many European diplomats and journalists: Walter Baring, the secretary of the British embassy, and Eugene Schuyler, the American consul in Istanbul; journalists Januarius Macgahan, an American, Robert More, an Englishman, and Ivan de Woestyne, a Frenchman, etc. It was also one of the few places where the Ottoman government took some care in rebuilding houses.[13]

Ahmed Aga and Destruction of Peruštica

It is a fact that Ahmed aga Tămrašlijata's name was connected with the suppression of the April Uprising from the very beginning. We find him mentioned in English and French, as well as Russian, diplomatic documents; but it is not always clear what massacre he is supposed to have participated in. He was very often confused with Ahmed aga Barutanlijata, also a Pomak leader, but from the Dospat range of the

---

[10] These shots were fired by Kočo Čestimenski, from Plovdiv; in our view he was in a large part responsible for the bloodshed of the repression. Čestimenski appears to have been a maximalist whose position only made matters worse. In Plovdiv he was the only one (together with D. Sveštarov) to set fire to his shop, a step decided upon by the Committee, to cause a big fire in the main town and to make any return impossible. He openly fired the first shots in Peruštica, causing the massacre (as is reported in George Natev's memoires). He resisted up until the last moment in the besieged church and killed with his own hand his wife and child before committing suicide. This attitude may be considered heroic, but it was highly uncharacteristic of Bulgarian behavior.

[11] Macgahan, *Turskite zverstva v Bălgarija* (Sofia, 1880), p. 72.

[12] *Istorija*, vol. 3, p. 413.

[13] Macgahan, *Turskite zverstva*, p. 72.

Rhodopes, who was responsible for the famous massacre of Batak. The American journalist Macgahan writes as early as June 1876 about Peruštica:

> This village was captured and burnt down by the Basi-božuks, led by Ahmed aga, who should not be confused with the other Ahmed aga, the even more disgusting massacrer of Batak.[14]

We find confusion, however, in a report by Prince Ceretelev to Giers in June 1876:

> Batak, 700 maisons, détruit par Ahmed aga Tymrychly, près de 2000 personnes y périrent après avoir rendu leurs armes.[15]

Russian and French sources agree about other villages:

> No. 15: Baikovo, l'école, l'église, 60 maisons, 20 personnes massacrées (commandant Ahmed aga). No. 16: Dedovo, détruit par Ismail aga, frère du précédent.[16]

In his report to Lord Derby, dated 7 August 1876, Hutton Dupuis, the British agent writes:

> Peroushtitza: with 2 churches and 2 schools, 320 houses, totally destroyed. One of the priests of this village, pope Stoimen, was massacred with his children and followers, while making their submission to the chief of Bashibozouks, Ahmed aga of Tumbrush.[17]

Robert More, who visited Peruštica in October 1876 with a bilingual interpreter, reports:

> During the time of their being in the lower church three women were sent to tell the commanders, three brothers from Rotroushlon Achmet Aga, Smil Aga, and Adil Aga, that the villagers would surrender. All the three women were shot on their way back.[18]

Even though the three negotiators were men, and it is difficult to identify "Rotroushian" with Tamras, the three names of the negotiators are accurately given. The American general consul in Istanbul, Schuyler, also accused Ahmed aga, as was confirmed later by his Bulgarian interpreter.[19]

---

[14]Ibid., p. 63.

[15]*Aprilsko Vǎstanie: Sbornik ot dokumenti*, vol. 1 (Sofia, 1954), p. 532.

[16]See Archives du Minitère des Affaires Etrangères, Correspondance Consulaire et Politique, Philippopolis 1876, pp. 330ff, and *Aprilsko Vǎstanie*, vol. 1, pp. 532.

[17]*Aprilsko Vǎstanie*, vol. 1, p. 521.

[18]R.J. More, *Under the Balkans* (London, 1876), p. 75.

[19]Petǎr Dimitrov, *Lični Spomeni* (Sofia, 1918), p. 15.

Contemporary Bulgarian sources considered Ahmed aga guilty, although less responsible than the Ottoman officials. In his letter to Dragan Cankov and Marko Balabanov, dated 16 September 1876, the exarchial archimandrit Metodij Kusev wrote:

> If the European cabinets want to discover the secrets and to establish that *the destruction in Bulgaria did not occur by chance,* it should be insisted on that an international commission be set up which will investigate firstly the above-named persons [Akif paša, vali from Plovdiv, and Sevket paša, who massacred Bojadžik] as well as Hafuz paša and Rašid paša, and, afterwards, the secondary figures, such as Tosun bey, Ahmed aa Tamrašli, Ahmed aa Barutanli, etc.[20]

Some ten years later Hristo pop Konstantinov, the first local Rhodopean historian, again accused Ahmed aga, who in the meantime had become leader of the so-called Pomak republic.[21] However, Bulgarian sources on the events in Peruštica are very rare. One survivor of the massacre, Georgi Natev, wrote his memoirs in 1901, and this almost unique document was to be abundantly used in the polemics of the 1970s.[22] (Two later histories of the events in Peruštica were written in 1930 and 1940, both using the last existing oral accounts, but we could not consult these works.)[23]

The tendency to exculpate Ahmed aga originated with the local Rhodopean historians. We mentioned in our introduction the very special historical sentiment that has flourished in the Rhodopes. This is probably the region of Bulgaria where local history is most actively studied; there are several publications concerned with the area (*Rodopski Zbornik, Rodopi,* etc.). One is aware of a certain exclusiveness, probably due to lengthy geographical and historical isolation, which was unique in Bulgaria (except perhaps in Pirin in Macedonia). In 1924 the most authoritative Rhodopean historian, Vasil Dečev wrote:

> We assert and can prove that Ahmed aga did not participate in person in the repression of the rebellion in Peruštica, and did not give any direct or indirect order to cut the throats of the rebels and their innocent wives and children. And this is not all. There is proof that Ahmed aga secretly agreed with the rebels, for many reasons of his own, mainly because he disagreed with the beys and rulers in Plovdiv, especially on questions and problems of a political and administrative character.[24]

This strange, undocumented statement remained unnoticed until 1958, when Nikolaj Hajtov used it to rehabilitate Ahmed aga, while writing the history of his home village, Javrovo. It is difficult to determine whether Hajtov is first and foremost a man of letters or a writer of local history, for both elements are part of his works. He became

---

[20]*Aprilsko Văstanie,* vol. 1, pp. 566-70.

[21]*Nepokornite sela,* Vol. 1, p. 7.

[22]*Spomeni,* pp. 459-93.

[23]I. Kepov, *Văstanieto v Peruštica* (Plovdiv, 1930) and K. Gălălbov, *Istorija na Vadltanieto v Peruštica* (Sofia, 1940).

[24]*Rodopski Pisma* (Sofia, 1924), published under the pseudonym, D. Smolyanski, cited in Vălčev, *Tămraš,* p. 165.

famous with his very brilliant *Wild Tales* (1967) but since then has almost renounced writing fiction. His passionate love for his natal Rhodopes, which leads him into partiality; his all too often affirmed confidence in oral tradition; and his tendency to present lively and picturesque descriptions of the past using dialogue and other devices of fiction betray him as no more than a good amateur historian. A remarkable stylist, he is also a ferocious polemicist, whose ultimate argument—even though not thus formally expressed—is, "If you are not a born Rhodopean, you cannot quite understand the whole question." In *Selo Javrovo, Plovdivsko* Hajtov portrays Ahmed aga Tămrašlijata as the defender of the honor of Christian women, as the protector of the Christian raja, and as the one whose authority saved the village of Javrovo from plunder by the *bāsibozuks* in 1876.[25] Similarly, he protected Lilkovo, Čepelare, Široka, Lăka, and the monastery of Sv. Petka Muldavska. Hajtov asserts that not Ahmed aga but his brother, Adil aga, was at Peruštica, and that the regular army as well as the Turks from Ustina were responsible for its destruction.

This apologetic point of view, brought to the fore once more with the publication of Dečev's complete works in 1968, provoked reactions from Marija and Manol Manolov.[26] They quote oral accounts showing Ahmed aga to be a petty tyrant who exploited the local population through corvée and illegal taxes and protected brigands and murderers. His presence, in Peruštica is proved by both western (Schuyler, etc.) and Bulgarian sources, they point out. Hajtov reacted sharply, for the most part accusing the Manolovs of believing western sources, especially the English Turkophile consuls.[27] The publication in 1973 of Colonel Vălčev's detailed book on Tămraš provided support for Hajtov's point of view.

The interesting question is, what lies behind these polemics? In our eyes, the answer is twofold: on the one hand, there is an overestimation of the importance of the April Uprising by the Bulgarian historians; on the other, having made this event so important in their historical narrations, they are confronted with the problem of Pomak participation in the suppression activities that are the major part of the story. The fact is that the April Uprising was comprised of only two narrative elements: the preparation of the insurrection and its crushing. Although the uprising in itself was a very important psychological turning point in the evolution of Bulgarian attitudes, it was too short-lived to develop a real organization or to result in a Bulgarian administration. Thus, the major task remaining to the historians is to describe the suppression of the insurrection, the heroic defense by the Bulgarians, and the merciless massacre and plundering by the *bašibozuks* and the Ottoman army. This scheme of things is very convenient for an analysis of the uprising in the Balkan and Sredna Gora ranges; but the events in the northern Rhodopes plainly implicate Pomak irregulars in the Batak and Peruštica atrocities. This was no real concern for historians up until the Balkan wars, so Konstantinov could openly accuse the Pomaks, and D. Strašimirov could point to their responsibility in a moderate way; but after Bulgaria was definitively confirmed within its present borders, and especially after the Communists took power in 1944, the

---

[25]First published as *Selo Javrovo, Asenovgradsko* (Sofia, 1958).

[26]"Ahmed aga Tămrašlijata."

[27]"Ošte za Ahmed aga Tămrašlijata i za edno tălkuvane na negovata rolja v potušavaneto na Aprilskoto Văstanie," *Istoričeski Pregled*, no. 5 (1972): 99-100.

integration of the Pomak population became of growing concern. A place had to be ascribed to them in Bulgarian history; but since their islamization in the seventeenth century, the Pomaks actually had played almost no role in that history (if we except the episode of Mehmed Sinap at the end of the eighteenth century). The participation of the Pomaks in Ottoman history, on the other hand, would be extremely interesting to document.

As we pointed out in the introduction, the Pomaks were "discovered" very late by the Bulgarians. The April Uprising was the date of their reentry into Bulgarian history, but, alas, on the wrong side. The fact that this group, who suffered most under the Ottoman regime (having been subjected to "denationalization," although succeeding in preserving their national language and customs), should appear at this "most Bulgarian time" with no national consciousness at all and, what is worse, contribute to crushing of the first Bulgarian attempt at independence, is far too paradoxical for a simplified nationalistic historiography. The whole polemic centered around Ahmed aga Tămrašlijata must be considered in this context: the Rhodopean historians (Dečev, Hajtov, Vălčev) by showing one Pomak leader to have been abusively accused during the uprising will demonstrate the existence of disinformation about the Pomaks; and thanks to the one proven innocent, the weight of the accusation resting on all the Pomaks will be lifted.

Vălčev's argument to explain why all western (and hence many Bulgarian) documents accuse Ahmed aga is quite subtle. It proceeds along the following line. The new regime, after overthrowing Sultan Abdulaziz, placed the responsibility for the Bulgarian massacres—which aroused condemnation in Europe—not only on the former administration but also on the Bulgarians themselves, misled as they were by Russian propaganda. For the main part, however, the blame is cast upon the *bašibozuks* who were called on to repress the insurrection.[28] Among the *bašibozuks*, Ahmed aga Tămrašlijata's name has been singled out for special attention because he was an independent local ruler, not over-respectful of Ottoman authority. According to both Vălčev and Hajtov, Ottoman officials, supported in this by the English diplomats, sought to put the blame on the heads of the Pomak irregular troops, first, in order to exculpate the regular army and, second, with incredibly far-sighted Machiavellianism, in order to spread animosity between Christian and Muslim Bulgarians. Thus, every historian who supports this Anglo-Turkish point of view is almost a traitor to the Muslim Bulgarians, as Vălčev imperturbably asserts:

> In our history the position and forgeries of Baring and Co. have long since been known and denied by everyone who honestly seeks the truth. But this does not prevent the Manolovs from referring once more to

---

[28]The question of how far the *bašibozuks* obeyed given orders or acted on their own is an important one, but seems one that is unlikely to get a clear response. During this troubled time the Turkish authorities did call upon the *bašibozuks*, but probably without assigning very precise tasks to them. They wanted the rebellion to be crushed; but did they really want one of the most flourishing regions of the Empire to be sacked? Or did they not really care, as long as the first goal was reached? The case of Javrovo, as described by Hajtov, is typical in our eyes: the *bašibozuks* arrived at the village, asked for food and shelter, tried by means of intimidation to obtain money and women, but waited for a signal to begin any real plundering or massacre and left the village untouched when Ahmed aga Tămrašlijata's men came to order them away.

these emissaries, thus consciously or not resurrecting the Anglo-Turkish interpretation of the insurrection. How could we otherwise explain their desire to prove that it was not the official Turkish authorities but the Bašibozuk leaders and, more particularly, Ahmed aga Tămrašlijata who crushed the insurrection; that Rašid paša "arrived late," that he neither commanded the repression nor displayed cruelty, and that all this was the doing of Ahmed aga Tămrašlijata. Wasn't this precisely what the Anglo-Turkish emissaries of the Turkish governmental commission tried to prove? Of course Ahmed aga did not do anything alone, he did not crush the insurrection alone; this was done by the Muslim Bulgarians he led. And from here to the question of the extent to which the Muslim Bulgarians are Bulgarians, there is only one step. If the Manolovs cannot make this step, there will be others ready to do so.[29]

Hajtov comes to the same conclusion:

> The Middle-Rhodopean historian Vasil Dečov, perfectly well understood the intentions of Ahmed aga Tămrašlijata's detractors, such as Hutton Dupuis and the foreign or national historical research workers of the April Uprising who confided naively in him. Moreover, Dečov understood with unmistakable intuition that it was not only a question of a conjunctural diplomatic maneuver, but of a long-lasting, serious accusation of fratricide against our brethren—the Rhodopean Muslim Bulgarians—whom some people 'well-intentioned' towards the Bulgarian nation wanted to drive like some sinister wedge between Bulgaria and the Muslim Bulgarians.[30]

Now that we have explored the far-reaching political and national considerations that lurked behind the polemical discussion about Ahmed aga Tămrašlijata, let us go back to Peruštica and the bloody days of May 1876. Did Ahmed aga make an appearance in person in Peruštica? Perhaps not, although the proofs of his presence else where at the crucial time—in Tatar Pazardžik (25 kilometers west of Peruštica) or near Stanimaka (Asenovgrad, 25 kilometers east of Peruštica)—are not very convincing. Were the Pomaks of Tămraš present in Peruštica? Yes; all authors are unanimous on this point, even Ahmed aga's defenders. Ahmed aga's brother, Adil aga, the leader, of the Pomak troops was there. The Pomaks of Tămraš remained until the last day, as the only witness, Georgi Natev, states:

> The people from Tămraš began the fight with us, they ended it as well.[31]

The Pomaks were not alone in attacking Peruštica; together with them were the Turks from Ustina and Kričim, some Tcherkess, and, from 10 May on, the regular army led by Rašid paša. Do they bear responsibility for the atrocities and, more particularly, for the first massacre of the surrendering notables? Hajtov goes to great pains to explain

---

[29]*Tămraš*, p. 158.

[30]"Ošte za Ahmed aga," p. 109.

[31]*Spomeni*, p. 492.

that the latter was the deed of the Turks from Ustina, one of whose leaders was also named Ahmed aga, surnamed Kărmadži. It seems to us, however, very difficult to attribute responsibility for individual events to any particular protaganist, for the detailed stories we have at our disposal were all recorded twenty-five or more years later. In any event, Rašid paša, head of the regular troops, *can* be accused of refusing to negotiate with the rebels for the sake of protecting the "civilian" population. However, it is evident that Ahmed aga Tămrašlijata had an immense influence on the men he commanded: the expressions "people from Tămraš" and "Ahmed aga's people" were synonymous. Whenever Ahmed aga gave orders to protect a place from plunder, he was obeyed. Apparently he decided not to protect Peruštica, which was beyond the limits of his *nahija* of Rupčos (nor did he protect Bojkovo or Dedovo, which were part of it). It should not be forgotten that Peruštica had provocatively killed three of his men.

This leads us to the underlying question: were Ahmed aga Tămrašlijata and/or the Pomaks as a whole anti-Bulgarian? In the black-and-white thinking of nationalistic Bulgarian historians the answer is either unequivocally "yes" (Manolovs)—because the uprising in Peruštica was crushed by him, or at least by his brother Adil aga, and the Pomak Ahmed aga Barutanlijata was in any event responsible for the massacre of Batak —or, equally unequivocally, "no," (Hajtov, Vălčev)—because he was a harsh but just ruler who protected Christians (as he did during the April Uprising in several towns), so that only some of the Pomaks are to be accused of participation in the atrocities.[32]

In our eyes the question of anti-Bulgarian feeling on the part of Ahmed aga does not really arise. As ruler of Rupčos, he exhibited justice and understanding towards his Christian subjects. Why should a Muslim ruler (whether Turk or Pomak) necessarily be a tyrant? Everything leads us to believe that Ahmed aga was a man of order: the most striking feature of his administration was the absence of robbery in his *nahija*. So order must reign between his Muslim and Christian subjects as well. Everyday relations between Christians and Muslims, especially when they spoke the same language, were not necessarily tense and were sometimes even rather cordial. As for robbery, it is probable that he did not object to it in principle, mountaineer from the Rhodopes that he was, as long as it did not interfere with his *nahija's* domestic life. The uprising in 1876 must, in his eyes, have seemed a disruption of order, as well as a good occasion for his young, poor *babaiti* to plunder the rich rebellious villages north of his *nahija,* toward the Thracian plain.

It is not certain that the national .character of the April Uprising was fully perceived by the Pomaks. Bulgarian historians begin with the *a priori* idea that national feeling is natural to man; so the national propagandists who were active in Bulgaria from about 1830 onwards must have "awakened" this feeling, which had not ceased to exist since the Middle Ages. We saw that the Pomaks, however, were unaffected by this national awakening. Their feeling of "togetherness," apart from local village or district identity, was derived from Islam; they did have a clear consciousness of their distinctness from the Turkish population, but this was secondary to them. If they perceived the national character of the uprising and if they fought consciously against it, it was for

---

[32]There was a later, ancillary polemic between the Manolovs and Hajtov concerning Ahmed aga Tămrašlijata's role in the 1865 revolt against high taxes in Aha-Čelebi; in this case, the issue was whether he was an anti-social, as well as anti-Bulgarian, leader.

religious, not national, reasons: they might have fought against a "giaur" kingdom, not necessarily against a "Bulgarian" kingdom.

All this is mere hypothesis, as we have no Pomak sources from this time and the few oral records at our disposal were all collected by Christian research workers; but we feel justified in considering the 1876 events in this way because of the behavior of the Pomak population during the period which followed.

The Turco-Russian War of 1877-78 : Ahmed Aga's "Pomak Republic":

The outbreak of the war in 1877, an indirect consequence of the April Uprising, polarized the positions of the various ethnic and religious groups concerned. The Rhodope area was not directly involved in the events of the war until the beginning of 1878. Between 16 and 18 January of 1876 Suleyman paša's army was definitively routed in the foothills of the Rhodopes south of Plovdiv, between Dermendere (Părvenec) and Stanimaka (Asenovgrad). As it could no longer retreat towards Edirne, it had to take the difficult way south, along the narrow snow-covered shepherds' paths of the Rhodopes. Together with the army, fleeing Muslim civilians tried to reach the Aegean plain by way of the mountains, under the most dramatic conditions. The local Pomak villages were flooded with refugees and disbanded soldiers, who plundered them in order to survive. Seized by the general panic, the Pomaks from Tămraš fled too, fearing reprisals from their Christian neighbors. Through Hvojna and Čepelare, Ahmed aga Tămrašlijata fled to his winter pastures of Kodžaorman in the Aegean plain, after having entrusted all movable goods to his Christian *kehaja*. (This did not prevent the two *čifliks* of Sredne and Tikla from being burnt down.) Most of the Pomaks of Rupčos fled in the same way, except in those villages with mixed populations, where the Christians could guarantee their security, just as they themselves had been protected by the Muslims in 1876.

The panic was not justified, as the Russian army had no intention of occupying the Rhodopes, especially not during the winter. Only two mountain brigades crossed over via the Haskovo-Kărdžali-Komotini and the Stanimaka (Asenovgrad)-Hvojna-Čepelare-Ustovo (Smoljan)-Darădere (Zlatograd)-Kušukavak (Krumovgrad)-Dimotika routes, without leaving behind any garrisons as they passed. On the northern slopes of the Rhodopes the Russian troops hardly penetrated the first villages before the end of January. The Bulgarians themselves raided and plundered, and in this way Tămraš was set on fire. On 31 January the armistice agreed to at Edirne fixed the line of demarcation at the watershed between Marica, Mesta, and Arda, thus according about two thirds of the Rhodopes to the Russians, who had not really set foot there. This diversion was confirmed by the treaty of San Stefano (3 March 1878). At the local level, this frontier line was unacceptable to both the Christian villages on the upper Arda (Ustovo, Rajkovo, etc.), which were left on the side of the Ottoman Empire, and to the Pomak villages that were included in Bulgaria. On the other hand, the decision remained almost hypothetical, as the whole Rhodope area served in fact as a buffer zone between the two armies.

The Rhodope insurrection that began at the end of February was a consequence of this undefined situation. It consisted of a series of skirmishes, directed mainly against the Christian villages in the regions not effectively controlled by the Russians. Under the leadership of the Englishman S.G.B. Saint Clair, the insurrection went as far as to threaten the railway line near Haskovo, but it was confined to the eastern Rhodopes. It spread later to the west, and the regions of Čepelare and Djovlen (Devin) in Rupčos became involved also, but to a lesser extent than the eastern villages. The local Christian population resisted these incursions under the leadership of Kapitan Petko Vojvoda, a very popular figure, whom the Russians only half trusted. In April 1878 the Russians engaged in some maneuvers in the northern Rhodopes, by which time the third *čiflik* of the Karahodžov family, that of Modăr, had been burned too. In May the insurrection led an offensive in the direction of Čepelare and Stanimaka. This provoked a reaction from the Russians, who penetrated deeper into the mountains, reaching Pavelsko and Savtăšte but not as far as Čepelare. The insurrection led by Saint Clair lasted until the end of the autumn of 1878. However, it never reached deeply into Rupčos and hardly affected those villages that were soon to be known as "insubordinate". It is interesting that the Rhodope insurrection should have been led by an Englishman. S.G.B. Saint Clair had formerly been with the British military, and Bulgarian historians assert that the revolt was, in fact, directed by England; however, research has not ascertained the truth of this belief. It is known that Saint Clair was bitterly anti-Russian and disliked the Bulgarians as well. He participated in the Polish insurrection of 1863, and then established himself in the Ottoman Empire: first in Djevarli in the eastern Balkan Range and then on an estate near Cape Emine on the Black Sea. Together with the British vice-consul in Burgas, Ch. A. Brophy, he wrote *A Residence in Bulgaria,* which was published in London in 1867 and republished, under the title *Twelve Years' Study of the Eastern Question in Bulgaria,* in 1877, again in London. His pro-Turkish sentiments are made clear in his book. He served in the Ottoman army in northeast Bulgaria in the 1877-78 war. As leader of the Rhodope insurrection he bore the name Hidaet pasha. Also involved in that revolt were Polish, Spanish (carlist), and other English adventurers.)[33]

The treaty of Berlin (13 July 1878) fixed the borders of the newly created autonomous province of Eastern Rumelia, attributing to it the whole *nahija* of Rupčos; but the new authorities soon appeared too weak to take possession of regions where the Russians had not already set up a Bulgarian administration. (Why the Russians omitted to do this in the villages of the Văcă valley before leaving Eastern Rumelia in July 1879 is unknown.) In October 1878 Petko Vojvoda tried to subjugate the southern part of Rupčos (Mugla, Breze, Beden) but was repelled. This was a very troubled period, and it is difficult to evaluate whether he acted on his own, as a local unofficial leader, or under orders. The fact is that he was temporarily arrested by the Russians, who were trying to placate world opinion that was very much against them as a result of Anglo-Turkish propaganda.

It is impossible to say who ruled Rupčos during the autumn and winter of 1878 and the spring of 1879. The region lived in isolation, and the Pomak emigrants

[33]See Michael Leo, *La Bulgarie et son peuple sous la domination ottomane tels que les ont vus les voyageurs anglo-saxons* (Sofia, 1949), pp. 30-31, and also James Baker, *La Turquie* (Paris, 1883), pp. 29-31, and Simeon Radev, *Stroitelite na savremenna Bălgarija* (Sofia, 1973), vol. 1, p. 34 and p. 811 (notes by E. Statelova).

gradually came back to their villages. During the spring of 1879 Eastern Rumelia was divided into territorial units by the provisional Russian administration. Within the *okrag* (department) of Plovdiv an *okolija* (district) of Rupčos was thus created, and Grigor Popov, a Bulgarian from Široka Laka, was nominated as *okolijski načalnik* (sub-prefect). This arrangement, however, was immediately changed by Aleko Bogoridi, Eastern Rumelia's new governor general, who arrived in Plovdiv on 27 May and two weeks later nominated the Turk Mehmed bey Karakehajolar to the post. This seems to have been a fatal mistake, resulting in the insubordination of the villages of the Văčă valley: it involved the introduction of an administrator foreign to the Rhodopes and, what is more, a Turk, whereas Rupčos had always been ruled by local Pomak leaders. Aleko Bogorodi, coming fresh from Istanbul, underestimated the silent hostility of the poor mountain Pomaks toward the rich beys of the Thracian towns.

To Ahmed aga Tămrašlijata the situation was intolerable: had he not, in the Turkish era, been almost independent of the Plovdiv authorities? Was he to accept a Turkish master, now that his country was in Bulgarian hands? Another mistake was to introduce Turkish as the official language in Rupčos, where the population, although mainly Muslim, was Bulgarian-speaking.[34] When, during the summer of 1879, Mehmed bey made his first attempt to be recognized by the villages of the Văča valley, he was stopped at Beden, where the village chief announced to him that a decision about whether to submit to him was to be taken by the neighboring villages. Some days later, indeed, a meeting of all local notables was organized at Trigrad. There the Pomaks of the Văča officially decided not to submit to the Plovdiv authorities and organized their own government, composed of Hadži Hasan of Trigrad, Hadži Mustafa Kjuljunk of Beden, and Molla Ejub of Mugla. The decisive authority was, however, to remain in the hands of the Karahodžov family, and Ahmed aga Tămrašlijata became "president" and his brother, Smail aga, chief of a police force of twenty men. The capital of this "Pomak republic" was at first designated as Nastan and later changed to Tămraš.

How many villages were part of this "Republic?" This is a complex question, as the different authors disagree. There were thirteen to start with: Osikovo, Čurekovo, Mihalkovo, Ljaskovo, Breze, Beden, Nastan, Grohotno, Gjovren, Balaban (now Jagodina), Trigrad, Mugla, and Kjustendžik (Kesten). Four other villages registered by the Rumeliot authorities in 1880 became dissenters in 1881: Čerešovo, Tămraš, Brezovica, and Petvar. These seventeen villages all belonged to the *nahija* of Rupčos. They were subsequently joined by four villages affiliated to the neighbouring *okolija* of Peštera (*okrág* of Tatar Pazardzik, not of Plovdiv): Selča, Djovlen (now Devin), Karabulak (Borino), and Naipli (Bujnovo). Vălčev adds to this list the village of Čilikli (now Stomanovo); but it is mentioned by no other author, and our guess is that is was not yet a village in the 1880s, as just before the Balkan Wars it numbered only thirty houses.[35] Stojanov and Dobruski list Kajinčală, which lies south ou the watershed of the Marica and the Mesta and was thus not part of Eastern Rumelia, as one of these

---

[34]*Marica*, no. 274 (3 April 1881); *Marica* was by that time the best-informed newspaper in Eastern Rumelia. Konstantinov (*Nepokomite sela*, Vol. 1,) considers that, in addition, the highly fanatical Pomaks were shocked by the lax Islamic ways of the urban Turks; but we have no evidence that the Pomaks were such puritans.

[35]Vălčev, *Tămraš* p. 283. Hajtov, in *Grad Devin* (p. 290), records an oral account about how Stomanovo became a village, but without any precise date.

insubordinate villages also. Brezovica was, for unknown reasons, not retroceded to the Ottoman Empire in 1886, although it was considered to be insubordinate.

The Rumeliot government was conscious of the problem raised by the Pomak "republic" but clearly decided to solve it in a pacific way. The reason for this attitude was that the Văča valley was not the only rebellious territory in Eastern Rumelia: the district of Kărdžali had been in open revolt since December 1879, and a military expedition of 1,200 men had been sent to pacify it in March 1880. As this action had taken on somewhat excessive dimensions, it had developed into an affair of international renown, compromising the image of the Bulgarian government in the autonomous province. It was nonetheless vital for the government to secure its southeastern border. Comparable incidents took place in May 1880 in the region of the Deli Kamčik River (now Luda Kamčija), following energetic pacification measures the principality of Bulgaria had launched in its own territory.[36] The main fear of the young Rumeliot administration had been that some kind of coalition would develop between the Turkish and the coastal Greek populations. Also insubordinate, i.e., refusing to pay taxes, was one mountain village north of Pirdop.[37] The sector of the Dospat range known as Babeški Kolibi, where brigands from Macedonia and Eastern Rumelia took refuge, resisted taxation also.

The problem of highway robbery within the "Pomak republic" was the most decisive element in favor of action on the Rumeliot side;[38] it was not so much the taxes these poor mountain villages refused to pay or the danger of rebellion spreading—as in the Kărdžali district—across valleys which hardly communicated with each other. However, the area being very difficult to reach, "pacification" might be difficult. During the first half of 1880 the Rumeliot government, which had had to intervene in Kărdžali and Deli Kamčik and had earned only criticism for this, remained totally inactive towards the Văča valley. It decided to resort to diplomacy. After a correspondence between Aleko Bogoridi and the Sublime Porte, a meeting was organized, in December 1880 in Djovlen (Devin), between the prefect of Tatar Pazardžik, Ivan Najdenov, and the *mutesarif* of Seres, who came escorted by Ahmed aga Barutanlijata, the slaughterer of Batak.[39] A document of submission was signed, but it soon became obvious that the Porte had no desire to see the affair settled. One of its devices in negotiation was always to separate the four villages affiliated to Peštera (which, in Ottoman eyes, fell under Nevrokop administration, *vilayet* of Thessaloniki) from the seventeen villages of Rupčos (under the authority of the *vilayet* of Edirne), even though there was no doubt that all of them were to become Rumeliot. In June 1881, Aleko Bogoridi went to Istanbul and pleaded the Rumeliot cause before the Porte and the foreign ambassadors, accusing the Ottoman administration of collecting taxes from the insubordinate villages. He only succeeded, however, in displaying the inefficiency of his administration. By this time public

---

[36]Bernard Lory, "Problèmes du brigandage en Bulgarie 1878-1883," in *Părvi Meždunaroden kongres po bălgaristika. Dokladi. Bălgarskata dărzăva prez vekovete, I* (Sofia, 1982), pp. 510-15.

[37]Vălčev, *Tămraš* p. 252.

[38]*Marica*, nos. 319, 369, 430, 629, etc.

[39]N. Hajtov erroneously gives 29 May as the date of this meeting (*Grad Devin*), p. 278). Vălčev, (*Tămraš*, p. 245) gives the date of 3 December 1880, but places, the meeting at Selča. We adopt here the version of Konstantinovc *Nekopornit, sela*, vol. 2, and *Marica*, no. 294 of 16 June 1881).

opinion in Eastern Rumelia had begun to react to the situation, and the affair was submitted to the regional parliament.[40]

Paradoxically, the populations of the Văča villages were not unanimous in approving the insubordination. Let us not forget that Ahmed aga was a derebey, who, despite a certain sense of justice, always put his personal interests first. In July 1880 the frontier commission had reported that the villages were ready to submit, but that they were terrorized by Ahmed aga Barutanlijata.[41] During the summer of 1882, a delegation of five inhabitants of Naipli came to Peštera asking that their village and Karabulak be administrated by Eastern Rumelia.[42] The village chief of Djovlen, was murdered for having asked that his village be integrated.[43] In the autumn of 1884 it was the turn of Mugla: Mehmed bey went there to organize the new administration but was expelled from the village by Hadži Ahmed Kjuljunk of Beden.[44] Nevertheless, it seems that even Ahmed aga Tămrašlijata himself would not have been opposed to submitting to Plovdiv, provided that he was named *okolijski načalnik* of Rupčos. Konstantinov is very harsh towards the Rumeliot authorities (whom he knew well, being secretary at the regional parliament):

> However, as a result of certain Byzantine considerations, the Rumeliot rulers did not agree to accord him this function. If Tămrašlijata had been given an autonomous service in Rupčos by Plovdiv, peace and tranquility would have reigned from the very beginning in that mountainous region.[45]

Our guess is that the "Byzantine considerations" were nothing less than the accusation that Ahmed aga had participated in the massacre of Peruštica, concerning which neither Konstantinov nor the Czech Dobruski, who visited Ahmed aga in Tămraš at that time, are in any doubt. If he was an innocent as Dečev, Hajtov, and Vălčev claim, why should the Rumeliot administration have balked at this very obvious solution? Why should it have entangled itself in humiliating negotiations with the Porte, from which it could expect nothing? In addition, the visit Ahmed aga made with his guards to the monastery of Bjala Cerkva in August 1883, as described by Stojanov, was not just that of a village chief refusing to pay taxes but that of a man who, if caught, was liable to be judged and perhaps condemned. So we can suppose that the "Byzantine considerations" involved questions of amnesty Ahmed aga Tămrašlijata had requested for himself (if he was guilty), or for his brothers Adil and Smail aga.

As the Rumeliot administration refused to acknowledge the autonomous status of the Văča villages through recognition of Ahmed aga Tămrašlijata's authority, and at the same time refused to intervene in force, the Ottoman government exploited the situation

---

[40]The first explicit article on this question was published (in French) in *Marica*, no. 294 (16 June 1881).

[41]*Marica*, no. 202 (22 July 1880).

[42]*Marica*, no. 245 (28 August 1882).

[43]Konstantinov, *Nepokornite sela*, vol. 1, p. 39. Hajtov quotes this fact in his monograph without any detail, omitting even the name of the murdered mayor (*Grad Devin*, p. 282).

[44]*Marica*, no. 657 (12 October 1884).

[45]*Nepokornite sela*, vol. 1, pp. 6-7; also vol. 2, p. 30.

for its own ends. The traditional taxes were collected by local (insubordinate) officials and paid to the Ottoman administration of the *kaza* of Aha-Čelebi.[46] For this reason the Plovdiv authorities threatened to reduce the tribute to the Porte by £10,000. The Porte answered that if this occurred, it would not consider the insubordinate villages to be part of Rumelian territory. According to Antoine Drandar, the Porte had already begun to recruit soldiers in the insubordinate villages in 1884.[47]

In August 1885 Zahari Stojanov made a mysterious visit to Ahmed aga in Tămraš. By that time Stojanov was actively preparing the Plovdiv revolution, which occurred only one month later on 18 September 1885. The revolutionary committee had to make sure that the Pomak republic would remain neutral towards the planned coup. It feared a military intervention from the Ottoman side, which was enabled to take such measures by the provisions of the treaty of Berlin. By coming along the insubordinate Văča valley, an Ottoman army could arrive unhindered at only a few hours distance from Plovdiv. Some days after this visit, Ahmed aga's son Hasan is said to have had a secret meeting in Dermendere with the opposition leader Georgi Stranski. Little more is known about these contacts. What did Ahmed aga ask in return for his neutrality? Was the function of *okolijski načalnik* still tempting for him? Or had the retrocession of the Văča valley to the Ottoman Empire already been decided by that time? If the latter were the case, this would tarnish the image of Stojanov as a pure patriot, but it does not seem incompatible with his pragmatic view of politics. The silence about these negotiations was probably due to the violent campaign of protest organized during the spring of 1886 against the Petko Karavelov government responsible for the return of the territory to the Ottomans.[48]

The history of the Plovdiv coup, the negotiations which followed it, the Serbo-Bulgarian war, and the negotiations leading to the Tophane convention of 5 April 1886 are well known, unlike the history of the insubordinate villages during the crisis. Immediately after the coup, a military detachment led by Captain Karaulanov tried unsuccessfully to occupy the "Pomak republic." Vălčev maintains that the Porte then proceeded overnight to occupy both the Văča villages and the Kărdžali district.[49] This seems highly improbable, as it would have meant a violation of the borders fixed by the treaty of Berlin and could not have passed unnoticed by diplomatic observers. The Ottoman army massed eighty *tabors* on the Rumeliot border but continued to respect it.[50] On 19 September the sultan gave an explicit order against any agression on the part of the regular army or the local Muslim population against Eastern Rumelia.[51] Konstantinov gives a slightly different account, but with little more detail:

---

[46]The tax system had been reorganized in Eastern Rumelia, so people thought they were paying more than previously.

[47]*Les événements politiques en Bulgarie depuis 1876 jusqu'à nos jours* (Brussels and Paris, 1896), pp. 373-81.

[48]Vălčev, *Tămraš*, pp. 261-70.

[49]Ibid., p. 257.

[50]*Istorija na srăbsko-bălgarskata vojna 1885* (Sofia, 1971), p. 46.

[51]*Dokumenti za bălgarskata istorija*, vol. 4, *Dokumenti iz turskite dăržavni arhivi (1863-1909)* (Sofia, 1942), p. 65.

The insubordinate villages of Rupčos, as well as the district of Kărdžali, were declared by the Porte to be under siege. The Pomaks, armed by the Turkish government, guarded their border with the help of Turkish soldiers.... From 6 September 1885 [Julian calendar] to 26 March 1886, the Pomaks of the insubordinate villages were vigilant.[52]

In January 1886, after the Bulgarian victory over Serbia, the Turkish representative in Sofia, Gabdan efendi, communicated to Prince Alexander von Battenberg the Ottoman conditions for the regularization of bilateral relations. The eleventh condition was the return to Ottoman administration of the insubordinate villages, the Kărdžali district, and the harbor of Burgas. This was unofficially agreed to by Prince Alexander, with the exception of the cession of Burgas.[53] The negotiations continued in Istanbul between Grand Vizier Said paša, the Bulgarian foreign minister, Ilija Canov, and the representatives of the Great Powers, resulting in the Tophane convention (5 April 1886), the second article of which stipulated as follows:

> As long as the administration of Eastern Rumelia and of the Principality of Bulgaria are in the hands of only one and the same person, the Muslim villages of the Kărdžali canton, as well as the Muslim villages lying in the Rhodopean region and left till now outside of the administration of Eastern Rumelia, will be separated from this province and administrated directly by the Imperial Government.... The delimitation of this canton and the villages in question will be executed by a technical commission, named by the Sublime Porte and the Bulgarian Prince. This will be done on the spot, naturally taking strategic conditions into account, and especially those of the Imperial Government.[54]

So the uncertain fate of the insubordinate villages was at last decided. Were they consulted in these negotiations? We do not know. We do not know either exactly when their territory was occupied by Ottoman troops. They lost the privileges of their intermediate position and soon discovered the disadvantage created by borders. For seven years they managed to live without borders, either to the north, in the direction of Plovdiv, where they could sell their wool, wood, and tar, or to the south, where their winter pastures lay. The new border transformed them into an appendage of the Ottoman state, a mountainous enclave deep in Bulgarian territory, and this was to cause their economic decline.

The fear of losing their Aegean winter pastures is often pointed to by Bulgarian historians as an argument to explain the insubordination of the Văča valley villages. Stock-breeding was undoubtedly the main occupation of the region, and a statistical report dating from the eve of the Balkan wars indicates that the region had 116,000 sheep and goats and 28,600 horses and cows to about 10,000 inhabitants.[55] It is convenient to assert that the Văča Pomaks had to refuse the Rumeliot administration in order to preserve their wealth, even though they had no national objection to the

---

[52]"Iz Rodopite - Rupčos—*Periodičesko Spisanie,* no. 60 (1899): 911.

[53]Radev, *Stroitelite* , vol. 1, pp. 726-27.

[54]*Bălgarskata dăržavnost v aktove i dokumenti* (Sofia, 1981), p. 268.

[55]Vălčev, *Tămraš,* p. 282.

Bulgarian state: historical materialism and nationalism are thus reconciled. But these two issues are separate. The economic point of view undoubtedly carried immense weight in the decision not to submit; but the fact that neighboring villages, with a comparable economy, took the opposite decision shows that there was no economic determinism involved. The ideological aspect of the question also had its importance: the neighboring villages had mixed populations of Christians and Muslims, whereas the insubordinate villages were purely Muslim (see map following this article).

In any event, whether subordinate or insubordinate, pro-Bulgarian or pro-Turkish, all Rhodopean villages entered a period of decay after 1878. The real disaster was the drawing of a frontier line that cut this very fragile mountain economy off from the Thracian, or the Aegean, plains. The provisional solution found by the Văča villages was initially to refuse any outside administration, which would have meant the establishment of borders. Why did they then accept integration into the Ottoman Empire? With that realignment they became an eccentric salient of Ottoman territory, lost their Thracian market because of customs regulations, and became dependent upon Drama, when Plovdiv was only six hours by foot from Tămrăs; they were thus economically doomed. The answer is quite simple: villages of the Văča valley submitted to Ottoman authority because they were under military occupation. Their independence up until 1886 had been due almost entirely to the weakness of the Rumeliot regime.

As for the ideological factor, a clear preference was shown by the Pomaks for the Ottoman regime at the end of the nineteenth century, as is proved by the emigration movements of the Rhodopean population. The Pomaks of Rupčos began to emigrate into Ottoman (later Turkish) territory from the beginning of the 1880s, leaving the villages of Sitovo and Pavelsko. This movement continued during the following thirty years as villagers from Narečen, Hvojna, and Orehovo emigrated. Then the main emigration flow was provoked by the Balkan Wars, and the villagers of Borovo, Pavelsko, Savtăšte, Mihalkovo, Stojkite, Naipli, Dospat, etc. were on the move. The Pomak population of Beden, however, emigrated northward to the Thracian plain.[56]

The history of the Pomak "republic" from 1886, when it became the *nahija* of Tămraš under the authority first of the *kaza* of Nevrokop, *vilayet* of Thessaloniki, and later of the *kaza* of Komotini, *vilayet* of Edirne, is little documented before 1912. A Turkish garrison was organized at Djovlen (Devin), and frontier posts were set up in the surrounding area. Life became more difficult. Tămraš, the biggest of the insubordinate villages with 350 houses, was at the tip of the salient, surrounded by the border on three sides. The old Ahmed aga Tămrašlijata died during the autumn of 1895. His brother Adil aga had already been directing local affairs for about ten years and remained a leading figure up until 1907 or 1908, when his eldest son Atem took over. By the time the Balkan War broke out, the wealth of the Karahodžov family had considerably declined. The old Smail aga died in 1913 in Smoljan, totally ruined economically.[57]

On 5 October 1912 the tip of the salient was attacked by the Bulgarian army. The population fled southward, leaving Tămraš deserted. The inhabitants of the neighboring Bulgarian villages—Lilkovo, Čuren, Orehovo, Sitovo, Dedovo, Bojkovo, Sotir, Brezovica, and Peruštica—arrived to plunder it. It seems that those from Peruštica,

[56] Anastas Primovski, *Bit i kultura na rodopskite Bălgari* (Sofia, 1973), pp. 114-55.
[57] Vălčev, Tămraš, pp. 271-93.

coming from further away and finding it impossible to carry off much booty, set fire to the village. So vengeance was wrought for the 1876 events. Tămraš was totally destroyed and never reconstructed. Its inhabitants were resettled in Turkey, near Izmir, near Edirne in the village of Elegöl, and near Çumra in a village that was given the name Tămraš.[58]

Thus ends the story of Tămraš. As we have already pointed out, the villages of Rupčos were left with rather positive memories of Ahmed aga Tămrašlijata. In Bulgarian historiography, and especially in Bulgarian literature, his name became synonymous with "bloody plunderer." In the last chapter of his masterwork, *Under the Yoke* (1894), Ivan Vazov tells that Ahmed aga even carried the severed heads of men and women on spears; and in a short story broadly inspired by the figure of Ahmed aga, Anton Strašimirov reports the legend of a child burnt alive in order to cure the flocks of disease ("Ramadanbeg's konak," 1901)—that legend being ascribed to Ahmed aga. In Genčo Stoev's novel *The Price of Gold* (1965), Ahmed aga's personage as destroyer of Peruštica is, very interestingly, tempered by his rivalry with the Turks: the Manichean element that usually irritates one in Bulgarian historical novels here gives way to a deeper, tragic vision of history.

It is not the historian's task to judge whether Ahmed aga Tămrašlijata was "bad" or "good." As a historical personage, this local derebey did not play a very important role. We have chosen to focus on him, however, because in the light of his personality the problem of the relationship between Christian Bulgarians and Pomaks is vividly perceptible. The Pomaks are but a small ethno-cultural group, scattered through many provinces, mainly in poor, mountainous regions. Their unique character resulted from a process of islamization, which integrated them with the Islamic structures of the Ottoman Empire. This process was, however, religious and not national. Bulgarian nationalism developed along different lines. It was first bound up with religious considerations (quarrels with the Greek clergy about liturgical language, etc.) and deeply marked by Orthodox Christianity. Later on, laic elements grew more important (language, consciousness of historical past, politics, etc). It was in terms of this new perspective that the Pomaks found their place in Bulgarian national ideology. As they were claimed by the Bulgarians for national reasons, they were simultaneously claimed by the Ottoman Empire for religious reasons. During the period considered here—the last quarter of the nineteenth century—the religious element was predominant; but this by no means prejudiced the evolution of group consciousness among the Pomaks at a later date.[*]

---

[58]Ibid., p. 331

[*] The map following was drawn by me, incorporating information on boundaries and populations gathered from various sources, including works cited in the text (Primovski, *Bit i kultura;* Vălčev, *Tămraš;* Hajtov, *Selo Devin*). Other sources are Stoju Šiškov, *Pomacite v trite oblasti Trakija, Makedonija i Mizija* (Plovdiv, 1914); Stefan Zahariev, *Geografiko-istoriko-statističesko opisanie na Tatar-Pazardžiškata kaaza* (Sofia, 1973); and Tevfik Guran, *Structure économique et sociale d'une région de campagne dans l'empire Ottoman vers le milieu du XIX siècle* (Sofia, 1979).

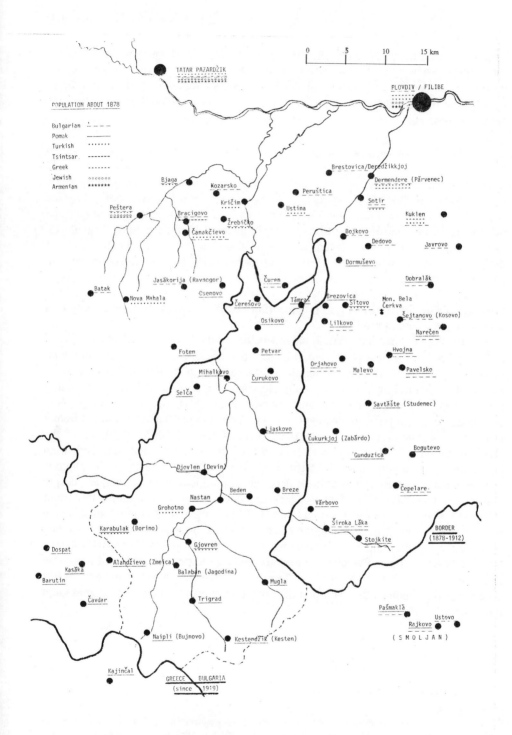

COMPOSITION OF THE POPULATIONS OF RHODOPEAN VILLAGES, 1878

Ali Eminov

THERE ARE NO TURKS IN BULGARIA: REWRITING HISTORY BY ADMINISTRATIVE FIAT*

During the winter of 1984-85 the Bulgarian government brought to a rapid close a ten-year-long, gradual and intermittent campaign to force Turks in Bulgaria to replace their Turkish-Muslim names with conventional Bulgarian names. Although reliable information is difficult to come by, it is clear that between November 1984 and March 1985 all Turks in Bulgaria had been forced to assume different names. The effort apparently began in the Turkish villages in the eastern Rhodope region during the last months of 1984 but quickly spread to central and northeastern Bulgaria. The campaign capped a twenty-five year government effort to assimilate the country's largest minorities— the Macedonians, Pomaks, gypsies, and Turks—and used tactics refined during the campaign against the Bulgarian-speaking Muslims a decade earlier. It is alleged that the name-changing campaign among Turkish Muslims was met with violent resistance—with predictable results. Hundreds of Turkish Muslims were killed, thousands were arrested and sent to hard labor camps, and scores were banished to different parts of Bulgaria, far away from their home communities. Because of the extremely unsettled situation among Turkish Muslims, Turkish areas of Bulgaria have been declared off-limits to foreigners for the forseeable future. As a result of these restrictions, independent verification of these allegations is not possible. Eyewitness accounts from many Muslims who have been able to escape from Bulgaria since the campaign began, however, speak eloquently to the truth of the allegations.

Since the name changing campaign began, the government crackdown on Turkish Muslims has been stepped up. Orders have been issued to store and restaurant managers and clerks not to serve Turkish and other Muslim women who wear traditional dress; Turks have been forbidden to speak in Turkish in public conveyances and other public places; radios and tape recorders have been confiscated so that Turkish Muslims can not listen to news programs from Radio Istanbul, Radio Free Europe, Voice of America, and similar independent sources. Bulgarian authorities have also begun to enforce strictly the ban against circumcision. It is reported that health officials regularly visit Muslim households to make sure that young Muslim boys remain uncircumcised. Tombstones with Turkish and Arabic inscriptions have been destroyed. Even the names of the

* A slightly different version of this paper was published under the title, "Are Turkish-speakers in Bulgaria of Ethnic Bulgarian Origin?" in *Journal of the Institute of Muslim Minority Affairs* 7, no 2 (1986): 503-518.

deceased Muslims have been replaced with Bulgarian names. Serious efforts have been made to discourage traditional Islamic funerary practices and to replace them with "socialist" funerary ceremonies. A broad attack has been launched on all Islamic beliefs, practices, and rituals.[1]

The Turkish and the West European press began roundly to condemn the persecution of the Turkish minority in early January of 1985. As expected, the Bulgarian press was absolutely silent on the events taking place in Bulgaria at that time. The Bulgarian ambassador to Turkey, Argir Konstantinov, when asked to respond to these allegations, dismissed them as completely untrue. He categorically denied the presence of any such campaign or pressure on Turks to change their names, citing the constitutional guarantee that names can be changed only through proper legal procedures.[2]

The initial Turkish government response to these allegations was very reserved and cautious. Turkish Foreign Minister Halefoğlu, in response to questions about the events in Bulgaria, said that Turkish leaders were carefully examining press reports at the highest levels of government. He went on to say:

> In doing so we keep in sight our close and neighborly relations with Bulgaria. If there are problems we want them to be solved without harming our mutual relations. We first must reduce tension.... We are motivated from the point that an escalation is in the interests of neither us, nor them.[3]

Reiterating that the matter would best be solved by dialogue between Bulgaria and Turkey, he urged those agitating for determined action against Bulgaria (primarily emigre organizations) to be patient. Prime Minister Özal was similarly careful.

The Turkish and western press continued to report the Bulgarian government's campaign against Turks throughout January and February, but the official position of the Turkish government still remained one of caution and optimisim that the problem could be resolved through friendly dialogue. However, as press reports continued to give prominent place to the persecution of Turks in Bulgaria, the Turkish government could no longer ignore the matter. Finally, on February 20, the question of the Turkish minority in Bulgaria was discussed in a long, closed-door session of the Turkish Parliament in Ankara, and on February 22 a diplomatic note was sent to Bulgaria through its ambassador in Turkey. In the note Turkey demanded an end to the persecution, requested a ministerial-level meeting to negotiate a new migration agreement by which all those Turks in Bulgaria who wanted to emigrate to Turkey would be able to do so, and requested that a Turkish parliamentary delegation or a delegation made up of Turkish and foreign diplomats be allowed to visit Turkish areas to

---

[1] Amnesty International, *Bulgaria, Imprisonment of Ethnic Turks: Human Rights Abuses during the Forced Assimilation of the Ethnic Turkish Minority* (London, 1986).

[2] *The Pulse*, 28 January 1985, p. 21. At a later date, Mr. Konstantinov acknowledged that there had been some disturbances in Turkish areas in Bulgaria, but according to him press accounts had exaggerated these "minor disturbances" beyond all recognition. He did not elaborate (ibid., 21 February 1985, p. 21.) Other Bulgarian officials also denied the allegations while at the same time denying permission to independent observers to visit Turkish areas in Bulgaria.

[3] Ibid., 28 January 1985, p. 21.

find out for themselves whether the allegations in the press were true.[4] The Bulgarian government's response to the issues raised in this note was found unsatisfactory, and additional diplomatic notes were sent to Sofia in March and April, seeking clarification and a more satisfactory answers to questions raised in the previous notes.

The response of the Bulgarian government to these suggestions and requests was entirely negative and uncompromising. It finally admitted that Turks were replacing their Turkish names with Bulgarian ones but insisted that they were doing so voluntarily on their own initiative. The Bulgarian government then launched a propaganda blitz, for both foreign and domestic consumption, in an attempt to repudiate the charges leveled against it in the international press. Seven members of the Central Committee Secretariat were sent to the districts of Blagoevgrad, Kurdzhali, Haskovo, Burgas, Ruse, Silistre, Veliko Turnovo, and Razgrad—districts with large Turkish and Muslim concentrations—to brief local party officials on the party line. Their speeches were published only in provincial newspapers, except for parts excerpted in the English-language weekly, *Sofia News*.[5] Newspapers with national distribution remained largely silent on the matter. The request of the Turkish government for a high level meeting to arrive at a comprehensive migration agreement was rejected on the grounds that there were no Turks in Bulgaria. The request for a Turkish parliamentary delegation to visit affected areas was rejected on the grounds that what was happening in Bulgaria was entirely an internal matter. Even the suggestion of such a visit was interpreted as meddling in the internal affairs of Bulgaria. The charge of persecution of Muslims and forcing them to change their names was false, Bulgarian officials said, because freedom of religion and freedom from deprivation of nationality were protected by the Constitution.[6]

In a commentary in *Sofia News* on Turkish demands and requests, it was stated that Bulgarian Muslims are the descendants of Bulgarians who were, according to Bulgarian officials, forced to convert to Islam during the Ottoman period and forgot their original identity over time.[7] Moreover, the commentary claimed that

> The rudiments of a process of resurgence of the national identity of Muslim Bulgarians can be traced back to as early as the second half of the 19th c. and especially in the 20th c. *It is based on the traditions common for the Bulgarian nationality (regardless of religion) in the domains of language, folklore, ethnography and others* [emphasis added].[8]

---

[4]Ibid., 25 February 1985, p. 20

[5]For the texts of these speeches, see the documentation section of *Südost-Europa Zeitschrift für Gegenwartsforschung:* "Von bulgarischen Türken und getürken Bulgaren," 6 (1985): 359-67, and "Aussenpolitische aspekte der bulgarishen Türken-politik," 9 no. 34 (1985): 477-487.

[6]*Sofia News*, "Lessons in religious tolerance," 10 April 1985, p. 9; see also the issue for June 19.

[7]Since January 1985 reference to "the Turks of Bulgaria" or "the Muslims of Bulgaria," which was still common until the fall of 1984, has been purged from the official vocabulary. Since then, such terms as "Bulgarian citizens," "our fellow citizens who reverted to their Bulgarian names," "our fellow countrymen who had Turkic-Arabic names," or "Muslim Bulgarians" have replaced previous designations.

[8]*Sofia News*, "No part of our people belongs to any other nation," 3 April 1985, pp. 1, 13.

Had there been a resurgence of Bulgarian ethnic identity among Muslims in Bulgaria as the commentator claims? No. The claim is pure ideological invention and has nothing to do with reality. Even the Pomaks, the Bulgarian-speaking Muslims, fought against the Bulgarian and Russian forces during the Russo-Turkish War of 1877-78; they also fought on the side of Turkish forces during the Balkan wars and World War I and worked for the establishment of a Muslim state in the eastern Rhodopes area. During and after the Balkan wars and World War I, the Pomaks were subject to intense and often brutal christianization campaigns, which the governments in power did little to curb. After the establishment of communist power in Bulgaria following World War II, the new government, asserting that they were of "pure Bulgarian origin" because of the fact that they spoke a Bulgarian dialect, mounted a determined assault on the Muslim identity of Pomaks.[9] Initially, government ideologues saw the campaign against the influence of Islam among Pomaks and other Muslims in Bulgaria simply as one of anti-Islamic propaganda and education. Nikolai Vranchev, writing soon after the establishment of communist power in Bulgaria, treats the problem of Islam among the Pomaks in the following way:

> There will be a struggle between ignorance and deception [Islam], on the one hand, and knowledge and truth on the other. The bearers of the former are the old Bulgarian Muslims, and the bearers of the latter are the members of the younger generation. Some day the older generation will pass away and take their ignorance with them. The young will remain and consolidate the new system with enlightenment and culture. And then there will not be even a memory of the Bulgarian Muslim problem that troubles us today.[10]

According to Vranchev, unlike the "barbaric" Turks, "a contemporary and democratic government" [of Bulgaria] would not need to resort to any threat or coercion to accomplish this task. Anti-Islamic propaganda and education alone would eradicate the influence of Islam among the Pomak population within a single generation. However, these words were soon forgotten, for the hold of Islam was found to be deep-seated and tenacious and did not show signs of loosening before the propaganda onslaught.

Between 1960 and 1976, as the result of threat and coercion, close to 200,000 Bulgarian-speaking Muslims replaced their Muslim names with conventional Bulgarian names. Religious schools and mosques were closed also; religious texts were confiscated and destroyed; many religious leaders and others who resisted this campaign were arrested, imprisoned, and even killed; Pomak women were forced to adopt Bulgarian dress; and the performance of Islamic rituals, such as fasting during the month of Ramazan, the slaughter of lambs during the Feast of Sacrifice, festivities following the two important Islamic holidays, the circuncision of boys, and traditional Islamic funerary practices, among others, were prohibited.[11]

---

[9] Bulgarian writers have always insisted that Bulgarian-speaking Muslims are of pure Bulgarian origin. The origin of Pomaks is problematic; see S. P. Kyriakides, *The Northern Boundaries of Hellenism* (Amsterdam, 1980), and A. Cevat Eren, "Pomaklar," *İslam Ansiklopedisi*, vol. 9 (1960), pp. 572-76.

[10] *Bulgari Mohamedani (Pomatsi)* (Sofia, 1948), p. 59.

[11] Amnesty International Yearbooks of 1976 through 1984 include stories of Pomak and Turkish prisoners who are serving long terms at hard labor for resisting government efforts to bulgarize them.

The attempts of various governments since the war of 1877-78 to impose a Bulgarian identity on the Pomaks and to eradicate the influence of Islam among them led to quite different results from those expected. Some among the Pomak population, especially those living close to Turkish villages, established a much closer relationship with the Turks than with the Bulgarians, and an increased rate of intermarriage between Pomaks and Turks during recent years has led to a process of turkification of the Pomaks.[12]

The turkification of the Pomaks is acknowledged even by Bulgarian writers. Mizov, in his *Islam in Bulgaria,* cites "the overall backwardness of the Turkish population, its religious fanaticism and the influence of [Turkish] bourgeois nationalism" as reasons for large numbers of Turks wanting to emigrate to Turkey. He goes on to say:

> These same reasons pushed a considerable number of gypsies, Tatars, and Bulgarians who profess Islam, toward turkification. Separate examinations [of data] have revealed that tens of thousands of gypsies, Tatars, and Bulgarian-Muslims are taking on Turkish identity. The majority of them, however, present themselves and consider themselves as Turks only outwardly, in their documents, based on the fact that they have the same religion as the latter. But some of them persistently imitate the Turks in many respects, learn their language and culture, try to impose it upon their children as "their own," etc.[13]

As Bulgarian-speaking Muslims and gypsy Muslims came under intense pressure to assimilate, some attempted to protect their Muslim identities by declaring themselves Turks.

What has been going on among Muslims in Bulgaria over the years is not the growth of Bulgarian consciousness but the growth of Muslim consciousness and of attempts to protect that identity by various means. This may have been one of the main reasons why, during the early 1970s, the government moved to bulgarize the Turkish villages close to Pomak areas in the Rhodope region.

Bulgarian commentators have also made a number of misleading, if not entirely false, claims. Do all Bulgarian citizens share common traditions as is claimed? No. Turkish identity has nothing in common with Bulgarian identity. Turks in Bulgaria speak Turkish, not Bulgarian; Turkish folk traditions draw their inspiration from sources quite different from the Bulgarian ones, Turks are overwhelmingly Muslim in religion, while Bulgarians traditionally profess the Bulgarian Orthodox faith; Turkish customs, culture, and worldview are products of a different set of historical experiences from those of the Bulgarians. Similarly, the cultures of Bulgarian-speaking Muslims and gypsy Muslims include tradition and customs that are unique to those minorities. To pretend

---

For example, the Yearbook for 1976 reports (p. 157) that, according to a Bulgarian refugee who was imprisoned in the notorious Belene Island prison in 1974, out of a total of 1,300 prisoners at Belene that year, approximately 500 were Pomaks, many of whom were there because they had resisted the government's name change campaign.

[12] During the campaign to force Pomaks to replace their Muslim names with Bulgarian ones, many Pomaks asserted that they were Turks who, over time, had lost their facility in the Turkish language; see Vladimir Ardenski, *Svoi, a Ne Chuzhdi* (Sofia, 1974).

[13] Mizov, *Isljamut vuv Bulgaria,* (Sofia, 1965), p. 15.

otherwise is to deliberately misrepresent the facts. The statement that the language, folklore, and style of life associated with one identity may survive awareness of a new identity is an attempt to reconcile the glaring contradiction between theoretically posited resurgence of Bulgarian self-consciousness among Muslims and the reality of the persistence of Turkish and/or Muslim identity as manifested in language, folklore, religion, customs and culture.

The commentary in *Sofia News,* quoted earlier, asserted further that the growth of awareness of original Bulgarian identity among Turks had intensified during the last several decades:

> The process gained particuler momentum in the later [sic] half of the [20th] century.... Anyhow, the 1960s witnessed the first big wave of resurging national self-consciousness among Muslim Bulgarians, which found expression in the renunciation by tens of thousands of people of the once assumed personal names of Arabic and Turkish origin. This virtually uninterrupted process continued into the 1970s too, and by the end of last year [1984] it had assumed the nature of a truly massive popular movement.[14]

The claim that renunciation of Muslim names assumed "massive" proportions during the latter part of 1984 is absolutely false. There never was such a movement to begin with. In Bulgaria in August 1984 I talked to several people who had recently been forced to replace their Turkish names with Bulgarian ones and were psychologically devastated by the experience. Others I talked to were presently under pressure to change names. Some who were living in overcrowded houses would not be assigned a new apartment or given permission to build a new house. Still others were denied transfer to another job or to another part of the country. They were told, in effect, "Replace your Arabic-Turkish name with a Bulgarian name, then we will talk about it." In the eastern Rhodopes there were quite a few Turks who had chosen to remain without passports because getting a new passport would have meant a compulsory name change. I spoke with many other Turks in as yet unaffected areas, all of whom lived with the constant fear that their turn would be next. Over the last several years I have increasingly observed the symptoms of demoralization among the Turkish-speaking population in Bulgaria.

The ideological myth about the resurgence of Bulgarian identity among Bulgarian Muslims, especially among Turks, is offered as justification for a wide-ranging assault on Muslim identity in general and Turkish identity in particular. The assault, which began in earnest among the Pomak population in the 1960s and was extended to the gypsies and several Turkish villages in the east-central Rhodope region in the early 1970s, was brought to a rapid and brutal conclusion during the winter of 1984-85. What has happened among the Muslim population in Bulgaria during the last twenty-five years has not been a "resurgence of Bulgarian identity" but a determined effort by a totalitarian regime to achieve ethnic homogeneity, in theory if not in fact. When anti-Islamic propaganda and education failed to accomplish the political purposes of the Bulgarian government, coercion and terror followed.

---

[14]"No part of our people," p. 12.

Ljubomir Shopov, chief of the Balkan department of the Ministry of Foreign Affairs, during a press conference for foreign journalists in late April 1985, more or less repeated the "resurgence" myth and then went even further, suggesting that there is no connection between Turkey and Bulgarian Muslims: "Turkey has no historical rights and no other grounds whatsoever to claim some 'Turkish national minority' or 'compatriots' in Bulgaria."[15] The affairs of the Muslim community in Bulgaria he concluded, are a purely internal matter. He reiterated the latest government position on the status of the Turks in the following words:

> The forcibly converted part of the population has become aware of the historical truth about their national identity and has been regaining national self-consciousness [as Bulgarians] in the whole course of a century after Bulgarian liberation in 1878.... *All this has found a final and categorical expression in the proccess of the restoration of Bulgarian names by the Bulgarian Muslim citizens of their own free will and on their own initiative* [emphasis added].[16]

Thus Bulgaria has categorically denied any use of force or terror to coerce Turks to assume Bulgarian names. It has also vigorously denied any encroachement on the religious rights and freedoms of Turks and other Muslims in the country.

Did Turks change their names voluntarily and on their own initiative without any threat or coercion as claimed? The idea that hundreds of thousands of Turks, during the bitter cold months of the winter of 1984-85, flocked to police stations throughout Bulgaria in droves and stood in line to change their names is absurd, to say the least.

Shopov also claimed that all Muslim Bulgarians [Turks] who felt in any way connected with Turkey had all emigrated to Turkey during the period when the Turco-Bulgarian Agreement on Partial Emigration was in force (1969-1979).[17] Hence, there are no Muslim Bulgarians who have any connection with Turkey or anyone in Turkey. Dimitur Stojanov, minister of internal affairs and Politburo candidate member, has put forth this claim even more adamantly:

> *All our countrymen who reverted to their Bulgarian names are Bulgarians.* They are the bone of the bone and the flesh of the flesh of the Bulgarian nation; although the Bulgarian national consciousness of some of them might still be blurred, they are of the same flesh and blood; they are children of the Bulgarian nation; they were forcibly torn away and now they are coming back home. *There are no Turks in Bulgaria* [emphasis added].[18]

The truth of the mater is that Bulgarian national consciousness among Turks is not blurred, as Stojanov suggested: it does not exist and has never existed. All assertions

---

[15]*Sofia News*, "Bulgaria has no spare citizens," 1 May 1985, p. 3.

[16]Ibid.

[17]It is interesting to note that lately the Soviet Union has used similar reasoning to explain the drastic reduction in the number of Soviet Jews who have emigrated from the Soviet Union during recent years: to wit, most Jews who wanted to leave the Soviet Union have already left.

[18]Quoted in *Radio Free Europe Situation Report*, "Officials say there are no Turks in Bulgaria," 28 March 1985, p. 5.

to the contrary by Bulgarian authorities seriously misrepresent well-known facts and distort Bulgarian history beyond recognition.

During the 1950s and 1960s there was an official government policy to encourage the maintenance of the Turkish identity as separate from the Bulgarian through specific programs such as Turkish language schools, Turkish teacher training institutes, a Turkish press, state supported regional Turkish theaters and folk groups, and the encouragement of amateur folk groups in Turkish villages throughout the country. With hindsight, however, it is now clear that these programs were not established because the Bulgarian government sincerely believed in cultural pluralism. On the contrary, they were initiated for pragmatic political reasons, in order to placate the very restive Turkish population, whose sensibilities had been badly wounded by the actions of the government towards them between 1948 and 1951. This period had seen not only the elimination of the semi-autonomous status the Turkish-speaking community had enjoyed in Bulgaria up to that time, but also a surge of active government interference in the life of the community. Such interference had begun in 1946, when all private Turkish schools were nationalized and placed under strict government supervision. In 1949 the religious affairs of the Muslim community came under government regulation, and in late 1949 the government began its initial collectivization drive in the fertile plains of Dobrudzha, where most of the land was owned by Turkish farmers. These and other similar actions were met with fierce and determined resistance on the part of Turks and other Muslims, and there was considerable agitation to be allowed to emigrate to Turkey. In early 1950 the Bulgarian government suddenly began to deport large numbers of Turks, especially from northeastern Bulgaria. The lands of the farmers were confiscated outright and the Turks were herded *en masse* to border stations, many with only the clothes on their backs. In 1949 only 1,525 Turks emigrated from Bulgaria to Turkey, while during the first nine months only of 1950 some 28,250 left Bulgaria. In September of 1950 Bulgaria informed Turkey that 250,000 additional Turks were willing to emigrate but that the transfer of this number must be completed by November 10.[19] This demand for the enormous transfer of population on such short notice and in such a short period of time was in clear contravention of the procedures for orderly migration established by the Ankara Agreement of 1925.[20] By the end of 1951 approximately 155,000 Bulgarian Turks had crossed into Turkey. Unable to absorb such a large influx of immigrants within such a short time, Turkey closed the border.[21]

These experiences generated widespread dissatisfaction among the Turks. The more liberal attitude of the Bulgarian government toward Turks after 1951 must be understood within this context. However, even during the period of apparent liberality in the 1950s, the underlying goal of the government remained the assimilation of the

[19]*The World Today*, "The expulsion of the Turkish minority from Bulgaria," 7 no. 1 (1951): 33.

[20]This agreement had a number of provisions to safeguard the life and property of prospective emigrants. Among these, the agreement required that all emigrants should have the right to take with them all their movable property and savings, as well as to dispose of all their immovable property without interference (ibid., p. 31). Even after signing the Ankara agreement, Bulgaria continued to ignore its provisions, leading Turkey to close the border. Between the end of 1951 and 1969, when a new agreement on emigration went into effect, the emigration of Turks from Bulgaria to Turkey virtually ceased.

[21]Huey L. Kostanick, *Turkish Settlement of Bulgarian Turks, 1950-1953* (Berkeley, 1957).

Turks into the dominant Slavic majority. Since the Turkish population was largely monolingual at that time, it was felt that the propaganda attack the government chose to use in the effort to accomplish that goal would be most effective if mounted in the Turkish language. Thus, both a wide-ranging attack on Islam among the Turks and a number of programs designed to foster the development of the Turkish language and culture date from this period.[22]

The new emphasis on the development of the Turkish language and culture ("national in form, socialist in content") was welcomed by many members of the Turkish-speaking community. As long as programs supporting Turkish-language schools, press, and theaters continued to function, many Turks became supporters of the regime. It was only after the elimination or drastic curtailment of many of these programs, starting in the early 1960s, that Turkish restiveness resurfaced and demands for emigration were heard once again.

Is There a Turkish Minority in Bulgaria?

To say now that there are no Turks in Bulgaria is ludicrous and represents a total reversal of previou Bulgarians positions. The presence of a sizable minority of Turkish Muslims has been acknowledged in a number of international agreements and several bilateral agreements between Bulgaria and Turkey, the last of which was the ten-year agreement on emigration of Turks from Bulgaria signed in late 1968.[23] Scholars in Bulgaria have written about the history and culture of this important minority in their midst, fully recognizing the distinctiveness of Turkish culture from the dominant Bulgarian culture. Mizov, discussing Islam in Bulgaria in 1965, wrote:

> The Islamic religion is mainly the religion of the Turkish population living in Bulgaria. In addition to the Turks, Islam is also the religion of the Tatars, who inhabit certain regions of northern Bulgaria, of approximately half of the gypsies, scattered throughout our country, and also of a certain number of Bulgarians, who were forcibly converted to Islam during the five-century long period of Turkish rule.[24]

---

[22]Mizov, in *Isljamjŭt*, treats Islam as nothing more than a collection of superstitions and prejudices and advocates a determined fight to eradicate it in Bulgaria.

[23]The Treaties of Berlin (1878), Neuilly (1919), Lausanne (1923), and Paris (1947) are among the international agreements. Bilateral agreements dealing specifically with the Turkish minority in Bulgaria include the Istanbul Protocol, the Turco-Bulgarian Peace Agreement of 1913, the Bulgarian-Turkish agreement signed in Ankara in 1925, the 1950 agreement reaffirming the principles of the Ankara agreement, and the 1968 emigration agreement. Bulgaria also signed the Covenant of the United Nations and a number of universal declarations of human rights, including the Helsinki Final Act of 1975. Also, her own Constitution has a number of articles devoted to the protection of the rights of citizens of non-Bulgarian origin. For an excellent discussion of the provisions of international and bilateral agreements dealing with the Turkish minority in Bulgaria, see Hamza Eroğlu, "Milletlerarası hukuk açısından Bulgaristan'daki Türk azınlığı sorunu," in *Bulgaristan'da Türk Varlığı: Bildiriler* (Ankara, 1985), pp. 15-46. (See also A. Mete Tuncoku, "The Rights of Minorities in International Treaties: The Case of the Turkish Minority in the People's Republic of Bulgaria" in this issue of *IJTS*. Ed.)

[24]*Isljamut*, p. 10.

Throughout the book Mizov made clear distinctions between the Turkish and Bulgarian population in areas of religion and culture. He noted that

> the main nucleus of Muslims in Bulgaria are Turks, who, by national origin and affiliation, differ from the Bulgarian nationality. Only 85 years ago they were the ruling nation, and their religion the ruling religion and ideology in our country.[25]

Moreover, until recently the Bulgarian government itself freely acknowledged the existence of a sizeable Turkish minority, as well as other minorities, in statistical yearbooks and censuses. For example, 1956 census figures published in Bulgaria provide a comprehensive breakdown of the country's population by national origin. (See Table 1 following this article.) Census statistics published by the Bulgarian government for the years through 1965 also provide valuable information on the nationality breakdown of populations in districts inhabited predominantly by Turks. The 1965 figures for the district of Kurdzhali in southeastern Bulgaria, for example, show that out of a population of 283,758 for the district as a whole, 204,981, or 72.6 percent were Turks; of these, 189,475, or 92 percent, lived in rural villages.[26]

The results of these censuses are instructive for the understanding of recent events in Bulgaria. The Bulgarian-speaking Muslims have always been counted among the Bulgarians. The gypsies disappeared entirely from official statistics after 1956, while the number of Macedonians was reduced by some 180,000 in the 1965 census. Since 1965, official statistical information on the Turkish minority has been difficult to come by. After the official announcement in March 1985 that there were no Turks in Bulgaria, the Bulgarian government is unlikely to provide any figures on national minorities in the country in the future. In the absence of official information on national minorities, we must rely on unofficial estimates (see Table 2).

During the 1950s the government of Bulgaria went to a lot of effort to demonstrate her goodwill toward the Turkish minority, emphasizing constitutional guarantees for the development of its language and culture. For example, Article 79 of the Constitution of the People's Republic of Bulgaria adopted in 1947 states:

---

[25]Ibid., p. 14. Of the many other works written by Bulgarian scholars about the Turkish minority, I cite only a few as follows: H. Memishev, *Uchastieto na Bulgarskite Turtsi vuv Borbata protiv Kapitalizma i Fashizma, 1914-1944* (Sofia, 1977), discussing the participation of Bulgarian Turks in World War II in the struggle against capitalism and fascism; M. Beitullov, *Zhivotut na Naselenieto ot Turski Proizhod vuv NRB* (Sofia, 1975) exploring the changes that have taken place in the lives of Turks in Bulgaria since World War II; a book published by Direktsija na Pecata (1951), *The Minority in the People's Republic of Bulgaria;* G. Ganev, *Selo Bezvodno vuv Minaloto i Dnes* (Sofia, 1969), discussing the history of a Turkish village in the eastern Rhodopes and concluding that the present-day inhabitants of the villages in the region all speak Turkish and feel themselves to be Turks; V. Marinov, *Prinos kum Izuchavaneto na bita i Culturata na Turtsite i Gagauzite vuv Severoiztochna Bulgaria* (Sofia, 1956), a monograph on the customs and cultures of Turks and Gagauz (Turkish-speaking Christians) in northeastern Bulgaria; Sh. Takhirov, *Bulgarskite Turtsi po Putja na Sotsializma* (Sofia, 1978), discussing the strides made by Turks in Bulgaria on the road to socialism; and A. Aliev, *Formiraneto na Nauchno-ateistichen Mirogled u Bulgarskite Turtsi* (Sofia, 1980), discussing the inroads of the scientific-atheistic worldview among Turks of Bulgaria.

[26]Tsentralno Statistichesko Upravlenie, *Rezultatite ot Prebrojavane na Naselenieto na 12.1.1965 g. - okrug Kurdzhali* (Sofia, 1967), pp. 157-158, 163-64.

Citizens have a right to education.... *National minorities have a right to be educated in their mother tongue and to develop their national culture,* while the study of Bulgarian is compulsory [emphasis added][27]

Todor Zhivkov, in his congratulatory message to *Yeni Hayat*, the Turkish-language monthly, on its tenth anniversary in 1964, said:

All possible opportunities have been created for the Turkish population to develop their culture and language freely.... The children of the Turkish population must learn their [mother] tongue and perfect it. To this end, it is necessary that the teaching [of the Turkish language] be improved in schools. *Now and in the future the Turkish population will speak their mother tongue; they will develop their progressive traditions in this language; they will write their contemporary literary works* [in Turkish]; *they will sing their wonderfully beautiful songs* [in Turkish].... *Many more books must be published in this country in Turkish, including the best works of progressive writers in Turkey* [emphasis added].[28]

It is ironic that Mr. Zhivkov was speaking these words precisely at the time when the government was busily engaged in dismantling the very programs intended to develop Turkish language and culture. It is also ironic that for the last fifteen years the Bulgarian government has been working hard at making null and void its policies of yesterday in order to achieve a homogeneous state. This is another instance of promises made for purely pragmatic, political reasons.

Between 1960 and 1970 all Turkish-language schools were eliminated. Since 1970 the Bulgarian authorities have stepped up the linguistic assimilation of the Turkish-Muslim minority in pursuit of their avowed goal of creating a single-nationality state. The implicit assumption behind this policy seems to be that once Turkish-Muslims become monolingual and use Bulgarian exclusively among themselves they will forget their separate ethnic and religious consciousness and be willing to be assimilated into the mainstream Bulgarian culture. To accomplish this linguistic goal the Bulgarian authorities have taken the following determined steps. "1) Turkish schools have been closed, and the teaching of Turkish has been banned. 2) The activities of the Turkish section of Narodna Prosveta Publishing House have been terminated. 3) The publication of Turkish newspapers and journals has been stopped. 4) Turkish theaters have been prohibited from staging Turkish programs. 5) Turks have been prohibited from receiving Turkish newspapers, journals, and books from outside. 6) All Turkish books published in Bulgaria have been taken off the shelves. 7) The publishing of Turkish books by poets and writers has been banned. 8) The singing of Turkish folk songs and other Turkish songs during ceremonies, weddings, and festivals

---

[27]Jan F. Triska, ed., "Bulgaria," in *Constitutions of the Communist Party States* (Stanford, 1968), p. 163. The Constitution as amended in 1961 maintains this article intact; see Triska, ed., *Constitutions*, pp. 176-77. The new Constitution, adopted in 1971, has a significant language change from the original; nevertheless it states that "citizens of non-Bulgarian extraction [meaning mainly Turks], in addition to the compulsory study of Bulgarian, are entitled to study their own language" (Sofia Press, *The Constitution of the Peoples' Republic of Bulgaria,* Sofia, 1971, op. cit., p. 17).

[28]Quoted in *Radio Free Europe Research,* 28 March 1985, p. 6.

has been banned. 9) The speaking of Turkish in public conveyances and on the streets has been banned. 10) In towns and villages Turks have been forced to learn Bulgarian. 11) Listening to Turkish radio programs has been banned."[29]

Similarly, the constitutional guarantees for the protection of the rights of minorities have been entirely ignored in practice. These guarantees include, among others, the freedom and inviolability of the individual; equality of all citizens before the law regardless of national origin; freedom of the press, of speech, and of assembly; and freedom of conscience and religion and performance of religious rites. A number of specific articles of the Bulgarian constitution are relevant for an understanding of the recent persecution of Turks. Section 2 of Article 48 states that "no privilege or limitation of rights based on nationality, origin, creed, sex, education, social and material status are allowed;" and section 4 of the same Article prohibits "the propagation of hate and humiliation of man because of race, national and religious affiliation." Article 50 guarantees the "right of defense against unlawful interference in a person's personal or family life and infringement upon a person's honor and good name." Article 51 protects the secrecy "of correspondence, telephone conversations, and telecommunications." Article 54 guarantees "freedom of speech, press, meetings, associations, and demonstrations."[30] And a number of articles in the penal code provide for punishment of individuals and groups who violate these constitutional guarantees. Even under ordinary circumstances most of these rights and freedoms have been routinely ignored. During the recent campaign against the Turks in Bulgaria *all* of these constitutional provisions were most blatantly violated.

Reasons for the "Bulgarization" of the Turks

Recent developments in Bulgaria should not be considered an abrupt change in government policy. The Bulgarian government has steadily sought, since the end of WWII, to create a single-nation Bulgarian state. This idea became set in concrete as the guiding principle of the Bulgarian Communist Party in the program of its 10th Congress in 1971, which stated that the development of the socialist nation would expand further henceforth and the citizens of Bulgaria "of different national origins will come ever closer together."[31] Around 1973 the phrase "unified Bulgarian nation" first began to be used by the news media. The assimilationist policy of the government was given further impetus by the Bulgarian Communist Party Central Committee Plenum of February 1974. Since then the campaign of "creating a unified socialist nation" has been speeded up to such an extent that one author in 1977 went so far as to claim that Bulgaria "is almost completely of one ethnic type and is moving toward complete national homogeneity";[32] and Todor Zhivkov confidently declared in 1979 that "the

---

[29]Eroğlu, "Milletlerarası," p. 19.

[30]Sofia Press, *The Constitution, op. cit.*, 1971, pp. 15, 18-20.

[31]The program of the 10th Congress of the Bulgarian Communist Party is described fully in the April 29 issue of the party newspaper, *Rabotnichesko Dela*. The coming together of different nations and nationalities and their eventual merger into a single socialist nation has been the guiding principle of Soviet nationality policy since the October Revolution of 1917; however, the merging of nations and nationalities in the Soviet Union has been postponed for the indefinite future.

[32]Rada Nikolaev, "Pressure on the Turkish minority reported," *Radio Free Europe Situation Report*, 30 January 1985, p. 2.

nationality question has been solved definitively and categorically by the population itself.... Bulgaria has no internal problems connected with the nationality question."[33] Finally, the climax was reached in 1985 in the categorical statement: "There are no Turks in Bulgaria."

Such claims have necessitated a drastic revision of Bulgarian history. Until the early 1970s, Bulgarian writers not only acknowledged the existence of a sizeable Turkish minority in Bulgaria but also located the origins of this minority outside the Balkan Peninsula:

> Turks are the largest national group after the Bulgarians (approximately 9 %). They were settled in the Bulgarian land between the 15th and 18th centuries, mainly in those areas in which the Ottoman Empire was most vulnerable to attacks.... Now Turks live in large concentrations in the eastern Rhodopes, Gerlovo, Dobrudzha, and Slannik. They are primarily workers in agricultural cooperatives. Bulgarians and Turks live amicably and together with all other nationalities participate in the building of socialism.[34]

Subsequently Bulgarian writers have brought their ideas in line with the Party dogma that Bulgaria is, for all intents and purposes, a one nationality state. Petrov, commenting on the ethnic make-up of the Bulgarian population in 1981, does not even mention the presence of Turks in the Rhodope region but confines them to a small pocket in northeastern Bulgaria:

> Bulgaria is a uninational state. The population throughout the country is Bulgarian. Only in the northeastern part—Shoumen, Turgovishte and Razgrad districts—are there communities of Bulgarian Turks.[35]

Another writer, talking about the Balkans in general in 1982, does not mention the existence of any Turks on the entire Balkan Peninsula!

> In terms of ethnic and linguistic affiliation, the population of the Balkan states as a whole belongs to the Indo-European group. In the Balkan lands there also live Russians, Armenians, Jews, gypsies, Tatars and other ethnic groups.[36]

All of this indicates that the assimilation of non-Bulgarian minorities into the dominant Bulgarian culture has been going on for some time now. However, until 1984 the forcible change of names among the Turkish population had been gradual, affecting only a few villages in the Rhodopes at a time, had generated little internal opposition, and had been all but ignored outside of the country. Why then did the Bulgarian government choose to accelerate this campaign and complete the bulgarization of Turks

---

[33]For Todor Zhivkov's speech, see the April 28 issue of *Rabotnichesko Delo*.

[34]Ljubomir Dinev and Kiril Mishev, *Bulgaria: Kratka Geografiia* (Sofia, 1969), p. 136," See also above, n. 14 and text.

[35]Petur Petrov, "Bulgaria on the geographical map," in Georgi Bokov, ed., *Modern Bulgarian History, Policy, Economy, and Culture* (Sofia, 1981), p. 145.

[36]Ts. Dimitrov, *Balkanite: Politiko-ekonomicheski Spravochnik* (Sofia, 1982), p. 14.

within a few months during the winter of 1984-85? In the following paragraphs I present some of the most plausible reasons that may have motivated Bulgarian authorities to rush ahead with the integration of the Turkish minority.

First, for the last twenty years or more there has been a serious concern among Bulgarian demographers about population trends in that country. It has been projected that if the present trend continues, by the 1990s the Bulgarian population may experience a zero or negative population growth. If this trend is seen against the backdrop of a projected increase in the demand for labor in the future, the concern is very understandable. Ethnic Turks and gypsies on the other hand, have registered much higher rates of population growth—twice as high—as the ethnic Bulgarian population. Higher growth rates among the Turks have been especially worrisome. On the one hand, Turkish citizens of Bulgaria are in a position to supply the future labor needs of Bulgaria. As Torsten Baest observes:

> A labor reserve of 1.2 to 1.5 million Bulgarian Muslims, two thirds of whom are Turks lacking appropriate education and "consciousness," can only be completely integrated when potential sources of conflict—e.g., national consciousness, religion, language, and education—are eliminated.[37]

On the other hand, a substantial rise in the number of Turks in Bulgaria might lead in the not too distant future to demands on their part for some sort of autonomy unless they are quickly assimilated. Bulgarian officials have intensified the fear of this by spreading panicky rumors that by the year 2000 Turks and gypsies will make up the majority of the population in Bulgaria. Such a projection is entirely off the mark, as Baest notes:

> Even allowing for a slight decline in the Bulgarian growth rate—for which there is some evidence—the proportions could alter only slightly. In fifteen years time a population of 83% Bulgarian would confront 15% Turks and Romani [gypsies], instead of 85% to 12.5%—hardly a dramatic shift.[38]

However, the longer large numbers of avowed Turks remain in Bulgaria, the longer the relations between Bulgaria and Turkey will be colored by their existence, and as economic conditions in Turkey improve, Turkey would be likely to ask for a comprehensive emigration agreement, under which Bulgaria might lose close to one million people. That would be a serious labor drain that Bulgaria could not tolerate. During the present crisis Turkey has already asked for such an agreement, and Bulgaria has flatly refused. Furthermore, the continued presence of a population of non-Bulgarian origin experiencing a rate of much higher natural growth than the ethnic Bulgarian population would have begun to retard severely the slow progress toward the goal of a homogeneous, one nationality socialist nation. An official reassessment of the implications of the demographic phenomenon of rapid Muslim population growth

---

[37]"Bulgaria's War at Home: The People's Republic and Its Turkish Minority (1944-1985)," *Across Frontiers* (Winter 1985), p. 26.
[38]Ibid.

versus Bulgarian population stagnation may have been one of the most important motivating factors in the recent name-change campaign among the Turks.[39]

Second, the census planned for December 1985 may have been another factor in the decision of the Bulgarian authorities to complete the bulgarization of Turks during the winter of 1984-85. Yugoslav commentators, looking back at what happened in the 1965 census, when most Macedonians were counted as Bulgarians and the teaching of the Macedonian language was abolished by decree, have called this procedure "administrative genocide". Similarly, the forcing of name changes among Turks may result in a significant reduction in their number in the 1985 census—if such figures are even published. It is noteworthy that very little of the information from the 1975 census has been published so far. It is likely that if any figures are published on the ethnic composition of the population in Bulgaria after the 1985 census, the numbers for Turks will be extremely low.

A third reason why the authorities decided to act now may have been the growing influence of Turkish and/or Muslim propaganda among the Turks in Bulgaria during recent years. Fundamentalism has increased significantly in Turkey during the last decade, with large amounts of air time devoted to religious programs on Turkish radio and television. There has been an increasing concern about these developments expressed in the Bulgarian news media recently.[40] Turks in Bulgaria listen to Turkish radio programs frequently, some exclusively; some even watch Turkish televison, modifying their television sets so as to be able to receive programs. Turks in Bulgaria also listen to the Turkish language broadcasts of the BBC, the Voice of Germany, and the Voice of America. Jamming activities against such broadcasts have not been as successful as Bulgaria would like. To counteract religious broadcasts from Turkey and elsewhere, Bulgaria has increased her own anti-Islamic propaganda output during recent years. Such propaganda in Bulgaria has portrayed Islam as the handmaiden of Turkish bourgeois nationalism and religious fanaticism.

Islam has been seen as the major obstacle to the integration of Turks and other Muslims into Bulgarian society.[41] The forced Bulgarization of the Turks is supposed to undercut the influence of Islam. The secretary of the Central Committee of Bulgarian Communist party, Vasil Tsanov, described the completion of the bulgarization program in early March as

> a revolutionary act, which dealt a strong blow to bourgeois nationalism [*read* Turkish nationalism] and rendered powerless its ceaseless attempts to confuse and poison the conciousness of some Bulgarian citizens [of Turkish origin], to alienate them from the socialist motherland, and to

---

[39]See Flora Lewis, "Bulgaria's Image Problem," *The New York Times,* 31 May 1985, p. 23, and Liliana Brisby, "Administrative Genocide in the Balkans?" *The World Today* 41 (1985): 69-70.

[40]I. Dzhambazov, in "Kakvo se krie zad 'reformata' na religioznoto obrazovanie vuv Turtsija?" *Ateistichna Tribuna* 6 (1981): 52-69, speculates, for example, about the hidden motives behind the renewed emphasis on religious education in Turkey during the last decade and sees such developments as a danger to the integration of Turks into Bulgarian society.

[41]S. Ilyazov, "Islajamit i turskijat burzhoazen natsionalizm," *Ateistichna Tribuna* 5 (1981): 22-27; Dzhambazov, "Kakvo se krie" see also Mizov, *Isljamut.*

turn them into tools of reactionary anticommunist forces [primarily Turkey].[42]

Can the Party officials really believe that forcing Turks to replace their Turkish names with Bulgarian names is going to obliterate the religious and ethnic consciousness among a population of almost one million of them? Bulgaria's own history of stubborn cultural survival in the face of oppression is one example that speaks eloquently against the notion. It is unfortunate that Bulgarian ideologues have turned a blind eye to this valuable historical lesson.

Any reasonable person must accept as fact that there are more than 800,000 Turks who live in Bulgaria today. Although the ancestral origins of some of these Turks may be obscure, today an overwhelming majority of them speak Turkish, identify themselves as Turks, and profess the Islamic faith. Membership in an ethnic group is not a matter of blood, as the current campaign of the Bulgarian government against Turks would have it. It is a matter of self ascription, combined with ascription by others. Turks in Bulgaria identify themselves as Turks and are so identified by those around them. No ideological statements, no replacement of names is likely to change that fact for a long time to come. On the contrary, the assault on Turkish identity in Bulgaria is likely to have the opposite effect: that of strengthening the resolve of Turks to cling to their ethnic and religious identities even more tenaciously.

Conclusions

Since the end of World War II Bulgarian authorities have been talking about creating neighborly relations among Balkan states and establishing the Balkans as a zone of peace. The latest events in Bulgaria cast serious doubts on Bulgarian intentions in the Balkans. These doubts are reflected in the question posed by the Yugoslav publicist Ranko Petrovic: "A zone of peace and cooperation in nuclear-free Balkans—or a Bulgaria without Macedonians, Turks, Gypsies, and other nationalities?"[43] We cannot help but conclude that the anti-Muslim stance of the government since World War II, the recent anti-Turkish and anti-Muslim campaigns in Bulgaria, and the declarations of Bulgarian officials in early 1985 clearly indicate that Bulgaria has opted for the latter. What has been the impact of such policies on Turkish and other Muslims in Bulgaria?

An observer who is familiar with the physical landscape of Muslim villages, towns, and cities in the Middle East and elsewhere is struck by the changes in the physical landscape of Muslim villages in Bulgaria. Traditionally, Muslim villages and Muslim neighborhoods in towns and cities in Bulgaria were organized around and dominated by the mosque. The mosque served not only as a place of worship but also as a focus of ceremonies associated with core events in Muslim life—birth, circumcision, marriage, and death—and as an assembly house where the elders of the community gathered to discuss community affairs. The religious leaders were also community leaders who served as teachers, mayors, and doctors. Often the only literate members of their communities, they were the source of both the civil and the religious authority,

---

[42]*Radio Free Europe Research,* 28 March 1985, p. 6.

[43]Quoted in Baest, "Bulgaria's war at home," p. 26.

which in Islamic practice were not considered to be separate domains. Since World War II that landscape has changed. Mosques have been closed, converted to warehouses or schools, neglected, or deliberately destroyed, and no new mosques have been built in Bulgaria.[44] Government policy has been to restore and maintain mosques and other religious buildings from the Ottoman period only if they have architectural and/or historical value and only in areas that are likely to be visited by foreign dignitaries and tourists. The government has allowed a small number of mosques continue to function normally, but this is essentially for propaganda purposes: the number of functioning mosques and the personnel serving in them is totally inadequate for a population of over one-and-a-half million Muslims in the country. As Baest observes, "The Islamic clergy, already severely weakened since 1948, were further decimated" during and after the winter campaign of 1984-85 against Turkish Muslims.[45]

Today the overwhelming majority of Muslim villages in Bulgaria are conspicuous by the absence of mosques. Those Muslims who want to participate in Friday prayers have to travel a considerable distance to find a functioning one. Another feature of the traditional Muslim village, the voice of the *muezzin* calling the faithful to prayer from the *minaret,* has been silenced. An important focus of community activity and solidarity has thus been eliminated. The eradication of mosques, the prohibition of the teaching of Islam at home as well as in schools, the imprisonment of religious teachers, the confiscation of Korans and other religious texts and, the laws against importation of religious texts from the outside have meant a general deterioration of knowledge about important Islamic beliefs and practices. This is especially true for those Muslims who were born during and following World War II. There has been a significant erosion of knowledge about the content and sources of the Five Pillars of Islam. These conditions cannot but have a negative impact on the future viability of Islam and the Muslim identity in Bulgaria.

The reaction of the international community to the policies of the Bulgarian government toward Muslims in Bulgaria has been very mild. Even Turkey and other Islamic countries have not done much beyond engaging in heated rhetoric. They have been unwilling to apply effective political and economic sanctions to try to force the Bulgarian government to change its policies. In the face of this, Turkish and other Muslims in Bulgaria must feel a deep sense of dread about their future.

What can the Turks in Bulgaria do? Any kind of militant separatist movement or prolonged military resistance is out of the question. Organized civil disobedience against repressive government policies is not an option available to the Turks, as the Bulgarian government has quashed all attempts to establish the infrastructure necessary to carry out such actions. Individual acts of civil disobedience and of sabotage against government targets are likely to continue, but the impact of such isolated actions on government policies is likely to be negligible. The last three years, since the end of forced name-changing campaign in Bulgaria, have made it clear to Turks in Bulgaria that they lack consistent ideological and moral support from the outside. Turkey, other Islamic countries, and western countries have roundly condemned human rights abuses in

---

[44]Lately government authorities have been closing mosques "for failure to comply with building codes," ibid, p. 22.

[45]Ibid.

Bulgaria but have been unwilling to go further. Nevertheless, ethnic conflict is likely to remain an important consideration in Bulgarian internal and external politics for some time to come. Continued repression and discrimination against Turks and the persistence of economic, political, and cultural inequalities between the ethnic Bulgarians and Turks, along with cultural traditions, will motivate Turks to assert themselves. For the time being, as in the past, the manifestation of Turkish identity in Bulgaria will revolve around attempts to activate cultural and religious support systems, to maintain and perpetuate ethnic identity and integrity. Attempts to maintain Turkish language will be an important aspect of this process.

Turks in Bulgaria continue and will continue to use Turkish as the primary medium of communication among themselves. Some Turkish parents are already teaching their children how to read and write in Turkish. Although Turkish children in kindergartens and schools are required to speak only Bulgarian, the language of communication in the home remains Turkish. Writing novels, stories, and poetry in Turkish is likely to continue. To what extent such works will circulate among Turks in a *samizdat* fashion is difficult to say, since such underground activity is controlled to a greater extent in Bulgaria than in the Soviet Union.

Turks continue and will continue to use their Turkish-Muslim names among themselves and give Turkish names to their children even though Bulgarian names are used exclusively for official purposes. Many Turkish women continue to wear *shalvars* (traditional baggy trousers) at home. Many Turks continue to defy the ban against circumcision. Turks continue to observe the important religious holidays, although their knowledge about Islamic beliefs, rituals, and practices continues to deteriorate. All indications are that the Turks are doing all they can, under the circumstances, to maintain their uniqueness and separateness by restricting their contacts with ethnic Bulgarians to the workplace alone. Government encouragement of mixed marriages has fallen on deaf ears. The pattern of endogamous marriages for Turkish and other Muslim women remains intact and is unlikely to change.

The survival of Turkish identity in Bulgaria may depend ultimately on how long the present regime survives and the repressive policies of the government remain in place. The younger Communist party leaders who will inherit the mantle of leadership from the old guard seem even more virulent Bulgarian nationalists than their predecessors. Although recent events in Bulgaria have strengthened the resolve of Turks to maintain their identity and integrity, if present policies remain in place for a generation or more, then the prospects for the Turkish minority in Bulgaria are not very promising.

Wayne State College, Detroit, Michigan

Table 1. The Ethnic Composition of the Bulgarian Population, 1956

Nationality	Number	Percent
Bulgarians	6,506,541	85.6
Macedonians	187,789	2.4
Russians	10,551	.1
Serbs	484	--
Czechs	1,199	--
other Slavs	1,100	--
Turks	656,025	8.6
Tatars	5,993	--
Gypsies	197,865	2.6
Armenians	21,954	.3
Rumanians	3,749	--
Greeks	7,437	.1
Jews	6,027	--
Albanians	1,105	--
Karakachans[a]	2,085	--
Kutsovlachs[b]	485	—
Hungarians	671	--
Germans	747	--
Other non-Slavs	1,900	--
Total	7,613,709	

SOURCE: Tsentralno Statistichesko *Upravlenie, Prebrojavane na Naselenieto vuv Narodna Republika Bulgaria na 12,1,1956 godina: Obshti Rezultati,* vol. 2. (Sofia, 1960), pp. 106-109.

[a] Greek-speaking nomadic shepherds

[b] Rumanian-speaking nomadic shepherds. Both the Karakachans and the Kutsovlachs were forced to settle during the 1950s and are largely assimilated by now.

Table 2. Ethnic Composition of the Population of Bulgaria, 1946-1980

Ethnic Group	1946 Numbers	Per-cent	1956 Numbers	Per-cent	1965 Numbers	Per-cent	1980 Numbers	Per-cent
Bulgarians	6,073,124	86.4	6,506,541	85.5	7,231,243	88.2	7,601,880	85.8
Turks	675,500	9.6	656,025	8.6	746,755	9.1	806,260[a]	9.1
Gypsies	-	-	197,865	2.6	148,874[b]	-	230,360	2.6
Macedonians	-	-	187,789	2.5	8,750[c]	0.1	221,360	2.5
Pomaks[d]	-	-	138,643[e]	-	-	-	80,000[f]	-
Others	280,725	4.0	65,489	0.8	211,912	2.6	-	-
Totals	7,029,349		7,613,709		8,226,564		8,860,000	

SOURCES: Figures for 1956 and 1965 are from R. R. King, *Minorities under Communism : Nationalities as a Source of Tension among Balkan Communist States* (Cambridge, Mass., 1973), p. 262; figures for 1946 are from Paul S. Shoup, *The East European and Soviet Data Handbook: Political, Social and Developmental Indicators, 1945-1975* (New York, 1981), p. 136; and the estimates for 1980 are from Walker Connor, *The National Question in Marxist-Leninist Theory and Strategy* (Princeton, New Jersey, 1984), p. 209.
[a]The 1980 estimate of the Turkish population by Connor is low. Given the high birth rate among Turks in Bulgaria, slightly over one million is a much more reasonable estimate.
[b]In the 1965 census, those gypsies who were forced to replace their Turkish-Muslim names with Bulgarian names were counted as Bulgarians.
[c]In the 1965 census most Macedonians in Bulgaria were counted as Bulgarians.
[d]The 1926 census counted 102,351 Pomaks by religious affiliation; the 1934 census counted 134, 125 Muslims who spoke Bulgarian as their mother tongue, most of whom were Pomaks (shoup, *Data Handbook*, p. 136).
[e]Mizov, *Isljamut*, p. 175; Mizov also gives figures for the number of *hodzhas* and the average number of Pomaks per *hodzha*, from which one arrives at a figure of 138,607 Pomaks for 1962, ibid., p. 195.
[f]This estimate of Pomaks is from R. V. Weekes, ed., *Muslim Peoples: A World Etnographic Survey, Vol. II* (Westport, Conn., 1984), p. 884; but this figure is extremely low: the actual figure must be at least twice that, if not more.

Alf Grannes

TURKISH INFLUENCE ON BULGARIAN[*]

> Baj Ganju znače ezici, po turski
> da ti prikazva kato turčin, ... (A.
> Konstantinov, *Baj Ganju*)

Introduction

From the end of the fourteenth century and up to the liberation in 1878 Bulgaria was dominated by the Turks militarily, politically, and economically. Thus, as stated by A. Vaillant: "La Bulgarie, immédiatement après le brillant développement de sa littérature du XIVe siècle, qui déclenche une renaissance du slavon dans tous les pays orthodoxes, est condamnée à un silence à peu près complet jusqu'à la fin du XVIIIe siècle".[1] Obviously the Ottoman bondage of nearly five centuries left a lasting imprint on Bulgarian culture and language. As late as the 1930s the Bulgarian author Ljudmil Stojanov could still write:

> There is no need to prove that we are today a semi-oriental state. The centuries-old Ottoman rule of our land and people has left indelible traces in our geography, ethnography, language, popular customs, and even in our mentality.[2]

There are several reasons for the strong Turkish influence in Bulgaria, some of the most obvious being the following.

a) The presence of Turkish military and administrative personnel.

b) The colonization of certain areas of Bulgaria (mainly eastern Bulgaria and the Rhodopes) by Turkish settlers, who were transferred by the Ottoman authorities or came on their own initiative. Even today Turks constitute probably close to 10 percent of the population of Bulgaria. The Turkish presence was more predominant in cities than in rural areas.[3]

c) The Islamization of a part of the Balkan population—primarily in Bosnia, Herzegovina, and Albania—was instrumental in spreading the influence of the Turkish Muslim culture and Turkish language. However, the role of the Bulgarian Muslims, the Pomaks (mainly in the Rhodopes), in this connexion seems to have been rather limited.

---

[*] This article appeared originally in *Folia Slavica*, which has kindly given permission to republish.

[1] "Les langues slaves méridionales et la conquête turque," *Byzantinoslavica* 16 (1953): 126.

[2] L. Stojanov, *Pătjat na maxcloto. Antifašistski statii* (Sofia, 1968), p. 90.

[3] G. K. Venediktov, *Iz istorii sovremennogo bolgarskogo jazyka* (Sofia, 1981), p. 77.

It is interesting that many leading figures in the Bulgarian national revival even considered the language of the Bulgarian Muslim population a model of linguistic purity![4]

The famous Bulgarian author Ivan Vazov gives a more plausible evaluation of a specific Pomak dialect: "They pronounce the numbers in Bulgarian and not in Turkish, like other Pomaks... the purity of their language is sullied by the presence of great quantities of Turkish words, that have crept into their language as a result of close contact with, and sympathy for, the Turks."[5] In Bulgaria there are still around 190,000 ethnic Bulgarians who are Muslims. As late as at the census of 1934, 13.51 percent of the Bulgarian population were Muslims, mostly Sunnis, but also a tiny minority of Shiites (Kăzălbaši).

d) The prestige of Turkish, the official language of the Ottoman Empire. As pointed out by P. Skok, "Ce n'était pas là seulement la langue des conquérants, des soldats et des représentants du governement, comme on le pensait faussement, mais aussi la langue d'une civilisation considérée par les sujets parlants balkaniques comme supérieure à la leur."[6] The attitude of the Bulgarians toward the language of their oppressors was undoubtedly more ambivalent than expressed by Skok, especially as the struggle for independence intensified during the nineteenth century. In his famous novel *Under the Yoke* (written over the period 1886-88), Ivan Vazov describes the hostility of the Bulgarians toward the Turkish language in the following passage:

> Only Merdevenjiev was a repulsive creature, with his devotion
> to the psalter and his love for the Turkish language. The first indicated
> a mildewed mind, the second—a votary of the scourge ; because for a
> Bulgarian to love the Turkish language meant love of the Turks
> themselves, or expectation of Turkish favour.[7]

On the other hand the prestige of Turkish language and culture is also well documented in Bulgarian literature, e.g. in L. Karavelov's novel, *Bulgarians of the Old Days*. The author, describing the people of his native village in the first half of the nineteenth century, writes with amused irony that "these Bulgarians love everything Turkish and never condescend to singing the old Bulgarian songs ... they are cultured and knowledgeable people, they know Turkish."[8]

In addition to the Osmanli Turkish dialects of the Balkans, Gagauz and Tatar dialects are also spoken by small groups in Bulgaria: Gagauz on the Black Sea, mainly the Varna region, and Tatar in the northeast (Dubrudja). The Gagauz and Tatar dialects are, however, of limited importance for the study of Turkic linguistic influence on Bulgarian. Osmanli Turkish dialects, commonly referred to as "Rumelian Turkish," constitute two vast dialect groups, an eastern (ERT) and a western (WRT). J. Németh

---

[4]Ibid., pp. 78-79.

[5]*Săbrani săčinenija v dvadeset toma* (hereafter SSDT), 20 vols. (Sofia, 1955-57); vol. 10, *Vnedrata na Rodopite* [In the bosom of the Rhodopes], p. 176.

[6]"Reste de la langue turque dans les Balkans," *Revue internationale des études balkaniques* 2 (1935): 258.

[7]M. Alexieva and Th. Atanassova, trs. (Sofia, 1955), p. 95.

[8]*Bălgari ot staro vreme,* The Pupil's Library ed., "Biblioteka za učenika" (Sofia, 1968), p. 91.

has established that "the respective areas are divided by a line starting east from Lom on the Danube, running southwards to the east of Vraca, Sofia and Samokov where it turns west and continues south of Küstendil."[9] As pointed out by several linguists, this dividing line between ERT and WRT follows roughly the Bulgarian *jat*-line (West-Bulgarian/East-Bulgarian).[10] The fact that both ERT and WRT are represented on Bulgarian territory complicates the study of Turkish linguistic influence on Bulgarian.

A phenomenon of basic importance for Turkish influence on the Bulgarian language was the widespread bilingualism prevalent, particularly, in eastern Bulgaria and other regions with a considerable proportion of Turkish population.[11] Often bilingualism would be more common among men than women: "When it was necessary to conceal something from their wives, the men spoke Turkish."[12]

Most Turkish influence on Bulgarian is the result of direct contact between speakers of the two languages in everyday life (intimate borrowing). As pointed out by Hazai, " la transmission littéraire, culturelle doit être considérée comme négligeable," while indirect literary loans are found mainly among the islamized population in the Balkans.[13] However, S. S. Bobčev's survey of Turkish influence on Bulgarian legal terminology gives a good example of literary transmission of influence.[14] It is no surprise that Turkish linguistic influence was strongest in eastern Bulgaria, where the proportion of Turkish population was greater than in the west.[15]

The Turkish linguistic influence was also particularly intense on the colloquial language in cities. Vazov, talking about the 1850s, states that "the spoken language in our cities was then half Turkish" and, according to V. Kjuvlieva, "Turkish influence—political, cultural and linguistic—was stronger in the cities than in the villages."[16] According to Mirčev, the Turkish linguistic influence on Bulgarian reached its apogee in the first quarter of the nineteenth century.[17] After the liberation in 1878 Turkish influence on Bulgarian came to an end, but the influence of Bulgarian on local Turkish dialects increased.[18] The change in status of the two languages reversed the direction of linguistic influence.

---

[9]"Traces of the Turkish Language in Albania", *Acta Orientalia Academiae Scientiarum Hungaricae* 13, nos. 1-2 (1961): 13.

[10]See G. Hazai, "Remarques sur les rapports des langues slaves des Balkans avec le turc-osmanli," *Studia Slavica Academiae scientiarum Hungaricae* (hereafter *SSlav*) 7 (1961): 119.

[11]K. Mirčev, "Za sădbata na turcizmite v bălgarski ezik," *Izvestia na instituta za bălgarski ezik* (hereafter *IIBz*) 2 (1952): 124; and see also idem, *Istoričeska gramatika na bălgarskija ezik*, 2nd ed. (Sofia, 1963), pp. 74-76.

[12]L. Stojanov, "Za turcizmite i dialektismite v bălgarska literaturen ezik", *Il B*,2 (1952), p. 218.

[13]"Remarques," pp. 111, 117.

[14]*Bălgarsko običajno nakazatelno pravo*, Sbornik na narodni umotvorenija i narodopis, no. 38 (Sofia, 1927), pp. 3-10.

[15]Mirčev, *Istoričeska gramatika*, p. 76.

[16]*SSDT*, vol. 19, pp. 355-56; "Morfologična adaptacija i asimilacija na turskite zaemki—săštestvitelni i prilagatelni—v bălgarskija ezik," in *Vǎprosi na sǎvremennija bǎlgarski ezik i negovata istorija* (Sofia, 1980), p. 79.

[17]"Za sadbata," p. 121.

[18]P. Mijatev, "Slavjanski leksikalni elementi v narodnite govori na turkskija ezik," *Bǎlgarski ezik* (hereafter *BEz*) 19, no. 2 (1969): 176-80.

Turkish influence by domains: vocabulary and proper names, phraseological calques, word-formation, the 'renarrative mood', syntax, phonetics, stylistics

Vocabulary is more open to foreign influence than other domains of language. As to the relative capacity of the other domains for interference, opinions differ, as pointed out by U. Weinreich:

> Whitney ... ranged words (nouns first), then suffixes, then sounds according to the freedom with which they are borrowed. Pritzwald ... lists the various domains in the order in which they are subject to foreign-language interference thus: vocabulary, sound system, word-formation and compounding, syntax, proper names. Dauzat ... asserts that vocabulary is most exposed to influence; then come the sounds, then syntax; while "morphology, ... the fortress of a language, surrenders last."[19]

In this connection, it is characteristic that the Turkish pluralizer *-lar/-ler*, frequently found in Turkish loanwords in Bulgarian, apparently never made its way into Bulgarian morphology, as it did in dialectal Albanian.[20]

The order in which the various domains are treated in the following does not reflect any ranking by "amounts of influence." We agree with Weinreich that " 'amounts of influence' in the various domains are incommensurable and that therefore no comparison is possible."[21] In our exposé we shall not limit ourselves to the literary language, although little information is available on the Turkish influence on Bulgarian dialects.

1. Vocabulary

The *Rečnik na săvremnija bălgarski knižoven ezik* (hereafter *RSBKE*) (Sofia 1954-59), contains about 850 Turkish loanwords (TLW). Compared to loans from other languages, TLWs occupy the fifth place in the *RSBKE* after Latin, Greek, French, and Russian. On the other hand, we know that in the early 1880s the great Bulgarian poet and writer Petko R. Slavejkov (1827-1895) compiled a dictionary of TLWs containing about 10,000 words. (Unfortunately this dictionary was never published, and to this day we lack a dictionary of TLWs in Bulgarian comparable to A. Škaljić's, (Sarajevo, 1966) for Serbo-Croatian, which contains 8,742 TLWs.) As can be seen from the great difference in the numbers of TLWs in a dictionary of the modern standard language like the *RSBKE* and a special dictionary compiled in the 1880s, most TLWs have either fallen into disuse or been relegated to non-standard varieties of Bulgarian. It is

---

[19]*Languages in Contact: Findings and Problems* (The Hague and Paris, 1974), p. 67.

[20]See A. Grannes, "The Use of the Turkish Pluralizer *-1x2r* in South Slavic and Albanian," *New Zealand Slavonic Journal* 11, no. 2 (1977): 91; W. Fiedler, "Die Pluralbildung bei den türkischen Elementen des Albanischen," *Linguistique balkanique* (hereafter *LB*) 20, nos. 1-2 (1977) : 143.

[21]*Languages in Contact*, p. 67.

characteristic that more than half of the Turkisms in *RSBKE* are stylistically marked as either *colloquial, popular, dialectal,* or *archaic.*[22]

The semantic value of Turkish loanwords: 'Sachgebiete'. As pointed out by K. Kazazis, Turkisms in the Balkan languages range "from culinary terms to obscenities."[23] A more explicit and detailed survey is given for Bulgarian by Mirčev:

> Today there is no Bulgarian city that does not show traces of Turkish terminology in the naming of streets, marketplaces, quarters, and places. Everything related to commercial life and to the administration of the city is full of Turkisms. The terminology of crafts and trades was nearly all Turkish; so was the terminology of architecture and furniture. In addition, great quantities of Turkisms were used in botanical and zoological terminology, in the naming of garments and parts of the human body. Even a considerable part of family and kindship terminology was of Turkish origin.... With the implantation of Oriental cuisine, Turkish terminology was taken over. Kitchen utensils had and still have Turkish names.... A great part of the civilities used by the Bulgarian people was also of Turkish origin.[24]

Mirčev focused on the borrowing of Turkish *terminology/nomenclature.* The strong impact of Turkish on professional terminology is well illustrated in the following passage from the local newspaper *Šumenski věsti* of 1924:

> Šivačite, koito se samosčitat za po-više săslovie ot *abadžiite* i se naričat s gordoto ime *frenkterzii,* s tănko izkustvo šijat razni *setreta, jaki, džebove kapaklii* i *djus, ildisvat,* pravjat *ilici, dikiši,* turgat *astar* om sebe si, šijat izkusno na *verev,* prišivat *toki* i *kopčeta,* kokaleni ili *čiličeni* za *askiite,* režat *jurtmeči* na pantalonite, koito poradi profesionalen atavizm napodobjavat nevolno *abadžijski bir-gjotlija poturi, jutjuldisvat* s osobena *jutija* novata drexa, kojato *čiračeto sabaxkarši* zanasja na obradovanija *mjušterija.*[25]

Strong Turkish influence in a very different field, maritime fishing terminology, is amply documented by A. Spasova, who stated that "Greekisms and Turkisms occupy a central place in contemporary Bulgarian maritime fishing terminology."[26] It should not be forgotten, however, that Turkish influence was strong also in the field of general

---

[22]S. Bojadžiev, "Za leksikata ot čužd proizxod v knižovnija bălgarski ezik," *IIBz* 19 (1970): 405; A. L. Grigor'ev, "Bolgarskie pisateli v bor'be protiv turkizmov," *Uč. zap. LGU,* no. 161, *Serija filol. nauk* 18 (1952): 149-72; L. Lakova, "Turcizmite v RSBKE ot stilistična gledna točka," *BEz* 22 (1972): 61.

[23]"The Status of Turkisms in the Present-Day Balkan Languages," *Aspects of the Balkans, Continuity and Change. (Contributions to the International Balkan Conference held at UCLA, October 23-28, 1969),* ed. H. Birnbaum and S. Vryonis (The Hague and Paris, 1972), p. 89.

[24]*Istoričeska gramatika,* pp. 75-76.

[25]Cited in A. Grannes, "Les turcismes dans un parler bulgare de la Bulgarie de l'Est," *Acta Orientalia Academiae scientiarum Hungaricae* 28, no. 2 (1974): 269-70 (with French translation).

[26]"Grăcki i turski elementy v bălgarskata morska ribarska terminologija," *BEz* 16, no. 4 (1966): 334.

228   *Alf Grannes*

abstract vocabulary.²⁷ Even the Christian religious vocabulary was affected at a certain period: *Kurtulija (kurtulu)*—'Savior', *kurtulisvam (kurtulmak)*—'to save', *xadžija (hacı)* —'Christian pilgrim to Jerusalem' (not only Muslim pilgrim to Mecca).²⁸

In spite of some exceptions, TLWs in Bulgarian have in general retained the same meaning they had in Turkish. As pointed out by M. Mollova:

> Les turcismes ont tellement conservé leurs caractères originaires dans la langue bulgare du point de vue... sémantique que l'on aurait pu penser qu'ils avaient été empruntés directement à la langue littéraire turque par un groupe de gens instruits.²⁹

Doublets— 'emprunts de luxe'. It is commonly assumed that in any language "the great majority of borrowed words are the names of *new* e.g. objects and materials." This might well be the case also for Bulgarian; but, as in any language exposed to a strong foreign linguistic influence, there are also a considerable number of 'emprunts de luxe' or doublets of native words: e.g. *pristǎp-juruš (yürüş)*—'assault', *griža-kaxǎr (kahır)*—'worry, anxiety', *prozorec-pendžera (pencere)*—'window'. In a special study of such doublets, E. Perniška points out that "during the Ottoman rule the inevitably strong influence of the Turkish language lends variety to the vocabulary of popular dialects with a number of words that duplicate the native ones."³⁰ Obviously the doublets were not restricted to 'popular dialects' (*narodni govori*) but were widely used also in the written language. Many of the so-called doublets (*dubleti*) were not absolute synonyms, and over a period of time some of them became more semantically and stylistically differentiated.

Lexical classes. Members of the 'open' lexical classes (nouns, verbs, and adjectives) are more readily borrowed than those of the 'closed' classes (pronouns, conjunctions, and prepositions).³¹ This is also the case for Bulgarian. Thus, on the basis of a presumably representative collection of 1,500 TLWs, Schaller has established that 73 percent are *nouns* (of which about 20 percent are *abstract* nouns). (Nouns are the most frequently borrowed class everywhere, so Schaller's finding is hardly a surprise.) He has further calculated a percentage of about 4 for *adjectives* and 1.6 for *verbs*.³² The latter percentage might as well have been calculated on the basis of Lakova's material, published a couple of years earlier, but not cited by Schaller. Lakova claims that in the

---

[27]C. Vranska, "Turskite naimenovanija na otvlečeni ponjatija v ezika na bǎlgarskija folklor," *BEz* 2 (1952): 220-21.

[28]See X. Pǎrvev, "Turcizmite v *Ogledalo* na K. Pejčinović," *IIBz* 16 (1968): 521-30; and O. Jašar-Nasteva, "Turcimite kaj K. Pejčinović so ogled na religioznata terminologija," in *Simpozium 1100-godišnina od smertta na Kiril Solunski. 2, 23-25 maj 1969. Skopje-Štip* (Skopje, 1970), pp. 257-67. For a more detailed study of the semantic value of TLWs, see B. Conev, *Istorija na bǎlgarskija ezik,* vol. 2 (Sofia, 1934), pp. 177-91, and H. Schaller, "Die türkischen Lehnwörter in der bulgarischen Sprache," *Zeitschrift für Balkanologie* 9, nos. 1-2 (1973): 174-86.

[29]"Etude phonétique sur les turcismes en bulgare," *LB* 12 (1967): 116.

[30]"Leksiko-semantičniti dubleti—otzvuk na obštestvenija život prez XIX v.," in *Izsledvanija iz istorijata na bǎlgarskija knižoven ezik ot minalija vek.* (Sofia, 1979), p. 62.

[31]Prof. Eric P. Hamp has pointed out to me that in contact situations, conjunctions especially discourse connectives, are often borrowed. I am indebted to Prof. Hamp for this information and for various useful suggestions.

[32]"Die türkischen Lehnwörter," p. 177.

two Bulgarian dictionaries, *RSBKE* and *Bălgarski tălkoven rečnik* (Sofia, 1963), there are about 2,000 TLWs, of which about 130 are verbs. Of these, about one-fourth, or 32, are borrowed as verbs from Turkish (*-disam, -tisam*).[33] Now, 32 verbs of 2,000 TLWs gives us exactly Schaller's percentage of 1.6.

The remaining lexical classes—*adverbs, interjections*, and *conjunctions*—constitute, according to Schaller, about 4.6 percent.[34] Borrowing of *grammatical words* from 'closed classes,' such as *conjunctions* and various *link-words*, is in general possible only "in situations of intense linguistic exchange"[35]—as in Bulgaria under the Ottoman rule. Grammatical words of Turkish origin were widely used not only in popular dialects but also in the written language.[36] Mirčev has pointed out, however, that these TLWs disappeared from the literary language particularly early:

> Turkish adverbs and link-words disappeared early. Words like *belki, karši, čunki, sanki, baja, baška, bile, dip, sal, adžeba*, have completely disappeared from contemporary literary Bulgarian, although they may be heard in dialectal and colloquial speech. Still used are *barem* and *zer*, but with a special stylistic value. The only link-word that is solidly established in Bulgarian and that is no longer perceived as a TLW is *čak*.[37]

2. Proper names

Toponyms. Toponyms of Turkish origin are common in Bulgaria, although many have been replaced by Bulgarian names. As pointed out by St. Ilčev, "In the toponomy, Turkish names of cities, villages, mountain peaks, and places have been reduced to a minimum."[38] The negative attitude of the great Bulgarian author Ivan Vazov to Turkish toponyms is interesting and typical:

> We stopped to spend the night in the most beautiful and most affluent village in that area. I would have preferred to call it by some poetical and sonorous name that would have appealed to your imagination. Unfortunately, for the Bulgarian and the poet, that village is entirely Turkish and carries the name Teke![39]

> The hillock *Kurubaglar*, in spite of the barbarism of its name, is the only place in the vicinity of Sofia where one can find green deciduous wood.[40]

---

[33]"Struktura i značenie na glagolite ot turski proizxod v bălgarski ezik," *BEz* 20, no. 5 (1970): 431.

[34]"Die türkischen Lehnwörter," p. 177.

[35]Th. Bynon, *Historical Linguistics* (Cambridge, London, New York, and Melbourne, 1978), p. 231.

[36]G. dell'Agata, "A proposito di alcuni prestiti grammaticali greci e turchi nelle lingue slave dell'area balcanica," *Richerche Slavistiche* 14 (1966): 17-28; Părvev, "Turcizmite," p. 527.

[37]"Za sădbata, p. 126.

[38]*Rečnik na ličnite i familni imena u bălgarite* (Sofia, 1969), p. 35.

[39]*SSDT*, vol. 11, *Bogdan. Izlet iz Sredna Gora*, pp. 105-106.

[40]Ibid.. vol., 6. *Pokolenie*, p. 337.

Until quite recently Turkish toponyms in Bulgaria seem to have been little studied. As late as 1965, H.-J. Kissling called this topic "ein bisher so gut wie völlig vernachlässigtes Gebiet."[41] A few years later W. Zajączkowski contributed to our knowledge with a small study, based mainly on Bulgarian material, in which he states that "the Turkish toponomy of the Balkan Peninsula follows basically the same principles of formation and creation as the toponomy of any other country."[42]

Characteristically enough, the most common type of Turkish toponym in Bulgaria is *adjective plus noun*, e.g. *Kara tepe*—'Black hill,' *Ak bunar*—'White spring,' *Egri dere*—'Sinuous river.' There are of course other types, many of which are exemplified in Zajączkowski's article e.g. *numeral + nouns : Juč tepe*—'Three hills,' *Beš tepe*—'Five hills,' and *plural forms of nouns denoting ethnic, social, professional of religious groups, e.g. Agalar*— 'agas,' *Karabašlar*—'monks'.

Another type of Turkish influence on the toponomy of Bulgaria is exemplified by Bulgarian toponyms that have undergone phonetic changes due to Turkish pronounciation, For example, *Ištip* from Bulgarian Štip (name of a town). Sometimes the Turkish variant supplanted the original Bulgarian form.[43]

Personal names and surnames. According to Ilčev,

> Turkish personal names [*lični imena]* were not adopted by the Bulgarians owing to the difference in religion. Muslim names (mainly of Arab origin) are found only in the Pomak population. In addition we find a small number of names in which a Turkish root is concealed, but these are formed on Bulgarian soil from known Turkish words. Such are, e.g., *Demir, Kurti, Karo, Sevda, Sultana, Sarma* [among others]. There are also a few nicknames or pseudonyms by which well-known *hajdouks* concealed their real names, e.g., *Čavdar, Indže, Atmadža*. While personal names of Turkish origin are few (except among the Pomaks), surnames (*familni imena*) of Turkish origin are numerous.[44]

Ilčev, in a book remarkable both for its outspokenly negative evaluation of Turkish surnames and its valuable information, asserts that

> Another, and indeed very unsound [*bolesnen*], flaw in our surnames is the great number of Turkish roots. Sometimes one can find lists of name like *Abadžiev, Avdžiev, Ajdžiev, Ajnaliev, Ajrandžiev, ... Bakalbašiev, Baldžiev, Baltadžiev, Balǎkčiev,... Bunardžiev, Burgudžiev, Bučakčiev, Bjuljukbašiev*, and some others even uglier [*po-grozni*] and more incomprehensible.

---

[41] "Die türkische geographische Nomenklatur auf dem Balkan als Erkenntnismittel für die Südosteuropa-forschung," *Zeitschrift für Balkanologie* 3 (1965): 142.

[42] "Tureckie elementy v toponimii Balkanskogo poluostrova," *Actes du Premier congrès international des études balkaniques et sud-est européennes, VI Linguistique* (Sofia, 1968), p. 105.

[43] At. T. Iliev, "Turski izgovor na bǎlgarski městni imena," *Spisanie na bǎlgarskata Akademija na naukite* 14 (1917): 104, 105.

[44] *Rečnik na lični te*, p. 10.

From the National Revival and onwards a great number of Turkish words have disappeared from our language... *only in anthroponymy do the Turkish nicknames and surnames still remain intact, nearly as during the Ottoman bondage.* At that time, however, more Bulgarians knew Turkish so that the names were understandable to them. Today it is not like that, and tomorrow they will be even more outlandish and unintelligible [emphasis added].[45]

He adds that since the time of the National Revival efforts have been made to Bulgarize Turkish surnames, most often by translation: e.g., *Saxatčiev* to *Časovnikarov*, *Bǎkardžiev* to *Mednikarov*.[46] This is easy enough with, e.g., the many Turkish surnames ending in *-džija* / *-čija*, denoting craftsmen engaged in various traditional trades, but hardly desirable with surnames denoting negative qualities: e.g., *Berbatov* (from *berbat*—'dirty'), *Bitliev* (from *bitli*—'lousy'), *Gebešev* (from *gebeş*—'simpleton') or signifying infirmities, e.g. *Iribadžakov* (from *eğri bacak*—'bow-legged').

In the early 1970s new and intense efforts were made to do away with Turkish names. Bulgarian Muslims with Turkish names were given new Bulgarian or 'international' names.

3. *Phraseological calques*

In her article on phraseological calques from Turkish, C. Makedonska states that very little research has been done on the subject. She distinguishes between calques and demi-calques, considering the latter as a result of Bulgarizing efforts during the period of National Revival. The demi-calques are also the most numerous: e.g., *stoja divan capraz* (*divan çapraz durmak*)—'stand demurely'; *storja zarar (zarar etmek)* 'to cause harm'. Some demi-calques, such as the latter, are still used in colloquial Bulgarian. As an example of a full calque from Turkish, Makedonska cites among others *bera um (aklını toplamak)*— 'become wise, reasonable'. She concludes that the Turkish language has played "an important role in the development of the phraseological system of the Bulgarian literary language."[47]

4. *Word-formation*

Suffixation. In Bulgarian, as in the other Balkan languages, a small number of Turkish suffixes were separated from loan words and began to be used with non-Turkish stems. The most important of these suffixes are *-džija* / *-čija (-ci, -cı, -cü, -cu* / *-çi, -çi, -çü, -çu), -lǎk (-lik, -lık, -lük, -luk), and -lija (-li, -lı, -lü, -lu).* The suffix *-ana*, productive in Serbo-Croatian (*elektrana*—'power station') is not used with native stems. B. Markov's statement that the suffix is used with native stems "in Macedonian and the neighboring Slavic languages" (presumably including Bulgarian) ought to be

---

[45]Ibid., p. 35.

[46]Ibid.

[47]"Turski frazeologični zaemki v bǎlgarski ezik," *BEz* 16, no. 4 (1966): 322, 328, 331.

modified.[48] It is characteristic that no examples of this suffix with a non-Turkish stem are listed in *Obraten rečnik na săvremennija bălgarski ezik* (Sofia, 1975), so the suffix has hardly ever had any place in literary Bulgarian nor even, judging from dialect materials at the Institute of Bulgarian Language of the Bulgarian Academy of Science (about which Dr. Kiril Kostov has provided information), in dialects. The examples from Macedonian cited by Markov might well be Serbo-Croatian loan words. On the other hand, Bulgarian did take over some TLWs (most of which are now obsolete) with this suffix: e.g., *baruthana*—'powder magazine,' *xapuzhana*—'prison'.[49]

Hundreds of TLWs with the *-džija / -čija* suffix invaded Bulgarian and the other Balkan languages. These TLWs are found even in the writings of the best authors of nineteenth- and twentieth-century Bulgarian literature. They include, for example, *avdžija*—'huntsman,' *axčija*—'cook,' *kazandžija*—'boilermaker,' *kaikčija*—'boatman,' and *kavgadžija*—'quarrelsome person'.[50] The suffix was borrowed and used also with Bulgarian stems. In Bulgarian, as in Turkish, this suffix is used in two main functions: 1) to form the *nomina agentis*—referring to various traditional or newer and more temporary occupations: *lovdžija*—'huntsman,' *cirkadžija*—'circus actor,' *tramvajdžija*—'tramworker,' *kurortadžija*—'vacationist';[51] 2) to form nouns indicating personality traits, usually negative or risible, e.g. *skăpčija*—'tightwad,' *ljubovčija*—'womanizer'. The TLW *kafedžija* can illustrate both functions: 'coffeehouse keeper, coffee seller' and 'great coffee drinker'.[52]

Whereas most TLWs with the sufix *-džija / -čija* have disappeared from contemporary Bulgarian, the suffix is still very productive with non-Turkish stems, particularly in colloquial and non-standard varieties of the contemporary language. This productivity is, however, limited to the second function of the suffix (see above) with its ironical-pejorative connotation. This connotation is now so strong that possible new formations of type one, *nomina agentis,* such as *compjuterdžija*—'computerologist' (it is suggested that this may be American-Bulgarian), could only have ironical or humorous connotations.[53]

The Turkish suffix *-li (-lı/-lü/-lu)* is found in numerous TLWs in Bulgarian where it has been enlarged with the segment *-ja* (as in *-dži-ja / -či-ja* above) as, e.g., in *šekerlija*—'sugared', *esnaflija*—'tradesman'.[54] As can be seen from these examples, the TLWs of this type in Bulgarian can function both as indeclinable adjectives and as

[48]"Nekoi aspekti od vlijanieto na turskiot jazik," *Makedonski jazik* (hereafter *MJa*) 28 (1977): 11.

[49]The latter word is listed in the three-volume dictionary of N. Gerov, *Rečnik na bălgarskija jazyk* (Plovdiv, 1895-1908).

[50]These examples are to be found, respectively, in V. Vazov, *SSDT,* vol. 12, p. 15; L. Karavelov, *Săbrani săčinenija,* vol. 1, p. 196; Petko R. Slavejkov, vol. 5, p. 129; Vazov, *SSDT,* vol. 13, p. 88; and N. Xajtov, *Šumki ot gabăr* (Sofia, 1966), p. 18.

[51]Vazov, *SSDT,* vol. 11, p. 314.

[52]K. Cankov, "Kăm slovoobrazovatelnata i akcentnata xarakteristika na săštestvitelnite s nastavki-*džija /-čija* i *-lija* v săvremennija bălgarski ezik," *BEz* 23, no. 1 (1982): 71.

[53]St. Stefanov, "Kam văprosa za značenieto na nastavkata *-džija,"BEz* 13 (1962): 101; S. Radewa, "Przyrostki tureckie *-dži(ja), -či(ja)* w języku bułgarskim," *Zeszyty naukowe Universitetu Jagiellońskiego,* vol. 114, *Prace językoznawcze* 15 (1965): 32; Cankov, "Kăm slovoobrazovatelnata," p. 71; D. Čizmarov, *Stilistični osobenosti na săštestvitelnoto ime v bălgarskija knižoven ezik* (Sofia, 1978), p. 151; Kazazis, "The Status of Turkisms," p. 104.

[54]Vazov, *SSDT,* vol. 12, p. 160; A. Konstantinov, *Săčinenija v dva toma* (Sofia, 1957), p. 286.

nouns. With non-Turkish stems the suffix was primarily used to form adjectives, e.g. *kremăklija*—'flintgun' (*kremăklija puška*—'flintgun'), *zvezdalija*—'decorated with a star' or 'nice'. According to Cankov, the suffix is still productive in Bulgarian, but only in the more limited function of forming nouns indicating a person's geographical origin (*žitelski imena*): e.g., *burgaslija*—'person from Burgas'. There are around 300 nouns of this type in Bulgaria. In most cases, however, there is a choice between the form with the Turkish suffix and one with a Bulgarian suffix: e.g., *gabrovlija /gabrovec* — 'person from Gabrovo', *tărnovlija / tărnovec, tărnovčanin, tărnovjanin*—'person from Tarnovo'. The 'pure' Bulgarian form is then recommended.[55] In some cases, e.g., *burgaslija* (see above) and *banskalija*—'person from Bansko', there is no variant with a native suffix.

The suffix *-lija* is little used in contemporary Bulgarian compared to the suffix *-džija / -čija*, and Cankov's characterisation of it as *productive* with '*žitelski imena*' is not based on material presented in his article. One suspects that he uses *productive* (*produktiven*) in the sense 'still used in some words', since he gives no examples of *new* formations.

The Turkish suffix *-lik / -lık / -lük / -luk* is found in many hundred TLWs in Bulgarian: e.g., *ergenlik*—bachelorhood', *kalabalăk*—'crowd', 'confused mass', *bokluk*—'garbage'.[56] As early as the seventeenth century this Turkish suffix began to be used with Bulgarian stems. It was taken over in the generalized form *-lăk:* e.g., *vojniklăk*—'military service', *ovčarlăk*—'shepherd's trade'. Of the many functions of this suffix in Turkish, only two were transferred with the borrowed suffix into Bulgarian: 1) its most characteristic function, forming abstract nouns (see above) and 2) its 'locative' function, indicating a place: e.g., the dialectal *s'ankâlăk*—'shady place' (from *sjanka*—'shade'). The latter function is limited to dialectal usage. In its function as a suffix for forming abstract nouns *-lăk* was widely used in dialects and in the language of folklore.[57] Particularly in dialects and folk language *-lăk* became the predominant suffix for forming abstract nouns.

Although it was used also in the literary language, in the last decades of the nineteenth century literary usage of abstract nouns formed with the suffix *-lăk* and TLWs containing the same suffix in its various forms became increasingly unpopular. As stated by K. Gutschmidt, "Man vermeidet vor allem türkische Abstrakta, deren Zahl in den Mundarten und auch in der Volksdichtung recht stattlich ist."[58] Both in TLWs and in Bulgarian formations the suffix *-lăk* was replaced mainly by the native suffix *-stvo:* e.g., *avdžilăk*—'hunting' became *avdžijstvo*, which was replaced by *lov* (i.e., replacement by a Bulgarian synonym); or sometimes (with stems having negative

[55]"Kăm slovoobrazovatelnata," pp. 72, 74.

[56]Gerov, *Rečnik na bălgarskija*; Vazov, *SSDT*, vol. 20, p. 152. See also A. Grannes, "Bulgare de l'Est *kaxpelik*, bulgare de l'Ouest *kaxpelăk?* (La réalisation de l'i turc dans le suffixe *-lik* dans les turcismes bulgare à l'harmonie vocalique palatale par *i* ou *e*)," *Scando-Slavica* 19 (1973): 207-15; and idem, "Bălgărskite nastavki *-stvo, -ština* kato zamestnici na turskata nastavka *-lăk, -lik, -luk, -ljuk (-1x4k)* v turski zaemki: Stadii na 'deorientalizacija' na rečnikovija fond na bălgarskija ezik," in *Bălgaristični Izsledvanija* (Sofia, 1981), pp. 107-17.

[57]T. Szymański, *Słowotwórstvo rzeczownika w bułgarskich tekstach XVII-XVIII wieku* (Wrocław, Warsaw, and Krakow, 1968), p. 146; Grannes, "Bălgărskite nastavki," p. 109; Vranska, "Turskite naimenovanija," p. 221.

[58]"Anfänge einer Normalisierung des Wortschatzes der bulgarischen Schriftsprache vor 1878," *Zeitschrift für Slawistik* 13 (1968): 124.

connotations) by the suffix -*ština*: e.g., *budalalǎk*—'stupidity' became *budal(a)ština*.[59] Most TLWs with the suffix -*lik* (-*lık* / -*lük* / -*luk*) have disappeared from the literary language, and hybrid formations with the suffix -*lǎk* are no longer used "as stylistically neutral nouns."[60]

Compounding. In eighteenth- and nineteenth-century Bulgarian, loan compounds of Turkish origin were widely used, and some of them were so well assimilated that they were no longer deemed 'foreign' words. A good illustration of this is the following statement of I. Vazov, in which he lists the Turkish loan compound *demir-čiček* (*demir çiçek*) among the 'Bulgarian names' of plants: "our botanical terminology has a limited number of Bulgarian names, such as, among others: *neven, zvǎnče, gorocvet, demir-čiček, div karamfil, diva temenuga*."[61]

The compound *demir-čiček* reflects the Turkish 'attributive izafet' (*unvanlı izafet*). Reflexes of this izafet-construction are quite common in Bulgarian: e.g., *kexlibar čibuk*—'amber pipe', *samur kalpak*—'sable cap'. As can be seen from these examples, the first component of the compound denotes a substance or material of which the second component is made. In Turkish, this semantic type is only one of several which together constitute the 'attributive' izafet; but precisely this type was so frequently reflected in Bulgarian that it reinforced an already existing, but rare, Slavic N + N-model: e.g., *srebro ploči*—'silver horseshoes', *zlato klinci*—'golden horseshoe-nails'.[62]

Another izafet-construction, the so-called 'indefinite' izafet, is reflected in Bulgarian in two ways, viz., with or without the third person possessive suffix -i^4 (> -*i*, -*ǎ, -ju, -u*), -si^4 (> -*si, -sǎ, -sju, -su*). In most cases the suffix is dropped in Bulgarian, as in *taskebap* (*taskebabı*), but in various dictionaries and literary works I have found approximately 150 loan compounds with the suffix preserved: e.g., *džeb-parasǎ*—'pocket money'.[63] In the typical Slavic appositional compound, the second constituent specifies more closely the first: i.e., the element order *determinatum—determinans* prevails, as in *vagon xladilnik*—'refrigerator car'. In the Turkish izafet-constructions and their reflexes in Bulgarian the second nominal element is the *determinatum* and the first is the *determinans*; e.g., in both the Turkish *cep parası,* and the Bulgarian *džeb-parasǎ* the first element *cep* / *džeb*—'pocket' determines, or specifies more closely, the second element 'money', as opposed to, e.g., *kan parası* / *kan parasǎ*—'blood money'. The same element order is typical of the Germanic languages, as can be seen in the English translations above and in the following German loan compound in Bulgarian with the corresponding Turkish compound: Bulgarian, *bormašina*—German, *Bohrmaschine* (cf. *Burgu makinesi*). It is quite clear that the type of compound described here, *determinans* plus *determinatum,* was not introduced with recent West European loans. It was amply represented in Bulgarian much earlier by suffix. Accordingly, in the development of

---

[59]Grannes, "Bǎlgarskite nastavki," p. 112.

[60]L. Andejčin, K. Popov, and St. Stojanov, *Gramatika na bǎlgarskija ezik* (Sofia, 1977), pp. 97-98.

[61]*SSDT*, vol. 10, p. 104.

[62]K. Kostov, "Zur Enstehung und Andwendung einer substantivischen Fügung in den balkanslavischen Sprachen," *Die Welt der Slaven* 2 (1968): 169, 196; Grannes, *Loan Compounds in Bulgarian Reflecting the Turkish Indefinite izafet-Construction*, Det Norske Videnskaps Akademi, II, Hist.-Filos. Klasse Skrifter, n.s. no. 15 (Oslo, Bergen, and Tromsö, 1980), p. 35, and idem, "Loan Compounds in Bulgarian Reflecting Three Types of Turkish izafet-constructions." (Paper presented at the First International Congress on Bulgarian Studies, Sofia, May 23-June 3, 1981), pp. 2-3.

[63]Grannes, *Loan Compounds*, pp. 15-84.

compounding constructions, Turkish has played a role both in furnishing new loanwords and in reinforcing the already existing, but rare, *determinans plus determinatum* pattern in Bulgarian compounds. This type is still productive.[64]

The affective reduplication by initial m-. The affective reduplication by initial *m-*, so typical of colloquial Turkish, as in *et-met*—'meat and suchlike', *kitap- mitap*—'book/books or such things', has been taken over by all Balkan languages, including Bulgarian.[65] As can be seen from the above-cited example, the reduplication confers an idea of approximation with a pejorative and/or playful nuance. The pejorative nuance is well illustrated in the following example from Vazov's novel, *Under the Yoke:*

> Spomenuvaneto na Stefčova razbudi neprijatno čuvstvo. Posle pribavi:-
> Sega *Stefčov-Mefčov* i drugi podobni bezobrazija nazad ostajat.[66]

This type of reduplication is still used in colloquial Bulgarian.

5. *The 'renarrative mood' (preiskazno naklonenie)*

It is a widely held opinion that the semantic relationship between the *di-* and *miş-* pasts of Turkish and the definite and indefinite pasts of Bulgarian (and Macedonian) is one of lender/borrower. Thus, C. Keesan affirms that:

> A second borrowing is found in the usage of the Balkan Slavic perfect tense forms in other meanings, variously termed 'distanced' forms (Lunt), or renarrative forms.... No one seems quite sure just what sort of verbal category is involved here. *One certainty is that the extension is from Turkish influence.* Turkish past-tense forms in *-miş* with a perfect type of temporal meaning, are also used in nontemporal ways. Forms in *-miş* are either considered as a whole (tense) or split between tense and mood (Kononov). In Macedonian and Bulgarian, grammarians draw the dividing line differently, splitting the usages regarded as temporal in Turkish between pure temporal and cases in which the speaker is not vouching for the truth of the information, and grouping the latter with cases of renarration as modal forms [emphasis added].[67]

It is possible that if Keesan had been familiar with V.A. Friedman's 1978 paper on the subject, her certitude about Turkish influence might have been weakened. Friedman argues convincingly that

> From a diachronic wiewpoint, it appears that the usual presentation of the so-called reported forms in Balkan Slavic as calques of the Turkish *miş-* past and therefore a Balkan areal phenomenon should be modified to say

---

[64]Grannes, *"Loan Compounds,"* p. 9.

[65]Grannes, "Le redoublement turk à M-initial en bulgare," *LB* 21 (1978): 37-38.

[66]*SSDT*, vol. 12, p. 202.

[67]"Renarration in Turkish and Macedonian: A Study in the Borrowing of Verbal Categories," *MJa* 30 (1979): 100.

rather that Balkan Slavic and Turkish share a common development whereby their past definites evolved into marked affirmative forms. ... Along with this development, and perhaps to some extent due to it, the past indefinite—originally a perfect in all these languages—developed into an unmarked past with a nonaffirmative chief contextual variant meaning, i.e. 'reported' in most instances, in contrast to the marked affirmative.[68]

The problem of possible *borrowing* from Turkish as opposed to *influence* from Turkish (by reinforcement of an already existing pattern) or to *parallel, completely independent development* is very complex and will certainly continue to be discussed in the future. The complexity of the matter increases if we add to the comparison other forms such as the Balkan Slavic present and the various imperfects and the Turkish present progressive in *-iyor* and the compound pasts using *-iyor* with the *di-* and *miş-* pasts of 'be' (3sg *idi, imiş*)."[69]

6. Syntax

Foreign influence on syntax is difficult to assess since it is covert, not overt like loan words and borrowed suffixes. As with the category of the 'renarrative' mood, it is often difficult to resolve the problem of borrowing or *influence* versus *parallel, independent development*, and findings and assessments in this field will often be more controversial.

Turkish influence on Bulgarian syntax has not been studied much, but Markov's survey of "Some aspects of the influence of the Turkish language on the grammatical structure of the Macedonian language" (in Macedonian) is useful also for Bulgarian.[70]

Indeclinable adjectives

From Turkish, Bulgarian has taken over a small number of adjectives (and nouns) which have remained indeclinable in Bulgarian with regard to both gender number and thereby added a new feature to Bulgarian syntax: e.g., *serbez*—'fierce, bold' (*serbez čovek, serbez bulka, serbez dete, serbez momičeta*). This and some other TLWs of the same category can also function as *adverbs:* e.g., *otgovarja serbez*—'answer boldly'.[71]

Adjectives (and nouns) in *-lija* are indeclinable with regard to gender, but not with regard to number, e.g., *kăsmetlija măž / žena / dete* but *kăsmetlii măže* (pl.).

It is important to note that the indeclinability of some adjectives of Turkish origin is an isolated phenomenon that has not changed the general rule for agreement between adjective and noun in Bulgarian. It is therefore more an example of adaptation (or, rather, *lack of adaptation*) of Turkish elements than an example of *influence*.

---

[68]"On the Semantic and Morphological Influence of Turkish on Balkan Slavic," in *Papers from the Fourteenth Regional Meeting, Chicago Linguistic Society* (Chicago, 1978), p. 115.

[69]Ibid., p. 118.

[70]"Nekoi aspeckti," *MJa* 28 (1977): 5-21.

[71]Kjuvlieva, "Morfologična adaptacija," p. 123.

Turkish influence on the Bulgarian prepositional system? V. Šaur suggests a possible influence from the Turkish case system (particularly the ablative) on Bulgarian prepositional usage;[72] but in a detailed study of the uses of the preposition *ot* (which in Bulgarian has replaced *iz* and *s* in many of their functions), A. Minčeva finds little evidence of Turkish influence. According to Minčeva, Turkish influence might, however, be one of many factors that have shaped the semantic spectrum of the preposition *ot*.[73] N. Boretzky draws attention to the peculiar use of the Bulgarian preposition *iz* with the meaning 'in, on, through, over', as in *pătuvam iz cjalata strana*—'travel all over the country', as a possible calque (*Lehnübertragung*) from Turkish (*ablativ*).[74]

Has the analytical Turkish comparison influenced a similar development in Bulgarian? The analytical Bulgarian comparison, which dates back to the fourteenth century, is structurally similar to the Turkish one: e.g., in Turkish it is *güzel*—beautiful', *daha güzel*—more beautiful', *en güzel*—'most beautiful' and in Bulgarian *gjuzel* (TLW), *po-gjuzel, naj-gjuzel*. Even if the analytical comparison should be considered an 'internal' Bulgarian development, it is probable that in a largely bilingual population the presence of a parallel Turkish model has reinforced the new Bulgarian pattern. The Turkish-Bulgarian parallelism also includes the correspondence between the function of the Bulgarian preposition *ot* and the Turkish ablative: e.g., in Bulgarian one says *tova e po-dobro ot onova*— 'this is better than that' and in Turkish *bu, şudan (daha) iyidir*.[75]

Turkish influence in the usage of the possessives? Keesan argues that "both Bulgarian and Macedonian usages of the possessive have been changed to more closely approximate the Turkish usage." She refers to parallel constructions such as (Turkish) *benim kitap*, (Bulgarian) *mojata kniga* and (Turkish) *kitabım*, (Bulgarian) *knigata mi*— 'my book'. In the latter example, where the dative enclitic pronoun is used, Keesan sees a Turkish influence and erroneously qualifies it as 'a new usage in Bulgarian'.[76] This usage goes back to Old Bulgarian;[77] it is, of course, possible that it might have been reinforced by the Turkish model (*kitabım*, as opposed to *benim kitap*).

7. Phonetics

Little is known or written about a possible Turkish influence on Bulgarian phonetics, but Kazazis is undoubtedly correct in affirming that "Turkish influence on the

---

[72]"K otázce ovlivnění dialektů jihoslovanských jazyků balkánskými konvergencemi," in *Československé přednášky pro VI.1 mezinárodní sjezd slavistů v Praze* (Prague, 1968), pp. 161-64.

[73]"Za turskoto vlijanie vărxu semantičnija spektăr na bălgarskija predlog *ot*," *IIBEz* 19 (1970): 891.

[74]"Ein semantischer Turzismus in den Balkansprachen," *Zeitschrift für Balkanologie* 7, nos. 1-2 (1969-70): 16-21.

[75]Ibid.

[76]"Renarration," p. 99.

[77]Mirčev, *Istoričeska gramatika*, p. 246.

sound system of the standard Balkan languages has been minimal."[78] In the following we shall briefly mention five phenomena.

Phonemic /dž/. Keesan maintains that "the presence of phonemic /dž/ in Balkan Slavic is due mainly to its use in Turkish loans; *džamija*—'mosque' (from *cami*), *džeb* —'pocket' (*cep*)".[79] As pointed out by Kazazis, the sound did, however, already occur in Bulgarian and other Balkan languages as "a voiced positional variant of the sound t, as the result of voicing assimilation: for instance, Bulgarian *ličba* (pronounced lidjba) 'sign; symptom'."[80]

Phonemic /k'/ and /g'/. The phonemic status of /k'/ and /g'/ is also the result of Turkish influence, v. minimal pairs such as *koše* (dim. of *kos*—'basket')/ *k'oše* (Turkish köşe—'corner'), *gol*—'naked' / *g'ol* (Turkish *göl*—'pool').

[f]. Kazazis adds that "Turkish also helped spread the Sound [f] in Balkan Slavic, but it was preceded by Greek and also by other languages."[81]

[ǎ]. A similar 'statistical' influence occurred when the Turkish [ɪ] was rendered as the Bulgarian [ǎ] in the numerous TLWs.

Soft, final consonants (non-phonemic and non-etymological). I.V. Kočev has pointed out that in Bulgarian dialects (both East- and West-Bulgarian) a new, non-etymological softness of final consonants has developped. The source of this new softness is Turkish loan words such as *g'ol'*—'lake' (Turkish *göl*), *bair'*—'hill' (Turkish *bayır*). From TLWs the softness has spread to native Bulgarian words (mainly nouns). Kočev emphasizes that the TLWs only served as the 'first spur' (*pervjy tolčok*) to this development.[82]

8. *The retreat of Turkisms and their status in contemporary Bulgarian*

From the point of view of contemporary Bulgarian, Turkisms (lexical and grammatical) can be divided into three categories: 1) stylistically neutral Turkisms, 2) non-standard Turkisms, and 3) archaic Turkisms.

Stylistically neutral Turkisms. In the field of vocabulary the stylistically neutral Turkisms are limited basically to those for which there is no native Bulgarian equivalent, e.g., *barut*—'gunpowder'. Possible reflexes of Turkish influence on Bulgarian grammar are covert and stylistically unmarked.

Non-standard Turkisms. Up until the first half of the nineteenth century Turkisms were stylistically unmarked and freely used in the literary language. The 'pejorization' (*pejorizacija*) of Turkisms is a phenomenon characteristic of the second half of the century.[83] This is to a large extent a result of deliberate puristic efforts. As stated by Kazazis: "The avoidance and replacement in higher styles of a number of Turkisms in

---

[78]"The Status of Turkisms," p. 99.

[79]"Renarration," p. 97.

[80]"The Status of Turkisms," p. 99.

[81]Ibid.

[82]"O balkanskom xaraktere mjagkix soglasnyx v pozicii konca slova v bolgarskom jazyke," in *Actes du Premier congrès internationale des études balkaniques et sud-est européennes. VI, Linguistique* (Sofia, 1968), pp. 452-53, 455.

[83]Pǎrvev, "Turcizimite," p. 528; Gutschmidt, "Anfänge," p. 242.

each language did not necessarily push them *out* of the language. In many cases it simply meant that they were pushed *down* stylistically, that they were 'demoted' as it were." (see Section 1). Over the years this has happened with suffixation with Turkish suffixes: productive suffixation (*-džija* / *-čija*) is stylistically marked in the contemporary language. On the other hand, one should not forget that some Turkisms, like the reduplication by initial *m-* never really made their way into the literary language: they were and have remained non-standard.

In non-standard Bulgarian, and particularly in slang, Turkish elements are still quite frequent. M. Stajnova even observes that 'quite recently' many jocular expressions have been created on Bulgarian ground from TLWs. Among these recent 'quasi-Turkisms' she cites: *kaxǎr suratlǎ babait*—'the Knight of the Sorrowful Countenance', *čadǎr asker*— 'parachutist', literally 'umbrella-soldier'.[84]

Archaic Turkisms. The majority of TLWs have become obsolete, and editions of nineteenth century classics often have to be provided with glossaries to enable the modern Bulgarian reader to cope with the Turkisms. In fact, classial Bulgarian authors like Karavelov, Botev, Vazov, and Z. Stojanov used more TLWs than the authors of the first half of the nineteenth century.[85] This reflects the main theme of their works: Bulgaria under the Ottoman rule and the fight for national freedom. Even modern writers like Talev and Xajtov make extensive use of 'archaic' TLWs when dealing with historical themes. Thus archaic Turkisms have survived to a certain extent as 'historical' words.

The gradual retreat of Turkisms has several causes. Deliberate puristic efforts have already been mentioned. The disappearance of Ottoman institutions (army, administration, law, monetary system, etc.) also obviously led to a rather spontaneous falling into disuse of certain TLWs. Other TLWs disappeared more gradually as a result of socio-economic changes in Bulgarian society: e.g., terms related to disappearing trades such as *samardžija*—'saddlemaker', *abadžija* — 'weaver of/dealer in frieze; tailor'.[86]

Many Bulgarian linguists who have written about Turkish influence on their language express satisfaction over the fact that the 'battle' against Turkisms has been so successful. Purifying the language of these undesirable elements connected with "the oriental culture of the Turks"[87] is considered a progressive task.[88] West European and, particularly, Russian influence is more positively evaluated.

Russian Institute, University of Bergen, Bergen, Norway

---

[84]"The Status of Turkisms,"k p. 95.

[85]"Za pejorizacija na turcizmite v bǎlgarskija ezik," BEz 14, nos. 2-3 (1964): 185.

[86]Gutschmidt, "Anfänge," p. 241.

[87]Kjuvlieva, "Morfologična adaptacija," p. 81.

[88]Stajnova, "Za pejorizacija," p. 186.

A. Mete Tuncoku

THE RIGHTS OF MINORITIES IN INTERNATIONAL LAW AND TREATIES: THE CASE OF TURKISH MINORITY IN THE PEOPLE'S REPUBLIC OF BULGARIA

In international law the term minority generally refers to those ethnic groups distinctly different from the majority of the population of a country in terms of race, religion, language, and culture. Their legal status and the protection of their rights have always been the subject matter of discussion in many treaties and documents. Especially in contemporary international relations, minorities and their rights constitute one of the most frequently discussed and delicate topics. The violation of the rights and freedoms of the Turkish minority in Bulgaria, the subject of this paper, is the main cause of the recent crisis in Turkish-Bulgarian bilateral relations.

The existence of a Turkish minority in Bulgaria today is a matter of historical record and current political reality. Those Turkish people constitute not only the most populous Turkish minority inherited from the Ottoman Empire living outside Turkey today but also the largest non-Bulgarian ethnic group in Bulgaria. Reliable sources put their number at about one million out of a total Bulgarian population of nine millions.[1] The recent acceleration of the ongoing assimilation tactics employed by the Bulgarian authorities against the Turks, such as the forcible change of their names, restrictions on the freedom of religion, and the prohibition of the public use of the Turkish language are in many respects contravening the fundamental principles of international law and those treaties that determine the legal status of the ethnic Turks in Bulgaria. In spite of the denials of the Bulgarian government, the news that comes out of Bulgaria is, unfortunately, true and reflects the situation of the Turks in that country.[2] It has aroused a strong reaction not only in Turkey but in many other countries too. Several governments and various international institutions and bodies, including the Council of Europe, Amnesty International, the North Atlantic Assembly, and the Organization of

---

[1]This figure is not exact because the Bulgarian authorities have made no reliable data available since 1965. According to the last official figures issued by the Bulgarian government, which were based on the census of 1965, the number of the Turks was 746,755; see *A Report from Helsinki Watch, Destroying Ethnic Identity: The Case of Turks of Bulgaria* (June 1986), p.1.

[2]For further information about the recent developments in Bulgaria, see the following international sources: Anton Kolendic, "The Position of the Turks in Bulgaria," *Review of International Affairs* 36, no. 837 (20 February 1985); "Reports on the Situation of the Turks in Bulgaria," *Time*, 26 February 1985; "The Experience of Being Bulgarized," *The Economist*, 14 December 1985; "Bulgaria's Turks Tell of Terror in Forced Assimilation Drive," *The Washington Post*, 8 April 1986.

the Islamic Conference, have severely denounced the oppressive procedures applied by the Bulgarian government and the military to the Turkish people.

The main purpose of this article, however, is not to deal with the political and humanitarian aspects of the present crisis. It aims to discuss the question of the legal rights and freedoms of the Turkish minority in Bulgaria vis-à-vis international laws and existing treaties. Since the Bulgarians, like the other Balkan peoples, lived under the rule of the Ottoman Empire until the end the Balkan wars in 1912 and 1913, a brief account of the history of Turkish-Bulgarian relations is necessary to the understanding of the nature and the scope of the present problems between the two countries.

Turkish-Bulgarian Relations in Historical Perspective

Ottoman rule in Bulgaria was established in 1396. From that time on, as a part of the traditional Ottoman policy of populating the newly conquered lands with ethnic people loyal to the Ottomans, the settlement of Turks began there.[3] In other words, the present Turkish people in Bulgaria were originally brought from different parts of Anatolia; but they have been living there uninterrupted for more than 500 years. They belong to the Anatolian branch of the Turkish race, and even today thousands of them have relatives in Turkey.

Every historian studying Ottoman history acknowledges the fact that the Ottomans, long before such concepts as "minority" and "human" rights came to be recognized internationally, were advocating pluralism in both theory and practice. It was under the just and tolerant Ottoman administration, which lasted for nearly 500 years, that the Bulgarians, like other people under Ottoman rule, were able to preserve their religion, culture, and ethnic identity. Before the conquest by the Ottoman Turks, Bulgaria had lived under the political domination of Byzantium, which had facilitated the oppression exerted by the Byzantine church. During the 350 years of Byzantine administration, the Bulgarian community in the Balkans was absorbed by the Byzantine church, which ultimately brought them to the point of losing even their native language, whereas, under the policy of religious, cultural, and communal tolerance and autonomy with regard to the ethnic groups that prevailed in the Ottoman Empire, the Bulgarian people enjoyed autonomy in their communal affairs.[4]

This policy of the Ottomans, however, combined with the pressure of the nineteenth-century liberal and nationalist movements in the Balkan Peninsula, led to the gradual disintegration of the Empire and prepared a favorable environment for the establishment of independent states in this part of Europe. Additionally, as the Ottoman central authority weakened, foreign intervention increased and the Balkans gradually

---

[3]On the population settlement policy of the Ottoman Empire, see Barbara Jelavich, *History of the Balkans* (Cambridge, 1983), vol. 1, pp. 95-96, and Halil İnalcık, *The Ottoman Empire: The Classical Age, 1300-1600* (London, 1973), pp. 6-16.

[4]Jelavich, *History*, pp. 39-45, 48-53; İnalcık, *Ottoman Empire*, pp. 7-15; Nagata Yuzo, *Chuto Gendai Shi,Vol. I, Toruko, Sekai Gendai Shi* (Tokyo, 1982; Shupansha, 1982), vol. 9. p. 49.

became the center of a great power conflict that, in turn, accelerated the rise of independence movements in the region.[5]

At the end of the nineteenth century the Bulgarians like many other peoples in the Balkans, revolted; and by the terms of the Berlin Treaty, signed in 1878, the autonomous Bulgarian principality was established. Later, in 1908, Bulgaria became an independent kingdom. A protocol signed in 1909 between the Kingdom of Bulgaria and the Ottoman State confirmed this new status for Bulgaria.

It should be emphasized that both the 1878 Berlin Treaty and the 1909 Protocol secured the ethnic rights of the Muslim-Turkish minority in Bulgaria. Thus, from the very beginning of Bulgaria's establishment as an independent entity, Bulgarian authorities formally guaranteed respect for the minority rights and freedoms of the Turkish people in their country. The Treaty of Istanbul, which was signed after the end of the Second Balkan War in 1913, not only regulates border disputes between the participant countries but also contains provisions reconfirming the rights of the Turks in Bulgaria. Then, after the establishment of the Turkish Republic in 1923, Turkey and Bulgaria in 1925 signed the Ankara Treaty of Friendship and Cooperation. This treaty, which is still in force, provides mutual rights and guarantees for both the Turkish minority in Bulgaria and the Bulgarian minority in Turkey.

From 1925 until the beginning of the Second World War in 1939, despite the complexity of the problems that existed in their bilateral relations, the Balkan states tried, in the face of the growing German and Italian threat in Eastern Europe and the Mediterranean, to establish cooperation among themselves. The Balkan Entente of 1934 was the most important outcome of these persistent efforts.[6] However, in the post-WWII era the Balkan Peninsula was faced with radical political changes. The Cold War that had started between the eastern and western blocs had its repercussions in the region, and the loyalties of the Balkan countries were divided between the two hostile blocs. These unfavorable developments naturally affected Turkish-Bulgarian relations as well.

Following the establishment of the communist regime in 1944, Bulgaria promulgated a new constitution that still made promises to all the ethnic minorities in that country. By the end of 1947, however, Bulgarian authorities had initiated a policy of forceful assimilation of the minorities. One of the fundamental goals of the new Bulgarian regime was the creation of a "One Nation Integrated Bulgarian State," and the purpose of that policy was the assimilation of the Turks, who constituted the largest ethnic minority in the country protected under the international guarantees. This policy of assimilation has remained unchanged since 1947. Only the techniques and the procedures employed in its implementation have changed. In 1950 Bulgarian authorities put great pressure on Turks to emigrate, despite contrary provisions in the 1925 Treaty of Friendship and Cooperation. This naturally created considerable friction in the relations between Bulgaria and Turkey. Furthermore, as the relations between East and

---

[5] For detailed information about the eighteenth- and nineteenth-century Balkan developments, see Jelavich, *History*, pp. 171-327, 329-73; Nagata, *Chuto Gendai Shi*, p. 70-89; Fahir Armaoğlu, *Siyasal Tarih (1789-1960)* (Ankara, 1961), pp. 75-80, 359-87; Gewehr Wesley, *The Rise of Nationalism in the Balkans, 1800-1930* (U.S.A., 1967), pp. 41-79; and Dimitrihe Djordjevic and Stephen Fischer-Galati, *The Balkan Revolutionary Tradition* (New York, 1981), pp. 67-161.

[6] Armaoğlu, *Siyasi Tarih*, pp. 185-90, 321-26; Oral Sander, *Balkan Gelişmeleri ve Türkiye, 1945-1965* (Ankara, 1964), pp. 5-14.

West deteriorated over these years, Bulgaria moved into the eastern communist camp opposing Turkey, who remained with the West. In the 1960s, however, there was a marked improvement in Turkish-Bulgarian relations, mainly the result of the easing of strained relations in Europe. Under these favorable international conditions, a Migration Agreement was signed in 1968. It provided for the migration of the Turks to Turkey for the purpose of uniting those families divided as a result of the forced emigration in the 1950s. This treaty would remain in force for ten years, and during that ten-year period about 150,000 Turks migrated to Turkey.

Beginning in January 1985 the policy of employing forcible measures designed to bulgarize the Turks suddenly gained momentum. It appears that the emigrations, compulsory and voluntary, had not greatly helped in the drive toward the policy goal of "One Nation Integrated Bulgarian State." Disturbed by the existence of a large minority that continued to assert its national identity under minority rights confirmed by several agreements, the Bulgarian government decided to intensify its efforts at the forced assimilation of the Turks. (It appears, however, that in their recent attempts the authorities are trying to exterminate the whole Turkish population in Bulgaria and to thus achieve their "Integrated State.") Such a policy of oppression is against the fundamental principles of international law, existing bilateral and multilateral treaties, and other legal documents, which are reviewed below. The text of the relevant portions of these documents is provided in appendices following this article or in the body of the discussion of their provisions.

The Status of the Turkish Minority in Bulgaria in International Treaties and Other Documents

An examination of the international treaties and legal documents related to this subject clearly shows that the Turkish people living in Bulgaria have been recognized as a distinct ethnic group and that their rights have been under the guarantee of international law since the establishment of the Bulgarian Autonomous Principality in 1878. These rights are assured either specifically, under provisions on minority rights, or more generally as human rights at the international level.[7]

I discuss below, in a document-by-document analysis, these two separate types of international guarantee, beginning with the provisions directed specifically toward minority rights.

The Berlin Treaty. Article 5 of this treaty, which was signed between the Ottoman Empire and the European Great Powers on 13 July 1878, set forth the fundamental principles to be applied to the rights and freedoms of the minorities living in Bulgaria: communities of different religions would be protected, they would have freedom of religion and enjoy rights and liberties on a par with ethnic Bulgarians, and these principles were to be embodied in Bulgarian Public Law. In signing this treaty Bulgaria thus, from the very beginning of its existence as a separate political entity,

---

[7]Hüseyin Pazarci, "Rights of the Turks in Bulgaria vis-à-vis International Laws and Treaties," *Turkish Review Quarterly Digest* 1 (November 1985): 79-91.

pledged to respect the rights of the Turks and other minorities within its borders. (The text of Article 5 is reproduced as Appendix I.)

The Istanbul Protocol and Convention. By this Protocol and its annexed convention, signed by the Kingdom of Bulgaria and the Ottoman Empire on 19 April 1909, the minority rights of the Turks in Bulgaria were restated. Under Article 2 of the Protocol, the Bulgarian state undertook to provide the Turkish minority with the religious liberty and other freedoms and rights. They were to benefit from all civil and political rights enjoyed by the other ethnic groups and be equal to the Bulgarians before the law. In the convention annexed to the Protocol, the rules governing the responsibilities of the Muslim religious leader (*Mufti*) are described in detail.

The Treaty of 20 September 1913 and the Convention on Muftis. Articles 7 and 8 of this treaty, which was signed in Istanbul at the end of the Second Balkan War, contain the provisions on minority rights and freedoms in Bulgaria, while the Convention on Muftis includes articles detailing the rights, religious freedoms, and rules governing the administration of the religious affairs of Bulgaria's Muslims. An examination of the articles of the 1913 Treaty and Convention reveals that status of the Turkish minority in Bulgaria has always been important to Turkey. (Appendix II contains the text of the relevant articles of these documents.)

Neuilly Peace Treaty. This treaty was signed on 27 November 1919 after the defeat of Bulgaria in the First World War. Turkey was not a party to this treaty, but it includes articles recognizing the rights and freedoms of all the ethnic groups in Bulgaria, which naturally includes the Turkish minority. Furthermore, with this treaty the legal status of the minorities was defined in accordance with the general principles adopted by the newly-created League of Nations. All the articles in Section 4 of the Neuilly treaty deal with the protection of minorities in Bulgaria. The Bulgarian government also agreed that the provisions in this section had the same value as the state constitution: that is to say, that the Bulgarian constitution, public and private laws, decrees, and regulations could not contain any provision contrary to the provisions of this treaty on minority rights and freedoms. (See Appendix III for the articles of Section 4 of this treaty.)

5. *The Turkish-Bulgarian Treaty of Friendship and Convention of Establishment.* After the establishment of the Turkish Republic (1923) the two countries started negotiations and finally signed a Friendship Treaty and Convention of Establishment on 18 October 1925. This is the basic international agreement on the legal status of the Turks in Bulgaria, and it is still in force; thus it still is binding on both Bulgaria and Turkey. According to the Paragraph A of the annexed Protocol of this treaty, the articles of the Lausanne Peace Treaty on the rights of non-Muslim minorities, apply to the Bulgarians living in Turkey, while the Muslim minorities in Bulgaria come under the provisions of the 1919 Neuilly Treaty regarding protection of minority rights. In other words, Section 4 of the Neuilly agreement was made an integral part of the 1925 Turkish-Bulgarian friendship treaty, thus giving Turkey, which was not one of the signatories of the 1919 document, the guarantee that the Muslim Turks specifically would benefit from the provisions of the earlier accord. The Protocol, in addition, gave the Turkish government the legal right to concern itself with the Turks living in Bulgaria. As is known, Neuilly Treaty ceased to be in effect after the signing of the Paris Peace Treaty of 1947; but the Turkish-Bulgarian Treaty of Friendship of 1925 and its provisions regarding the rights of Turkish minority in Bulgaria are still in force and

the Bulgarian government is still today legally obliged to respect its terms. (For the text of the relevant articles of the 1925 Turkish-Bulgarian treaty and annexed Protocol, see Appendices IV and V.)

The Turkish-Bulgarian Convention of Establishment, which was signed at the same time as the the Friendship Treaty, introduced articles guaranteeing the free emigration of Bulgarian Turks. Article 2 of the Convention provided that Bulgarian authorities would not create obstacles to the emigration of Turks from Bulgaria but would facilitate their migration and help them in the liquidation of non-movable properties. Since this Convention, like the Treaty of Friendship, is still in force, Bulgarian authorities are under the obligation not to prevent the voluntary emigration of the Turks to Turkey. The provisions of both the Treaty of Friendship and the Convention of Establishment in this respect are clear and precise. (Appendix VI reproduces the text of the Convention of Establishment.)

The Bulgarian Peace Treaty. After the end of the Second World War, on 10 February 1947, Bulgaria signed a treaty with the Allied Powers. In the Peace Treaty of 1947, which is still in force, the Bulgarian government undertook to respect the human rights of all its people. Article 2 of the treaty listed a variety of "fundamental liberties" that the Bulgarian authorities were to ensure by whatever measures necessary to all those under its jurisdiction without regard to differences of race, sex, language, or religious creed:

> Art. 2- La Bulgarie prendra toutes les mesures nécessaires pour assurer à toutes les personnes relevant de sa juridiction, sans distinction de race, de sexe, de langue ou de religion, la jouissance des droits de l'homme et de libertés fondamentales, y compris la liberté d'expression, de la pensée, la liberté de presse et de publication, la liberté de culte, la liberté d'opinion et de réunion.

This language was inspired by that of the United Nations Charter. Thus, Bulgaria's conduct toward its minorities became, in a way, the concern of all the member countries of the UN (which was joined by Bulgaria in 1955).

The Turkish-Bulgarian Migration Agreement. Under the favorable conditions of international relations in the 1960s, Turkey and Bulgaria were able to improve their bilateral relations and sign a Migration Treaty on 22 March 1968. According to the treaty provisions, however, only close relatives of those who had left Bulgaria in the 1950s would be able to migrate to Turkey. Consequently, while some families were united, several thousands of them remained divided. This treaty would remain in force for ten years, during which time about 150,000 Turks were able to emigrate to Turkey. It had been hoped that the agreement would constitute a first step for the union of all the divided families, but, unfortunately, after its expiration in 1978, no further steps were taken in this respect. (For an unofficial translation of the Agreement on Migration, see Appendix VII.)

The general issue of protecting minority rights was addressed as early as the post-WWI period by the League of Nations. Under the charter of the League, those minority rights recognized by treaties were to be accepted as having the power of constitutional provisions in domestic public law of signatories and were guaranteed by the League. After the Second World War, however, the question became that of protecting the rights of the individual on an international scale. Within this new framework the rights of the

Turks in Bulgaria were secured by a number of international declarations described below.

The Charter of the United Nations. This charter, which is signed by Turkey, and by Bulgaria as well, is the most important international legal document. The various human rights provisions of the United Nations Charter are *jus cogens* and binding upon the UN organization itself and its member nations, Bulgaria included.

The Universal Declaration of Human Rights. This declaration, proclaimed by the United Nations in 1948, is another international document recognized by both Turkey and Bulgaria. Being simply a decision of the General Assembly of the UN, this document is not legally binding. However, it certainly has moral implications for the states that signed it. Several provisions of this Declaration are relative to the protection of human rights and freedoms.

The Helsinki Final Act. This document, which was signed on 1 August 1975, aims essentially at creating security and cooperation in Europe. Again, both Bulgaria and Turkey are among the signatory states. Although generally considered to be an international agreement, the Helsinki Final Act is not a document imposing legal obligations on the signers. It is the political and moral character of the Act that give it force. Several articles address human rights and freedoms, such as the freedom of thought, religion, faith, and conscience. The Act states:

> The participating states on whose territory national minorities exist will respect the right of persons belonging to such minorities to equality before the law, will afford them the full opportunity for the actual enjoyment of human rights and fundamental freedoms and will, in this manner, protect their legitimate interests in this sphere.

Other International Documents. There are several other documents, signed within the framework of the Charter of the United Nations, and ratified by the Bulgarian government. Some of these international agreements are 1°) the International Covenant on Civil and Political Rights (21 September 1970); 2°) the Genocide Agreement (September 1948); 3°) the Economic, Social and Cultural Rights Agreement (16 December 1966); and 4°) the Civil and Political Rights Agreement (December 1966).

Furthermore, the principles of international custom and tradition, and various general and particular principles of law also give importance to the protection of the minority rights. (These non-written principles of law are the source of the provisions in many international written agreements.)

Finally, besides these written agreements and non-written principles of international law, the 1947 Constitution of Bulgaria itself contains special articles on the protection of minority rights. Articles 45, 71, and 78 clearly define those rights and the obligations of the Bulgarian government in this respect.

Conclusion

In the light of the above it is possible to reach conclusions about the rights of the Turkish minority in Bulgaria and the legal implications of their treatment. First, the Turks were officially recognized as one of Bulgaria's minority groups in the Berlin

Treaty of 1878, which laid down rules for the protection of these minorities in the same document that created Bulgaria as a political entity. Numerous subsequent international treaties, world agreements, and related documents have reiterated, in both specific and general terms, Bulgaria's obligation to deal equitably with her minority populations. Contrary to the claims of the Bulgarian government, the fate of the Turks within her borders cannot be considered a purely internal affair: the provisions on minority rights that exist in the Bulgarian constitution are there by virtue of international treaties giving her legitimacy, and their violation is a violation also of international law.

The legal basis for Turkey's special interest in Bulgaria's Turkish population was established by the Berlin Treaty and has been reinforced by the later documents on the rights of minorities in Bulgaria and elsewhere. Furthermore, in the Turkish-Bulgarian Treaty of Friendship of 1925 Bulgaria explicitly recognized Turkey's legal right to concern herself with the Turks there. Since the inception of the severe assimilation policies, Turkey has sought to exercise her legal right to intervene to protect the Bulgarian Turks but, taking into consideration the importance of friendly relations with this neighboring state, has carefully refrained from attitudes that would inflame the Turkish public opinion.

Turkey has been seeking to settle this dispute through bilateral negotiations for a new emigration treaty, having declared several times that she is ready to receive all those Turks who would like to emigrate. However, Turkey's appeal to discuss the problems at a high-level conference and for a new emigration treaty has been continuously rejected by the Bulgarian government. Acting on the basis of her legal rights, Turkey brings this question before international fora on every occasion. (It is, in fact, presently under consideration by various international bodies.) All the aspects of this forceful assimilation campaign in Bulgaria are by now widely known in the international arena.

In taking such unjust and inhumane measures against one part of her own people, Bulgaria, which is ethnically a very heterogenous society, may have lost indefinitely the opportunity to establish a climate of harmony and peace inside the country as well as earned international opprobrium as a result of her conduct. The continuation of the forcible assimilation of the Turkish minority will not only increase the legal and moral culpability of the Bulgarian state in the eyes of the world but will also heighten the tension and cause even further instability within Bulgaria.

Middle East Technical University, Ankara, Turkey

APPENDIX I. ARTICLE V OF THE BERLIN TREATY OF 1878

Bulgaria. Basis of Public Law

ART. V. The following points shall form the basis of the public law of Bulgaria:

Bulgaria. Civil and Political Rights. Exercise of Professions and Industries by all, irrespective of Religious Creeds.

The difference of religious creeds and confessions shall not be alleged against any person as a ground for exclusion or incapacity in matters relating to the enjoyment of civil and political rights, admission to public employment, functions, and honours, or the exercise of the various professions industries in any locality whatsoever.

Bulgaria. Freedom of Religious Worship.

The freedom and outward exercise of all forms of worship are assured to all persons belonging to Bulgaria, as well as the foreigners, and no hindrance shall be offered either to the hierarchical organization of the different communions, or to their relations with their spiritual chiefs.

APPENDIX II. EXTRAIT DU TRAITÉ DE PAIX ENTRE LA TURQUIE ET LA BULGARIE SIGNÉ A CONSTANTINOPLE LE 16/29 SEPTEMBRE 1913

ARTICLE 7.

Les originaires des territoires cédés par l'Empire Ottoman au Gouvernment Royal de Bulgarie et qui y sont domicilés deviendront sujets bulgares.

Ces originaires devenus sujets bulgares auront, pendant un délai de quatre ans, la faculté d'opter sur place en faveur de la nationalité ottomane, par une simple déclaration aux Autorités locales bulgare et un enregistrement aux Consulats Impériaux Ottomans. Cette déclaration sera remise, à l'étranger, aux chancelleries des Consulats Bulgares et enregistrée par les Consulats Ottomans. L'option sera individuelle et n'est pas obligatorie pour le Gouvernement Impérial Ottoman.

Les mineurs actuels useront de l'option dans les quatre ans qui suivent leur majorité.

Les Musulmans des territoires cédés devenus sujets bulgaresm ne seront pos assujettis pendant ce délai au service militaire, ni ne payeront aucune texe militaire.

Après avoir usé de leur faculté d'option, ces Musulmans quitteront les territoires cédés, et cela, jusqu'à échéance du délai de quatre ans prévu plus haut, en ayant la faculté de faire passer en franchise de droits de sortie leurs biens meubles. Ils peuvent toutefois conserver leurs biens immeubles de toutes catégories, urbains et ruraux, et les faire administrer par des tiers.

ARTICLE 8.

Les sujets bulgares musulmans de tous les territoires de la Bulgarie jouiront des mêmes droits civils et politiques que les sujets d'origine bulgare.

Ils jouiront de la liberté de conscience, de la liberté et de la pratique extérieure du culte. Les coutumes des musulmans seront respectées.

Le nom de Sa Majesté Impériale le Sultan, comme Khalife, continuera à être prononcé dans les prières publiques des musulmans.

Les communautés musulmanes, constituées actuellement ou qui se constitueront à l'avenir, leur organisation hiérarchique, leurs patrimoines reconnus et respectés; elles reléveront sans entraves de leurs chefs spirituels.

ARTICLE 9.

Les communautés bulgares en Turquie jouiront des mémes droits dont jouissent actuellement les autres communautés chrétiennes de l'Empire Ottoman.

Les Bulgares sujets Ottomans conserveront leurs biens meubles et immeubles et ne seront aucunément inquiétés dans l'exercice et la jouissance de leurs droits de l'homme et de propriété. Ceux qui ont quitté leurs foyers lors des derniers événements pourront retourner dans un délai de deux ans au plus tard.

ARTICLE 10.

Les droits acquis antérieurement à l'annexion territoires, ainsi que les actes judiciaires et titres officiels émanent des Autorités Ottomanes compétentes, seront respectés et inviolables jusqu'à la preuve légale du contraire.

ARTICLE 11.

Le droit de propriété fonciére dans les territories cédés, tel qu'il résulte de la loi ottomane sur les immeubles urbains et ruraux, sera reconnue sans aucune restriction.

Les propriétaires d'immeubles ou de meubles dans lesdits territoires continueront à jouir de tous leurs droits de propriété, méme s'ils fixent, à titre provisoire ou définitif, leur résidence personnelle hors de la Bulgarie. Ils pourront affermer leurs biens ou les administer par des tiers.

ARTICLE 12.

Les vakoufs Mustesna, Mulhaka, idjarétein, Moukataa, Idjaréi-Vahidé, ainsi que les dimes vakoufs, dans les territories cédés, tels qu'ils résultent actuellement des lois ottomanes, seront repectés.

Ils seront gérés par qui de droit.

Leurs regimes ne pourront être modifés que par indemnisation juste et préalable.

Les droits des établissements religieux et de bienfaisance de l'Empire Ottoman sur les revenues vakoufs dans les territoires cédés, à titre d'Idjaréi-Vahidé, de Moukataa, de droits divers, de contrevaleur des dimes vakoufs et auters, sur les vakoufs bâtis seront respectés.

ARTICLE 13.

Les biens particuliers de Sa Majesté Impériale le Sultan, ainsi que ceux des Members de la Dynastie Impériale seront maintenus et respectés. Sa Majesté et les Membres de la Dynastie Impériale pourront les vendre ou les affermer par des fondés de pouvoirs.

Il en sera de même pour les biens du domaine privé qui appartiendraient a l'Etat.

En cas d'aliénation, préférence sera accordée, à conditions égales, aux sujets bulgares.

ARTICLE 14.

Les Hautes Parties contractantes s'engagent à donner à Leurs Autorités provinciales des ordres afin de faire respecter les cimetiéres et particuliérement les tombeaux des soldats tombés sur le champ d'honneur.

Les Autorités n'empêcheront pas les parents et amis d'enlever les ossements des victimes inhumées en terre étrangére.

ARTICLE 20.

Le présent Traité entrera en vigueur immédiatement après sa signature.

Les ratifications en seront échangée dans la quinzaine à dater de ce jour.

En foi de quoi, les Plénipontentiaires respecteifs l'ons signé et y ont apposé leurs cachets.

Fait en double exemplaire à Constantinople, le 16/29 Septembre 1913.

Pour la Turquie: Pour la Bulgarie:
Signé :   Signé :
TALAAT   SAVOFF
MAHMOUD   G. D. NATCHOVITS
HALIL   A. TOCHEFF

APPENDIX III. TREATY OF PEACE BETWEEN BELGIUM, THE BRITISH EMPIRE, CHINA, CUBA, CZECHOSLOVAKIA, FRANCE, GREECE, THE HEDJAZ, ITALY, JAPAN, POLAND, PORTUGAL, THE SERB-CROAT-SLOVENE STATE, SIAM AND THE UNITED STATES, AND BULGARIA, SIGNED AT NEUILLY-SUR-SEINE ON 27 NOVEMBER 1919

Section IV.-Protection of Minorities

49. Bulgaria undertakes that the stipulations contained in this section shall be recognised as fundamental laws, and that no law, regulation or official action shall conflict or interfere with these stipulations, nor shall any law, regulation or official action prevail over them.

50. Bulgaria undertakes to assure full and complete protection of life and liberty to all inhabitants of Bulgaria without distinction of birth, nationality, language, race or religion.

All inhabitants of Bulgaria shall be entitled to the free exercise, whether public or private, of any creed, religion or belief, whose pratices are not inconsistent with public order or public morals.

51. Bulgaria admits and declares to be Bulgarian nationals ipso facto and without the requirement of any formality all persons who are habitually resident within Bulgarian territory at the date of the coming into force of the present Treaty and who are not nationals of any other State.

52. All persons born in Bulgarian territory who are not nationals of another State shall ipso facto become Bulgarian nationals.

53. All Bulgarian nationals shall be equal before the law and shall enjoy the same civil and political rights without distinction as to race, language or religion.

Difference of religion, creed or profession shall not prejudice any Bulgarian national in matters relating to the enjoyment of civil or political rights, as, for instance, admission to public employments, functions and honours, or the exercise of professions and industries.

No restrictions shall be imposed on the free use by any Bulgarian national of any language in private intercourse, in commerce, in religion, in the press or in publications of any kinds, or at public meetings.

Notwithstanding any establishment by the Bulgarian Government of an official language, adequate facilities shall be given to Bulgarian nationals of non-Bulgarian speech for the use of their language, either orally or in writing, before the Courts.

54. Bulgarian nationals who belong to racial, religious or linguistic minorities shall enjoy the same treatment and security in law and in fact as the other Bulgarian nationals. In particular they shall have an equal right to establish, manage and control at their own expense charitable, religious and social institutions, schools and other educational establishments, with the right to use their own language and to exercise their religion freely therein.

55. Bulgaria will provide in the public educational system in towns and districts in which a considerable proportion of Bulgarian nationals of other than Bulgarian speech are resident adequate facilities for ensuring that in the primary schools the instruction shall be given to the children of such Bulgarian nationals through the medium of their own language. This provision shall not prevent the Bulgarian Government from making the teaching of the Bulgarian language obligatory in the said schools.

In towns and districts where there is a considerable proportion of Bulgarian nationals belonging to racial, religious or linguistic minorities, these minorities shall be assured an equitable share in the enjoyment and application of sums which may be provided out of public funds under the State, municipal or other budgets, for education, religious or charitable purposes.

56. Bulgaria undertakes to place no obtacles in the way of the exercise of the right which persons may have under the present Treaty, or under the Treaties concluded by the Allied and Associated Powers with Germany, Austria, Hungary, Russia or Turkey, or with any of the Allied and Associated Powers themselves, to choose whether or not they will recover Bulgarian nationality.

Bulgaria untertakes to recognise such provisions as the Principal Allied and Associated Powers may consider opportune with respect to the reciprocal and voluntary emigration of persons belonging to racial minorities.

57. Bulgaria agrees that the stipulations in the foregoing articles of this section, so far as they affect persons belonging to racial, religious or linguistic minorities, constitute obligations of international concern and shall be placed under the guarantee of the League of Nations. They shall not be modified without the assent of a majority of the Council of the League of Nations. The Allied and

Associated Powers represented on the Council severally agree not to withold their assent from any modification in these articles which is in due form assented to by a majority of the Council of the League of Nations.

Bulgaria agrees that any member of the Council of the League of Nations shall have the right to bring to the attention of the Council any infraction, or any danger of infraction, of any of these obligations, and that the Council may thereupon take such action and give such direction as it may deem proper and effective in the circumstances.

Bulgaria further agrees that any difference of opinion as to questions of law or fact arising out of these articles between the Bulgarian Government and any one of the Principal Allied and Associated Powers, or ony other Power, a member of the Council of the League of Nations, shall be held to be a dispute of an international character under Article 14 of the Covenant of the League of Nations. The Bulgarian Government hereby consents that any such dispute shall, if the other party thereto demands, be referred to the Permanent Court of International Justice. The decision of the Permanent Court shall be final and shall have the same force and effect as an award under Article 13 of the Covenant.

APPENDIX IV. TRAITÉ D'AMITIÉ ENTRE LA TURQUIE ET LA BULGARIE SIGNÉ À ANKARA LE 18 OCTOBRE 1925 : LA TURQUIE, D'UNE PART, ET LA BULGARIE, D'AUTRE PART

Egalement et sincèrement désireuses d'établir et de consolider les liens de sincére amitié entre la République Turque et le Royaume de Bulgarie, et pénétrées de la même conviction que les relations entre les deux Etats, une fois établies, serviront à la prospérité et au bienêtre de leurs relations respectives, ont résolu de conclure un Traité d'Amitié et ont, à cet effet, nommé pour leurs Plénipotentiaires, savoir:
Le Président de la République Turque:
Tewfik Kiamil Bey, Sous-Secrétaire d'Etat au Ministére des Affaires Etrangéres à Angora
Sa Majesté le Roi des Bulgares:
Monsieur Simeon Radeff, Envoyé Extraordinaire et Ministre Plénipotentiaire de Bulgarie à Washington:
Lesquels, après s'être commiqué leurs pleins pouvoirs, trouvés en bonne et due forme sont convenus des dispositions suivantes:

ARTICLE 1.
Il y aura paix inviolable et amitié sincère et perpétuelle entre la République Turque et le Royaume de Bulgarie.

ARTICLE 2.
Les Hautes Parties Contranctantes sont d'accord pour établir les relations diplomatiques entre les deux Etats conformément aux principes du droit des gens; Elles conviennent que les Représentants diplomatiques de chacune d'Elles recevront, à charge de réciprocité, dans le territorie de l'Autre, le traitement consacré par les principes généraux du droit international public général.

ARTICLE 3.
Les Hautes Parties Contractantes sont d'accord pour conclure une Convention de Commerce et une Convention d'Etablissement et un Traité d'Arbitrage.

ARTICLE 4.
Le présent Traité sera ratifié et les ratifications en seront échangées à Angora le plustôt que faire se pourra, 11 entrera en vigueur le quinziéme jour après l'échange des ratifications.

ARTICLE 5.

Le protocole annexé au Présent Traité en fait partie intégrante.

En foi de uoi, les Plénipotentiaires respectifs ont signé le présent Traité et y ont apposé leurs screaux.

Fait en double à Angora, le 18 Octobre 1925

(L.S.) Tewfik Kiamil   (L.S.) S. Radeff

APPENDIX V. PROTOCOLE ANNEXÉ AU TRAITÉ D'AMITIÉ ENTRE LA TURQUIE ET LA BULGARIE SIGNÉ À ANKARA LE 18 OCTOBRE 1925

A.

Les deux Gouvernements s'engagent l'un envers l'autre de faire jouir respectivement les minorités musulmane's en Bulgarie de toutes les dispositions relatives à la protection des minorités stipulées dans le traité de Neuilly et les minorités bulgares en Turquie de toutes les dispositions relatives à la protection des minorités stipulées dans le Traité de Lausanne.

La Bulgarie reconnait à la Turquie et le Turquie reconnait à la Bulgarie tous les droits dont sont investis, en ce qui concerne les clauses des minorités les Puissances signataires respectivement des Traités de Neuilly et de Lausanne.

Remarque.— Sont considérés comme appartenant à la minorité bulgare les ressortissants tucs de religion chrétienne et dont le bulgare est la langue maternelle.

B.

Le Gouvernement turc reconnaît la qualité des ressortissants bulgares à tous les bulgares nés sur le territoire de la Turquie de 1912 et qui, ayant émigré en Bulgarie jusqu'à a signature du présent Protocole, ont acquis la nationalité bulgare en vertu de la législation intérieure en vigueur dans le Rayaume.

Le Gouvernement Bulgare reconnait la qualité des ressortissants turcs à tous les musulmans, nés dans les limites de la Bulgarie de 1912, et que, ayant émigré, jusqu'à la ont acquis la nationalité turque en vertu de la législation intérieure en viguere dans République.

Les femmes martiées suivront la condition de leurs maris et les enfants âgés de moins de 18 ans celle de leurs père.

Il reste bien entendu que les ressortissants turcs et bulgares des deux catégories susmentionnées conservent leurs droits de propriété sur leurs biens situés respectivement en Bulgarie et en Turquie, sauf les catégories mentionéées à l'Article C.

Si des Bulgares nés sur le territorie européen de la Turquie, la ville de Constantinople exceptée, ayant émigré en Bulgarie voulaient se réétablir dans le territoire ci-dessus mentionné le gouvernement turc se réserve son consentement à cet effet.

Le Gouvernement bulgare se réserve exactement le même droit en ce qui concerne les musulmans nés districts annexés à la Bulgarie en 1913 et ayant émigré en Turquie, au cas ou ceuxci voudraient se réétablir dans le territoire ci-dessus mentionné.

Remarque.— Constantinople comprent aux termes du présent Protocole, les circonscriptions de la Préfecture de la ville de ce nom, telles qu'elles sont délimitées par la loi de 1912.

C.

Les biens immobiliers de quelque nature qu'ils soient appartenant aux Bulgares originaires du territoire européen de la République Turque, la ville de Constantinople exceptée qui, postérieurement au 5/18 Octobre 1912, auraient immigré en Bulgarie jusqu'à a signature du présent Protocole de même que les biens immobiliers de quelque nature qu'ils soient, appartenant aux musulmans originaires des territoires détachés de l'Empire Ottoman à la suite de la guerre balkanique, et qui postérieurement au 5/18 Octobre 1912 auraient immigré en Turquie jusqu'à la signature du présent Protocole, seront acquis respectivement à l'Etat sur le territoire duquel ils sont situés.

D.

Les biens immobiliers de quelque nature qu'ils soient situés en Bulgarie et appartenant à des ressortissant turcs ou bien situés en Turqie et appartenant à des ressortissants bulgares et qui restent en dehors de l'application de l'Article précédent, si leurs propriétaires légitimes n'en sont pas actuellement en possession seront restitués à ceux-ci. à leur ayants-droit ou à leurs mandataires. Toutes les mesures et dispositions exceptionnelles qui, pour quelque motif que ce soit, auraient frappé les dits biens seront levés dès la mise en vigueur du présent Protocole.

Les revenues des biens qui auraient été sequestrés seront intégralement versés à leurs propriètaires.

Dans le cas de biens occupés par les immigrants ou des indigènes, il sera alloué aux propriétaires intéressés un loyer équitable.

Les intéressés devront établir réciproquement devant les juridictions des pays respectifs par tous les moyens de preuve légaux fait d'avoir quitté leur pays d'origine avant le 5/18 Octobre 1912.

Il reste bien entendu que toutes les clauses ci-dessus s'appliquent également, chacune suivant le cas qu'elles vise, aux biens des personnes visées dans les deux premiers alinéas du § B.

E.

Les droits acquis antérieurement à l'annexion du nouveau territoire bulgare ainsi que les actes judiciaires et titres officiels émanant des organes compétents de l'Empire Ottoman seront respectés et inviolables jusqu'à preuve légale du contraire.

F.

Les deux Parties Contractantes sont d'accord pour considérer comme ayant cessé d'exister et perdu toute validité les stipulations du Traité de Constantinople et de ses annexes, sauf celles fixant la frontière entre les deux Etats.

G.

La lettre adressée par le Plénipotentiaire Bulgare au Plénipotentiaire Turc, au sujet du mode d'application aux ressortissants turcs en Bulgarie de la loi sur la propriété foncière du travail fait partie intégrante du Présent Protocole et entrera en vigueur en même teps que lui.

Les difficultés qui pourraient surgir au sujet de l'application du Présent Protocole feront l'objet de négociations diplomatiques entre les Deux Gouvernements.

Fait à Angora, e double exemplaire, le 18 Octobre 1925.

(L.S.) TEWFIK KIAMIL   (L.S.) S. RADEFF

APPENDIX VI. EXTRAIT DE LA CONVENTION D'ETABLISSEMENT ENTRE LA TURQUIE ET LA BULGARIE SIGNÉE A ANKARA LE 18 OCTOBRE 1925

ARTICLE 1

Les ressortissants de chacune des Parties Contractantes auront le droit de s'établir et de séjourner sur le territoire de l'Autre et pourront en conséquence, aller, venir et circular librement, en se conformant aux lois et règlements en vigueur dans le pays.

ARTICLE 2

Les Parties Contractantes agréent qu'il ne sera porté aucun obstacle à l'émigration volontaire des Turcs de Bulgarie et des Bulgares de Turquie.

Les émigrés auront le droit d'emporter avec eux leurs biens meubles et leur bétail et de liquider leurs biens immobiliers en toute liberté. Ceux qui n'auraient pas voulu liquider leurs biens immobiliers avant leur départ définitif devront le faire dans le délai de deux ans aprés leur émigration.

Une entente interviendra entre les deux Gouvernements au sujet de la maniére dont les intéressés exporteront le produit de la liquidation de leurs biens.

APPENDIX VII. AGREEMENT BETWEEN THE REPUBLIC OF TURKEY AND THE PEOPLE'S REPUBLIC OF BULGARIA

The Migration to Turkey from the People's Republic of Bulgria of the Bulgarian Citizens of Turkish Descendent Whose Close Relatives Have Already Immigrated to Turkey before the Year of 1952.

The Republic of Turkey and the People's Republic of Bulgaria,

Considering the developments recorded in various fields in the relations between the two countries,

Convinced that the concluding of an Agreement on the voluntary migration to Turkey from Bulgaria of Bulgarian citizens of Turkish descendent whose relatives have already immigrated to Turkey before the year of 1952 would positively contribute to the good-neighbourly relations between the two countries,

Agree to the following :

ARTICLE 1

The immigration of Bulgarian citizens of Turkish descendent whose family and relatives, also former Bulgarian citizens of Turkish descendent, immigrated to Turkey before 1952 and obtained Turkish citizenship, who fall within the described categories below, and who wish to immigrate to Turkey will be implemented under the provisions of this Agreement :

a) Husband, wife

b) Mother, father, grandmother, grandfather, and their mothers and fathers,

c) Children and grandchildren and their spouses and children,

d) The non-married sisters and brothers and single adult and non-adult children of
   sisters and brothers dead before the date this Agreement goes into effect.

ARTICLE 2

The persons falling within the categories in Article 1 and wishing to immigrate should apply to the Bulgarian Authorities within six months following the entry into force of this Agreement.

Bulgarian competent Authorities can issue passports to those persons falling within the above categories within 45 days following their application.

Turkish missions in Bulgaria can issue entry visas to such persons within 45 days following their application.

ARTICLE 3

The migration shall be accomplished within the period from 1 April to 30 November.

The number of immigrants shall not exceed 300 persons per week.

ARTICLE 4

The transportation of the immigrants and the implementation of the immigration shall be made through highway (Kapitan Andreejev-Kapıkule) and existing railway border check point gates.

ARTICLE 5

The immigrants can take with them documents concerning their marital status and their immovable properties (title deeds and documents about purchase or sale of real estate), as well as educational and professional certificates and other documents about their military service and its duration, including those indicating that there is no legal obtacle to be exiled from the country, etc.

ARTICLE 6

The immigrants will be eligible to take with them their personal and household effects, except those the export of which are forbidden at the date of the immigration, exempt from all export duties whatsoever.

ARTICLE 7

Immigrating craftsmen and farmers are eligible to export tools, instruments, work-benches, and machines, as well as other used properties of movable nature which are in their personal ownership and necessary for their professional and private business, exempt from all export duties whatsoever, except those the exports of which are forbiddent at the date of the immigration.

Craftsmen and farmers are eligible to export, also exempt from all export duties, machines which are necessary for their craft, profession, and private business and which are part of the immovable property in use.

ARTICLE 8

The immigrants are eligible to take with them, according to the regulations in force at the date of the immigration, their foodstuffs, domestic products, and agricultural produce of their private business.

The immigrants are also allowed to take with them an amount of wheat sufficient for their family's consumption for one to two months.

ARTICLE 9

The immigrants shall, by an official certificate issued by the Public Community of their place of legal residence, prove their ownership of the properties mentioned under Articles 6,7, and 8 above.

ARTICLE 10

The immigrants will be eligible freely to dispose of the animals in their ownership before their immigration. The liquidation procedure will be implemented according to the regulation in force and the existing market conditions.

ARTICLE 11

The immigrants will be eligible freely to liquidate their immovable properties before their immigration, according to the Bulgarian laws and regulations existing at the date of entry into force of this Agreement.

The competent Bulgarian Authorities shall assist such liquidatioh.

ARTICLE 12

The immigrants shall receive an appropriate compensation in lieu of their rights, such as labor accident, retirement compensation, and other retirement and social insurance benefits which they are eligible to receive abroad, according to the Bulgarian laws and regulations in force at the date of immigration.

The conditions of payments of indemnity will be determined among the Parties subsequently.

ARTICLE 13

The use and transfer of funds of the immigrants stemming from the liquidation of their animals and immovable properties and other funds in their ownership shall be implemented as follows:

The immigrants shall be permitted to export from Bulgaria, to import to Turkey, and to purchase there properties under the laws and restrictions in force in the respective countries at the date of immigration and afterwards.

ARTICLE 14

The Articles of this Agreement are applicable to the persons falling under the categories under Article 1 only.

The Agreement is subject to ratification and enters into force from the date of the exchange of ratification instruments.

The Agreement is made in the Turkish and Bulgarian languages and both of the texts are equally valid.

Ankara, 22 March 1968.

On behalf of the
Government of the Republic
of Turkey
   (signed)
İhsan Sabri Çağlayangil
(Minister of Foreign Affairs)

On behalf of the
Government of the People's
Republic of Bulgaria
   (signed)
Ivan Başev
(Minister of Foreign Affairs)